DECISION IN GERMANY

DECISION

by Lucius D. Clay

IN GERMANY

GREENWOOD PRESS, PUBLISHERS
WESTPORT, CONNECTICUT

Contents

Illustrations

ALL ILLUSTRATIONS ARE U. S. ARMY PHOTOGRAPHS

Introduction

THIS record of four years in Germany is written in the hope that it will contribute to a better understanding of the German problem. We are well on the way to its solution within a framework acceptable to the free countries of Europe. We have not reached the goal. A self-supporting and self-responsible Germany is essential to the restoration of stability, and without a stable Europe lasting peace is impossible.

The American people have a huge stake in peace. Twice within the century, still only half run, we have given of our lives and our resources to prevent the domination of Europe by force. We recognize that a threat to freedom anywhere is a threat to our own freedom. We remain determined that free people shall not be enslaved by alien dictatorship. To this end, in time of peace we are giving substantially of our own resources at real sacrifice to rebuild a Europe in which the economic and, we hope, the political co-operation of the independent and peace-loving countries will soon make the threat of aggression remote. Meanwhile we have declared our intent to share in the common defense in our support of and adherence to the North Atlantic Pact.

Solving the German problem will be a major constructive step toward peace. It is a complex task. A new political and economic life had to be reconstructed from the chaos of total defeat. Under these conditions the administration of the American Zone of Occupation alone was a difficult undertaking. The establishment for the four zones of occupation of a government responsible to the people, and the rehabilitation of economic life sufficiently to promise them a reasonable standard of living under security measures which would make future aggression impossible, would have taxed the competence of the Allied Control Council even if there had been full co-operation among its members and between it and the German people.

Unfortunately there was never full co-operation. Three of the four occupying powers had signed the Potsdam Protocol which formed the directive for the occupation. France was not a party to this understanding and therefore did not feel bound by its provisions. But French unwillingness to abide by the Potsdam decisions was the major cause for dissent within the Control Council for only a few months. It soon became apparent that the Soviet Government interpreted the decisions very differently than did the British and American governments. The Russians wanted to create conditions that would provide opportunity for Communist penetration and domination of German political life and economic resources.

Thus the effort to rule Germany by unanimous agreement of the representatives of the four occupying powers failed. As this failure became evident, vital decisions had to be made in Germany. The American and British zones of occupation were merged into an economic unit to facilitate and expedite the industrial activity which was required for recovery in Europe. While the French had stood firmly with us and with the British in resisting the Soviet effort to build a Communist Germany, they were not satisfied with security measures and therefore did not join their zone with the bizonal area. Although plans to this end were laid, they did not become a reality until the North Atlantic Pact united the Atlantic countries for the common defense. Then France agreed to the setting up of a West German Government, elected by the people and given a large measure of responsibility for internal affairs and the development of economic self-sufficiency.

The success of the European Recovery Program and the planned formation of West German Government led to the Soviet blockade of Berlin, a ruthless attempt to use starvation to drive out the Western Powers, thus re-creating in Europe the fear which favored Communist expansion. The airlift prevented the blockade from accomplishing its purpose. There were risks involved in our determination not to be driven out of the former German capital. We understood and accepted these risks as my story will show. To do so was essential if we were to maintain the cause of freedom. The firm stand of the Western Powers in undertaking the airlift not only prevented terror from again engulfing Europe but also convinced its free people of our intent to hold our position until peace is assured.

Western Germany is a reality. It is a member in its own right of the Organization for European Economic Co-operation and is learning to work with others in a common cause. Its people have lived next door to Communism for four years and have decided that they do not want to live under Communist domination. Its government has been given only limited responsibility. It has not been received back in the comity of nations. Germany remains divided. Even when it is united security measures, if enforced, will suffice to prevent it from again becoming a threat. The German people also have a right to security, and it remains to be determined how this will be provided. Germany's free neighbors, who have suffered much from German hands, must be willing to accept its return to a free and independent status. This is the German problem which must be solved finally and fully before we can be certain of lasting peace.

Time, patience, and understanding are required, for we *must* find the right answer. American policy, taking into account the views of Germany's neighbors, is proving successful in clearing the way to solution. This policy must be continued in the months and perhaps years ahead until full success is achieved. It will be continued if it has the firm support of the American people. It will receive that support if they are fully informed and understand the problem in its many aspects.

This understanding cannot come about merely from a study of our administration of German affairs. During the past four years many international discussions have been devoted to the attempt to reconcile the conflicting views of the four governments and, when it became apparent that this was impossible, to bring the three Western governments together. Quadripartite conferences broke down because the earnest effort of the Western representatives to reach accord failed to prevent Soviet representatives from using the meetings for invective and propaganda purposes. Each of these international gatherings immediately affected relationships among the occupying powers in Germany, and thus at least indirectly the administration of their separate responsibilities.

Therefore, to understand the situation it is necessary to know something of the task of administering military government, the influence of international conferences, the difficulties encountered in political and economic reconstruction, and the security measures effected so that a revived Germany will not be a threat to peace.

I had not planned to write of my four years in Germany, and in fact for three years intentionally avoided keeping a record so that I would not be tempted. In January 1948 a draft of the official history of Military Government, prepared in the Historical Section of the Military Government staff, was placed on my desk. It was an admirable compilation of important documents combined with an accurate chronology of major events. It did not record the many discussions and exchanges of cables which led to major decisions, and thus it lacked spirit and animation. These cannot be provided from files. After reading the official draft I began to dictate from memory the incidents and discussions which preceded the principal decisions so that I should have a record of my participation if only for my own use. My associates, who had access to this record, urged that it be used as the basis of a book which might prove helpful to those interested in the German problem.

During my four years in Germany I served as deputy military governor to Generals Dwight D. Eisenhower and Joseph T. McNarney for two years, and as military governor for two years. In these capacities I served under three Secretaries of War (Army)— Henry L. Stimson, Robert P. Patterson, and Kenneth Royall; and under four Secretaries of State—Edward R. Stettinius, Jr., Justice James F. Byrnes, General George C. Marshall, and Dean Acheson.

With my political adviser, Robert D. Murphy, I attended two four-power conferences in Paris, one in New York, one in Moscow, and one in London, at which the United States was represented by the Secretary of State. I also attended six conferences in London, Paris, and Washington which were held to resolve differences among the Western Powers. Ambassadors W. Averell Harriman and Walter Bedell Smith from Moscow, and Ambassador Lewis W. Douglas from London visited Berlin frequently to keep abreast of current developments. Each day in Germany significant events were reported by radio to both the State and War (Army) Departments.

Of course in these four years many different American viewpoints had to be reconciled. They resulted from the honest thinking of able and sincere officials, and were presented and argued vigorously in sound democratic tradition, until agreements were reached or decisions made by the responsible authorities. Except for occasional flare-ups which quickly died out and made it possible for us to work more closely together, they created no personal antagonisms among the group which worked together for so many months in the endeavor to find a solution to the German problem. Some familiarity with the causes of these differences is necessary to a full understanding of how our policy developed and was reconciled with the policies of the other countries interested in Germany.

It is difficult to select from an eventful period of four years the significant events, items, and discussions which convey the magnitude of the task and the spirit in which it was executed. It is, however, the only way to tell the story, and it should be told so that in future the mistakes of the past may be avoided and the successes continued in application.

Having taken part in these events and discussions, I have formed deep convictions and can write of my experiences only with them in mind. I do not claim to be dispassionate in my recording of these years.

We have created a West German Government which has assumed major responsibility for the internal affairs of 45,000,000 persons. They form a force which must be duly considered if we want a stable Europe with an economy which offers the promise of reasonable life. They are separated from 20,000,000 Germans in the Soviet Zone. No lasting stability may be expected as long as 65,000,000 persons in the heart of Europe are divided against their will. Their natural desire for a unified country will remain until east and west Germany are reunited. Extreme nationalism is certain to develop from this division.

Of utmost importance to the future of the world are the questions of how and when West Germany is readmitted to the fellowship of nations and how and when it may reunite with eastern Germany, from which is it separated now by the barrier of Communism. In executing the measures which guarantee that Germany will not again become an aggressive threat we should not forget that there must also be security for its people, and that security against Germany must be considered in its relationship to world security. Now that we have created a partial government we must determine its place in world affairs, and in this determination lies the hope of peace.

Since this is largely a record of events in which I participated and as I remember their occurrence, it has been impossible to avoid the use of the personal pronoun. I am convinced that the small group of devoted and able Americans who were my close associates in Military Government will understand that its use does not in any way detract from their contribution, individually and collectively, which made possible any accomplishments Military Government may have achieved. It is because of my faith that their work was well done, and that consistent adherence to the established program for Germany will prove of lasting value in its contribution to peace, that I have written this book.

DECISION IN GERMANY

CHAPTER 1

Occupation and Military Government Begin

O N May 12, 1949, at 12:01 A.M., our trains and trucks, carrying food and coal, crossed the boundaries between the Anglo-American zones and the Soviet Zone en route to Berlin. The steady drone of the airlift planes was still heard overhead. They had broken the Soviet attempt to drive the Western Powers from Berlin by denying them access by land and water. That same morning I flew to Frankfurt to join my British and French colleagues in approving the Basic Law which would bring into being the federal state of West Germany.

For four years we had struggled for understanding among the four occupying powers and found that it would result only from acceptance of the Soviet will to dominate Germany. We were forced to combine the American and British zones to achieve economic progress and subsequently to include the French Zone to form a West Germany in which 45,000,000 German people are separated from 20,000,000 German people by the Soviet-constructed "Iron Curtain."

How had this come about? Why was it impossible for four countries who had fought to victory in a common cause to co-operate in peace? Why had the Soviet Government imposed a blockade on Berlin? Why was it necessary to create a West German Government? Neither these questions nor the decisions which they made necessary occurred to me in the spring of 1945.

In late March I was occupying an office in the Reconstruction Finance Corporation Building as deputy to Justice James F. Byrnes, who was then director of War Mobilization and Reconversion. My secretary announced that a Mr. Murphy was waiting to see me. Although I had heard much of Robert D. Murphy and the work he had accomplished in North Africa in saving many American lives at the expense of much unwarranted criticism, I had not met him personally. I did not identify my visitor until he introduced himself as General Eisenhower's political adviser. He told me that he was briefly visiting Washington to report to the State Department and had dropped in to congratulate me on my coming assignment as deputy to General Eisenhower for Military Government. I replied somewhat to his amazement that he must be mistaken as I had heard nothing of it.

My denial to Mr. Murphy held valid for only a few minutes. He had hardly left the room when I received a telephone call from Justice Byrnes asking me to come over to his office in the White House. There he told me that Secretary of War Henry L. Stimson had just telephoned him that I was to be immediately designated as deputy military governor to General Eisenhower. Now it was my turn to be amazed because the limited discussion I had heard of this appointment had pointed to the selection of a civilian; Under Secretary Robert Patterson and Assistant Secretary John J. McCloy were both mentioned frequently.

My assignment in late November 1944 to work with Justice Byrnes as his deputy had also come as a surprise. In October, at General Eisenhower's request, I had been sent to France on a four-month loan by General Brehon B. Somervell, commanding general of the Army Service Forces. When I reported to General Eisenhower he told me that my first job was to take over the Normandy base, including Cherbourg and its port activities, a bottleneck in the shipment of supplies to the front. It was at Cherbourg that I had my first experience with civil affairs, as I found on my staff a Civil Affairs Section primarily engaged in the maintenance of good relations between the French civil authorities and our Army administration. Fortunately I discovered that the bottleneck in Cherbourg was mainly due to the fact that the efficient port director was receiving too much supervision. By the simple process of giving him the authority he needed I was able to eliminate it very quickly, and in fact received undue credit for the remarkable improvement he achieved within a few days.

There were more than 200,000 troops under my command in Normandy. It was a staging area through which the combat divisions passed on the way to the front. Thousands of tons of supplies were stored in open fields adjacent to the beaches over which they had been unloaded and from which they were moved forward to meet requirements at the front. Ships were unloaded in the dry docks and locks of the French naval yard, inside and along the breakwater, and from harbor anchorages by lighters and amphibious trucks. While the scene may have appeared confusing to the casual observer, it was my command and I was certain of my responsibility. The bureaucratic struggle for jurisdiction in war production and procurement which never ended in Washington had no parallel in Cherbourg. I was happy in my work, which lasted only three weeks, when General Eisenhower sent for me to say that my mission was accomplished. He wanted me to visit our Army groups with one of his staff directors, General Harold R. Bull, to make an accurate appraisal of the need for heavy ammunition, after which we were to go home to convince the War Department of its urgency. When I told General Eisenhower I was apprehensive that my trip to Washington would lead to my retention there, he promised me he would send a personal letter to General Marshall which would assure my prompt return.

When General Bull and I reached Washington we reported immediately to General Marshall, who was worried that the ammunition shortage might delay the final assault. Our competent ordnance officers met with me to develop the possibility of making additional ammunition available by compressing the pipe line. Our calculations proved we could deliver enough so that the final assault could be staged, provided production-line output was increased promptly to insure an adequate future flow. We reported back to General Marshall on the day after our arrival, Friday afternoon. He was pleased with the result and both General Bull and I were cheerful over the report we could now take back to General Eisenhower.

We planned to leave on Sunday. Thus for the first time since the beginning of the war I had a free Saturday on my hands, which just happened to be the day of the Army-Navy football game in Baltimore. I managed to obtain seats and stopped by the Pentagon early that morning to finish up last-minute chores. Hardly had I sat down at my desk when I received a call from Justice Byrnes advising me that he was requesting my services as his deputy for War Production and that it would be my particular mission to see that more heavy ammunition was produced quickly. I rushed to my chief, General Somervell, to ask his assistance in securing my return to Europe, and I told him of the letter General Eisenhower had written to General Marshall. Somervell remarked that this would be easy and that he would see General Marshall immediately. However, whatever he may have said to General Marshall or General Eisenhower may have written in his letter had little effect, as I was shortly told to report for duty to Justice Byrnes on the following day for an assignment to last four months. I am afraid that I failed to appreciate fully the achievements of Blanchard and Davis as they led the Army football team to victory that Saturday afternoon.

The four months were drawing to an end when Justice Byrnes told me that I was to go to Germany as deputy military governor. Immediately after receiving this information I drove to the War Department to ask both General Somervell and Assistant Secretary McCloy to try to find someone else. I did so because it looked then as if the Japanese war would last for some time and I hoped for a tour of duty in the Pacific which would carry with it some combat experience. I had been a soldier in two wars, and like any other professional soldier, I believed that my career would be a failure without combat experience. My plea was ineffective.

After seeing General Somervell I had another talk with Justice Byrnes, who recognized the difficulties which would confront me in Germany and felt strongly that my responsibilities must be clearly defined. He said that I should be General Eisenhower's deputy in fact, reporting directly to him and not through the General Staff. He was insistent that my appointment be announced from the White House by the President, and Secretary Stimson agreed.

On the following day, when the appointment was to be announced (I believe it was March 31, 1945), Justice Byrnes took me to see President Roosevelt. On the way over he told me that I should be prepared to answer a test question which the President would put to me but which he did not feel that he could disclose. But the President never asked the question. When we left, Byrnes told me that the President had indicated that he would inquire what action I would take if there should be a series of murders of American soldiers by unknown hands in one of the occupied cities. I still do not know what my answer would have been. (Some weeks later I was to hear staff discussions over the actions we might take if we met with resistance. Suggestions ranged from the destruction by fire of the block or blocks of buildings in which gunshots originated to the seizure, imprisonment, and even execution of hostages. I became convinced that advance planning was of little value, since the action to be taken would be dictated by the circumstances, the extent and kind of resistance, and the temper of the population. In any circumstances there had to be prompt, firm action justified by events and not ruthless and oppressive beyond need.)

Actually President Roosevelt spoke of his youth in Germany, where he had attended school and had formed an early distaste for German arrogance and provincialism. He spoke particularly of the need for developing a more inquisitive mind in German youth, and at some length of Europe's need for hydroelectric power. He believed that a huge hydroelectric power development serving several of the European countries—a sort of international TVA—was essential to economic rehabilitation and would lead to better co-operation among the participating countries. While the President was most gracious, I did not have an opportunity to say very much, for which I was thankful, because I was so shocked at his physical appearance that I found it difficult to say anything. I remarked as we left that the President was a dangerously ill man, and I remember well that Justice Byrnes replied that my comment worried him, as perhaps he and the others who saw the President daily did not realize how ill and worn he looked. Two weeks later he was dead.

When we returned to Byrnes's office I said good-by to him and his associates and went to the Pentagon to collect my thoughts and to select some competent personnel to assist me in the task ahead. I had very little time, because the War Department wished me to report to General Eisenhower within a few days. My first action was to call on General John H. Hilldring (later Assistant Secretary of State), director of the Civil Affairs Division of the War Department. He told me, to my astonishment, that my appointment as deputy had not been made known in advance to General Eisenhower, who had requested me to be director of the Civil Affairs (G-5) Division of his General Staff, a status quite different than reporting directly to him. I was certain that a staff division would not prove the proper place to put military government responsibility. I was not at all sure that General Eisenhower's General Staff would agree with me. Shortly afterward, when I reported to Assistant Secretary McCloy, I found that he shared my apprehension, because he brought up the subject and said that he proposed to visit General Eisenhower soon after my arrival to discuss the problem.

Before my departure I reported to Secretary Stimson. His long experience with government had given him a clear view of the difficulties and responsibilities ahead and he told me that he knew of no more difficult task than that which confronted General Eisenhower and me. He gave us both his full confidence and assurance of support. When I left his office I called to say good-by to General Marshall. Although he was still beset with all the problems of war, he gave me much of his time on a busy day. In assuring me of his interest and continuing support he urged me to write him at any time that I needed his assistance.

I used the three or four days at my disposal to persuade General William H. Draper, Jr., to become my economics adviser and to follow me to Germany within a few weeks after he had recruited some key personnel to assist us in the establishment of military government.

As I look back I find it amazing that I did not visit the State Department or talk with any of its officials. Nor was it suggested that I do so. No one at that time advised me of the role of the State Department in occupation matters or of its relationship to military government, and I am inclined to believe that no one had thought it out. Fortified by the support which I had received from my chiefs and by the assurance which came from General Draper's agreement to serve as my economics adviser, I left New York by air on April 6, 1945, to land in Paris the following day. I had said good-by to Mrs. Clay in our quarters at Fort Myer, Virginia, which she would now have to leave to seek an apartment in crowded Washington.

In the Army one becomes accustomed over many years to new assignments and, having no say in them, takes them in stride without anxiety or exultation. In my civil work with the Corps of Engineers, in my responsibilities for war production, and in my four months with Justice Byrnes I had learned enough about government to realize that the task ahead would be filled with perplexing problems and difficulties. I had served in the Philippines and had become sufficiently interested to read of our experience in occupying these islands. My responsibility for procurement had given me some knowledge of the supply problem involved in the maintenance of civilian populations in the wake of battle—as in Italy, where it had been necessary to sacrifice badly needed war cargo to deliver food to sustain the Italian population behind our advancing armies.

When I left Washington I knew nothing of JCS (Joint Chiefs of Staff) 1067, the top-secret policy directive which was to be my guide but which was then still in preparation. Nor did I know anything of the policies and agreements which had been established in international conferences with Russia and the United Kingdom prior to the surrender of Germany. As I sat in the plane flying across the Atlantic I had time to wonder whether the task ahead could be accomplished and what experience, talents, or training that were mine could give me any hope of confidence. I was thinking of the task as an administrative problem and little did I realize what decisions would result from international differences and misunderstandings and what firmness of purpose would be required to carry them out.

I found that General Eisenhower was spending most of his time in his headquarters at Reims, where I reported to him on April 8. I also reported to his chief of staff, Lieutenant General Walter Bedell Smith, and learned from this forthright officer that he was not particularly favorable to the designation of a deputy to General Eisenhower for Military Government. General Smith had valid reasons for his views, as civil affairs were then under the supervision of an integrated group of American and British officers which was a part of the staff he directed for General Eisenhower. This group, known as G-5, one of the five divisions of the General Staff, was establishing policy guidance for military government in Germany, which was administered in the rear areas by trained teams under the Army commanders.

I could not help but agree with the logic of General Smith's position. Divided responsibilities were unthinkable at the moment and I did not even take up the question with General Eisenhower. I felt certain that with his good sense and sound judgment he would see the wisdom of separating military government responsibility from direct military command as soon as the war ended. But in those last rushing days of victory his problems were too great to add another.

A few days later McCloy arrived to discuss the problem with Eisenhower and Smith. I was not present at these talks. On April 17 the order designating me deputy military governor was issued, although it was then a title without a job. Military government remained a combined Anglo-American responsibility under the SHAEF Civil Affairs Division. I was placed in command of the United States Group Control Council, the nucleus for the American delegation in the Allied Control Council, which was to govern Germany under an agreement reached in London between the Russian, British, and American governments.

In addition I was made deputy chief of staff for the United States Forces, European Theater, with the redeployment of troops for the Pacific war as my special responsibility. In this capacity I hoped to relieve General Smith from a small part of the heavy burden which rested on his shoulders. I also received notice from the War Department of my promotion to a lieutenant generalcy.

When I arrived in Paris I had heard only vaguely of the U. S. Group Control Council which was now under my command, and knew little of its functions. I did know that, while the actual supervision of military government was a staff function of Supreme Headquarters, there was an American group planning our participation in military government after the defeat of Germany and the dissolution of combined command. I had heard that this group had prepared a manual for military government that aroused indignation in Washington because allegedly it proposed a liberal treatment of Germany, which was displeasing to those who were preparing a much more drastic policy directive. Our government ordered the suppression of this manual with consequent devastating effect on the morale of the U. S. Group Control Council, although reading it now will show that it deviated little from the American policy which was to develop for Germany and to be proclaimed first by Secretary of State Byrnes in his Stuttgart speech.

When I assumed command I found that this group had been in existence for many months under the able and personable Brigadier General Cornelius Wickersham, in civil life a well-known lawyer in New York City. It had its headquarters in Versailles and its tail—and a substantial tail indeed—just outside London. It was composed of several hundred officers and a few civilians selected as experts in specific fields of government.

It was organized into divisions paralleling the German ministries which were to be seized on surrender and continued in operation under Allied control. I was certain the German Government was already so scattered that complete collapse was inevitable. Thus the concept of finding and utilizing working ministries had ceased to have reality. The group had studied German government carefully and its accumulated knowledge and considered planning were to prove of great and lasting value to our work. For the moment I felt that these experts were badly needed in the practical task of military government and, moreover, that experience in the field would prove of benefit to our future task, so I arranged with the chief of the Civil Affairs Division for substantial numbers to join the Military Government teams working in the field.

I found also that corresponding British and French groups had been organized and had their headquarters in Paris under Generals Stanley Woodburn Kirby and Louis Marie Koeltz respectively. The three groups could thus form committees to discuss subjects of mutual interest.

I was sitting in my office in Versailles in the late afternoon of May 6 when General Bedell Smith telephoned me to come to Reims at once. I knew something was about to happen and I rushed to a nearby airport to get a ride. When I reached the school building which served as headquarters I went immediately to my office, which was in a wing set aside for General Eisenhower, General Smith, and the secretary of the General Staff. As I passed the guard I noticed he was smiling. I opened the door to my office and to my surprise saw sitting at my desk an immaculately turned-out general officer of the German Army. Not knowing what this meant, I backed out quickly. General Smith's secretary advised me that in my absence my office had been loaned to General Jodl, who had come to negotiate surrender. The next morning the German officials had surrendered unconditionally and were waiting in a small anteroom for their return transportation.

There was little outward celebration of victory in General Eisenhower's headquarters. Rather, there was a quiet satisfaction that one phase of our war effort was ended. We were still at war with Japan, and already orders were being issued to transfer troops and supplies to the Pacific. We did not then expect the Japanese collapse would come so soon. General Eisenhower had his close associates, British and Americans, join him for lunch at his residence. There little was said as his guests realized this would be the last official gathering for many of those present.

SHAEF had already planned its forward move to Frankfurt, and I had arranged with General Smith for the U. S. Group Control Council to move forward at the same time to the nearby industrial suburb of Hoechst, where accommodations were available in the office buildings of a large I. G. Farben subsidiary. This move was started in late May and completed in early June. At last the U. S. Group Control Council was assembled in one place. That place was in Germany and adjacent to Supreme Headquarters.

Its future was by no means certain. General Eisenhower had favored the continuation of SHAEF in an integrated joint occupation of western Germany. This would never have been acceptable to the Soviet Government, which was even then suspicious of the formation of a "Western bloc." Churchill was alleged to favor both the continuation of SHAEF and the joint occupation of all the territory held by our armies, rather than withdrawal to the agreed boundaries for occupation purposes. None of the occupying powers appeared willing to make the initial overture toward establishing four-power government. Since I was not a part of SHAEF I knew nothing at first hand of these matters but I had been too long in the Army not to discount the rumors which were flying thick and fast.

I did know now of the international agreements which were to affect our occupation of Germany and I had received JCS/1067, the document which was to be our policy guide in administering the American Zone of Occupation and in negotiating with the other members of quadripartite government.

A knowledge of these agreements and documents is essential to an understanding of the negotiations which were shortly to take place in Berlin. In fact it may well be said that the German problem as it then stood originated in international conference and finally it was already becoming evident that it could be resolved only in international conference. While much was written at the time about United States policy, based on expediency, being improvised in Germany, this appeared to be the case only because the international discussions had been held in secrecy and neither the resulting agreements nor the basic policy directive had been or were to be published for some time. A study of these conferences reveals the degree to which they influenced and molded our early German policy. While the full story of all these conferences is still not available, the published record suffices to show their import and to explain many of the administrative actions and decisions which were taken in Germany.

The first of these conferences was the meeting between President Roosevelt and Prime Minister Churchill "somewhere in the Atlantic" which resulted on August 14, 1941, in the Atlantic Charter. This document in its sixth point formulated a policy for the re-establishment of a German nation in the words:

After the final destruction of the Nazi tyranny, they hope to see established a peace which will afford to all nations the means of dwelling in safety within their own boundaries, and which will afford assurance that all the men in all the lands may live out their lives in freedom from fear and want.

The Inter-Allied Declaration of London, January 5, 1943, served warning to the German nation that it could not expect to hold the loot of war and expressed the intent of the Allied Nations "to reserve all their rights to declare invalid any transfers, or dealings with, property, rights and interests . . . of open looting or plunder, or of transactions apparently legal in form."

It is understood, although no record is available, that in the second Quebec Conference of September 11–16, 1944, attended by President Roosevelt and Prime Minister Churchill, we gave up our previous insistence on American occupation of northwest Germany and accepted an occupation of south Germany in exchange for the United Kingdom's acceptance in principle of our proposed policy for the treatment of Germany. This was the policy advocated by Secretary of the Treasury Henry Morgenthau, Jr., who had been at Quebec, and was subsequently expressed with some modification in JCS/1067. In any event it is certain that the occupation areas of the United States and the United Kingdom were defined at this time.

The major presurrender conference affecting Germany was attended by President Roosevelt, Prime Minister Churchill, and Generalissimo Stalin at Yalta on February 3–11, 1945.[1] I was deputy to Justice Byrnes at the time and I know of his concern with some of its provisions. It was agreed at Yalta that the forces of the three powers should each occupy a separate zone of Germany. It was further agreed that co-ordination and control should be exercised through a central Control Commission, composed of the supreme commanders of the three powers, with headquarters in Berlin. The

Soviet Government also agreed that France, if the French Government should so desire, could have a zone of occupation provided it was made available from the British and American zones, and could participate as a fourth member of the Commission. Thus Yalta confirmed the pattern of occupation which had been worked out by the European Advisory Commission in London, and unfortunately, as it turned out, laid the basis for a split Germany.

It was at Yalta that the Allied Powers formulated their purposes with regard to Germany: to destroy Nazism and militarism to ensure that Germany would never again disturb the peace of the world, to disarm and disband Germany's armed forces, to break up the General Staff, to remove or destroy all war equipment, to eliminate or control industry having war potential, to punish war criminals, to exact reparations in kind for the destruction wrought by the Germans, to wipe out the Nazi party, laws, and institutions, and to remove Nazis and militaristic influences from public office and from cultural and economic life.

It was at Yalta that the eastern frontier of Poland was fixed and that Poland was promised, in exchange for the territory thus transferred to Russia, compensation in the form of "substantial accessions of territory in the north and west." This led to the present Polish-German boundary which has still not been accepted by the Western governments as complying with the terms of the Yalta Agreement.

The Yalta Conference also arranged to establish a Commission for Compensation of Damage to determine the amount and kind of reparations to be exacted, the Commission to meet later in Moscow. It was at this conference that the Soviet Government first announced its claim for $10,000,000,000 in reparations. Because the British and American representatives were willing to consider this in relation to other claims, the Soviets later asserted again and again that it had been accepted at Yalta.

Although it does not appear in the agreement, I am of the opinion that it was also here that we accepted the principle later formally agreed at Potsdam of the expulsion of persons of German origin from the areas outside postsurrender Germany and their resettlement in Germany.[2] This led to a substantial increase in the population of western Germany and created a new and difficult problem of absorption.

However, the Yalta Conference was not devoted entirely to punitive and security measures. It reaffirmed the principle of the Atlantic Charter in declaring that it was not the Allied purpose to destroy the German people and that they could hope for a decent life and a return to the family of nations when Nazism and militarism were extirpated.

The influence of Yalta cannot be overemphasized. It formed the basis for such joint Allied policy as did result and, while the different interpretations subsequently given to its provisions by the signatory powers showed how different were their purposes and understandings, each of the powers did claim that its policy was based on its announced understanding of the Yalta Agreement.

In many respects the Yalta Conference affirmed the agreements and understandings reached in London, where the European Advisory Commission had been meeting for some months to formulate a written agreement for the control of Germany. On this Commission we were represented by Ambassador John G. Winant, the British by Sir William Strang, and the Russians by Mr. F. T. Gusev. On November 14, 1944, the Commission agreed to three documents[3] which were to be issued by the three commanders in chief in Berlin, and on a map which defined the boundaries between the zones of occupation with Germany and the sectors of occupation in Berlin. When this was affirmed in principle at Yalta with provision for French participation, it became necessary for the Commission to meet with the French representative, René Massigli. An amended agreement was signed on May 2, 1945, with a revised map to indicate the French Zone of Occupation. This was drawn to meet French desires on the one hand and military requirements on the other and, in spite of specific protest by Mr. Murphy, resulted in the division of the traditional states of Wuerttemberg and Baden between the American and French zones. The French Sector in Berlin was not yet defined, although it was understood that it would come from either the British or the American Sector.

The three documents agreed on by the European Advisory Commission have been made public. Since they are not readily available and their context is essential to an understanding of the German problem as it existed at the time military government was established, it seems desirable to summarize them.

The first of these documents was the "Declaration Regarding the Defeat of Germany"[4] and was to be signed and issued in Berlin in the name of their governments by the four commanders in chief. In the preamble the four governments assumed supreme authority in Germany by virtue of its unconditional surrender and the absence of competent authority which resulted. The four governments announced their intent to establish the boundaries of Germany. They required the transfer of all war equipment, aircraft, and merchant vessels, the remaining in place of all German armed forces, the provision of labor and services necessary to disarmament, the furnishing of any information and records which might be requested, and the provision of adequate transport facilities. The declaration provided for the immediate release of all prisoners of war, nationals of the United Nations, and persecutees, although this had been accomplished in fact by the victorious Allied armies prior to its issue. It required German authorities to turn over to Allied representatives as requested any Nazi leaders, suspected war criminals, or officers. German authorities were required to furnish information of mines and mine fields and to retain for Allied use all property, records, or archives. Communications facilities were taken under Allied control. Provision was made for the stationing of Allied forces and civil agencies in any or all parts of Germany and for Allied representatives to impose any additional political, administrative, economic, financial, military, and other requirements which might arise from the complete defeat of Germany. The German authorities and people were charged with the unconditional execution of Allied requirements. Thus, in this declaration, the four occupying governments eliminated the last vestige of national government in Germany and replaced it with four commanders in chief. It was a fateful decision which can be judged fairly in its effect only by time and history.

The second proclamation,[5] which was to be issued simultaneously, carried the disintegration of Germany a step further by establishing in each zone the commander in chief as the supreme authority subject only to the four commanders in chief acting in unanimous agreement in matters affecting Germany as a whole. This was the veto which blocked our efforts for four years. Each commander in chief was to be assisted by a political adviser. They were to meet at regular intervals in the Allied Control Council, which would establish a permanent co-ordinating committee composed of the deputies to the commanders in chief and a control staff of military and civil personnel to form twelve directorates. The Control Council was to arrange for liaison with other United Nations governments. It was charged with the administration of "Greater Berlin" under the immediate direction of the four commandants, who would rotate monthly in the chair. This proclamation established the life of its arrangements as the period in which Germany was meeting basic requirements and until arrangements were reached for the subsequent period by separate agreement of the four governments.

The third proclamation[6] announced the boundaries of the four zones of occupation and the occupation of Berlin by the troops of all four powers.

It is interesting to note that all of these documents accepted a common occupation of Berlin and yet no one of them contained any guarantee of access or specific provision for truck, rail, and air right of way. This omission was not accidental and had been discussed with our representative on the European Advisory Commission by Mr. Murphy. Ambassador Winant believed that the right to be in Berlin carried with it right of access and that it would only confuse the issue to raise it in connection with the agreement. He felt strongly that it would arouse Soviet suspicion and make mutual understanding more difficult to attain. He believed it possible to develop a mutual friendly understanding in which differences would disappear.

To judge the full effects of these international agreements, it is necessary to visualize the Germany which resulted from total defeat. All central and state government had collapsed; county and city government no longer existed. Mail service had stopped; communications were taken over completely for security and for the use of the invading armies. More than 3,000,000 American troops were in Europe, mostly in Germany, and these troops and their equipment were to be moved rapidly to the Pacific war areas. In fact more than 2,000,000 of these troops were out by November, a rate in excess of 400,000 per month. Seven million German prisoners had surrendered to the Western armies, and almost 5,000,000 were to be processed for discharge by our forces. Perhaps 1,500,000 more were held in France, England, and the United States for return to and discharge in Germany.

In our zone alone more than 2,000,000 displaced persons had been repatriated by November 1945, while more than 500,000 remained in our care. Meanwhile additional refugees from Poland (German refugees and the expellees from Poland), Czechoslovakia, and Hungary poured into west Germany to augment its population by almost 4,500,000 persons by the end of 1946. The scenes on highway and railway were indescribable as these huge mass migrations took place. Transport was never sufficient to meet the demand and the roads were filled with destitute human beings searching desperately for a place to live.

Hundreds of thousands of tons of German war material had to be guarded and destroyed while more than 8,000,000 tons of our own equipment were moved into Germany from the liberated areas for disposal or for utilization by our occupation forces. Navigation on the Rhine and its auxiliary canals was impossible until sunken barges and tugs and destroyed bridges were removed. Normal highway and rail facilities were usable only in part because of the destruction of innumerable bridges.

In July 1945 we estimated that only 1200 of the 12,000 plants in our zone were in limited production. Many school buildings had been destroyed or were occupied either by our troops or by displaced persons. Only our own press and radio were in operation. Hospitals everywhere were filled with wounded German soldiers.

In looking back, I think that if we had then realized the confusion and chaos which existed we would indeed have thought ours a hopeless task. Certainly the authorities in Washington who had prepared our policy directive did not visualize these conditions. They did not know of the heavy burden performed so well under the circumstances by the Military Government teams which accompanied the combat troops and were engaged even before the surrender of Germany in re-creating some form of local administrative machinery at the city and county level and in re-establishing at least locally law, order, and public services.

Our policy directive, which was to guide us for many months (except as modified in the Potsdam Protocol) in our deliberations with our Allies and in the administration of our zone, was distributed to key personnel on May 21. It had been issued as JCS 1067/6 on April 26, amended on May 10, approved by President Truman, and issued finally on May 14, 1945, classified as top secret.[7] Thus for some months we were carrying out a policy whose existence we could not even admit. It was difficult indeed to make our press representatives in Germany believe that we were not conducting our administration on a basis of expediency but frequent requests for the removal of the security classification were refused and the policy directive was not made public until October 1945.

While this document was intended as a guide only for the initial postwar period rather than as an ultimate statement of policy, it was not replaced in full until 1947. For many months we were to urge the adoption of its principles by the Allied Control Council. JCS/1067 authorized the assumption of sovereign power by our commander in chief, based upon unconditional surrender and his participation in the Allied Control Council. It required the decentralization of the German political and administrative structure and the complete severance of all ties between Germany and Austria. This became the expressed objective of all four powers and yet determining what it meant became a principal controversial issue between the Western Powers and Russia, and then among the Western Powers. Consistently we supported a structure which gave adequate but limited powers to a federal government.

By the provisions of JCS/1067 Germany was to be occupied as a defeated nation under a just, firm, and aloof administration which would discourage any fraternization. The German economy was to be controlled only to the extent necessary to meet the needs of the occupation forces or to produce the goods which would prevent disease and unrest, which might endanger the occupying forces. The Nazi party and its affiliates were to be dissolved, Nazi laws and regulations annulled. Members and associates of the party who had been more than nominal participants in party activities were to be excluded from places of prominence in public and private life, and party property and records were to be taken into our custody. The German armed forces were to be disbanded and arms, ammunition, and implements of war were to be seized and destroyed. War criminals and persons suspected as dangerous to the accomplishment of our objectives were to be arrested. To broaden the effect of this provision, the document listed a large number of organizations such as the Nazi party, Nazi youth and women's groups, the Gestapo, the SS, the SA, the police, the General Staff, the ministries, and less important groups whose key officials, officers, and non-commissioned officers were to be seized and held in internment because of the positions which they had held.

While political activities to include parades of any kind were prohibited, freedom of speech, press, and religious worship were to be permitted so long as the exercise of these freedoms did not prejudice military interests. Educational institutions were to be permitted to reopen when Nazi personnel was eliminated.

JCS/1067 gave only limited authority to Military Government. It specifically prohibited us from taking any steps to rehabilitate or maintain the German economy except to maximize agricultural production. Land reform was to be effected. Trade unions were to be encouraged and social insurance and poor relief to be continued. Patents and trade processes were declared subject to seizure. Production in war plants was to be stopped and plants equipped for such production were to be removed without awaiting action by the Allied Control Council. Until agreement was reached in the Council, there was to be no production of iron, steel, chemicals, machine tools, radio and electrical equipment, automobiles, or heavy machinery. Only the production of light consumer goods and the mining of coal were to be encouraged. Large concentrations of economic power were to be broken up, and all cartels and cartellike organizations disbanded. We were permitted to undertake such fiscal measures as seemed essential to prevent or restrain inflation.

When I was sent to Germany I had been fortunate in securing with Justice Byrnes's help the services of Lewis Douglas as my financial adviser. My work in production had brought me into frequent touch with his work in the Maritime Commission, and I had formed a great admiration for his ability. I was relieved of much anxiety when he joined me shortly after my arrival in Paris. He and I had been shown a draft of the proposed directive in late April. We were shocked—not at its punitive provisions but at its failure to grasp the realities of the financial and economic conditions which confronted us. Like the four basic documents which directed Allied policy, it had been drafted before Germany surrendered and without knowledge of the conditions we should find.

It seemed obvious to us even then that Germany would starve unless it could produce for export and that immediate steps would have to be taken to revise industrial production. Since there was no German Government to initiate these steps, Military Government perforce would be responsible. Nevertheless, we were not only prohibited from taking such steps but were also required to stop production in many fields until agreement could be obtained in the Control Council, and such agreement could be blocked indefinitely by a single veto. The original draft also prohibited financial controls, although the inflation of currency within Germany was already apparent.

At my request Douglas made a hurried trip to Washington to report our fears to McCloy and to attempt to obtain modification of the directive sufficient to permit the exercise of economic and financial controls. His efforts to this end were successful in limited degree only; all that he could accomplish was to have added the authority to exercise financial control if essential to prevent inflation. One of the results of this directive was that Douglas soon resigned. I am sure his feeling that our economic efforts would be futile in the economic field under the restrictions led to his early return home.

Fortunately the provisions of JCS/1067 were in some respects general in nature, so that the degree of application was left to the judgment of the military governor and some of its more drastic economic and financial provisions were tempered by the agreements reached in Potsdam. Still, there was no doubt that JCS/1067 contemplated the Carthaginian peace which dominated our operations in Germany during the early months of occupation.

CHAPTER 2

Commanders in Chief
Meet in Berlin

WE took off from Frankfurt by air on the morning of June 5 for Berlin to sign and issue the three documents prepared by the European Advisory Commission. The date for a meeting of General Eisenhower, Field Marshal Sir Bernard Montgomery, Marshal Grigori Zhukov, and General Jean de Lattre de Tassigny was fixed in an exchange of communications between governments through diplomatic channels. We traveled in several planes. General Eisenhower planned to return the same day, while Mr. Murphy and I were prepared to stay if it proved possible to negotiate our entry into Berlin and the start of quadripartite government. We carried with us radio transmitting equipment and operators which we proposed to use to maintain communications with Frankfurt, with or without Russian concurrence. When we climbed into the planes we remembered Soviet reluctance to participate in the first surrender ceremony in Reims and Soviet insistence on a second ceremony in Berlin, and we could not but wonder at what might lie ahead. The delay in arranging this meeting and the realization that previous international agreements did not suffice had already resulted in diplomatic exchanges which were to lead to the Potsdam Conference.

The three Western commanders in chief arrived in Berlin separately in the forenoon. The signature ceremony was scheduled for twelve o'clock noon. Although SHAEF was still in existence, the French and British commanders in chief were there as representatives of their respective countries and not as a part of the SHAEF Command.

When we landed at Tempelhof airport General Eisenhower was received with appropriate honors by a Soviet contingent of troops roughly corresponding in size to one of our battalions, about 800 men. It was the first Soviet military unit I had seen. While it was evident that their uniforms and equipment were war-worn, they were clean and tidy. The men appeared to be in splendid physical condition and well disciplined, and I was impressed.

After General Eisenhower inspected the guard of honor we were escorted to waiting cars which, paced by motorcycle escort, led us through Berlin to Karlshorst in eastern Berlin, where Marshal Zhukov had his headquarters. This ride passed quickly for us as we were having our first view of the city. A few of our senior officers had visited Berlin for the signing of the second surrender document on May 8 and had reported on their return the almost complete destruction of the city. Later I found the report exaggerated, but I could well understand why they reached such a conclusion. Wherever we looked we saw desolation. The streets were piled high with debris which left in many places only a narrow one-way passage between high mounds of rubble, and frequent detours had to be made where bridges and viaducts were destroyed. Apparently the Germans along the route, which was lined with Soviet soldiers, had been ordered to remain indoors, and it was only at the intersections that a few could be seen on the streets which crossed our route. They seemed weak, cowed, and furtive and not yet recovered from the shock of the Battle of Berlin. It was like a city of the dead. I had seen nothing quite comparable in western Germany, and I must confess that my exultation in victory was diminished as I witnessed this degradation of man. I decided then and there never to forget that we were responsible for the government of human beings.

As soon as we arrived at Karlshorst we were taken to a residence which had been prepared as a billet and were served an excellent lunch by Red Army women. So far only minor Soviet officials had greeted us and if they knew anything of the ceremony which was to take place they were unwilling to impart their knowledge to us.

Shortly after lunch, and already well past the hour scheduled for the signing ceremony, Montgomery and De Lattre de Tassigny walked over from their nearby billets. All three commanders in chief were now impatient with the delay and with the unexplained lack of courtesy. We discovered that the trouble came from a clause in the agreement which would have required the Soviet Government to place Japanese citizens in Russia under arrest. Obviously this was a mistake, since the Soviet Government was not at war then with Japan and the Western governments would never have asked that this provision be applied. Nevertheless, it was an early example of the meticulous care with which Soviet representatives scrutinized the exact wording of each document.

Although the agreement had been confirmed by the four governments, I accepted responsibility for the deletion of this provision and assured the Soviet representative, V. S. Semeonov (who was later to become political adviser to the Soviet commander in chief in Germany), that General Eisenhower would initial it. British and French representatives also agreed, so it looked as if the way was now clear to proceed with the signing. This proved not to be the case, perhaps because of the usual desire of Soviet representatives to obtain the approval of the next higher authority. In any event it was several hours before transportation and guides arrived at approximately five o'clock in the afternoon to take us to the building where the declaration was to be signed. Marshal Zhukov, Andrei Vishinsky, and a small group of service officers met us on the porch. The officers were in field uniform and the diplomatic representatives in the gray service uniform of the Soviet diplomatic corps. They were smiling and affable and noticeably enthusiastic in greeting General Eisenhower.

Inside, a large round table had been set up with places marked for the four delegations. In the glare of flashlights and with photographers everywhere, the documents in English, French, Russian, and German were signed without further delay, and the formal ceremony was concluded in a few minutes.

Marshal Zhukov then led the three delegations back to the porch, where wine and vodka were served, after which he invited us to be his guests at a banquet. General Eisenhower reminded the marshal that he had been in Berlin many hours for a simple ceremony and that while he would be glad to attend the banquet it was necessary for him to leave at six o'clock as he had to return to Frankfurt that day. He said further that he would like to leave a small staff in Berlin to arrange the details of our entry into the city. It was apparent that Zhukov did not have the Kremlin's answer to this request, because he replied that he did not believe it would be useful, since such arrangements could be made only when the troops were in the prescribed occupation areas. At this time troops under SHAEF were not only occupying the three western zones but were also well into Saxony and Thuringia. General Eisenhower said he understood that the withdrawal of occupation troops to prescribed areas would be concurrent with our entry into Berlin. He did not press the issue since it was obvious that Marshal Zhukov was not prepared to discuss it.

After a few minutes on the porch we proceeded to the banquet table. A large soldier chorus was on an improvised stage at one end of the hall, and it thrilled us with the fine quality of its singing. Choral singing is a field in which the Russians excel, and this chorus had been assembled without doubt from a large group, as it was unusually good. The banquet table was filled with caviar, smoked salmon, cold fish, and cold cuts, and several bottles of vodka and wine stood in front of each plate but we had time for only a few bites and, with the urging of the Soviet hosts on either side, a few drinks of vodka. It was my initiation into the Soviet custom of frequent toasts throughout the meal. I must confess that if the ability to enjoy vodka comes from experience I never passed the first stage. In addition to the toasts between those sitting next to each other, formal toasts were also started by Marshal Zhukov, who soon after we sat down raised his glass to the four heads of state, extending a welcome to the three Western commanders in chief. He spoke briefly and warmly. General Eisenhower in response also spoke warmly of the victorious Red Army and its accomplished military leaders, and expressed his satisfaction that the four powers which had worked so successfully together in war were now to work together in peace. However, he remembered the hours of delay which he did not believe conformed to the dignity of his position as a representative of the United States. Therefore he closed his response quickly, expressing regret that the long delay had prevented an earlier start as he now had to thank his hosts and say good-by. I am sure the Russians did not expect him to leave on schedule and that it proved an effective lesson. Henceforth their appointments with him were kept as sedulously as he kept his own appointments.

When we returned to Frankfurt we still did not know when the Allied Control Council would be established and when our troops would move into Berlin. A further exchange of messages between governments resulted in a second talk with Marshal Zhukov at his headquarters in Berlin on June 29, 1945. I represented General Eisenhower at this meeting to which I was accompanied by Murphy and by Major General Floyd Parks, who had been designated to command the contingent of troops which was to form our Berlin garrison. The British representative was my newly designated opposite, Lieutenant General Sir Ronald Weeks. He was accompanied by Sir William Strang and by the British troop commander for their Berlin garrison. General Weeks had been deputy chief of the Imperial General Staff and in that capacity had participated in several military Lend-Lease conferences which I too had attended. He was an able industrialist brought into military service by the war and I welcomed his appointment. Although French participation in quadripartite government had been agreed to, there were no French representatives present in these early discussions, since Marshal Zhukov was unwilling to meet them until the French Sector of Berlin had been determined.

While this meeting of June 29 was to result in agreement on our entry into Berlin, two subsequent meetings were required to effect the arrangements for four-power control. All three of these talks were held in Zhukov's headquarters. Although we had met him on June 5, this was the first time that we had been with him long enough to appraise his personality. He was below medium height, heavy-set but powerful rather than fat, and his bearing indicated that he had become accustomed to wield power and authority. It was largely the bearing of a professional soldier who has exercised high command with perhaps a little more consciousness of position than would be normal with us. He was polite, even affable, with a sense of humor and with the obvious desire to seem friendly. I liked the marshal instinctively and never had reason to feel otherwise. He had with him his deputy, General of the Army Vassily Sokolovsky, and his political adviser, Arkady Sobolev (later a deputy to Trygve Lie, secretary general of the United Nations); he conducted the negotiations personally and appeared to be in full control of the Soviet position.

The discussions were directed principally to the taking over of

Berlin and the withdrawal of Allied troops to their agreed occupation zones. We fixed quickly the number of troops to be quartered in Berlin at approximately 25,000 each. We had previously discussed with Soviet field commanders the time required for the withdrawal of our troops and the movement of Soviet troops to replace them, and had agreed tentatively to accomplish it in a nine-day period. Zhukov believed this much too long. I agreed with him, particularly because I knew we could certainly move as rapidly as he could. Therefore we arranged for a four-day period starting July 1, which would enable our men to enter Berlin on the Fourth of July. Soviet troops were to follow our withdrawing troops at intervals of not less than one kilometer. Liaison representatives were to be exchanged directly between the field commanders responsible for the movements. Soviet reconnaissance parties were permitted to enter the areas to be occupied by Soviet troops at once, and our reconnaissance parties were permitted to enter Berlin.

Arrangements were made for the armies to take with them all German prisoners including the wounded and all displaced persons who desired to move, other than Soviet citizens. I refused to require the movement of displaced persons who wished to remain and I also made it clear that our use of the term "Soviet citizens" applied only to those our government so recognized and not for example to citizens of the Baltic States, which we did not recognize as a part of the Soviet Union. General Weeks agreed with me. Neither of us was willing to leave five days' food supply for the displaced persons who elected to remain but, recognizing the justice of the Soviet contention that some time would be required to arrange this supply, we did agree to leave enough for two days. It was an academic argument as few if any displaced persons failed to leave in front of our withdrawing troops.

The remaining matters we discussed were not so easy to resolve. We had explained our intent to move into Berlin utilizing three rail lines and two highways and such air space as we needed. Zhukov would not recognize that these routes were essential and pointed out that the demobilization of Soviet forces was taxing existing facilities. I countered that we were not demanding exclusive use of these routes but merely access over them without restrictions other than the normal traffic control and regulations which the Soviet administration would establish for its own use. General Weeks supported my contention strongly. We both knew there was no provision covering access to Berlin in the agreement reached by the European Advisory Commission. We did not wish to accept specific routes which might be interpreted as a denial of our right of access over all routes but there was merit to the Soviet contention that existing routes were needed for demobilization purposes. We had already found transport a bottleneck to our own redeployment. Therefore Weeks and I accepted as a temporary arrangement the allocation of a main highway and rail line and two air corridors, reserving the right to reopen the question in the Allied Control Council. I must admit that we did not then fully realize that the requirement of unanimous consent would enable a Soviet veto in the Allied Control Council to block all of our future efforts. While no record was kept at this meeting, I dictated my notes that evening and they include the following:

It was agreed that all traffic—air, road and rail, . . . would be free from border search or control by customs or military authorities.

I had no way of knowing that Soviet insistence on border and customs control would serve as the excuse for the initial imposition of the blockade of Berlin.

I think now that I was mistaken in not at this time making free access to Berlin a condition to our withdrawal into our occupation zone. The import of the issue was recognized but I did not want an agreement in writing which established anything less than the right of unrestricted access. We were sincere in our desire to move into Berlin for the purpose of establishing quadripartite government, which we hoped would develop better understanding and solve many problems. Also we had a large and combat-experienced army in Germany which at the moment prevented us from having any worries over the possibility of being blockaded there. However, I doubt very much if anything in writing would have done any more to prevent the events which took place than the verbal agreement which we made. The Soviet Government seems to be able to find technical reasons at will to justify the violation of understandings whether verbal or written. In any event General Eisenhower had delegated full authority to me to conduct the negotiations and the responsibility for the decision was mine. The die had been cast and for better or worse the Western Allies were now committed to withdraw to their separate zones of occupation and to start the move into Berlin on July 1. The first step toward four-power government had been taken.

During this meeting we discussed and reached agreement on communications from Berlin, which included the assignment for our use of certain main cables which traversed the Soviet Zone and the use of the Berlin airports. We made arrangements also for certain specific facilities to be made available during the Potsdam Conference, which had been announced by this time.

Two major questions were left unsettled: the provision of food and of coal for the city of Berlin. Before joining Marshal Zhukov for refreshments we agreed to meet in a few days to resolve them. We returned by air to Frankfurt, leaving Major General Parks in Berlin as chief of our liaison group to arrange for the entry of our troops, and for the accommodations of the American delegation, which we knew would include the President, at the Potsdam Conference.

Before our second meeting, which took place with Zhukov at his headquarters on July 7, 1945, Murphy and I had moved a small staff into Berlin and had established temporary billets and offices. A reconnaissance group from my headquarters in Hoechst was searching for adequate office space and billets to permit the early movement of our section of the Allied Control Council. We had only two phones connected with Frankfurt, one in my office and the other in Murphy's office. This made it a very simple matter to keep in touch with the progress of arrangements, as almost everyone who called our Hoechst office had to do so from my telephone. On July 4 the leading elements of the 2d Armorea Division arrived and paraded in honor of our national holiday, thus announcing publicly not only their arrival but also the assumption of American responsibility. For the first time we felt established in Berlin, with equal rights and responsibilities for its government.

The July 7 meeting was devoted mainly to a continuation of the discussion concerning the supply of food and fuel for the city and the establishment of the quadripartite government of Berlin. Zhukov insisted that the Western Powers bring in food to support the population of the western sector. He said that there was a shortage of food not only in eastern Germany but also in Russia, and that the Soviet Government could no longer continue to feed the whole city of Berlin. He maintained that supplies had been furnished from Soviet Army reserves and that they would last for only five to seven more days. I suspected then and found out later that while the food being sent to the city did come from their Army stocks, it had been requisitioned in eastern Germany. General Weeks and I both insisted that Berlin should continue to receive the bulk of its food from the surrounding country since it had depended on eastern Germany in the past: Marshal Zhukov pointed out that the eastern German farm belt had been reduced substantially by the cession of territory to Poland and to the Soviet Union. Moreover, food was not available for Berlin from eastern Germany and it was impossible for the Soviet Union to make any supplies available since its people were already on a minimum sustaining ration. Weeks and I knew there was a definite shortage in both eastern Germany and the Soviet Union. Fighting between the ground forces in eastern Germany had gone on for a much longer period than in western Germany and was certain to have cut down its resources. We could not expect the ill-nourished Russians to eat less in order to feed Berlin. Therefore, subject to the establishment of a common ration in all sectors of Berlin and with the understanding that the Control Council when it was established would arrange for the exchange of food between all zones of occupation to equalize the ration throughout Germany, I accepted the responsibility for bringing in the food necessary to support the population in the American Sector.

Again I did not realize how futile our efforts to arrange for the exchange of food on an equal basis throughout Germany would prove. This was later to become one of the major disagreements with Soviet representatives on the Allied Control Council. General Weeks agreed with me tentatively, though he wished to consult his government before giving a final reply.

Zhukov also insisted at this meeting that coal for Berlin be made available from the Ruhr. Since there was only a negligible amount in our zone of occupation, this was principally an argument between Zhukov and Weeks. Weeks urged that coal be provided from Silesia. Zhukov rejected this proposal, insisting that Silesian production now belonged to Poland and that the Soviet Government had no jurisdiction whatsoever over how it was allocated. After long discussion it was agreed that a fair proportion would be provided from the Ruhr, with some brown coal and hydroelectric power to come from eastern Germany.

At this meeting we also agreed to the formation of a Kommandatura, to be composed of the four Berlin commandants with the chairmanship rotating each month, to serve as the top Allied governing body for the city. While the French had not as yet been assigned a sector in Berlin, their troops had entered with us and their participation in the government of the city was recognized. It was agreed that French representatives should attend further meetings. On the date that the Kommandatura was established the responsibility of each commandant for his sector was to begin, subject to his compliance with its general instructions. We suggested that the Kommandatura be instructed to meet immediately to organize the several departments necessary to govern the city and that each of these departments—including utilities, public safety, food distribution, public health and welfare, and such others as appeared necessary—be supervised by a quadripartite committee of experts responsible to the Kommandatura. Transportation and movement within the city were to be unrestricted between the sectors. Zhukov was fully in accord with my proposals but he wanted them embodied in a written document which he agreed to prepare for our signature at a meeting to be held on July 10.

I have described these two meetings with Marshal Zhukov in considerable detail because they illustrate the difficulties we were to face in negotiating with Soviet representatives and which became apparent in these first talks. Thus we were entering into the Allied Control Council with no illusions and we knew that the path ahead would be filled with obstacles. Our government had accepted the principle of four-power control and we had determined on our part to try in every way to allay Soviet suspicion, to create the mutual understanding that might make it successful. It is possible that this desire to make a success of quadripartite government led us in the early months to take compromise positions which merely deferred the real issues that finally forced the breakdown of the effort. I still feel that we had no alternative other than to attempt wholeheartedly to work in the four-power harmony to which as a nation we had subscribed at Yalta and in the European Advisory Commission.

I had prepared a paper which contained our general proposal for the organization of the Control Council including the establishment of the German administrative departments which were provided for in the agreement setting up the Council. I presented it to my colleagues in the hope that it would obtain their approval when we met on July 10. While we were quickly able to confirm the establishment of the Kommandatura and to approve the paper which Zhukov had prepared so that it could hold its opening session the next day, we were not able to give formal approval to the proposal for organizing the Control Council. Zhukov said he was satisfied with it but would have to withhold his concurrence until it had been referred to his government. He would notify us promptly when he had heard so that the Control Council could hold its first meeting. He further agreed that our responsibility for providing food and fuel for Berlin would start on July 15.

Before these three talks with Zhukov and during the period in which we were arranging for our entry into Berlin and the establishment of quadripartite government, the French, British, and American deputy military governors met regularly at intervals of two weeks. In these conferences we arranged for the co-ordination of transport, the release of grain from SHAEF reserves, the allocation of coal from the Ruhr, and similar measures which were of mutual benefit. Their value lessened when the Potsdam Conference convened without French representation. Moreover, as we were apprehensive that their continuance would be viewed with suspicion by the Russians, we discontinued them when the Control Council was established. They were not to be resumed until 1948, after the London meeting of the Council of Foreign Ministers had adjourned without agreeing to meet again.

In the few days between our July 7 and 10 meetings with Marshal Zhukov, Mr. Murphy and I were to have our first real opportunity to look at Berlin where we were to live for almost four years and where we were to strive so hard to develop a working four-power government. Even the start was not auspicious. In placing under way the movement of troops to Berlin on July 1, General Parks sent in his advance reconnaissance party a day early. It included his deputy for Military Government, then Colonel (later Brigadier General) Frank Howley, and a selected Military Government team composed of approximately 500 officers and enlisted men. They had hardly got under way when they were halted at the Dessau bridge across the Elbe by the Soviet outposts with the demand that their number be reduced to 37 officers and 175 enlisted men. Where these figures came from was always a mystery; it was another early incident of arbitrary action. After much argument Colonel Howley separated this number from the party and the smaller group continued to Berlin.

In his report Howley states that he passed several "Red Army supply trains reminiscent of our Civil War." He was not accustomed to seeing horse-drawn supply trains. He found the country largely deserted, with fields unattended and very few Germans in sight, and was shocked even then at the difference from conditions in west Germany, where every effort was being made to maximize agricultural activity.

His men did not reach Berlin that day, although it was only a short journey. Without explanation they were halted and forced to spend the night in Babelsberg, a Berlin suburb just outside the city limits. The following day, July 1, they continued to Berlin and pitched camp in the Grunewald Forest. They were ready to assume responsibility for the government of the American Sector. Although Soviet representatives had already agreed to withdraw, conferences to arrange for this brought no results, and on July 4, General Parks instructed Colonel Howley to take over in our sector, adding "but don't get in too much trouble." The next day Howley moved his *Verwaltungsbezirk* (borough) commanders and their detachments into offices requisitioned on the spot in each of the boroughs in our sector, raised the American flag before each office, and announced to the German borough officials that henceforth they would receive their orders from the American representatives. Soviet representatives, who rise late in the day, rushed to protest, but as usual the *fait accompli* was accepted and we had learned our first lesson in how to obtain Russian consent.

After Howley and his men had taken over we had our first real look at Berlin. Three million people were packed into the remaining buildings of a city which had suffered frightful destruction. Their meager official ration of 1240 calories a day was being met by only two thirds that amount. Workmen whom we employed to rehabilitate the buildings selected for Military Government offices fainted from exhaustion on the job until we brought in sufficient food to provide them with hot noon meals. Shortage of fuel had stopped the wheels of industry. Suffering and shock were visible in every face. Police and fire protection had broken down. The city was paralyzed.

Perhaps the picture can be shown by a few statistics. There were only 20 fire department stations in operation compared to a normal total of more than 80. Almost 3000 breaks in water mains were still to be repaired and gas was available to only a small portion of the city. Hospital beds were limited in number and far below demand. Medical supplies were scarce and many of the hospitals were completely out of narcotics. Motor ambulances were not available and transport of the sick and the dead was by hand stretcher or by cart. Dead bodies still remained in canals and lakes and were being dug out from under bomb debris. It was a common sight to see a headstone of wood on top of a mound of debris with flowers placed at its foot. Large quantities of untreated sewage had to be discharged in the canals, creating an additional health hazard, and only 23 of 84 sewage pumping stations were in operation. In the borough of Steglitz it was estimated that out of 14,000 homes 3260 had been destroyed, 3200 uninhabitable, and in the remaining 7500 which were considered habitable 10,000 out of 43,000 rooms were seriously damaged. In the borough of Schoeneberg, 45 per cent of the housing was completely destroyed, 15 per cent heavily damaged, and only 5 per cent undamaged.

Often I wondered how Howley and his team accomplished so much, how they maintained the courage to go ahead. Several years later Howley was to be criticized by some for his forthright denunciation of communist tactics in Berlin. Perhaps his language was not always diplomatic, certainly sometimes it was not timely, but I had only to think back to the successful effort he had made, working day and night, to bring order out of chaos, to relieve human suffering beyond reason, and to bring the humanitarian touch of America to the stern task of occupation. Then it would seem to me that he had well earned the commendation not only of Americans but of his fellow men.

This was the city in which we had established temporary advance offices on June 25 and to which we were to bring our element of the Group Control Council on July 10. We had to move slowly. The offices we were to occupy were badly bomb-damaged; and while our billets were more than ample in number, there were few which did not require extensive repairs to be habitable with any degree of comfort. I cannot say too much for the willingness of our personnel in those early days to accept inconvenience and discomfort cheerfully. In spite of these conditions we were prepared for the initial meeting of the Allied Control Council which took place on July 30. In August, when we received visits from Assistant Secretary McCloy and General Hilldring, they were surprised and commented favorably that we had been able to establish working machinery for our part in quadripartite government so quickly.

The date of July 30 for the opening of the Control Council was arranged as soon as Marshal Zhukov had received the approval of his government, in an informal meeting of the deputies held in my office. It is interesting to note that the Soviet delegation insisted that the headquarters of the Allied Control Council be in the United States Sector, which was accepted by all of the delegations. The discussion as to who should be the first chairman ended quickly when General Sokolovsky stated with considerable emphasis that it was the view of the Soviet delegation that this honor should go to General Eisenhower.

Thus the Allied Control Council was formally convened in the main conference room of our Berlin headquarters. General Eisenhower was in the chair with me on his right and Mr. Murphy on his left. General Parks, the Berlin commandant, and the senior staff secretary also sat with us at the table. The British were represented by Field Marshal Montgomery; his deputy, General Weeks; his political adviser, Sir William Strang (now permanent Under Secretary of the British Foreign Office); and General J. F. M. Whiteley. The Soviet representatives included Marshal Zhukov; Mr. Vishinsky (who was not present for later meetings); Mr. Sobolev, the political adviser; and General Sokolovsky. The French were represented by their deputy military governor, General Koeltz; as the French commander, General de Lattre de Tassigny was not assigned to the Control Council and General Pierre Koenig, who was to be the French military governor, had not reported for duty.

General Eisenhower and each of the other three commanders in chief expressed their pleasure briefly in the opportunity that the Allied Control Council would give them to work together. General Eisenhower then presented for the consideration of the Council the paper which would establish it and its machinery.[1] Action on this paper was deferred until the next meeting. However, agreement[2] was reached that the Control Council should meet thereafter three times monthly on the tenth, twentieth, and thirtieth, except as these dates fell on Sunday, when the meetings would be held on the following Monday. It was decided also that the chairmanship should rotate monthly and that the Co-ordinating Committee of deputies should meet informally to prepare the agenda for the next meetings, but that its formal meetings should await ratification of the Control Council paper. General Eisenhower, in a gesture of good will, then extended the welcome not only of the United States Sector in Berlin but also of the United States Zone to members of the other occupying forces at all times. It is interesting to note that he received no reciprocal offer.

As soon as the Council had adjourned the four commanders in chief, their deputies and political advisers sat down around the same table for refreshments. This became a custom with much merit, since the heat of argument which developed around the council table was usually dissipated in the friendly conversation at the refreshment table. We were careful to provide only light food and drink at this first meeting but later gatherings tended to become more and more elaborate with each rotation of chairmanship. Both General Eisenhower and I felt that these hearty refreshments were inconsistent with conditions in Germany and with the work we had before us, so we persuaded our colleagues to limit them to sandwiches and drinks. In spite of this agreement, time and time again the same tendency developed, although usually our month in the chair served to bring about a return to simplicity.

Prior to the second session of the Control Council, which was to be held on August 10, the deputy military governors met four times as an informal Co-ordinating Committee to prepare for the future meetings of the Council. These informal discussions arranged for the formal establishment of the office of the Council in our sector, in an Allied building to be administered by one of our representatives under the Control Council. Nominations were made to the directorates, committees, and subcommittees provided for in the paper to be considered by the Control Council, so that with the approval of the paper the personnel would likewise be approved and the real work of the Council could get under way.

Meanwhile our engineers made heroic efforts to prepare the conference room of the building selected for the headquarters of the Control Council so that it would be ready for the meeting of August 10. We chose a 546-room German court building known as the Kammergericht (Appellate Court) and located at 32 Elscholz Strasse in the borough of Schoeneberg. Although it had been damaged considerably and was bomb-scarred everywhere, it had dignity, particularly when the park in which it was located had been landscaped beautifully. Each day until the Soviet representatives broke up the Control Council and shortly thereafter pulled down their flag, the four national colors were raised high on four identical flagstaffs in front of the building, the colors on the right being those of the nation which was in the chair at the moment. The conference room itself had been the scene of the notorious People's Court in which the fiendish Nazi judge, Dr. Roland Freissler, had sentenced to death after a travesty of a trial the leaders in the July 20, 1944, effort to kill Hitler. Later it seemed fitting—and I am sure that the Germans who gave their lives in the July putsch would have felt likewise—that it was in this same room that final judgments of the International Tribunal sentencing the Nazi leaders were approved.

At its meeting of August 10 the Control Council approved the paper establishing its organization.[3] This had been prepared carefully and in detail by my staff under the direction of Lieutenant Colonel Robert Bowie. It provided for the Co-ordinating Committee, composed of the four deputy military governors, to have broad delegated powers which included the supervision of the Allied Secretariat, the Liaison and Protocol Section which would serve the foreign missions accredited to the Council, the Administrative Bureau, the directorates of government, and the Berlin Kommandatura. The functions of the governmental directorates were indicated by their designations: Military, Naval and Air, later to be combined into a single Combined Services Directorate; Transport; Political; Economic; Finance; Reparations, Deliveries and Restitutions; Internal Affairs and Communications; Legal, Prisoners of War and Displaced Persons; Manpower; and German External Property. The American delegation proposed that the Transport, Economic, Finance, Internal Affairs and Communications, and Legal directorates proceed forthwith to establish German administrative agencies in Berlin under German state secretaries to have jurisdiction in their respective fields throughout Germany under Allied supervision. This proposal was made in anticipation of the Potsdam Protocol, which had been signed but not yet transmitted to us officially. It was taken under consideration by the Council for future action.

We had the form and, we thought, the substance for the exercise of four-power government. We did not foresee the long hours of wrangling ending in deadlock which would characterize the work of the committees and directorates.

CHAPTER 3

Heads of State
Meet in Potsdam

PRESIDENT TRUMAN and the American delegation flew into Berlin to land at Gatow airport in the
British Sector for the Potsdam Conference, which started on July
17 and ended on August 2. We arranged with the Russians and the
British for flight control of our own planes and for the use of our
own troops for security purposes.

It was at Potsdam that I had my first experience with Soviet
security. On a visit to Babelsberg to inspect the American residences,
the Soviet guide had been delighted to show me not only the
residences prepared for President Truman and his staff but also
those prepared for Prime Minister Churchill and his staff. Inno-
cently I inquired if I might see what had been arranged for Generalissimo Stalin. I did not receive a reply.

Once when I landed at Gatow airport, which was only a few miles
from Babelsberg, I tried to take a short cut running through the
British Sector; one block on this route was in the Soviet Zone. I was
stopped at the entrance to this short block. Innumerable badges,
passes, and other documentary evidence in Russian which I had
taken care to obtain had no effect. I had to turn around and go by
the much longer official route.

At the time I was not dissatisfied with the extreme Soviet precautions. The security of the President of the United States is not
a responsibility to be taken lightly at any time, and certainly not in
the heart of a defeated country only a few weeks after its surrender.

With selected troops from one of our seasoned combat divisions providing internal security, the Soviet arrangements for effective external security relieved me of much anxiety.

This was really my first attendance at an international conference in which the German problem was discussed. Although I had been present with the military staff at the Quebec Conference which fixed our occupation areas and our joint policy for Germany with the British, we were there to discuss military problems and did not even hear of the German discussion.

I do not know of any reason, other than its relatively central location, why Potsdam was chosen as the conference site. But it seemed fitting that this conference to determine the fate of Germany should be held in the city of the kings of Prussia, where German aggression had its origin. I was not a member of the American delegation (I attended only the special discussions, to which I had been invited by Secretary of State Byrnes) but I had been given the responsibility for making arrangements for the conference with the Soviet commander in chief. The details were handled almost entirely by Major General Parks in his capacity as Berlin commandant.

Mr. Murphy attended the conference in an advisory capacity. He and I had discussed at great length the many problems certain to arise. We were both apprehensive that restrictions in the financial and economic fields might be imposed, thus preventing the economic recovery which even then we believed essential to a healthy Europe. We felt it was much too soon to determine Germany's minimum needs in industrial production, and we wished to urge that any effort to define these minimum needs be in general terms with sufficient flexibility to permit intelligent appraisal and decision when more detailed information was available. We had heard that some of the advisers to the American delegation favored production for reparations purposes. It was clear to us that for many months to come German production would not suffice to keep the German people alive, and that the use of any part of it for reparations would mean that once again the United States would be not only supporting Germany but also paying the bill for reparations.

Throughout the conference the foreign ministers (Byrnes, Molotov, and first Eden and then Bevin) met frequently to resolve many differences in viewpoint which otherwise would have had to be discussed in the meetings of the chiefs of state (President Truman, Generalissimo Stalin, and first Prime Minister Churchill and then Attlee). When as a result of the British general election Attlee and Bevin replaced Churchill and Eden on July 28, everyone at the conference believed it a remarkable demonstration of the continuity of British foreign policy. The diction and the words of debate may have changed; their meaning was the same.

Almost to the very end of the Potsdam Conference it looked as if agreement would prove impossible. The Soviet representatives, with frequent reference to Yalta, were endeavoring to have accepted their claim for reparations to the value of $10,000,000,000. Time after time Secretary Byrnes reminded them that at Yalta it had been agreed only to consider this amount in relation to other claims and that it was obvious war-damaged Germany could not satisfy all claims in full. The British representatives were most anxious to fix Germany's eastern boundary so that the country would retain enough of its eastern agricultural area to reduce the need for importing food to keep its people alive. Already in northwest Germany, and particularly in the Ruhr, they were faced with a deficit economy and saw the burden which occupation would present to the British people.

Last-minute compromises and provisions in general rather than specific terms permitted the protocol[1] to be signed on August 2, 1945. For the next four years this was the most important document bearing on the German problem. Familiarity with its principal provisions is essential to an understanding of our administration in Germany and the relationships which developed with our Allies. In fact the part pertaining to German affairs was the "rule of law" for three of the occupying powers in the months ahead. Unfortunately it could not become the rule of law for the Allied Control Council. The Council could act only by unanimous consent and one of its members, France, was not a party to and never accepted the protocol in full. Time and time again, when the Council attempted to implement the provisions to which France objected, the French member in exercising his veto power reminded us that his government had not been represented at Potsdam. On several occasions my Soviet colleague suggested to me that France was receiving too much financial assistance from the United States to maintain such strong opposition unless it was with our acquiescence. I doubt if I ever convinced him that our aid was not extended for such purposes. On the other hand, my French colleague later remarked that it had become obvious that early Soviet willingness to establish central administrative agencies was not sincere, and that fortunately the French veto had prevented us from creating agencies which would have been vehicles for Communist expansion.

To summarize the Potsdam Protocol is to say that in general it reaffirmed and elaborated the Yalta Declaration. Once again it pointed out that the occupying powers desired not to destroy or enslave the German people but rather to give them the opportunity to reconstruct their country and their lives on a democratic and peaceful basis.

It reasserted the supreme authority of the four commanders in chief, acting in unanimous consent for the whole of Germany, and acting separately in their respective zones of occupation. It required that the population of Germany be treated as uniformly as possible in all four zones.

In the interest of security, demilitarization and disarmament were to be complete, and industry having major war potential was to be eliminated. The Nazi party was to be destroyed, its laws abolished, its leaders arrested and interned, and members who were more than nominal participants in its activities banned from public office and places of prominence in private undertakings. War criminals were to be tried and punished.

In the interest of democratic growth, education was to be controlled and the judicial system reorganized. The political structure was to be decentralized to encourage the development of greater local responsibility. The right of free assembly and discussion were to be given to democratic political parties to encourage their growth. Elective councils were to be established quickly at local levels and as soon thereafter as possible at regional, provincial, and state levels.

However, German government at national level was to be limited to the establishment of the essential central administrative agencies headed by German state secretaries under the immediate supervision of the Allied Control Council. It should be noted here that the Council never succeeded in establishing these agencies for the administration of Germany as a whole, and hence such agreements as it did reach had to be implemented separately and independently in each zone by its military governor.

Subject only to security requirements, which, however, were not further defined, the protocol provided for freedom of speech, press, and religion, and for the encouragement of free trade unions.

In the field of economics the production of war equipment was prohibited and the production from industries which could support war production was limited to peacetime needs. Excessive concentrations of economic power were to be broken up and cartels disbanded. Here again a general directive was to develop controversy among American officials and among the Allies as to just what constituted too large an enterprise. Agricultural production and the peaceful domestic industries were to be maximized. Germany was to be treated as a *single economic unit* and common policies were to be made applicable in all zones for mining and production, agricultural products, wages, prices, and rations; imports and exports, currency and banking, central taxation and customs, reparations, transport, and communications. Allied controls were to be exercised to meet the needs of the occupation, to ensure an *equitable distribution* of essential commodities among the several zones, to develop a balanced economy, and to control scientific research. These controls were to be exercised by German administrative agencies established for the purpose. Germany's external assets were to be taken into the custody of the Allied Control Council. *Payment of reparations* was to leave enough resources to enable the German people to subsist *without external assistance*. An economic balance was to be worked out with proceeds of exports from current production and stock available in the first place to pay for imports. These provisions clearly contemplated the early establishment of a single economic life for the whole of Germany which would enable it to be self-supporting. This was the field in which we first began to encounter the Soviet veto and it was our failure to obtain a common utilization of German products which led to the breakup of quadripartite government.

It should be noted that these provisions in the fields of finance and economics negated the provisions of JCS/1067 under which we could exercise no control over financial and economic matters except as required to prevent inflation. Now we were specifically charged with the development of a balanced economy which would place Germany on a self-sustaining basis. This was a policy change of major import which influenced our administration of Germany almost from the start. It was an early appreciation that until Germany was able to produce again it not only would require assistance from the occupying powers but also would be a drag on recovery in Europe.

In establishing the principles governing reparations, provision was made for the Soviet and Polish claims to be met from removals in eastern Germany to which were to be added twenty-five per cent of the removals from western Germany. However, payment was to be made by the Soviet Government in commodity products for three fifths of the equipment made available from west Germany. In addition the Soviet Government was to receive German external assets in eastern Europe. Other countries were to obtain their reparations from western Germany and Germany's remaining external assets. Any claim to gold captured by SHAEF was waived by the Soviet Government. A special commission representing the three governments was to divide German naval and merchant vessels. Removal of plants to be made available for reparations was to be completed within two years, and commodity products in payment thereof to be delivered within five years. Advance deliveries of plants selected for the purpose were to be made without waiting for final agreement on the full list of plants to be removed from Germany by the Allied Control Council.

The protocol also provided for the trial of war criminals, taking note of the separate negotiations which were then under way at London to establish the International Tribunal. It authorized the expulsion of ethnic Germans from Poland, Czechoslovakia, and Hungary and their resettlement in Germany providing this transfer of persons was orderly and humane.

This document was to serve as a common directive to three of the four members of the Allied Control Council, although its provisions were to receive very different interpretations. The events which henceforth take place in Germany can always be traced back to Potsdam. It is too early to appraise it. Perhaps without the French veto we could have created central administrative agencies for Germany as a whole within the first six months and struggled within and through them for a common economic policy. Certainly our economic and later our political differences with the Soviet Government would have arisen anyway. It might have been more difficult for these differences to have split a Germany in which central agencies were directing affairs everywhere. Four-power government could not succeed without German administrative agencies to carry out its directives. Six months after Potsdam the Soviet expansion program was under way. The Communist drive to power in the satellite countries was gaining in form and strength; agreement in Germany was no longer possible.

The Potsdam Conference expedited the establishment of the Allied Control Council. Moreover, it provided an opportunity for those of us who were responsible for military government to discuss with the responsible government officials who represented us at the conference the problems we had already encountered. I was delighted to see Secretary Byrnes again. During my service as his deputy I had learned to know and respect his devotion to public duty, his deep knowledge of government, and his rare human understanding. At that time his staff met with him at six o'clock each evening to discuss events of the day and these meetings were always inspirational to me. I had formed a sincere and lasting affection for this great and good American. He had taught me to appreciate a special brand of old bourbon which was difficult to obtain in Europe. To greet his arrival in Potsdam I managed to obtain four bottles which I wrapped up very carefully and handed to an old friend and associate, Walter Brown, who was then working with Secretary Byrnes. Brown was glad to deliver my package but at the same time gave me a package from Byrnes. When I returned home and opened mine I found that it contained four bottles of the same brand brought all the way from the United States.

During the conference I was honored to dine once and lunch twice with the President and the Secretary of State, and learned from their conversations much of the progress of the discussions. I also discussed economic problems with Assistant Secretary of State William L. Clayton, whom I had come to admire in Washington during the war, and with my friend and former associate in War Mobilization and Reconversion, Benjamin Cohen, counselor of the Department of State. I discussed our relations with Soviet representatives with Averell Harriman, and the reparations problem with Edwin Pauley, who was chief of our Reparations Mission, on its way to Moscow to negotiate a reparations agreement with the Soviet Government. I was happy to pay my respects again to General Marshall and to my old chief, General Somervell.

An inspiring occasion during the President's stay in Potsdam was his review of the 2d Armored Division, which was then the principal unit in our Berlin garrison. All the tanks of the division, cleaned and oiled to immaculate but warlike appearance, were aligned side by side, guns to the front, along the autobahn between Potsdam and Berlin, and the battle-seasoned troops stood at attention before them as the President drove slowly down the line. It was an impressive demonstration of American military power which, I might say, did not go unnoticed by the Russians. I must admit that several years later, with two battalions of infantry in Berlin, I wondered whether the blockade would have occurred if the 2d Armored Division or its equivalent had remained. Obviously there is no answer to this type of conjecture which the soldier can never avoid. Certainly military strength can and does lead to aggressive action when the strength becomes relatively too great. It seems equally certain to the soldier that there is a relationship between military preparedness and maintenance of peace, and that war is most apt to occur at a time when countries have neglected their national defense or have permitted it to fall below the demands of reality.

The presence of President Truman at Potsdam made possible another event which became a lasting inspiration to all of us who were there. He agreed to attend the official raising of our national colors on the staff in front of our Berlin headquarters. The flag which we used that day had flown over the Capitol on December 7, 1941, had been raised over Rome, and now on July 22, 1945, was raised over Berlin before being sent to General MacArthur to be raised over Tokyo and returned home. We had arranged a simple ceremony for this occasion with troops lined up on both sides of the short entrance drive which led from the street to the small courtyard in front of the headquarters. President Truman, accompanied by Secretary Byrnes and Secretary of War Stimson, Generals Eisenhower, Bradley, Patton, and me, walked down the entrance drive between the aligned ranks to stand in front of the flagstaff. A special honor guard of troops was on one side of the court and the band on the other. Slowly, with the soldiers at Present Arms and with the band playing "The Star-Spangled Banner," the flag was raised to full mast. President Truman spoke briefly but impressively to say that the United States wanted neither material gain nor territorial expansion from victory, that it wanted and would work only to secure a world of peace and of mutual understanding.

While the soldier is schooled against emotion, I have never forgotten that short ceremony as our flag rose to the staff. When in later days anyone suggested the possibility of our departure from Berlin before, of our own choice, we left a free Berlin, I could not help thinking that no one who had seen our flag raised by right of victory but dedicated to the preservation of freedom and peace could possibly see it withdrawn until peace and freedom had been established.

When the Allied Control Council approved its own organization on August 10, it had not received officially the Potsdam Protocol of August 2. However, the machinery which it established began to function quickly. Its secretariat prepared special briefs on all papers emanating from the various directorates in three languages—English, French, and Russian—to permit their ready discussion. Public documents were prepared also in German. The Co-ordinating Committee of the deputies met twice in the ten-day intervals between meetings of the Control Council. The agenda for each session was prepared in time for the experts in the directorates to brief me in advance on agreements and disagreements with their colleagues. The attendance was limited to principals and a few key assistants. The conference table was arranged around a hollow square with each delegation seated on one side of the square. Each delegation had two interpreters—in my case, one French and one Russian—who translated the remarks of the head of the delegation. All of us soon found that long speeches necessarily interpreted twice wasted time unduly and thus we learned to economize in words until the Council in its closing days became the setting for long and vitriolic Soviet propaganda attacks.

The Allied Control Council quickly became a beehive of activity. Each directorate had several committees and these in turn established additional subcommittees and working parties. At the peak of activity directorates, committees, subcommittees, and working parties exceeded 175 in number, with perhaps as many as 12 or more working on the same day. An Allied mess was run in the Control Council building. It was always interesting to watch Russians, British, French, and Americans eating together and talking through interpreters, in sign language or in some mutually spoken language (usually German) in which few were fluent. General Eisenhower and Marshal Zhukov had established a friendly personal relationship based on mutual respect. Outwardly good will and good intent pervaded everywhere. Most of us began to think that perhaps this experiment in international co-operation would work. Perhaps it might even lead to the understanding necessary to lasting peace.

The Allied Control Council recognized that many of its actions would have the force of law, and agreed to issue those actions which affected the German people either as proclamations or ordinances, while actions affecting zone commanders only were issued as directives.[2] The proclamations or ordinances were promulgated as separate documents and also published in the German language in the official *Gazette* which was issued periodically.[3]

Thus, a short while after the Potsdam Conference had adjourned, it looked, at least on the surface, as if the Allied Control Council had become an effective functioning body to govern Germany and to carry out the provisions of the Potsdam Protocol. The record of the next few months indicates the assiduous manner in which the United States delegation worked to carry out these provisions with some initial but always decreasing success. These successes and failures henceforth were reflected in the relationships among the four powers in Germany and in the later international conferences concerning the German problem.

General Eisenhower continued to take the lead in the development of friendly relations among the representatives of the occupying powers, and particularly with Soviet representatives. On June 10 Marshal Zhukov visited Frankfurt as his personal guest. The marshal was received at the airport by an escort of honor from an airborne division which was at its unexcelled best in appearance, and escorted to General Eisenhower's office in the I. G. Farben building in Frankfurt along a highway lined with tanks and armored cars. As we were assembling for lunch a review of more than 500 fighter aircraft passed overhead. It was an impressive ceremony which had its climax in a formal luncheon for at least 100 guests. Zhukov made a witty speech in which he said that the soldier had done his job, which had become necessary because of the failure of the diplomats, and that it was now up to the diplomats to try again to secure a lasting and worthwhile peace. Vishinsky

General Clay, who already has established headquarters in Berlin, meets General Eisenhower at Tempelhof Airport upon his arrival for the 1945 Potsdam Conference.

One of the first photographs taken of Premier Stalin and President Truman just before the Potsdam Conference. To the right are Secretary Byrnes and Mr. Molotov.

An early visitor to Berlin was Mrs. Eleanor Roosevelt. With her are General Clay and members of a WAC detachment.

then said that, speaking for the diplomats, they were prepared to accept the challenge of the soldier but that the soldier should not be too critical of the diplomat, for if the latter always succeeded there would be no further need for the soldier. Montgomery, who rose to toast the guest of honor, quite unconsciously, I am sure, sounded the only note of discord—or at least it was a note of discord to me. He said that it was particularly fitting for him to pay tribute to Marshal Zhukov as there had been two decisive battles in the war—Stalingrad, where victory was won by Zhukov, and El Alamein, where victory was won by Montgomery. However, the British political adviser to SHAEF, Sir Yvonne Kirkpatrick, rose quickly to the occasion, saying that while he was not a military man and hence unable to evaluate specific victories he could understand and pay tribute to the genius of the man who with patient understanding and skill had welded together all of the Western Allies to form a magnificent fighting machine—the Supreme Commander, General Eisenhower.

There was an excellent troupe of Negro entertainers visiting the theater at the time and they had volunteered to provide the entertainment. By the time lunch was over General Eisenhower, who likes to sing, had broken the ice and the party wound up with him and Marshal Zhukov joining with the Negro performers and guests in singing, humming, or trying to sing, in whatever language one could use, "Old Man River" and other old favorites.

It had proved to be a successful day and was to be followed shortly by General Eisenhower's official trip to Moscow as the guest of the Soviet Government.

This visit was made between August 10 and 15. General Eisenhower took with him an old friend from our days in Manila, Brigadier General T. J. Davis; his son, Lieutenant John Eisenhower; and me. Marshal Zhukov accompanied us in General Eisenhower's plane to act as his personal escort. Our flight to Moscow was uneventful except that it was made for much of the distance at an elevation of less than a thousand feet as the Soviet navigator who had been loaned to us apparently took his bearings by direct observation and not by instrument. General Eisenhower and Marshal Zhukov exchanged views on the use of troops and movement of supplies in combat. When we arrived at the Moscow airport we were met with appropriate honors by Soviet troops and taken directly to our embassy, where we were to stay during our visit as the guests of Ambassador Harriman and his charming hostess daughter, Miss Kathleen Harriman.

I am sure that General Eisenhower's invitation had been timed to permit him to see the spectacular annual Sports Parade, in which thousands of well-trained athletes of both sexes, from all parts of the Soviet Union, pass in review before Generalissimo Stalin and other Russian dignitaries and stage in Red Square their superbly executed folk dances, acrobatic and gymnastic feats. It is a colorful event and the various representatives from the several republics, dressed in regional costumes, vie with each other in performances, which inevitably end with homage to Stalin. It was at this review that Generalissimo Stalin invited General Eisenhower, who took along our senior military representative, General John. R. Deane, to stand with him on the top of Lenin's tomb as the review passed by. Mr. Harriman was amazed at this evidence of good will, although I believe he was equally astonished a day later when on our return from a trip to both a collective and a state farm Marshal Zhukov accepted General Eisenhower's informal invitation to join us in the embassy for light refreshments. Harriman told us then that it was the first instance of an informal, spur-of-the-moment visit that the embassy had received from a high Soviet official during his stay. We visited also an art gallery, the truly amazing Moscow subway, and attended a championship football game held in a huge stadium which was completely filled. The warmth with which General Eisenhower was received everywhere was encouraging, particularly at the stadium, where the audience gave both him and Marshal Zhukov an ovation. We were taken through a Soviet aircraft factory and saw one of its planes test-flown by a very competent pilot. Later we went through the historic rooms and museum of the Kremlin.

We dined at the Kremlin at a state dinner given in General Eisenhower's honor by Generalissimo Stalin during which Mr. Molotov was toastmaster. Stalin wore a finely tailored field uniform with natural ease. He was smaller than I had expected but his well-proportioned chest and shoulders gave the appearance of solid strength. He was smiling and affable. In the few minutes in which his face lost animation, in repose, somewhat heavy features gave the impression of determined will. There was a genuinely friendly atmosphere at this dinner beyond that induced by the drinking of many toasts. The Soviet general who sat on my right took compassion on me as the number of vodkas increased and showed me how I could keep my vodka glass reasonably filled with white wine from one of the bottles in front of my plate so that it could not be refilled so often with the vodka which the attendants were pouring assiduously. After the dinner we adjourned to Stalin's well-appointed motion picture lounge, where we saw our friend Marshal Zhukov in the *Battle of Berlin*, as we sat in easy chairs sipping champagne or eating the delicious fruit which was placed on tables adjacent to our chairs. In spite of language difficulties it was a pleasant evening which seemed to reflect a desire by the Soviet Government to pay sincere respect to General Eisenhower and to create friendly relations.

Before our departure from Moscow Mr. Harriman gave a large buffet supper which was attended by a large number of Soviet officials including a number of their high military leaders. During this reception Harriman received the cable reporting the unconditional surrender of Japan. Most of us had expected months more of fighting and the news was a welcome release from anxiety. The party thereupon became very gay, winding up with Russians and Americans all trying to sing the authentic "Volga Boat Song" to show their mutual desire for friendship between our countries. When the party broke up in the early morning both Ambassador Harriman and General Deane expressed doubt as to Soviet willingness to accept surrender until Soviet forces had completed the occupation of Manchuria. Like so many Americans, I was skeptical of their views, discounting their experience. I did not make this mistake again.

While our visit to Moscow had increased hopes for the success of our relationship in Germany, neither Harriman nor Deane was optimistic. They told us of their difficulties in the stress of war in trying to offer help to the Soviet Government without arousing new suspicions and their failure to develop any real co-operation. Mr. Pauley, who had been in Moscow for a few weeks to discuss reparations, had already concluded that agreement was impossible. On the way back we stopped for lunch and a short visit in Leningrad, where we were again entertained warmly. On our arrival in Berlin

General Eisenhower and I agreed that we had enjoyed our trip and that we had found a sincere friend in Marshal Zhukov.

The Allied Control Council was established, and our friend Zhukov was the Soviet representative. We had the Potsdam Protocol, agreed to by at least three of the occupying powers, including Russia, to serve as the directive for our future actions. There seemed to be no further reason why quadripartite government could not be made to succeed. General Eisenhower and I determined to do our part.

CHAPTER 4

Military Government
Finds Its Place

T HERE was still uncertainty as to the part to be played by the United States Group Control Council in administering military government. When it moved to Berlin it became our representative in quadripartite government. However, our zone was still being administered by the Army Command which had taken over the duties of SHAEF on July 14. Thus the Group Control Council was like an embassy representing the Army Command in its international negotiations.

It was certain that this would lead to a conflict of responsibilities. For instance, at an early meeting I encouraged German party leaders to engage in political activities as a first step in the restoration of political life. A few days later our director in Munich called me to report that Army intelligence agents had raided a party gathering the preceding night and had arrested several of the Germans including two who had heard my talk. It is true this was a left-wing gathering, but this only made the arrest more difficult to explain, since it was interpreted to mean that our policy of political freedom was restricted beyond the exclusion of active Nazis from such activities.

It was evident that there were differences in thinking as to how our administration in Germany should be conducted. It was possible for the Army to administer our zone through its field commanders with supervision in the General Staff. Army headquarters in Frankfurt would receive policy instructions from Washington to transmit to Berlin for use in negotiation with the other powers, and to the field commanders for execution in our zone. General Bedell Smith and most of the General Staff favored this method.

It was at complete variance with my concept. I had no doubt that the Army had the ability to do an effective job of administration. However, we were after more than that. We were trying to recreate civil government in Germany on a democratic basis. This was our principal mission and it did not belong in one of five staff divisions at theater headquarters. Moreover, it was our task to build a civilian organization which could be transferred at any time to one of the civil departments of government. To accomplish this it was imperative that Military Government be organized separately from the Army Command under a deputy responsible directly to the theater commander. This deputy would have a staff or cabinet serving the same purpose for Military Government as the General Staff for Army administration. Thus the two organizations would complement each other, neither being subordinate and both reporting to the theater commander. The deputy military governor would receive policy instructions direct from Washington. Subject always to the approval of the commander, he would be guided in his relationships with the representatives of the other powers by these instructions. He would also be responsible for the execution of these policies in our zone, setting up field offices in the states directly responsible to him and not to the field commanders. This organization would be staffed with civilian experts as rapidly as they could be obtained.

We did not start off this way. Our zone was divided into two military districts: the Eastern District of Bavaria under General George Patton, and the Western District of Wuerttemberg-Baden and Hesse under General Geoffrey Keyes. The port of Bremen and our sector of Berlin were separate commands reporting directly to the theater commander. Each of these four commanders supervised military government in his area, utilizing the G-5 Division of his staff for the purpose. General policy direction and supervision were exercised by the G-5 Division of the theater commander's General Staff.

International agreements, and particularly the Potsdam Protocol, placed policy control in the Allied Control Council, thus making it clear that policy directions for the United States Zone would emanate from our representation on the Council. At first these directions could be transmitted to the field only through the G-5 Division of the theater General Staff and through the district commanders. This arrangement was cumbersome and confusing. There was also confusion as to the responsibility for the receipt and dispatch of important cables bearing on occupation policies between the Berlin and Frankfurt offices in Germany and between the State and War Departments in Washington.

It was difficult to convince the General Staff that our civil functions would soon become our primary mission in Germany. At the moment the redeployment of our forces to the Pacific and the care and repatriation of displaced persons were the major administrative tasks. Both of these were unquestionably Army problems which required the control and use of available transport facilities within our zone.

It was fortunate that the G-5 Division of the theater General Staff was headed by my lifelong friend, Major General C. L. Adcock, who shared my views on organization. He was personable and able, and carried out his assignment to satisfy both General Smith and me, which under the circumstances was no mean feat as neither of us was a negative character. General Adcock made his staff division a part of a single Military Government team without creating friction and hostility, even though it reported elsewhere.

I might have made an issue of this problem then as I knew General Eisenhower agreed with me that we should build promptly an organization which could be transferred bodily to a civil branch of government. During the Potsdam Conference we visited President Truman together and General Eisenhower told him of our thinking. I expressed the view that we could have such an organization by July 1946. The President listened attentively and, I felt, sympathetically, although he did not express himself except to ask General Eisenhower to put his views in writing. This was done in November. However, I did not press the issue because there was much to General Smith's view that we should break up the existing pattern slowly and only as we were certain of the next step, and I had both respect and friendship for General Smith. Besides, there were so many problems to be solved that it seemed better on the whole to move slowly in developing our organization and procedures.

I was helped far more than I then realized by Secretary Stimson's visit during the Potsdam Conference in the early phases of our efforts to organize Military Government. General Eisenhower invited me to lunch with Secretary Stimson, after which we sat on the terrace of his pleasant Bad Homburg house in the warm sunlight of a beautiful July day and listened to the Secretary express his philosophy of occupation. He had not even thought of military government as part of the Army Command. He visualized it as a separate and distinct task to be executed by an organization directly under the theater commander. He recognized the need for controls, favored adequate security measures, and believed that the arrest and trial of the Nazi leaders and war criminals were of utmost importance to future peace. He would have no part of a policy based on vindictiveness and was certain that the American people would in the long run give their approval only to an occupation which was decent and humane and which was conducted under a rule of law. He could see no purpose in the deliberate destruction of the German economy, because he was convinced that its reconstruction was essential to create an atmosphere in which it might be possible to develop a true spirit of democracy. He knew that the innate kindliness and decency of the American people would lead them to disapprove the exercise of our supreme authority in Germany in other than the traditional American way. Both General Eisenhower and I were impressed by his talk and it had a lasting effect on my conduct of responsibilities. We went to the airport to see Secretary Stimson off, and as we stood at salute when his plane roared down the runway I felt once again that we had been in the presence of a great American whose contributions to the public service were beyond measure.

Military Government officials were also helped in the early organizational problems by another visit from Assistant Secretary McCloy in August. While we stood in the late afternoon in the courtyard of our Berlin headquarters a shot rang out and one of his assistants, Colonel Ammi Cutter, who had contributed much to our discussions, collapsed. Rushing to him, we found that he had been shot through the leg with a .45-caliber bullet. Immediately it was surmised that a Nazi die-hard had tried to assassinate Mr. McCloy, but a careful investigation determined in a few hours that there was no secret plan to do away with the American high command. The shot had been fired carelessly from the basement of a nearby building by a young officer cleaning his pistol. This, too, taught me a lesson, for we were already considering the steps we should take in reprisal when we discovered the truth. Thereafter I was unwilling to accept reports of German resistance and defiance until they had been investigated and verified. Contemplating such measures as a daylight curfew, I couldn't help thinking back to the test question President Roosevelt had told Justice Byrnes he would ask me. I am afraid that our young officer, who was a regular and a West Pointer, had some difficult moments, in spite of his courage in voluntarily acknowledging his responsibility.

At this stage Military Government in the field consisted of a large number of detachments running village, city, and county governments, and reporting directly to the responsible Army commander. By September we had created three states in our zone and had established their state administrations. Bremen and our sector of Berlin were kept as separate organizations. Each state office was headed by a director of Military Government who also exercised supervision over the local governments within the state.[1] These directors of state Military Governments were: Brigadier General Walter Muller, and later former Governor Murray D. Van Wagoner of Michigan, in Bavaria; Colonel William Dawson, and later former Congressman Charles M. LaFollette, and Major General Charles P. Gross in Wuerttemberg-Baden; Dr. James Newman in Hesse; Thomas F. Dunn and later Captain Charles R. Jeffs (USN) in Bremen; and Colonel Frank Howley in Berlin. They were our field representatives, in daily touch with the German authorities and responsible for the prompt organization of German local and state administrations. Their influence was of inestimable value to the accomplishment of our purposes. In September 1945 they were still under the Army district commanders although there was a free exchange of information between their offices and mine. Actually the district commanders delegated broad authority to their state directors, who accepted our policy instructions so that the divided responsibility which existed at the time was not as serious as it looked on paper.

In October 1945 the G-5 staff divisions were divorced from Military Government responsibilities and the personnel engaged in these responsibilities were placed in the Office of Military Government.[2] There were still two offices of Military Government: Berlin, which was under my command; and Frankfurt, which remained a part of the General Staff. The Berlin office was designated the Office of

Military Government, United States, which was soon called OMGUS. It now had full responsibility for representation in the Allied Control Council, for the issuance of all policy directives, and for all matters pertaining to finance, economics, reparations, restitution, and manpower. Since the Army Command felt keenly its responsibility to prevent disorders, the Frankfurt office retained control of legal matters, administration, public health and welfare, and public safety.

General Eisenhower promised me that this would be a temporary arrangement. At one of our regular monthly meetings with the Army district commanders he made it clear that it was his purpose to support the development of a Military Government organization which could be transferred to civilian control on twenty-four hours' notice and that everyone was to understand that our troops were in Germany primarily to support Military Government. This eliminated further effective opposition to the gradual continued separation of Military Government from the Army Command.

It now seemed necessary to clarify our relationships with our government and with the State Department. Many cables relating to Military Government were received in Berlin from the War Department, while others were received in Frankfurt. State Department cables would sometimes be dispatched to us through the War Department and at other times to Robert Murphy, who was political adviser to both General Eisenhower and me. General Eisenhower agreed with me that all communications which dealt with civil functions should be sent to Berlin for action, with the understanding, of course, that I would take up with him such matters as were sufficiently important to require his decision. This arrangement was accepted immediately by the War Department. There thus remained only the clarification of our communications with the State Department. Murphy had a staff of approximately 140 persons to maintain liaison with all of the divisions of Military Government and to attend in advisory capacity the quadripartite meetings of the Control Council, its Co-ordinating Committee, directorates, committees, and subcommittees. Thus his staff was in immediate possession of all important information to be transmitted directly to the State Department over its wires. Likewise his staff was receiving directly information and suggestions which were difficult for me to evaluate. We did not know from what office in the State Department they had been dispatched, or what consideration they had received there and in the War Department. This resulted in some confusion and led me to send a cable on November 17 which I hoped would clarify the situation. I pointed out substantially:

We are getting mixed up here in our channels of instructions. We are prepared to receive instructions from either War or State, and we fully recognize State Department responsibility. However, we feel State Department instructions should come to this office either through War Department or direct rather than through State Department representatives here. Political Affairs Division composed of State Department representatives is authorized direct communication with State Department in latter's code for information exchange, which is desirable to permit State Department representatives to be sufficiently well informed to give us current advice. . . . However, it is to be expected that this is to result in frequent reporting of views of subordinates which may not be my views, and instructions based on such views may have to be reopened by me.

I feel Military Governor and/or Deputy are working for State Department even though channel is through War. We will lean heavily on Political Adviser but we remain responsible for all decisions and are entitled to receive our instructions direct from government. . . . OMGUS is fully prepared to accept that State Department orders be sent through War, or if not, direct to OMGUS. Military Governor and Deputy regardless of channel should be considered as working for State. There are no personality clashes involved. I have highest respect for Murphy as counselor, and affection for him as friend. I do feel strongly that one channel of instructions is essential under either Military Governor or High Commissioner and that channel should follow chain of responsibility.

I quote from this cable extensively because an early impression, which was never entirely erased, was created that Military Government was unwilling to work for the State Department.

As a result it was arranged that instructions should always be sent through the War Department and that State Department messages to the political adviser were to be considered as suggestions. Throughout the occupation we received many of these suggestions which were accepted in large part. When they were not, Murphy was free, if he thought it important enough, to advise the State Department so that those rejected could be repeated as instructions. To me this arrangement seemed simple and satisfactory. In any event I am sure that government has never been better informed than it was on our operations in Germany. There was a constant exchange of cables between the Office of Military Government and the War Department and between the State Department and the political adviser. In fact between July 1945 and April 1949 the State Department sent 18,970 cable dispatches to Germany and received 17,298 from the political adviser. Military Government received 50,000 cables and dispatched 23,000 cables to the War Department. In addition to these cable exchanges there were frequent teleconferences, the monthly report of the military governor, and many special reports by mail.

The teleconference was the most satisfactory medium of exchange for important matters since it permitted senior officials to confer directly with high officials in Washington. The teleconference is an adaptation of teletype in code, and incoming messages are received, decoded, and flashed on a screen in the teleconference room. They can be answered immediately and flashed on a corresponding screen in Washington. While this system is not as rapid as a telephone conference, questions can be answered as quickly as the answers can be written and transcribed on the typewriter and the teleconference avoids the always possible misunderstandings of telephone conversation.

So that both Murphy and I could be fully informed, he came to my office at least twice a day with the major cables he had received, and my daily cable book, which contained the important messages I had received or dispatched, was sent to him each day. Neither of us ever kept a cable to his department secret from the other. Thus, daily, major messages were discussed and analyzed so that their principles could be applied in our negotiations and decisions. The majority of cables relating to negotiations which were sent to us from Washington made it clear that their content was informational, leaving me considerable discretion. Such was the relationship between Murphy and me that I know of no decision taken during the four years in which we were in Germany from which he dissented. Nor were we ever advised that any decision was at variance with our instructions or with the general policy under which we operated.

This does not mean that as time progressed I failed to develop definite views with respect to the German problem which I would present vigorously in the exchange of cables. Usually the War Department supported me, which was logical, for I would have been replaced if it had lost confidence in my judgment. Differences in thinking between War and State Departments were much less numerous than appeared to be the case and arose largely from the differences in their respective responsibilities to Congress. The State Department worked with Congress on occupation policies and matters through the congressional committees on foreign relations, whereas the Army worked with Congress on these matters through the appropriations committees. To obtain funds to support the occupation, certain commitments were made to the appropriations committees and sometimes these commitments did not fit in with the ways in which the State Department would have liked the funds used to support foreign policy. Such an instance was the unwillingness of Military Government to use Low Country ports in which port charges had to be paid in dollars, while German ports handled cargo destined for Germany in Reichsmarks provided by German government. The State Department would have liked to see the Low Country ports used to restore a more normal transport system and to assist these countries, which were badly in need of dollars. However, the Army, while willing to use the Low Country ports if dollars were made available elsewhere, did not feel that it could use its own appropriations. There were some who argued that the loans and other financial assistance being extended by the United States to western Europe justified the use of funds appropriated for Germany for the same purpose. I had handled appropriated funds for many years and I felt strongly that they must be used zealously only for the purposes for which they were voted by Congress. Neither the War Department nor I could accept any deviation from this principle.

In November 1945 General McNarney arrived to take General Eisenhower's place. Because of my close friendship for the latter I was glad to see him go, for it seemed unfair to me that the victorious Allied commander should remain in Germany to command a small army of occupation and be faced with the almost impossible task of governing Germany to satisfy the conflict of public opinion at home as to how the occupation should be conducted. Nevertheless, I felt his loss keenly. I have known him for many years and as a friend for fifteen years. We had served together on General MacArthur's staff in Manila when it was engaged in developing an army for the Philippine Commonwealth. I had for him not only the deep and lasting affection of sincere friendship but also admiration and respect for his rare abilities and achievements. His companionship made working for him a constant pleasure. General Eisenhower was keenly interested in military government and on his three visits to Berlin each month to attend the meetings of the Control Council kept free the preceding evening and morning so that we could have a full discussion of the issues which were to arise in the Control Council and of other problems. His prestige and personality created an early friendly atmosphere in Allied meetings. His concept of our mission was clear. He believed that we must execute it with firm justice but this did not mean oppression and starvation. He felt strongly, for instance, that the output of the Ruhr must be raised in the interests of Europe as a whole. I was to miss his counsel and support, and even more his warmth and genuine kindness.

I also had respect for General Eisenhower's successor, who had proved himself a capable administrator. His leadership in the reorganization of the War Department in the early days of the war had resulted in a sound and efficient administration. I found quickly that he accepted my concept of the relationship between Military Government and the occupation troops and was prepared to support its continued implementation.

Thus we proceeded with further separation from the Army Command. On December 11, 1945, Information and Transportation Services were transferred from Army hands. By this time the Laenderrat, the German administration which we had established for our zone, was functioning and a German transport directorate in charge of rail traffic was set up under it. Our chief of transport predicted a transport collapse when the Army gave up control. Although I had confidence in the ability of our Army Transport Service, I did not believe this, because I was certain that German railway technicians were competent to direct their own rail operations. In the first month after the transfer the German directorate removed several thousand Nazi employees whom the Army had found indispensable to adequate service and, while doing so, appreciably increased passenger traffic and freight tonnage.

On March 9, 1946, the separation from the Army Command was completed.[3] The Frankfurt Office of Military Government was abolished. The directors in the several states were placed directly under the Office of Military Government in Berlin. The G-5 Division of the General Staff was re-established at theater headquarters in Frankfurt to maintain liaison with Military Government. Operational responsibility for the care of displaced persons, war trials before military tribunals, discharge of German prisoners of war, the destruction of military installations and equipment, and the arrest and detention of war criminals and Germans considered dangerous to the occupation were the sole functions relating to the administration of German affairs left in Army hands. They were left because the Army was better equipped to complete them.

A temporary exception was made for telephone and telegraph communications, which were kept under the supervision of the chief signal officer. Armies are always zealous to control their own communications, which is understandable, although I did believe that a much larger proportion of the German network was used for this purpose than was necessary. Later, in September 1947, this activity was also transferred and resulted in no real interference with Army needs while making a much greater proportion of the network available to the German economy.

Thus the Army had accepted as its principal mission the support of Military Government. We now had a compact organization responsible to a single head which worked with German officials at the state level through our state directors, and with the German Laenderrat[4] on matters pertaining to the zone as a whole through our Coordinator of Regional Government.[5] This simple and sound organization continued throughout except as it was modified to provide for bizonal administration when the British and American zones were joined in economic unity.

During this period I had no direct military responsibility, nor in fact was I to assume any except for the command of our troops in Berlin until I succeeded General McNarney in March 1947. Of course there was necessarily a close relationship between Military Government and the occupation forces, so that the conditions which affected one also affected the other.

When General McNarney assumed command in November 1945 there were still more than 1,000,000 troops in the theater. Our redeployment program was based on a point system designed to supply troops for the Pacific war and at the same time releasing those not needed for the Pacific war who had experienced long or arduous combat service. This had required the breaking up of combat units, with the inevitable loss of morale which follows when men and officers associated in battle are separated. Moreover, the point system resulted in the return of those with longer service and deprived the units which remained of their more experienced officers and soldiers. When Japan surrendered it was deemed too late to change the system. There was no longer the pressure of war to maintain morale. Only General Eisenhower's prestige and the high personal regard in which he was held kept the command together until his departure. General McNarney was not so well known to the troops, and shortly after his arrival their demand to be returned home became a clamor.

While it was announced that the occupation force would be cut to 300,000 men and the surplus sent home as quickly as transportation became available, the men who were to remain were still in the Army through induction and many of them did not desire Army careers. There were several mass demonstrations, including a march of several thousand malcontents to headquarters in Frankfurt. General McNarney wisely rode out the storm while maintaining control of the rudder, and thus avoided the uglier demonstrations which occurred in the Pacific. In late 1945 and early 1946 replacements began to arrive but they were principally young inductees who were to serve for a year only.

Elaborate entertainment and sports programs were arranged and helped to improve morale. An early order prohibiting fraternization, required under our directives,[6] prevented the normal "boy meets girl" process, and the soldier who could not be kept away from the opposite sex was forced to meet German girls in dark halls and alleys and under cover of darkness. Obviously only the lowest type of girl, the tramp, would meet with soldiers under such conditions. Drinking and venereal disease increased. Our Allies experienced the same problem, and the fraternization rule was lifted by mutual agreement in the Allied Control Council in September 1945. Special Services then began to invite carefully screened German girls to the clubs provided for our soldiers. However, the reputation left by the tramps made attracting decent girls a difficult and slow process. Our regulations prohibited the serving of food to Germans in our military installations and hence the soldiers could offer the German girls only liquor. It was some time before clubs were provided where soldiers could take girls and obtain food and soft drinks for them.

General Clay (extreme left) and Ambassador Murphy (far right) conferred frequently with American labor leaders. Here they are shown with George Harrison and David Dubinsky.

After four years of active duty in Berlin General Clay and Mrs. Clay are greeted in Washington by Secretary of Defense Louis Johnson.

General Clay and Ambassador Murphy meet for one of their daily exchanges of information and ideas.

Bob Hope helped entertain American troops in blockaded Berlin. Secretary of the Army Kenneth C. Royall looks on while he chats with General Clay.

The black market was rampant. Our Allies used the same Allied military marks. The Russians had agreed to use them, as a result of negotiation at government level, only if they were provided with a duplicate set of plates to print their own supply, although they obtained these plates by promising a strict accounting for the marks they placed in circulation. We never received this accounting, though we pressed for it in many meetings of the Control Council. Our soldiers were able to buy items in the Post Exchanges which could be sold at high profit for Allied military marks, and these marks could then be reconverted into dollars. While it was difficult to tell the combat soldier that Allied marks in his possession could not be reconverted, the problem was of such magnitude that in July 1945 regulations were issued to the effect that a soldier could convert only his pay. Even then, officers, soldiers, and civilians could sell Post Exchange items for enough Allied marks to meet all their needs, thus retaining their pay intact. In Berlin we introduced an elaborate coupon book system in November 1945. The coupon book had to be purchased in dollars and only its coupons were acceptable in our installations. It was an effective if complex system. At this time our personnel in Germany had to carry so many papers for the simplest transaction that one wallet proved insufficient. Finally on December 16, 1946, we obtained military scrip printed in the United States, which from then on was used for pay purposes and assured a full control of our currency.

During much of the rampant black market period large sums of Allied military marks without dollar backing reached our finance offices. Thus we became responsible to our Treasury Department for $300,000,000. In payment we could offer only marks, which the Treasury Department would not accept. One of the problems I inherited when I became theater commander was settling this account. Through the purchase of these marks to meet dollar obligations in Germany which were not properly occupation costs (such as the pay of servants, personal services, telephone service, transportation) and through their use by our Post Exchanges to have products made in Germany and to pay its employees, and to pay German prisoners of war, we were able to retire the entire amount without loss to our government.

During this period of unavoidable confusion, charges of almost every kind appeared to be a part of the daily fare—loose living by officers, luxurious living, black marketing, looting, cruelty toward the Germans, softness toward the Germans, failure to remove Nazis from office. Unfortunately many of them had some basis in fact. A victorious army of combat veterans had defeated the enemy in hard fighting. Released from the discipline of combat, it was not ready to accept the more rigorous discipline of garrison and peacetime training. Unpleasant as this condition was, I felt then that it was caused by a minority and that the great majority of Americans in Germany were living according to their normal standards and pursuing their daily tasks with sincerity and ability. I knew also of the administrative steps being taken to control the situation and that it would be only a matter of time until they became effective.

It was regrettable that the actions of a small minority in the early days of occupation should discredit the efforts of the whole. Certainly there was some looting, highlighted by the sensational Kronberg Castle jewelry theft. Yet this was the same Army which had found and stored in Frankfurt vaults almost $300,000,000 in gold bars and additional millions in non-monetary gold, jewels, and securities for restoration to their rightful owners or their heirs. This was the Army that with utmost diligence uncovered more than 1500 repositories of art and cultural objects and with meticulous care returned these objects of inestimable value to the nations from which they were looted. Moreover, the same assiduous attention was given to German works of art placed in the repositories for safekeeping from bomb damage. Perhaps never in the history of the world has a conquering army sought so little for its own and worked so faithfully to preserve the treasures of others.

Also the natural kindness of the American soldier was becoming evident, and more and more he was seen giving candy to German children and playing games with them. Here and there others were emulating Sergeant Patrick J. Moriarity, who started a club in Bremen for German youths to try to give them a chance to play in grim, postsurrender Germany. As this movement grew, General McNarney adopted it as an Army program in early 1946, and at its peak more than 600,000 boys and girls participated in its activities. Later Marshal Sokolovsky charged in the Allied Control Council that German boys were being taught baseball to keep alive their military spirit. The GYA (German Youth Assistance) program was continued. It was not allowed to interfere with the German organizations for young people, but under Military Government counsel was directed to bring about a close co-operation with German movements through their own offices, now established in almost every county.

General McNarney's program to improve morale and discipline faced many difficulties. The size of the occupation force was cut again and again, faster than military units which formed the occupation army could be reorganized to absorb the cuts. The German police were still ineffective and the guard requirements for our supplies, internment camps, railway transport, and military installations made training of our soldiers impossible. Hence there was established in January 1946, under Major General Ernest Harmon, a special Constabulary force of 30,000 men for police and riot duty, stationed throughout the zone and linked together with radio and telephone equipment. They were provided with enough vehicles to be a highly mobile force which could be concentrated quickly if needed. No better commander could have been selected for this purpose than General Harmon, and from the start the Constabulary with its bright yellow scarf, its special uniform, and its important mission had high morale, excellent discipline, and soldierly bearing. It won the respect and admiration of all, including the German population.

When we had completed the separation of Military Government from the Army in April 1946, we cut its staff from a peak in December 1945 of approximately 12,000 (much less than either the British peak, which I understand exceeded 26,000, or even the French peak for a much smaller zone of occupation) to 7600 persons. This was accomplished largely through attrition, as no effort was made to replace Army personnel in the field teams lost through redeployment. This reduction in personnel caused some public criticism at the time but it was a part of our program to return the responsibility for local government to the Germans as quickly as possible. At the same time we were gradually replacing military with civilian personnel in our headquarters and regional offices. This was accomplished in part by retaining as civilians officers and soldiers due for redeployment and in part by recruiting civilian specialists from the United States.

By now we had established German administrations at all levels of government so that there were two parallel organizations to carry out our directives; one was our Military Government administration and the other the German administration. This led to some confusion and overlapping of responsibility. It seemed clear that this could be avoided and that we would in fact have more positive control if our instructions and directions were sent only to our directors of Military Government at the state level for transmission to the German state governments, which would then be held responsible for their execution by the German administrations. Our personnel in the field working under the director of Military Government for the state would then be charged with observing and reporting- on German compliance. This enabled us to reduce our field strength further and to fix on April 1, 1946, our total strength at 6524 persons. Field personnel remained officers and enlisted men as there were obvious advantages to having the uniform worn by those who associated daily with German officials. In all other offices military personnel was to be replaced by civilians until the latter represented two thirds of our total strength. It was my view that this ratio would provide us with a predominantly civilian organization which could be taken over by the State Department at any time and that the remaining officers and soldiers could be returned to military duties as rapidly as desired by my civilian successor.

Confident that German administration would improve in efficiency, the total strength of Military Government for the forthcoming new year starting January 1, 1947, was fixed at 5000 persons, to be reached by normal attrition. We did reduce to this figure as scheduled. Moreover, our civilians made up 50 per cent of our total strength. These reductions were continued as German state administrations became effective and as the German bizonal organization for the British and American zones was established, so that our total strength just prior to my departure from Germany in the spring of 1949 was approximately 2500 persons, of whom only 94 were officers and enlisted men. Corresponding British strength was then about 12,000 and French strength about 8000. These reductions in our strength were largely responsible for the improvement in the efficiency of local German government, which was forced to accept responsibility in our zone, and no real loss of control resulted in comparison with other zones. Our budget for the fiscal year beginning July 1, 1949, contemplated an average strength of 2000 persons for the year ahead, as the development of the West German Government would further lessen our responsibilities. This meant we would end the fiscal year with less than 1500.

I think that in the fall of 1945 and spring of 1946, when we had to establish local German administrations and appoint key German officials, our major administrative problem was to find reasonably competent Germans who had not been affiliated or associated in some way with the Nazi regime. The first report to government which I had prepared for General Eisenhower to cover our operations through July 1945 stressed the perplexing problem which denazification presented to the Military Government officer, confronted with administrative and communal problems of considerable magnitude.

His mission is to find capable public officials . . . at the same time, he must seek out and remove the Nazis. All too often, it seems that the only men with the qualifications . . . are the career civil servants . . . a great proportion of whom were more than nominal participants (by our definition) in the activities of the Nazi Party.

The size of the problem is evident when it is realized that more than 300,000 government employees were required in our zone alone, not counting replacement of the Nazis who had to be removed in schools, churches, hospitals, and places of prominence in private enterprise. It was relatively simple to carry out our directives[7] to locate and intern dangerous Nazis, to repeal Nazi laws, to seize Nazi property and block Nazi bank accounts, and to disband Nazi and affiliated organizations. There still remained the search for the individual German who was more than a nominal participant in Nazi activities so that he could be denied access to positions in which he could further influence German life.

On the one hand, it was certain the 12,000,000 or more Germans who were identified in varying degree with Nazi activities could not be kept forever from political and economic life. On the other hand, it was clearly essential to any hope of a democratic Germany that the real Nazis be identified so that they could be excluded from positions of leadership until new leaders emerged who would resist any effort on the part of former Nazis to exert influence again on German thinking. Nazism, under that name, was dead through disastrous failure, but those who had helped to create it might raise anew false creeds under other names and carefully changed phraseologies. I had become convinced that this real task could not be accomplished by occupation officials without at some time making martyrs out of those we sought to condemn in the eyes of their countrymen, and that the long-range job was one for the Germans to undertake. Until there was German administration and legal procedures, we had to perform the task.

To detect the Nazis we developed elaborate questionnaires or *Fragebogen* to be submitted by applicants for key positions and checked by our Public Safety officers, with severe penalties for those who falsified or withheld information. The tendency of the Germans to keep detailed and accurate records facilitated our check. Early in the occupation one of our officers was advised by telephone that valuable papers were lying in a Munich paper mill ready to be made into new paper. A hurried trip to this plant found a large mass of water-soaked documents which on examination proved to be the individual records of the members of the Nazi party and its auxiliaries. These files were transferred to Berlin, sorted, and prepared for ready access. Thenceforth it was almost impossible to falsify a questionnaire without detection. These records indicated the careful Nazi search for evidence of loyalty, including investigation of ancestry, which was convincing proof that few were forced to join the Nazi party; that, in fact, it was difficult to become a member. They cleared some who had joined the party in its early days without fully realizing its sinister objectives and who had been dropped later because of lukewarm support or doubtful loyalty. However, no matter how painstaking the search, it was always possible for some to escape the screening process and to hold public office for some months.

Of course there were many weaknesses in the system, particularly as the questionnaire had to be answered only by applicants for positions. Thus Nazis who had cash in their possession or in the hands of their families could escape by remaining idle at a time when there was a need for the work of every able-bodied citizen. To extend the field, Military Government enacted the widely publicized Law No. 8[8] which made it illegal for private enterprises to be managed or owned by those who had not passed the test of the *Fragebogen*.

Our Public Safety officers had to apply arbitrary definitions to determine the degree of participation which would exclude the individual and frequently this led to injustices which punished the nominal participant as severely as the active one. A story which became widespread was of two former Berlin bank officials who had become street cleaners in the fall of 1945, one employed within the

Military Government grounds in Berlin and the other by the borough of Zehlendorf in which these grounds were located. One day they met while pursuing their street-cleaning activities and recognized each other. Their mutual question was "What are you doing here?" The Military Government employee spoke up proudly: "I was able to get work and a hot noon meal here as a street cleaner because of my clean record in never having associated with the Nazis." The other replied: "Under the law I am required to work too, so I applied to the borough office where I was told that since I had belonged to the party the only job open to me was to be a street cleaner, so here I am."

Whether this story is true or not, there is no question that we were excluding former Nazis from even the most menial tasks. Once there was a commotion among our people, who had found that one of the scrubwomen in our headquarters had belonged to the Nazi organization for women in a very minor capacity. It seemed to me unnecessary to discharge her since I could think of no more fitting task to be performed by a former Nazi.

However, our work was not undertaken lightly. I insisted that real Nazis be identified and kept from office. At the same time I was apprehensive that in our search we would find and condemn many who had held membership in affiliated organizations but had not otherwise participated in Nazi activities and that this mass condemnation would fail to receive the support of even those Germans known to have opposed Nazism. By the end of 1945 there were in our zone alone more than 100,000 Nazis, classified as dangerous under our definitions, in internment camps under guard. There was no law to govern their trials and it was against our tradition to hold them indefinitely without trial. It was clear that American tribunals could not be established, since we had been able to secure competent personnel for the smaller Nuremberg and Dachau trials only with great difficulty. Our Public Safety officers had received and examined more than 1,650,000 *Fragebogen* and had refused employment to more than 300,000 persons in other than common labor. These persons had been excluded by administrative decision without benefit of trial.

I believed it was sensible to develop a German law which would require the registration of all adults and would make possible a final determination of the Nazis and Nazi associates who should be tried and punished in German tribunals established for this purpose. My legal adviser, former Solicitor General of the United States Charles Fahy, and my two personal assistants, who were also splendid lawyers, Robert Bowie, now professor of law at Harvard University, and Donald S. McLean, now with the legal office of Socony-Vacuum, shared my views and worked together with others to draft a model law. In the spring of 1946 the Laenderrat, or Council of States, in our zone accepted the responsibility for drafting a German law which would embody the purpose of our model. They were assisted by Lieutenant Colonel Fritz Oppenheimer, who combined understanding of and loyalty to our objectives with an exceptional knowledge of the German judicial system. This law[9] was enacted in March 1946 to relieve us from further direct responsibility in denazification proceedings, although we maintained our right to observe and supervise its execution.

The decision to turn over to the Germans further denazification was controversial when it was made. Factual analysis of the administrative problem was sufficient to convince me that there was no other solution to this problem. Moreover, it seemed to me of major import that German officials had voluntarily assumed the responsibility of judging their fellow Germans who had supported the Nazi party and enabled it to bring destruction to so much of the world and to the German people. They were far better able than we to determine the real Nazi who had profited from the misdeeds of the Nazi regime.

A significant event in the spring of 1946 which I believe to have been of direct value to our occupation was the arrival of our families in Germany. The decision to let them come was debated for some months. There was some opposition in the theater General Staff, which had not entirely discarded the possibility of "werewolf" or other resistance movements and believed that dependents would have to be placed in carefully guarded areas. I urged General Mc-Narney to recommend favorable action to the War Department, as I believed their arrival would bring normal home life to our communities. It would be convincing evidence that we were in Germany for a long stay. Of course there would be an additional burden on the German economy, principally for housing, but this would be compensated for by the further reduction in the number of occupation troops. Since our dependents would comply with the established policy to import all our food and commodity needs, they would not, other than in housing, draw from the meager German supply. Finally, I was convinced that Military Government would not obtain qualified personnel willing to spend several years in Germany if it meant separation from their families.

I have never regretted my recommendation or General McNarney's favorable decision. While we were not permitted to tax limited transport facilities in order to welcome our wives and children as they landed in Bremen, it was a gala occasion and in each community we waited patiently for the arrival of the first train. In Berlin this proved to be a wait of several hours as locomotive troubles delayed the train. In a few months our dependents in Germany aggregated about 30,000 persons, scattered in many communities. Shortly after their arrival one of our press correspondents in Berlin remarked that our life in Germany had become a replica of American suburban life.

Priority to receive relatives was based on length of service in Germany. I did not have sufficient time to my credit to expect Mrs. Clay on the first ship and I was fortunate that she was ready and hence was able to make it because others higher on the list were not ready. She was accompanied by the wife of our elder son (who had a much higher priority than mine). It was an especially happy arrival for Mrs. Clay. She had not seen our two sons, who were now stationed in Germany, since they had left the United States for combat duty in 1942 and 1943. While she had no difficulty in recognizing them, they were now experienced veterans of months of combat, one a major of tanks who had campaigned with the 1st Armored Division from Africa until final surrender in Italy and its march into Germany to join the occupation forces, and the other a lieutenant colonel in the Air Forces, who had flown more than seventy B-26 missions with the Ninth Air Force. Unfortunately her hopes for a real family reunion did not materialize, for one was stationed in Frankfurt and the other near Munich, both some distance from Berlin. We did see them and their families separately from time to time in the few months before the demands of the service transferred them back to the United States.

Mrs. Clay busied herself quickly in the founding of the American Women's Club of Berlin, which embarked on a community and charity program to be paralleled soon in our other communities. The good work which such clubs accomplished was remarkable and contributed much toward making the Germans understand the humane characteristics of the American people. Spending much of my time in Berlin, I became more familiar with the work of its club than with others, although I appreciated and was grateful for the contribution which all made to the accomplishment of our objectives. At one Christmas season the Berlin club sponsored a community drive which raised more than $40,000 from the relatively small American contingent in Berlin and some of our visitors. During the blockade it published an *Operation Vittles* cookbook which earned more than $10,000 in its initial publication. This was a collection of recipes spiced with the humor of occupation, as for instance the American who ordered a dry martini and got three (*drei*). While these funds were used for general charitable purposes, they were applied largely to the support of hospitals for the young and to help needy and ailing children. Supplies were distributed by members of the club, giving a valuable personal touch to its work. Not enough has been said of the part played by our American women and children in Germany, and too much of what was said was devoted to the few who lived lavishly in the midst of poverty. Perhaps as a group we did tend to live too much together. If so, this did not prevent our women and children from giving freely of their time to work without stint to relieve distress. This they did while living in a deficit economy in which needed articles had to be ordered from the United States, but they brought the touch of home into everyday life.

The spring of 1946 was significant, too, in that it marked the first meeting of the Council of Foreign Ministers to consider the German problem. Although the Council had held its initial meeting in London in September 1945, it had not at that time discussed Germany. Murphy and I used the 1945 occasion to report to Secretary Byrnes on our program in Germany. I must admit we were more optimistic then with respect to the possible success of quadripartite government than was warranted by future events. By the spring of 1946 much of this optimism had gone.

Shortly after reporting to Secretary Byrnes with General Eisenhower's approval in October 1945, I had returned to the United States to discuss the revision of our policy directive JCS/1067, which had been modified to some extent by the Potsdam Protocol. There seemed to be no difference in thinking among the representatives of the several departments in Washington charged with its preparation, and my own suggestions were received with favorable comment. James Riddleberger, of the State Department, headed the drafting committee and was confident that the revised directive would be in our hands in a few weeks. Actually it had not materialized in the spring of 1946, and did not reach us until July 1947.[10]

Therefore I believed it was timely to submit a report on the general situation in Germany together with my recommendations to Secretary Byrnes and his advisers in the State Department before the first Paris meeting of the Council of Foreign Ministers. My report was in letter form and as it apparently did not reach the heads of departments I decided to repeat it, somewhat condensed, by cable. General McNarney concurred and authorized me to dispatch this cable, which was submitted in May. Since it was my first comprehensive review of the German problem, I repeat it almost in full:[11]

Further progress in settlement of German problems requires firm definition of economic unity agreed at Potsdam. De-industrialization and reparations policies are based on treatment of Germany as an economic unit, which has always been interpreted as fully inclusive of that part remaining after the allocation of territory to Poland and Russia. If a common economic policy is to be fully implemented in all zones of Germany, central administrative agencies are essential. If they cannot be obtained and/or the boundaries of Germany are to be changed, the present concept of Potsdam becomes meaningless.

After one year of occupation, zones represent air-tight territories with almost no free exchange of commodities, persons, and ideas. Germany now consists of four small economic units which can deal with each other only through treaties, in spite of the fact that no one unit can be regarded as self-supporting, although British and Russian zones could become so. Economic unity can be obtained only through free trade in Germany and a common policy for foreign trade designed to serve Germany as a whole. A common financial policy is equally essential. Runaway inflation accompanied by economic paralysis may develop at any moment. Drastic fiscal reforms to reduce currency and monetary claims, and to deal with debt structure, are essential at earliest possible date. These can not be obtained by independent action of the several zones. Common policies and nationwide implementation are equally essential for transportation, communications, food and agriculture, industry and foreign trade, if economic recovery is to be made possible.

Immediate decisions are imperative that the Rhineland and Ruhr are to remain within the German political and economic structure even if internationalized; that the Saar is or is not to be ceded to France; that the indigenous resources of Germany are to be equally available throughout Germany and where used for exports proceeds are to be available to provide essential imports for all Germany; that zonal boundaries serve only to delineate areas of occupation and not as internal barriers for the German people; that central administrative agencies either under a provisional government or to be placed under a provisional government, should be established without delay. As it now stands, economic integration is becoming less each day, with Soviet and French Zones requiring approval for practically each item leaving their zones, and with the British and our zones in self defense moving in the same direction.

The post-war level of industry to be left Germany, which serves as a basis for reparations, is based on treatment of Germany as an economic unit. Its execution under other conditions would be absolutely impossible as it would leave economic chaos in Germany. It would particularly affect the U. S. Zone which has no raw materials and would create a continuing financial liability for the United States for many years. In the absence of agreements essential to economic unity, we have discontinued the dismantling of reparations plants except those approved for advance deliveries, as further dismantling would result in disaster if we are unable to obtain economic unity. If economic unity proves impossible, only those plants in the U. S. Zone which were designed solely for production of war munitions should be removed. If economic unity is obtained, there is no reason why the reparations plan should not be implemented promptly. Much pressure is developing to revise the reparations plan in favor of production for reparations. This ignores the real danger which Germany would still present if restored to full industrial strength. Much has been written relative to importance of German industry to the recovery of Europe. It is my considered opinion that it will take from three to five years to bring German industry to the level now agreed, and that the removal of plants for reparations purposes has no major bearing on the extent of economic recovery during this period. Unfortunately, the level of industry plan does not make specific provisions for small numbers of miscellaneous peaceful industries, and hence such industries can be removed from the eastern zone without violation of either Potsdam or the level of industry plan. Implementation of the reparations plan should also require a cessation in the taking of products as reparations until and unless an import-export balance is obtained. Finally, it must be recognized that any modification in the boundaries of occupied Germany will require a revision of the program. The loss of the Saar would not require a serious revision. The loss of the Rhineland and the Ruhr would require complete revision.

(Political Structure) It is feasible now to establish concurrently (with the administrative agencies agreed at Potsdam) a provisional government to which these agencies would report. We would propose that the initial provisional government would correspond roughly to the Council of Minister Presidents now established in the U. S. Zone. A Council of Minister Presidents of the States of all four zones would be established with the requisite coordinating committees to supervise the approved central agencies and to effect coordination on other matters of internal policy. This council would be charged with the preliminary draft of a constitution to be placed before an elected constitutional convention, which would prepare for ratification by the people the future constitution for the German state, subject to approval of the Allied Control Authority. We believe the following principles should be fundamental:

a. Germany should be a federal state composed of between 9 and 15 states, organized either by economic areas or by traditional political divisions. Each of these states would be politically autonomous, except for the specific functions ceded to the federal government. Bavaria and Gross Hesse in U. S. Zone would be ideal states. The present amalgamation of North Wuerttemberg and North Baden would be discontinued in favor either of two states or of a combined Wuerttemberg-Baden state. Similar state units have been or could be established in the other zones.

b. The constitution must contain the essentials of democracy, to wit: All political power must originate with the people and be subject to their control; there must be frequent reference of programs and leadership to popular elections; elections must be held under competitive conditions in which there are at least two competing parties; political parties must be democratic in character and clearly distinguished from governmental instrumentalities; the basic rights of the individual must be preserved by law; government must be exercised through rule of law; and the powers of the federal government must be limited in the constitution to those agreed by the several states composing the federal government. While the constitutions of individual states need not agree, they must be democratic in makeup and must provide for some delegation of powers to the county and the community level. The constitutions of the several states must provide for the exercise of all powers reserved to the states and not given to the federal government.

c. Prior to the writing and adoption of the new constitution, a provisional central government of the type previously indicated should be established at the earliest possible date. As soon as the central administrative agencies are established they should work directly with state organizations, and zonal organizations established by the occupying powers should be dissolved.

A special paper on the Ruhr has been presented to the Secretary of State at his request. It points out that Ruhr coal and steel represent Germany's chief assets. Under the present boundary of Germany, practically all of its steel and all of its industrial coal come from the Ruhr. It would be impossible to obtain a balanced export-import program with the removal of the Ruhr. The separation of the Ruhr-Rhineland area would in itself turn the remainder of Germany into a pastoral economy. It would particularly affect the U. S. Zone where industry is largely of the assembly type and can not exist without coal and steel from the Ruhr. If it had to pay for this coal and steel in a separate currency, it would have a continuing deficit for many years. Politically, the separation of the Ruhr-Rhineland area would create permanent political unrest and every patriotic German citizen would begin now to plan for such political and military alliances as would promise some day to return this area to Germany. It violates the principle of self-determination. Facing reality, the United States agreed to the transfer of certain areas in Germany to Russia, Poland and Czechoslovakia. However, recognizing the impossibility of a successful incorporation of these areas into the respective countries as long as the population was German, it was further agreed to remove their entire German population. Manifestly, the large population in the Ruhr could not be removed. Its removal would cripple industry in the area. Moreover, it is clear that there is no place available to which this population could be moved. Hence, it is our view that the political or economic separation of the Ruhr-Rhineland would be a world disaster.

We would propose the establishment of a Ruhr Control Authority for only the coal and steel industry in the area. This Authority would take over ownership and possession of the properties, issuing Class A common stock to those present owners cleared from Nazi associations, which would be the only stock entitled to dividends. Control would be exercised through Class B stock in the hands of the Ruhr Control Authority composed of such nations as may be agreed. The proposed authority would operate under existing quadripartite government until a German government is established and its relationship to that government would be specified in the peace treaty. The Authority would have complete control over the volume of production and would require such exports as are agreed in the Allied Control Authority or specified in the peace settlement. Under this Authority, general management would be left in German hands and the Authority itself would operate within the political and economic framework of Germany. The creation of the Ruhr and the Rhineland as separate states in a federal structure should facilitate the operation of the Ruhr Control Authority.

In concluding, we are of the view that our proposals herein will be generally acceptable to the British. In theory, since they accord with Potsdam, they should be acceptable to the Russians, although in detail many difficulties will arise with the Russian representatives. Basically, it is expected that these proposals will be strongly resisted by the French. However, if agreement cannot be obtained along these broad lines in the immediate future, we face a deteriorating German economy which will create a political unrest favorable to the development of communism in Germany and a deterrent to its democratization. The next winter will be critical under any circumstances and a failure to obtain economic unity before the next winter sets in will make it almost unbearable. The sufferings of the German people will be a serious charge against democracy and will develop a sympathy which may well defeat our other objectives in Germany.

The British and U. S. Zones together could, within a few years, be-
come self-supporting although food would have to be provided
during this period until industry could be rehabilitated sufficiently
to provide requisite exports to support food imports. Recognizing
fully the political implications of such a merger it is our belief here
that even these implications would not be as serious as the contin-
uation of the present air-tight zones. If French and Russian agree-
ment to these basic principles cannot be obtained, we would
recommend strongly that the British be approached to determine
their willingness to combine their zone of occupation with ours.
If the British are willing for this merger to be accomplished, the
French and Russian representatives should be advised that it is our
proposal to effect this merger before winter, even though we would
much prefer to obtain Allied unity in the treatment of Germany as
a whole.

This report contained the first proposal for bizonal merger. I had
discussed its substance with Secretary Byrnes in Paris in the spring
of 1946, but the cable itself had somehow been lost in the maze of
bureaucracy and never reached him. When he returned to Paris
for the next meeting, in July, I pointed out to him the positive nature
of Communist propaganda in Germany and the necessity for an
early public statement of United States policy which would nullify
the effectiveness of the Communist appeal. Secretary Byrnes, Senators Connally and Vandenberg, and Mr. Cohen agreed that a statement was needed. Byrnes believed it was an announcement of
major import which should be delivered by the Secretary of State
at an appropriate time and place, which pleased me very much.
When Molotov used two Paris conferences to spread Soviet propaganda, Byrnes determined that the appropriate place for his statement was in Germany. He discussed this with Connally and Vandenberg and the latter in particular felt strongly that the Secretary
should make the statement in the form of a speech and in Germany
as soon as feasible. As a result September 6 was fixed as the date on
which Byrnes would address an audience composed largely of
occupation personnel, but with key German officials included, in
Stuttgart.

This was the major development of the occupation so far. Our
Secretary of State came to Germany to announce a constructive

policy which we would follow alone if necessary because we believed it in the interest of all Europe. Byrnes came first to Berlin by air. His party included Mrs. Byrnes, Senator and Mrs. Connally, Senator and Mrs. Vandenberg, Mr. H. Freeman Matthews (later our Ambassador to Sweden), Miss Cassie Connor, private secretary to Secretary Byrnes and an old friend, and Mr. and Mrs. Frank (Anne O'Hare) McCormick. Mr. Charles E. Bohlen and Mr. Michael McDermott of the State Department went directly to Stuttgart to check arrangements for the address and for the handling of news by the large number of correspondents assembled in that city.

Byrnes discussed his speech with me in Berlin. I was impressed both with its straightforward simplicity and with its constructive tone. At the time he was considering the elimination or at least the modification of a sentence which read: "As long as an occupation force is required in Germany, the Army of the United States will be a part of that occupation force." I urged him with all the persuasion at my power not to change one word because it would be the most welcome part of his speech, not just in Germany but throughout Europe. It seemed essential even then to express the determination of the United States to remain in Europe until stability came to alleviate the terror which resulted from Communist expansion. Byrnes agreed with me but felt that this statement was so important that it should be cleared with the President. As he was unable to reach Truman by telephone, he cabled the proposed sentence so that he could be advised if change was felt desirable. No reply was received, and the statement not only had the desired effect but also was the first expression by a high American official of our firm intent to maintain our position in Europe.

We went from Berlin to Stuttgart on the same evening that Byrnes arrived in Berlin, using a private train designed for Hitler's use and heavily armor-plated underneath. While the decoration of the train was heavy from our point of view, it was luxuriously equipped to include sunken black marble bathtubs in the private suites prepared for Hitler and his immediate staff. Before we arrived in Stuttgart I arranged for the four minister-presidents of the states in our zone to call at the train to pay their respects. They remained for a brief talk with Byrnes, Connally, and Vandenberg, during which they expressed their appreciation for American assistance and for the co-operation of military government in their effort to re-create German administration. They made an excellent impression on this short visit, and both Connally and Vandenberg commented favorably on their intelligent replies to questions and their dignified bearing.

The setting for the speech at Stuttgart was dramatic. The streets leading to the Opera House where it was delivered were lined with immaculate troops from the Constabulary, and with armored cars at the intersections. Behind these aligned troops were thousands of Germans. It was a friendly gathering. The auditorium was filled with officers, soldiers, and civilian officials of Military Government, and with the invited German officials who were seated in a reserved section in the front orchestra rows. As we entered the rear of the Opera House, I left the party to sit immediately in back of those Germans so that I could observe their reactions and also obtain the full effect of the occasion. The stage contained the podium and four chairs, and was decorated only with a few flowers. Our national colors and the flag of the Secretary of State stood on either side of the chairs. The Secretary, accompanied by the two senators, was escorted to the stage by General McNarney while one of our Army bands played a patriotic air. McNarney introduced the Secretary of State in the simplest possible words: "Ladies and Gentlemen: The Secretary of State, the Honorable James F. Byrnes." While all four of the minister-presidents were able to read and understand the English language to some degree, they had been furnished with translations of the speech in German so that they could follow it without difficulty. It was interesting to watch the hope which came into their eyes as our Secretary of State sounded the first constructive note which had come from the Western occupying powers. After the speech, Dr. Karl Geiler, minister-president of Hesse, had tears in his eyes as he expressed his appreciation.

Our Secretary of State had not made a soft speech nor had he minced words in defining Germany's responsibilities. He reiterated our determination to demilitarize and denazify Germany and to exact reparations. He announced that we would support the French claim to the Saar in international conferences. He reaffirmed our right and our intent to punish war criminals. He recognized the right of Poland to annex territory in east Germany in compensation for the territory ceded by Poland to Russia, but refused to affirm the boundary claimed by Russia and Poland.

On the constructive phases of military government, he pointed out that it was timely for the German people to have self-government and the opportunity to earn their living. He favored retention of the Rhineland and the Ruhr within the German framework subject to imposition of security controls. In expressing our desire for a unified Germany he stated that it would not alter our invitation to other zones to join our zone in economic unification to provide greater opportunity for the people in the enlarged area. He voiced our concern lest Germany should become a pawn between East and West, and concluded with the words: "The American people want to help the German people to win their way back to an honorable place among the free and peace-loving nations of the world." While the major requirements of JCS/1067 remained, the punitive tone was replaced with constructive purpose. The German people were promised the opportunity and assistance to rejoin the family of nations.

The band then played "The Star-Spangled Banner" and the audience remained standing as Secretary Byrnes and his party withdrew. I walked backstage to meet them in the wings and to congratulate him on a speech which I believed would live through the years. Senator Vandenberg, whose eyes were moist, as were mine, remarked: "And they played 'The Star-Spangled Banner' with the same authority as if they were on the steps of the Capitol." The speech had reached a large German audience. It had been broadcast in German with Secretary Byrnes's voice in the background as it was delivered. Moreover, the German extras were already reaching the streets as we left the auditorium.

After the speech Mrs. Clay and I gave a buffet luncheon so that our visitors could meet the senior army officers and the officials of Military Government. We then left by diesel-electric train for Murnau, a lovely village at the foot of the Bavarian Alps where we were to spend a couple of days which were for Mrs. Clay and me, and we hoped for our guests, delightful and memorable. We traveled by automobile from Murnau through beautiful Bavarian scenery, stopping for lunch at Himmler's former home, which had been converted to an American club, and then up the winding mountain road to fabulous Eagle's Nest. We had to transfer to jeeps for the mountain climb because of the steep grades and hairpin turns. While security precautions were ample, I was apprehensive that the sudden change in altitude might adversely affect some of our guests. Fortunately this proved a needless worry and we were soon in the elevator, which carried us through a shaft excavated in solid rock to the peak, six hundred feet above. Here was the mountain home built by Martin Bormann, at a total cost of several millions of dollars, for Hitler to visit only a few times. From the living room of this chalet, looking through an enormous picture window, could be seen the towering peaks of the Austrian and Bavarian Alps and between the peaks the broad valleys beyond. As Senator Vandenberg remarked: "I can understand now how this madman, self-isolated by overwhelming egoism, could look from this peak and in his madness say to himself, 'What I see is mine, and why not the world?'" We paused briefly on the way down to look at the home where Hitler lived on his Berchtesgaden visits, and where he had so often summoned his vassals. It was now in ruins. We were enchanted by the beautiful little town which had nestled in this tiny valley through the centuries, surrounded on all sides by towering, snow-capped Alpine peaks. Returning to Murnau by train, we passed through many small Bavarian villages whose people had gathered at the station to watch the passage of the train.

On the following day we stopped in Munich so that Secretary Byrnes and his party could visit the export show, which we had organized to encourage the redevelopment of Bavaria's export trade. Then we drove to the airport from which the party left for Paris in midafternoon. While security precautions were taken everywhere, there had not been a single indication of hostility.

To be with Secretary Byrnes is always a pleasure and an inspiration for me. During this visit I had many opportunities to talk with him and also with Senators Connally and Vandenberg at length, and to appreciate their deep interest and understanding of the German problem.

In November 1946 Mr. Murphy and I returned to the United States to attend the Anglo-American conference in Washington on bizonal fusion and also the meeting in New York of the Council of Foreign Ministers. I believed we had accomplished the mission which General Eisenhower and I had assigned ourselves—to develop a military organization staffed largely with civilians, able to stand on its own feet—and that our German administration was advanced as far as was possible in our zone until we obtained quadripartite agreement on government for Germany as a whole. I had General McNarney's consent in again urging transfer of military government to civilian authority. In any event I believed that my mission was accomplished and if I was not to be replaced by civilian authority I wanted to be replaced by another soldier.

I found that Secretary Byrnes remained unalterably opposed to the transfer. He was convinced that the State Department should keep aloof from operating responsibilities which might interfere with its policy-making functions. Robert Patterson, who was then Secretary of War, urged me to continue in Germany, expressing once again his confidence in my work. During the war, while working directly under the able and outstanding General Somervell, I had also worked closely with and under Patterson, who was the civil authority responsible for war procurement. I respected and admired his integrity and his single-minded purpose to achieve the maximum war production of which he felt America capable. He was not satisfied with less than our utmost national effort. His simplicity and his loyalty to his subordinates added affection to respect. The views of one who had contributed so much to public service could not be disregarded and I agreed to remain in Germany until the spring of 1947, by which time I felt that bizonal fusion in Germany would be a reality under the agreement then being reached in Washington.

Two or three days later General Eisenhower advised me that General McNarney, with his experience in combined arms, was wanted as our senior military representative to the United Nations and that if he was assigned to this task I would take his place in Germany. I accepted subject to McNarney's willingness to accept the United Nation's assignment. I returned to Germany in December to discuss the assignments with McNarney, who told me a few days later that he would take the appointment provided it became effective in March 1947.

During 1945 and 1946 as we developed our organization for military government we were also establishing first appointed and then elected German administrations in our zone. To understand our administrative responsibilities, it is desirable to trace this development, which we hope will have a lasting effect on the growth of a democratic spirit in Germany.

CHAPTER 5

The Way to Democracy: Rebuilding Government in the American Zone

SUNDAY, January 20, and Sunday, January 27, 1946, were important days in our zone. On these two days, first in Wuerttemberg-Baden and then in Hesse and Bavaria, the Germans in the smaller towns and villages went to the polls to select their local councils, their first free exercise of the right of ballot since Hitler's rise to power.

I have listened to election returns in the United States many times and with eager interest, but never have I waited so anxiously to know how many voted as I did that first Sunday. Dr. James K. Pollock, chairman of the Political Science Department of the University of Michigan, and others of my staff were in the zone driving around the country to witness the voting. About noon Dr. Pollock called me to say that I could stop worrying. In every town and village long lines were waiting at the polling places in schools, town halls, and sometimes in the remains of bomb-damaged buildings, when they opened. Old and young, men and women, the well and the sick had turned out in cold winter weather to record their votes. Free elections had returned to Germany, and the German people had responded.

These elections were only a part of the program of political reconstruction which had started with the establishment of local German administrations and the designation of local officials even before our troops had withdrawn from forward areas to our own occupation zone. The next steps to be taken were the extension of these administrations beyond the local level to the county and then to the state.

In July 1945[1] the Military Government teams in the field had restored German county (*Landkreis*) and city (*Stadtkreis*) administrations throughout our zone and had appointed the key German officials. They had also established regional (*Regierungsbezirk*) administrations to supervise several counties. Our Military Government officials still retained final control but much of the detailed work was now in German hands. Local government was recovering from the paralysis which followed surrender.

Before we could move ahead with state governments we had to create the states. This was made more difficult by the boundaries between the zones. No real consideration was given to the traditional pattern or to convenience in administration in fixing the line between east and west Germany. It was drawn before we landed in Normandy, when there was a lack of confidence in some quarters as to its success. It has been alleged that Mr. Churchill and his associates, underestimating the power of the Allied forces, considered this line to represent a major diplomatic victory for the Western countries which would save western Europe from Soviet domination. It was the line which stopped the advance of Communism to the west but it was far behind the forward position of our armies.

Likewise little consideration was given to the maintenance of old state lines in delineating the boundaries of the three western zones. We had accepted southern Germany as our area of occupation with reluctance and then only with the Bremen area[2] included under our control to provide us with a port of entry. It was separated from our zone by the British Zone and depended upon the latter for economic support. In carving out an area for the French to occupy, we had cut the old states of Wuerttemberg and Baden each into two parts. Only in Bavaria did we have a traditional state, although it too had suffered from loss of territory to the French Zone. However, it was fairly easy to set up a state administration there, since it had maintained some of its traditional autonomy in administration under the Nazi regime. Even Hitler had paid some attention to the Bavarian pride which has resulted in many separatist movements.

Therefore we established the first German state administration[3] in Munich under a cabinet which included ministries for interior, finance, economics, education and religion, and labor. Then we decided that neither North Wuerttemberg nor North Baden was large enough to make into a state so we combined them into a single state, Wuerttemberg-Baden, with its capital in Stuttgart. We faced another problem in Hesse, where much of the area had been administered for years as a province of Prussia. Here our original plans to form the states of Hessen-Nassau, with its capital at Darmstadt, and Hesse, with its capital in Marburg, were changed in response to many requests from Germans to form the single state of Gross Hesse, later called Hesse, with its capital at Wiesbaden. The formation of this state was announced on September 19, 1945. We now had three states in our zone under German administrations headed by minister-presidents whom we had appointed.

These three states and the Bremen Enclave moved rapidly to form their government structures. In the absence of central government they were made responsible within their borders for many activities formerly conducted by the Reich, such as postal, telephone, and telegraph services, rail and highway transport. Of course these services should have been nationwide in scope or, since this was impossible, at least zone-wide. Thus we felt the need for some form of zonal co-ordinating machinery. It was desirable for the German states to start working together and preferably in an organization which would lead their officials to a better understanding of the federal type of government.

To accomplish this, on October 5, 1945, we established a Council of States or Laenderrat, composed of the minister-presidents of the three states in our zone (later Bremen was included). We did not want to have a capital for the United States Zone as it might lead to charges that we were setting up a separate government. Nevertheless, to facilitate the working of the Laenderrat, we authorized it to have a permanent secretariat in Stuttgart and to form working committees of lesser state officials to consider specific problems of common interest, such as the resettlement of refugees, the collection and distribution of food, and the allocation of transport and communications facilities. Although the Laenderrat was not given executive authority, its agreements, when approved by Military Government, could be issued as decrees in each state by its minister-president.

Its organization was worked out between Military Government

and the German minister-presidents by a small staff under Dr. Pollock. To provide direct liaison, an American representative who reported directly to me was designated as Co-ordinator of Regional Government and given an office in Stuttgart. Dr. Pollock was the logical choice for this important position. He spoke German well, was acquainted intimately with its past political history, and was an expert in modern political developments. His proved to be the right hand to guide the Laenderrat into a better understanding of the principles of democratic responsibility.

Our state problems were not ended, though, as the Bremen Enclave was in difficulty. A part of the enclave lay outside the city limits and really belonged to the British Zone. The three port cities —Bremen, Bremerhaven, and Wesermuende—depended on a hinterland which was entirely under British control. We worked with British Military Government to try to find a solution and finally transferred the area outside of the port cities proper back to British control. For a while we ran local government in Bremen under the policy control of British Military Government in the effort to fit the enclave into a higher pattern of political and economic life.

With the creation of the Laenderrat, by November 1945 we were able to report that German administrative machinery was functioning at village, city, county, and state level and was being co-ordinated on a zonal basis by the Laenderrat. Still the German officials were appointees of the occupying authority and were neither selected by nor responsible to the German people. We had set the stage for democratic government but had given it no life. Administration in itself was only a means to an end, the creation of responsible German government.

The overthrow of the Nazi regime which had ruled Germany for twelve years left a political vacuum. This had to be filled promptly with democratic leadership while we were still there to prevent the growth of new totalitarian systems under different names. I was convinced that we could neither hesitate nor delay.

In August we had authorized the formation within the *Kreis* or county of political parties[4] which subscribed to democratic principles, and had encouraged them to political activity. Organization meetings, which were held immediately, were well attended and orderly. This led us in November to extend authority for the political parties to organize on a state-wide basis. It also was timely to take the first step in making German administrations responsible to the people.

I was convinced that the soundest way to restore political government was from the ground up rather than from the top down, and that elections should be held progressively from the village to the state level. While my advisers in the Civil Administration Division had advocated elections for some time, they became lukewarm when I was ready to fix a date. Now it was too cold for the voters to turn out and too early in the occupation for them to have developed a real political interest which would draw them to the polls. Even Dr. Pollock, the foremost advocate of early elections, accepted their misgivings. I remember remarking to him that to learn to swim you have to get in the water. I think I also enjoyed teasing him a little about a liberal professor of political science trying to restrain a hard-boiled soldier running a military occupation from promptly restoring the ballot to a people who had been deprived of their right to vote.

The first elections were set in January 1946 to allow sufficient time for the states to issue electoral laws precluding former Nazis from becoming candidates and preventing active Nazis from voting. They were held in villages (*Gemeinden*) with fewer than 20,000 inhabitants. We took care to see that armed troops were not on duty in the election districts and asked occupation personnel to keep off the streets as much as possible. Final returns showed that 86 per cent of those eligible had voted, an 'extraordinarily high percentage for any local election and almost twice what we would expect at home. Thus we were able to give local government, which under the Nazis had little if any autonomy and since surrender necessarily had been dominated by military government, a base of popular support and understanding.

The next step was elections for county (*Landkreis*) councils, and councils in the larger towns (*Gemeinden*) having more than 20,000 inhabitants, held on April 28, 1946. They too were successful, and while not so large a percentage of the eligible voters participated, more than 71 per cent did, which was a satisfactory turnout. It was interesting to find that these elections returned to office a majority of the officials we had appointed, indicating that our appointees had not been branded as collaborators. In May the elections held for city (*Stadtkreis*) councils drew more than 80 per cent participation of the eligible voters. They completed the election cycle to return local governmental responsibility to elected public officials.

We were now ready for the next phase of our effort, the return of state governments to the German people. While the minister-presidents had in January 1946 established State Advisory Parliamentary Assemblies whose members were selected by political parties and other groups, these assemblies were not responsible to the electorate nor did they have any real power. Therefore, early in 1946 we requested the minister-presidents to have preliminary constitutions drawn up and to arrange for the election of constitutional assemblies to consider these drafts. Tentatively the work of the constitutional assemblies was to be completed by September 15 for submission to popular referendum not later than November 3. The drafting commissions were appointed promptly and had the draft constitutions ready for consideration by the constitutional assemblies which were elected on June 30. This voting also proceeded smoothly and attracted a heavy vote. The assemblies convened on July 15, completed their work in October, and submitted their work for our approval. While there were many differences of detail in the three constitutions,[5] all represented a high concept of democracy. Many of their clauses were taken word for word from the constitution of the Weimar Republic, and others from those adopted by the German states between 1919 and 1923. They did contain some provisions such as proportional representation which we did not favor but which could not be considered in violation of democratic principles and were therefore accepted as representing the wishes of the electorate. The three constitutions established parliamentary forms of government and guaranteed independent judiciaries with judicial review of the constitutionality of legislation. They contained excellent provisions which defined and safeguarded the basic rights of the individual.

In approving these documents it was made clear that Military Government maintained the right to intervene and exercise supreme authority to accomplish our objectives. Those powers necessary "to effectuate the basic policy of the occupation" were reserved. Likewise it was made clear that under the state constitutions measures could not be taken which would interfere with or make more difficult the exercise of national government either by Military Government or as subsequently established in a national constitution. The form of letters of approval with their express reservation of authority, and with their acceptance of certain provisions under specifically defined interpretations of their meaning, was used later by the three military governors in approving the Basic Law, or provisional constitution, for western Germany.

The constitutions were ratified[6] by large majorities. In Wuerttemberg-Baden more than 72 per cent of the eligible voters took part in the voting, on March 24, which at the same time elected members of the State Parliament or Landtag. On December 1 the voters in Bavaria and Hesse gave overwhelming approval to the constitutions and elected their parliaments. We were now ready to place state governments in the hands of elected officials.

The new parliaments met at once to form these governments. Dr. Geiler, our appointee in Hesse, now rector of Heidelberg University, was succeeded by Christian Stock of the SPD (Social Democratic party), a former trade union official. In Wuerttemberg-Baden Dr. Reinhold Maier of the FDP (Free Democratic party) continued to head a coalition government, and in Bavaria Dr. Wilhelm Hoegner of the SPD was replaced by Dr. Hans Ehard of the CSU (Christian Social Union). This represented only a change within the coalition cabinet in Bavaria, for Dr. Hoegner became deputy minister-president when Ehard moved over from the Ministry of Justice to take his place.

Thus the three states in our zone entered 1947 with almost full self-responsibility for government. To insure their freedom of action within our basic policy, a directive[7] was issued to define clearly the powers which Military Government would retain and the relationships which we expected between our state offices of Military Government and the state governments. So that it would be clear to the Germans in ratifying their constitutions that they were being granted real powers, it was published on September 30. It was the forerunner of the Occupation Statute which was to be given western Germany by the three Western occupying powers almost three years later. Elected governments now existed at all levels in our zone and these governments had backgrounds of legal authority subject to challenge in independent courts if deemed in violation of constitutional authority. It was up to them to win the respect and confidence of the German people.

When we moved ahead with these steps in the political reconstruction of our zone we hoped that parallel action would be taken in other zones so that the Allied Control Council would have no difficulty in setting up for all Germany the central administrations required by the Potsdam Agreement and so that these administrations would find the structures of state government available to facilitate their work. Our example in holding early elections was not followed in the other zones until September 1946, when municipal and county elections were held, and even then there was little choice left to the voters in the Soviet zone, as in many places the SED list of candidates was the only one placed before them.

However, when we started political reconstruction in 1945 we did not foresee its importance in the later development of West Germany. Soviet plans for expansion were then well concealed and their representatives and vassals had not yet succeeded in dominating the the states of eastern Europe which were soon to become Soviet satellites. When the issue was drawn, the elected German administrations in our zone were steadfast in their opposition to Communism and in this way alone proved their value.

Perhaps the most significant development in western Germany, and particularly in our zone and the British Zone, was the healthy growth of political parties.[8] In November 1945 they were authorized to form and work on a state-wide basis. The state parties in our zone were shortly co-operating through informal working committees which we made legal by approving their formal organization on a zone-wide basis.

The resulting rebirth of old and the formation of new parties is perhaps the most concrete outward evidence of political reconstruction. The authorization granted for the resumption of party activities was used almost immediately by political leaders first on a state and then on a zonal basis. A study of their development is essential to an understanding of present-day Germany.

Under Hitler there was only one party. In the Weimar Republic the left had been composed of Social Democrats, Democrats, and Communists; the center, of the Catholic Center party and the Bavarian People's Party; and the right, of the People's Party, the Nationalists, and the National Socialists. In the new Germany after Hitler, the rightist groups practically disappeared, the Communists were a small and extreme leftist group, and the two great parties were both moderates: the SPD (Social Democratic party), slightly left of center, and the CDU (Christian Democratic Union), slightly right. Smaller parties, also for the most part slightly to the right of center, held the balance of power.

The oldest party, the SPD, derives its basic strength from industrial workers. It advocates the socialization of means of production and distribution by peaceful and legal methods. It desires that the so-called monopolistic industries be taken from private owners and turned over to a system of ownership and management on a co-operative basis by the states, trade unions, and co-operatives. It opposes nationalization—that is, ownership by central government. It supports a strongly centralized government and proportional representation, and opposes Church influence in public schools. Its leader, Dr. Kurt Schumacher, lives in Hanover in the British Zone. However, it had able men in our zone, including the heads of state governments in Bremen and Hesse, Dr. Wilhelm Kaisen and Christian Stock. Other leaders in our zone were Erwin Schoettle in Wuerttemberg-Baden, and Waldemar von Knoeringen in Bavaria.

The other great party to emerge was the Christian Democratic Union. It is a combination of Catholics and Protestants founded in the belief that all Christians should band together against the rise of Communism. Its strength is derived principally from the rural districts. It supports a true federal structure of government. It opposes socialism but believes that the capitalistic system should be modified by having government participate together with private capital in the ownership of major industries. Otherwise, it favors a free economy. It supports the right of parents to determine the sort of school their children shall attend, and confessional schools. It opposes proportional representation. Of particular interest is the support which the CDU gives to a united western Europe and to a reconciliation with France. Its leader, Dr. Konrad Adenauer, became president of the Parliamentary Council and was appointed the first Chancellor of the West German Republic in September 1949. Leaders in our zone include Dr. Werner Hilpert, Dr. Erich Koehler, and Dr. Ludwig Erhard. Dr. Hilpert was Finance Minister in the coalition cabinet in Hesse; Dr. Koehler, the able president of the Economic Council; and Dr. Erhard, the director of economics for the bizonal area. Dr. Erhard is deserving of special mention as his advocacy of a free economy became a major issue in the first general elections held in 1949. He removed many controls following currency reform, which required moral courage. Despite the abilities of its leaders, the CDU is not as effectively organized as the SPD, nor does it have comparable party discipline.

The CDU combined with the CSU appears to have been stronger than the SPD. The CSU differs little from the CDU. It is more predominantly Catholic and exists only in Bavaria. It favors a weak federal structure of government. Its leaders are Dr. Hans Ehard, Dr. Josef Mueller, who founded this party, and Dr. Alois Hundhammer. Were it not for typical Bavarian insistence on going it alone, the CSU would amalgamate with the CDU.

In the same Bavarian spirit, two smaller parties have developed in that state. One of these, the Bavaria party, led by Joseph Baumgartner, is rightist and would be nationalist if it did not base its principal appeal on the cry "Bavaria for Bavarians." The other, the Economic Reconstruction party (WAV), headed by Alfred Loritz, opposes Bavarian separatism and supports a federal structure of government. It advocates a referendum for all important measures and government by experts. Its colorful leader, who alternates between palaces and jails, keeps it in the limelight. All in all, Bavarian politics, though varied, are never dull.

The third major party started in Hesse in 1946 as the organization of liberals. Other organizations with the same objectives started shortly thereafter under other names. Finally they joined together to form the FDP, or Free Democratic party. It is politically progressive and economically conservative, a true party of free enterprise. I suppose it might also be called a party of the "rugged individualists." Its leaders include Dr. Theodor Heuss and Dr. Reinhold Maier, minister-president of Wuerttemberg-Baden. This party joined the CDU to form the first government of West Germany.

The Communist party (KPD) has its main strength in our zone in the Mannheim area. However, its voting strength in the zone is just a little over 5 per cent. Its tight party discipline has not helped it to expand in the face of rising hatred of Russia. Its principal leader, Max Reimann, is in the British Zone. Its leaders in our zone, which include Walter Fisch, Oskar Mueller, and Albert Buchmann, are largely party hacks.

Two parties located largely in the British Zone have some adherents in our zone. One of these, the Center party (Zentrum), is left of the CDU. So far its strength is limited to North Rhine-Westphalia. The other, the German party (DP), is a rightist party in which nationalistic elements predominate. It has as yet developed little strength in western Germany as a whole, and practically none in our zone.

The growth of these political parties indicates to me that there is considerable vigor left in German political life. It is regrettable that there are so many. However, they have played their part in restoring state governments and in the work of the bizonal administration, the Economic Council and the Parliamentary Council at Bonn. Their presence and the heavy vote which they have drawn collectively in all elections indicate to me that the oft-heard charge of political apathy in Germany is difficult to prove. Certainly if the existence of well-organized political parties is valid evidence, political reconstruction in Germany has made considerable progress.

However, the story of political reconstruction within our zone is incomplete without a description of the contribution made by the Laenderrat.[9] While this was a temporary council of the states given only limited authority to co-ordinate the activities of the states in our zone, it developed a faith in democratic procedures and an experience in limited central authority which paved the way for West German Government in a form we could accept. Its members were to play active roles in creating the new government.

For more than a year the Laenderrat was aided in its work only by committees composed of state officials. As elections progressed, it became increasingly conscious of its lack of a popular base and in September 1946 asked permission to add an Advisory Parliamentary Council. This request was not approved until after state elections were held, and even then direct election of its members were prohibited. We still did not want to overemphasize the governmental nature of the Laenderrat. The Advisory Council was therefore composed of twenty-four representatives from the elected state parliaments. Indirectly it provided some measurement of popular support for the work of the Laenderrat.

In March 1947 the president of the Bremen Senate was permitted at his request to participate in the deliberations. Bremen[10] had been excluded from representation because it operated under British policy just as Berlin was excluded because it was under quadripartite control. Bremen was never satisfied with this arrangement.

It had always maintained strong trade ties with the United States and wanted to be under our policy control. The attempt which we had made to administer the enclave under British policy had failed. Therefore, by mutual consent, we abrogated the earlier agreement on October 30, 1946, and made the enclave a state in our zone. Its Senate was authorized to prepare its constitution, which was ratified by its electorate on October 12, 1947.

During the two years in which the Laenderrat served as the co-ordinating agency for our zone I met with it in Stuttgart once each month with rare exception. The first meeting turned out to be the pattern of future meetings. I arrived in Stuttgart in the early morning and went directly to Dr. Pollock's office. There, in the Villa Reitzenstein, he and his staff briefed me on current issues while the Laenderrat and its principal staff assistants assembled in one of the large drawing rooms. This attractive villa, set in landscaped gardens high on a hill overlooking the city, had been the headquarters of the Nazi Gauleiter. As soon as the Laenderrat was assembled, Mr. Murphy, Dr. Pollock, our state directors, and I walked in to take seats on a platform at one end. After a welcome by the chairman, I spoke informally on the issues raised by Dr. Pollock. Then the meeting was adjourned and the minister-presidents joined me in Dr. Pollock's office for coffee. This gathering around the coffee table provided the opportunity for frank and informal exchange of views.

Later, when the Advisory Parliamentary Council[11] was established, its members also attended the meeting at which I spoke to the Laenderrat. I agreed to consider questions from the floor. This monthly appearance of a military governor of an occupied area to answer members of a parliament representing the occupied people must have been unique in the annals of occupations. Regardless of lack of precedent, it was a democratic procedure which developed better understanding of our purposes. It may also have reminded German administrators of their responsibility to the elected representatives of the people.

Still, our main benefit came from the informal meetings with the minister-presidents over coffee. Dr. Pollock and I were usually present, and later the minister-presidents were joined by the president of the Advisory Parliamentary Council and by the secretary general.

The minister-presidents were interesting, able, and intelligent.

Dr. Hoegner was a Social Democrat who had opposed the Hitler regime until he was forced to escape to Switzerland. Slightly built, he had great energy and a real appreciation of sound democratic principles. His successor, Dr. Ehard, was a lawyer and jurist of repute, with a clear head and a firm belief in constitutional procedure. Beset by the difficulties of Bavarian politics, he remained a staunch defender of the democratic processes. Dr. Maier had been a deputy in the Reichstag of the Weimar Republic. Although heavily built, his health had suffered in the past years and the exacting duties of office were a severe physical strain. His intelligent and attractive wife was Jewish, and she had fled with their children to England so that our entry into Germany had united the family after eight years of separation. He was a kindly, gentle man who loved the Swabian inheritance and, through his understanding, contributed much to the harmony of the meetings. Dr. Geiler was dignified and impressive. His reputation as an able lawyer was outstanding. Perhaps more ambitious than his colleagues, he was less inclined to impulsive responses and remarks and always weighed his comments carefully. He was succeeded by Christian Stock, largely a self-made man, who probably did not have the educational background of his colleagues but was a man of the people, close to their thinking. Herr Kaisen from Bremen, a former journalist and civil servant, was businesslike at all times. Impatient with dialectics, he was practical and realistic, essentially a man of action.

We were fortunate to have a succession of able men as Co-ordinators of Regional Government. When Dr. Pollock returned to his university duties he was succeeded by Colonel William Dawson, a Cleveland lawyer and member of the staff of Western Reserve University. At my request he removed his uniform, as I felt it most desirable to have a civilian in this important political task. Colonel Dawson was intelligent, democratic to the core, kind, and endowed with a homespun philosophy and humor which won the respect and affection of all who were associated with him. His influence on German thinking and his contribution to a real understanding of basic democratic principles were of inestimable value. After his death on February 11, 1947, American associates raised a fund in his honor for a German scholarship at Western Reserve University and German admirers established an American scholarship at Heidelberg University. He was followed by his deputy, Dr. Charles

Winning of the faculty of New York University, who had been with Military Government from the start and was well qualified to carry on the work.

The informal meeting with the minister-presidents was always followed by an informal session with the press on the events of the day. It was at Stuttgart that these meetings were first opened to German press representatives. They must also have been the introduction to German reporters of the "question and answer" relationship which marks the American press conference. It gave them a concept of what we meant when speaking of the responsibility of public officials to the press. At the initial meeting they could not believe they were permitted to question the deputy military governor. They watched the give-and-take with the Allied press for several meetings before they gained enough confidence to ask questions freely, and on the whole intelligently. Later, German reporters attended conferences in Berlin and Frankfurt at which they also learned much from Allied press representatives. They were no longer overawed by their own officials. They learned to demand that their questions receive appropriate consideration and reply. Today, editorial condemnation is certain to result for the public official who refuses.

In the early afternoon I met with our state directors to discuss current problems and to keep them abreast of policy developments.

These monthly meetings were used sometimes to express major policy and at other times to ask for the assistance of the minister-presidents in the accomplishment of our democratic objectives. They provided the opportunity to charge the minister-presidents with specific responsibilities and to remind them of failures to carry out these responsibilities or of deviation from our expressed policies. Thus the record of these meetings in many ways reflects the development and execution of American policy.

In the first meeting the Laenderrat was told: "United States policy in Germany is a firm policy. It may seem hard but it has been made so to destroy the war potential of Germany. It does not have as its purpose the destruction of Germany as an economic unit, nor the destruction of the German people. It includes as a primary objective complete denazification. Our policy likewise includes complete demilitarization. This means not only a breaking up of military forces, but also a deindustrialization directed principally at heavy industries. Concentration of industrial power will be dispersed and will not be permitted to re-form."

On the other hand, it was told: "We propose to return to you as quickly as possible the responsibility for self-government. We propose to return to you a free press and a free radio at the earliest possible date. You now have complete freedom of religious worship. We also propose to remove any obstacles which we may find placed in the way of liberal educational opportunities. We do not wish to establish a zonal German capital. Therefore, we propose as an interim measure to establish here in Stuttgart a Council of Minister-Presidents. Since you will in fact develop the measures necessary for full co-ordination between your units, it must be assumed that each of you individually will carry out what you have agreed to collectively. I wish to emphasize that, within United States policy, yours is the responsibility. We will not dictate to you except as you violate expressed policy."

General McNarney, who had just assumed command, attended the December meeting. It was then that the election codes were approved and that the minister-presidents were charged with the responsibility for further denazification, including determining the extent to which active Nazis would be denied the franchise:

"We have recently received your proposed election codes. We have decided to approve those codes which exclude from the franchise certain categories of former Nazis as set forth in our directive. We do this in full recognition that such exclusion of a large number of voters is not a complete fulfillment of the democratic process. However, we feel strongly that those Germans who were not affiliated with the Nazi party must form an elected government. We are also most anxious that the minister-presidents prepare a program or a plan for continuing and completing denazification."

In the January 1947 meeting it was informed:

"It seems to me you have been given now the full measure of self-responsibility which is possible until some form of provisional government is established for Germany as a whole. . . . Although these constitutions provide for the requisite ceding of state power to a national or federal government, the exact powers which will be so ceded have not and cannot be formulated until a constitutional convention or congress has developed the final form of national government."

In the absence of a national constitution it would prove difficult to distinguish clearly between the legislative responsibility of the Laenderrat and the state parliaments. However, Military Government policy was "to maintain a high degree of local responsibility and to hold national (zonal) legislation to the essential minimum." State legislation must be confined to state matters and thus "must be examined prior to formal approval by Military Government to make sure that it does not conflict with quadripartite matters either enacted or under consideration, or with uniform measures adopted in the American Zone."

The Laenderrat accepted the responsibility for denazification. In March 1946 it completed measures for this purpose and asked to present them for approval in Munich. This was the city in which Hitler made his first effort to grasp power and the minister-presidents believed it fitting that it also be the scene of the closing chapter. We met in the council chamber of the old Rathaus, a mellow, paneled room dating back to the Middle Ages, which retained its beauty and dignity although much of the building was bomb-damaged. The minister-presidents of Bavaria and Wuerttemberg-Baden and the Minister of Denazification of Hesse made short speeches to indicate their sincerity of purpose. Dr. Hoegner stated:

"We are fully conscious of the difficulty of our task. Without a thorough purging, no democratic reconstruction and no re-education of the German people will be possible."

The law was signed by the minister-presidents in formal ceremony and then presented to me for signature. In signing in General McNarney's name, I said:

"It has been a basic policy and is a basic policy of Military Government to eliminate National Socialism and militarism—to that we are pledged. It has never been our desire to accomplish that by arbitrary methods. The responsibility for self-government of a people carries with it the responsibility for determining those who would destroy self-government and for taking measures which would prevent its ever happening again."

I then congratulated the minister-presidents on their sincerity and courage, and reminded them: "The rights of a people can be protected only when there is a leadership that has the vision and courage to protect these rights. To live as free men in a society of free men requires courage and determination."

Perhaps some instances of the use of these meetings to express our firm intent to accomplish our objectives will add to an understanding of their value. The November session provided the opportunity to express disappointment over the progress of denazification and regret that the political will and determination to punish those who deserved punishment had not yet developed.

When Bavaria protested rulings of the Laenderrat, it was necessary to speak sharply: "We are apprehensive that excessive state pride is beginning to arise. The Council must demonstrate to Germany and to the world its readiness and its capability for self-government."

On another occasion I was shocked with a German recommendation to lower the ration of displaced persons to the German level. It was necessary to remind the Laenderrat that other nations were sending in the additional food for the displaced persons and that Germany was fortunate not to be forced to assume the entire burden of support for these unfortunate people who were there through no fault or desire of their own but as a result of ruthless Nazi action. I refused to forward to our government a request to reduce the number of expellees, pointing out that if there had been no German aggression and if the expellees had been loyal to their country of residence the problem would not exist. We became distressed over the treatment being accorded to the expellees which came in part from wishful thinking that their stay in Germany was temporary. Therefore, in February 1947, the minister-presidents were advised of our concern in the words:

"These people are with you. They must be absorbed and your good citizenship in the future depends on the manner in which you absorb them. If it continues as at present, you will be establishing a minority group fostering hatred and hostility for years. You should know the difficulties that minority groups have caused in the past."

On several occasions it was necessary to insist on improved food collections as a requisite to continued American aid.

Fortunately it was seldom that meetings had to be devoted to admonitions. In December 1945 the Laenderrat was told: "We shall approve with the beginning of January 1 ration period a 1550-calorie ration. Hunger and starvation have never been United States objectives. My government has authorized me to say to you that it will support a 1550-calorie ration, the cost of which will be paid by Germany when it is able to pay."

Later our intent to return further responsibilities to German hands was announced: "It is our purpose to return the supervision of transportation (from the Army) to the Laender and its co-ordination to you."

In August 1946 the Laenderrat was informed of a special interest we had in the state constitutions: "Something which is always dear to the hearts of Americans is the provision which is made in the Constitution for the protection of the rights of the individual."

Also it was asked to support our effort to liberalize the education system, and reminded: "The future working people of the world will never be satisfied with an educational system that does not offer to the poorest child the same opportunity it offers to the most fortunate child. . . . Many civilizations which have lived in the past and contributed much to the world, because they lived in the past, have disappeared."

The Laenderrat was authorized soon after it was formed to meet at any time with the minister-presidents of other zones. It began to work with their associates in the British Zone to plan the economic merger of the two zones. However, this work was made difficult as their British Zone associates had no similar organization but were members only of a large Zonal Advisory Council which General Sir Brian Robertson had established. It made one unsuccessful effort to hold a conference of the minister-presidents of all four zones in Munich in June 1947. The French Zone officials were denied permission to attend and the Soviet Zone officials, puppets as they were, came only to use the occasion to create confusion and disruption. They attempted to repeat in thin disguise the Soviet charges against the Western Powers, but the Western officials refused to allow the meeting to be used for such purposes.

The task given to the Laenderrat was not an easy one. It had to undertake measures difficult for a strong government and depend upon mutual co-operation for their accomplishment. Some idea of the range of its activities may be obtained from a listing of only a few of the measures it enacted. They included laws for the redress of Nazi wrongs, the revision of civil procedures, the prevention of misuse of foreign relief, land resettlement and reform, the extension of social insurance benefits to expellees, the revision of the criminal code and court procedures, the placement of labor, and employment insurance.

Its most effective work was accomplished in 1946 and early 1947. By then, financial and economic matters were handled by the bizonal administration and there was little left for the Laenderrat. Its members sat in the upper house of this organization. Therefore it was discontinued on June 1, 1948, and its members joined with their British associates in meeting informally each month with General Robertson and me. The new group was advisory and had no governmental responsibility.

I regretted seeing it disband. Any personal influence which I may have exerted through these monthly meetings and the close association which they developed was reduced substantially. Although General Robertson and I saw most things alike, we could not know exactly how each would reply to questions raised when we talked with the minister-presidents of both zones. Thus our answers were less frank and more guarded, so that the meetings never became the friendly exchanges of views which had characterized my talks with the Laenderrat. Moreover, the forum provided by the monthly meeting was gone.

In our final session I praised the democratic character and constructive nature of the role it had played in the reconstruction of our zone, saying:

"In the more than two years the Laenderrat has been in existence, I have found it always striving to represent the interests of the German people. I have found the Laenderrat always trying to accomplish its results through democratic processes which they believe in and which we believe in. I have found the minister-presidents zealous of the rights of the states which they represent, but I think always willing to compromise these rights in the interests of the common good. It is for that reason that I regret being here for the last time."

In the spring of 1948 a second political cycle was started with the election of new local councils. The participation of eligible voters continued high in quiet and orderly voting, in which, significantly, there was a loss of ground by the Communist party which at no time represented more than 7 to 8 per cent of the electorate in our zone.

It is timely now to return to the work of the Allied Control

Council while German administration was being established in the four zones. It was in this period when it seemed as if the Allied Control Council might work successfully that different types of administration developed in each zone, which made for greater difficulty in bringing them together.

CHAPTER 6

The Control Council
Functions

A V-J PARADE of the troops of the four armies of occupation, held in Berlin on September 7, 1945, was more symbolic of the relationships which were to develop in the Allied Control Council than we realized at the time. This parade was arranged by the four Berlin commandants, who believed that it would demonstrate to the German people the unanimity of purpose and the will to co-operate of the occupying powers. Regardless of this high intent, it was almost called off at the last minute, owing to the insistence of Soviet representatives that it be led by their contingent of troops. Normally the details of such a ceremony would not have come to my attention. This time General Parks called to say that Marshal Zhukov had intervened to support his representatives in insisting that Soviet troops lead the parade. I approved General Parks's position that we would march anywhere provided our position was determined by lot.

When we arrived at the reviewing stand near the Brandenberg Gate we found that a large number of senior Soviet officers had pre-empted the most prominent place in the center of the stand. It was obvious that this was planned to hold the place for Marshal Zhukov. He was the senior commander present and no one questioned his right to the place of honor had it been taken gracefully. As it was, we were vexed. I had invited General Patton to be our senior reviewing officer. Marshal Zhukov drove up shortly after our arrival. No longer in field uniform, he presented a dazzling appearance in the blue dress uniform, decorated in red and gold, of a marshal of the Soviet Union. He was wearing all his medals and there was barely room on his broad chest to display them. General Patton turned to me and said: "Damn it, Lucius, why didn't you warn me? I would have worn mine and I would have matched him too." General Patton did not need his medals; his immaculate appearance and military bearing sufficed. Nevertheless, he was only partly joking, because he sensed, as did most of us, that this was a deliberate Soviet effort to take sole credit for the capture of Berlin and major credit for the defeat of Germany. The Soviet contingent had won first place in the lottery and, as I remember, we had drawn last place. Throughout the parade the Soviet commander and his staff acted as if the review was theirs alone, but when the head of our marching column reached the stand General Patton whispered to me: "This is where you and I step forward." We then stepped a pace forward, where we stood while our troops passed in review. I may say, too, we did so with great pride as the soldiers of the 82d Airborne Division and the armor of the 2d Armored Division were magnificent that day. General Patton's action was understood by them, and I believe by everyone present. Soviet acts had ruined the spirit in which the parade had been arranged and no further attempt to hold a combined review was ever made.

Meanwhile Army General Koenig became the French representative on the Control Council and French commander in chief in Germany. He had played a heroic part in the French fighting in North Africa and had won respect as an able military leader. He headed the organized French resistance after the Normandy landings and was an ardent supporter and admirer of General de Gaulle. Koenig had no confidence in our ability to restore a democratic German nation. In particular, he was opposed to Berlin's becoming the capital of a revived Germany, and during our four years of association he came to Berlin as infrequently as possible and always with reluctance. Even during the blockade, when I disliked leaving Berlin, I had to meet him in Frankfurt if we were to transact business. In our capacities as commanders in chief of American and French troops, we worked together closely and without friction. Otherwise our relations as military governors executing divergent policies would have been more difficult.

Relations among the occupying powers were reflected in the

debates of the Allied Control Council and even more in those of the Co-ordinating Committee of deputies, which met much oftener. It was customary for the Co-ordinating Committee to send to the Council only resolved issues requiring formal approval or issues which it could not settle after prolonged debate. The members of the Committee became intimately acquainted with each other and three of them later became representatives of their countries on the Council.

The original British member, General Weeks, remained in Germany only a few weeks because of ill-health and was succeeded by General Sir Brian Robertson, son of the distinguished field marshal who had been chief of the Imperial General Staff. Robertson had been with Montgomery in North Africa and with Alexander in Italy in senior administrative capacity and had worked closely with our staff and supply representatives. We had something in common as he too had started his Army service as an engineer officer. Later he served with the League of Nations and had then left the Army to follow a successful business career in South Africa. He returned for the second World War and had received rapid promotion. In appearance he was typical of what we have come to expect from the regular British officer—well groomed, poised, and reserved almost to the point of stiffness. It was difficult to break through this outward reserve, yet I found him sensitive, warm, and friendly. His was the intelligence of the educated and disciplined mind. In the later days of stress and strain he proved a staunch associate. In our bizonal affairs there were many times when we disagreed so vehemently as to threaten our relationship. However, neither of us let the day close after such a disagreement without getting in touch with the other to repair the damage and to further cement our partnership. We learned quickly not to pull punches but to deal frankly and openly in all matters.

General Koeltz, the French representative, was a sincere professional soldier of distinguished military background. He was older than the rest of us and handicapped in negotiation by the limited authority given him by his government, but his dignified courtesy and kindliness endeared him to his associates. Later he was succeeded by the younger General Roger Jean Charles Noiret, who had escaped to England with the surrender of France to continue the struggle. General Noiret had two sons in the army and was himself devoted to the military service. He was likewise handicapped by limited authority, within which he worked earnestly to maintain good will and friendship with his colleagues. Like General Koenig, he had little faith in a reformed Germany and would have been content with a policy directed to continued occupation and Allied control of German government over the years.

General, later Marshal of the Soviet Union, Sokolovsky was a more complex character than Zhukov. Quiet, unassuming, and dignified, he was ready in debate, which he flavored with a delightful sense of humor and the frequent use of Russian proverbs. I learned to respect his ability, and Mrs. Clay and I both developed a genuine friendship for him and for Mrs. Sokolovsky. In early charges against the Western Allies, he used a manner of presentation which somehow drew the sting and indicated that he was carrying out orders. This but added to the hurt when I found him without a trace of his former warmth and apparently enjoying the situation created in the early days of the attempted blockade, when it appeared that it might be successful. Still, he was in any circle a man of competence.

During 1945 the Control Council enacted a substantial number of measures.[1] Laws were promulgated to terminate and liquidate Nazi organizations, to increase taxes, to reorganize the German judicial system, to seize the I. G. Farben property, to vest and marshal German external assets, and to eliminate and prohibit military training. A law to punish persons found guilty of war crimes, crimes against peace, and crimes against humanity was based on the principles agreed to in London among the four powers and established a uniform legal basis for the prosecution of war criminals before tribunals other than the International Tribunal. Orders were issued to require the registration of all employables and the surrender of arms and ammunition. Directives for uniform rationing of gas and electricity, destruction of military installations, and limitation and demilitarization of sport activities were to be implemented by zone commanders. Nazi additions to the German criminal code were repealed.

However, the principal concern was with reparations. Under the formula of the Potsdam Protocol, Germany's productive capacity was limited to the industrial requirements which would provide a standard of living not greater than the average of the European countries, exclusive of Russia and the United Kingdom. Plants in excess of those needed for this productive output were to be made available for reparations. It is needless to discuss the complexities of this formula except to say that the Economic Directorate's progress in determining the level of industry which would result from application of the formula was slow.

Our experts under the leadership of an outstanding economist, Dr. Calvin Hoover of Duke University, had arrived at a steel capacity of 7,800,000 tons as essential to a minimum sustaining German economy. The French experts proposed 7,000,000 tons; the Russians, 4,500,000 tons based on a per capita allowance which when corrected after the population census became 4,900,000 tons; and the British, 9,000,000 tons. While we advocated a lower steel capacity than did the British, our proposed level of industry did not vary materially from their proposal in total productive output because it provided for larger capacities in other industries.[2]

Fixing the level of industry was impossible unless we could reach an agreement on steel production. I was convinced of the merits of the Hoover proposal and was amazed to receive a suggestion from the State Department that 3,500,000 tons would be adequate. This would have put the United States in favor of a more drastic program than any of the other powers. While I did not accept this suggestion, it influenced me considerably to propose figures below the 7,800,000 tons which in the hope of compromise we had settled on as the desirable capacity.

As a result, relations between Soviet and American representatives appeared to be friendlier than Soviet and British relations. This was only because our position was closer than Britain's to the Soviet stand, permitting us to urge the Russian delegation to accept a larger capacity and the British to lower their figures. This continued until we moved to stop further deliveries.

Compromise efforts lasted for weeks and some bitter exchanges between British and Soviet representatives developed. During this period I frequently visited General Sokolovsky and General Robertson separately, trying to persuade each to make concessions. Toward the end of December 1945 a compromise was reached which allowed 7,500,000 tons of capacity to remain in Germany but restricted annual production to 5,800,000 tons until and unless increased by the Allied Control Council. This broke the deadlock on the reparations plan and permitted the experts of the four powers to proceed further with its preparation.

In point of fact even the compromise figures drew some rebuke from the State Department, although we were not instructed to modify our position. As late as February 8, 1946, we were advised by cable from the State Department to Mr. Murphy that independent experts at home had calculated that from 5,000,000 to 5,500,000 tons per year would suffice for Germany's needs and that the additional capacity to be retained in Germany was more than was needed to sustain the agreed 5,800,000 tons of annual production. I bring this out not in implied criticism but only to show that at this time our thinking at home was still very close to a "scorched earth" policy.

The friendly relations which had been established between the commanders in chief and their deputies extended throughout the directorates, committees, and subcommittees. Privately given informal luncheons, dinners, and receptions were attended frequently by the invited representatives of all four powers and by members of the many missions from other countries then in Berlin. On January 6, 1946, an Allied Grand Ball was held in the Control Council building to which the representatives of each of the four powers contributed food, drink, and entertainment. In our everyday relations it also looked as though the quadripartite experiment was succeeding.

On the surface the record was promising, but analysis showed that the Council had enacted only measures which gave legal status in Germany to general international agreements providing for the destruction of war potential and the punishment and exclusion from office of Nazi leaders. Almost no progress was made toward democratic political reconstruction or the development of economic self-sufficiency with a reasonable standard of living for the German people. The real issues at stake were becoming evident. These included the establishment of central administrative agencies essential to co-ordination of administration in four zones, free movement across zonal boundaries, the determination of reparations, and the pooling of German resources.

On September 22, 1945, our formal proposal for the establishment of a central German transport administration[3] was rejected by General Koeltz in the following discussion:

General Koeltz: "The French position has been sufficiently shown in the document presented by the Transport Directorate [referring to a minority report by the French member]. The French government has made its reservations through diplomatic channels."

General Sokolovsky: "Our governments agreed on this point at the Potsdam Conference. . . . We must meet the creation of this Transport Department."

General Clay: "I feel the problem right now is the fundamental principle of how we are going to govern Germany. If the Control Council isn't going to establish German administrative machinery it might as well fold up as a governing agency and become a negotiating agency."

Again on this subject in the October 12 meeting:

General Koeltz: "I am perfectly agreed that there should be an American, French, British, and Soviet Council [which was in fact what the Transport Directorate was] but I can't agree that the Germans should have anything to do with it."

On October 16 General Sokolovsky replied:

"The Soviet delegation has always been of the opinion that German central agencies for transport and communications . . . should be created. . . . It is about time in my opinion to start establishing these central German agencies."

On November 23 another attempt was made but General Koeltz said once again that his government would not permit him to agree to the establishment of any central administrative agency. Badly as single control of rail traffic in the four zones was needed, failure to obtain this control was even more serious because it signified the defeat of our efforts to establish the administrative agencies which might have made quadripartite government possible.

French determination to decentralize activities in Germany was not confined to governmental institutions, and General Koeltz objected to a proposal which would have permitted the federation of trade unions throughout Germany,[4] saying:

"The objects of the administration of Germany will be the decentralization of political structure and the developing of local responsibilities. Thus trade unions are political structures and will be decentralized."

The consistency of the French position is illustrated by the refusal of French Military Government three years later, in February 1949, to permit trade unions in the French Zone to join a federation for the three western zones.

While French opposition prevented progress in setting up German administrative machinery, discussions in the Co-ordinating Committee raised doubts as to the sincerity of Soviet support of these agencies and German unification. Berlin University was located in the Soviet Sector of Berlin. It was not placed under the Allied Kommandatura. This gave rise to fear on our part that it would have a limited life as a free university, which turned out to be the case. In the meeting of October 3, 1945, General Robertson and I urged that it be administered by the city government of Berlin under the supervision of the Kommandatura, to which General Sokolovsky replied:[5]

"The point is that if the University of Berlin is situated in Berlin, it doesn't mean that only the people residing in Berlin are to use it. . . . This is going to be for the present the one and only university in the Soviet Zone."

On December 6 General Robertson and I proposed the reopening of consulates in Germany,[6] which would have enabled other nations to have observation posts in eastern Germany. General Sokolovsky objected, saying:

"This matter is not a matter for the authority of the Control Council but . . . lies within the authority of our governments. Therefore, the commanders of the zones have even less right to decide such questions."

Time and time again we resubmitted this proposal. The four powers had agreed in the Potsdam Protocol to receive in Berlin from the sixteen nations allied in the war against Germany missions accredited on the Allied Control Council. Soviet representatives would never agree to enlarge this list or to authorize consular representatives from these and other countries to be stationed in the several zones. In 1949 accredited representation in Berlin was still limited; in fact, when Brazil broke diplomatic relations with the Soviet Union, Soviet representatives attempted to withdraw the accreditization of the Brazilian Mission, a proposal which was rejected by the three other powers. Soviet unwillingness to accept consular representatives in eastern Germany foreshadowed the erection of the Iron Curtain. In the meantime the three western zones proceeded separately to receive missions and consulates from other countries, more than thirty of which were opened in our zone.

General Eisenhower had made our zone free to all of the occupying powers in the opening meeting of the Control Council. He and I hoped this would allay Soviet suspicion and might lead to reciprocal action by their representatives but over the months this proved to be a one-sided arrangement and even those Americans en route to Berlin who left the established corridor by accident were detained for hours and sometimes for several days while we negotiated with Soviet authorities to secure their release. In the meeting of November 27 General Robertson opened a discussion on air corridors and declared that there was no reason why air travel in Germany should be restricted at all except as required for safety. This led to a general discussion of travel between the zones.[7] I had talked over the situation with General McNarney and we agreed that this arrangement should be discontinued. Therefore I said:

"The United States delegation in its zone has been very free in the removal of all restrictions. . . . Henceforth, our boundaries will be open to all of our colleagues, but only as open as their zones are to ours."

In the meeting of December 17 General Robertson and I supported a proposal to open all zonal boundaries to the passage of Germans. General Koeltz objected without explanation. General Sokolovsky explained the Soviet viewpoint, using a technique which was later applied to many proposals: he agreed in principle since the proposal was in accord with the Potsdam Protocol, but "practical implementation at the present moment is impossible." We were unable to determine why he thought the proposed action was impracticable.

In the Control Council in November 1945 Marshal Zhukov charged the British representative with deliberate failure to break up the German General Staff and Army units.[8] In reply Field Marshal Montgomery stated:

"We do not consider a helpless mass of Germans on an island in the Baltic as a perpetuation of the Wehrmacht, nor the small administrative staffs to do the work of administration a perpetuation of the German General Staff. However, suspicions are detrimental to co-operation. We have therefore taken the measures [to break up these staffs] at considerable inconvenience in order that a complete atmosphere of mutual trust can be attained."

This action by the British commander did not satisfy Soviet purpose, as was demonstrated in the Paris meeting of the Council of Foreign Ministers when Molotov leveled this charge against the United Kingdom. It was to be repeated again and again in conference and its intent was to keep alive the fears of Germany's neighbors to the east who depended largely on Soviet-supplied information for their knowledge of conditions in Germany. Soviet representatives were working, regardless of fact, to build up the record for their own propaganda purposes.

When we appeared to be deadlocked in reaching agreement in the steel capacity to be retained in Germany, we decided on a token list of about 74 plants to be delivered as advance reparations pending determination of the final list. We then had to determine how to divide this token list between East and West and how to evaluate the plants for allocation purposes and for reciprocal deliveries. While evaluation on any common basis was satisfactory for allocation purposes, it would be used also to determine the value of the reciprocal deliveries which the Soviet Government was to make for three fifths of the plants it would receive from west Germany. Thus the formula determined the bill which the Soviet government would pay and General Sokolovsky wanted it to be as low as possible. In discussions I had in mind not only the agreement but also the intent of our delegation at Potsdam to determine quickly and finally the reparations to be made available in the form of capital equipment, so that these plants could be removed to end the problem. On October 22 I pointed out that reparations had as its primary purpose the destruction of Germany's war potential,[9] adding: "We have been here six months and have destroyed none." I then recommended that the 74 plants selected for advance reparations be delivered at once without awaiting final agreement in evaluation and allocation:

"I have in mind particularly that if we actually start moving one or two of these plants from Germany to one or two of the Allies it would be really worth while . . . a token delivery."

Generals Sokolovsky and Koeltz accepted, but General Robertson refused, because he believed, with much merit, that no plants should be moved until the conditions of removal had been agreed to in detail. This led Sokolovsky to place in the minutes:

"The British delegation not only does not want to carry out in time the decision of the Potsdam Conference but insists categorically and handicaps the others in the fulfillment of those decisions."

Obviously this was an unfair charge, as Soviet intransigence had prevented agreement on an evaluation formula. It was again an opportunity to build up the record.

The surface climate of apparent agreement had not obscured the development of issues nor had friendly personal relations fully covered an undercurrent of impending difficulties which could be felt if not seen and which occasionally broke through the surface in minor incidents such as the victory parade.

On General Eisenhower's return from Moscow, he had asked the War Department to invite Marshal Zhukov to visit the United States as its guest. The request was approved and I was with him when he extended the invitation. There was no question as to the genuine enthusiasm with which it was accepted. We even discussed details with Zhukov and he said that he would take along two bodyguards. Eisenhower tried to explain that they were unnecessary in our country, but Zhukov brushed the explanation away by declaring that bodyguards always accompanied a marshal of the Soviet Union. He also asked for me to be designated as his escort and for General Eisenhower's son, Lieutenant John Eisenhower, to accompany the party. I must admit that I wondered about the impression I would make if I escorted Marshal Zhukov into an American hotel accompanied by his two armed bodyguards. You cannot disguise Soviet bodyguards; they look the part. Still, we believed that the visit would be most helpful to the maintenance of good relations and that our country would be warm in its greeting to the great military victor. On the day prior to the scheduled departure of the aircraft which was to take us to the United States, I received word for transmission to General Eisenhower that Marshal Zhukov was ill in Moscow and would have to postpone his visit. Members of our embassy staff thought they had seen him at the ballet that same evening. In any case, although we repeated the invitation, it was clear that Zhukov was not to be permitted to visit the United States. To avoid possible embarrassment to him, we did not press the invitation.

While conditions in Berlin at this time were conducive to trouble, they were kept firmly in hand. Soldiers, just out of combat, carrying arms and meeting with the soldiers of three other nations in a conquered city with a destroyed economy, provide the ingredients for an explosive mixture. The four commanders in chief recognized the necessity for firm discipline and, when prevention failed, they refused to let disorder develop into international incidents.

As early as 1945 we experienced our first difficulties in the operation of our train service to Berlin, when Soviet soldiers tried to enter these trains to check the identities of passengers. I discussed this problem in the Control Council without results, so I determined to see General Sokolovsky about it. I went to his office and reminded him of the discussions relating to our entry into Berlin and said that I would have to place armed guards on our trains to prevent access by others, if all else failed. Sokolovsky would not waive his claim to the right of inspection, which he applied in particular to German passengers. I advised him that our military trains would carry only such Germans as were employed by us, and all others would apply for quadripartite-issued permits.[10] I also told him that our use of armed guards could create a most unhappy incident for both of us. Sokolovsky then suggested, without waiving his claim, that we would have no further trouble. I replied in the same spirit that a "gentleman's agreement" was satisfactory to me but that I wanted to make it clear that we would not recognize any right on their part to inspect our trains. This understanding remained effective until the spring of 1948.

We began to receive frequent Soviet protests concerning our air flights into our Berlin airport at Tempelhof. They charged violation of air safety regulations and digressions from the air corridor to fly over Soviet military installations. If there were such flights, they were not made by planes engaged on the Berlin run. We were not yet running an airlift and the few planes which flew into Berlin each day could be checked easily. It was clear that the charges were exaggerated in fact and designed to build up a record for later use.

Another incident, unimportant in itself but characteristic of the undercurrent, resulted from our effort in the fall of 1945 to hold an international military track meet in Berlin in the interest of good will and to increase athletic opportunities available to occupation troops. The four commandants in Berlin made the practical arrangements with apparent enthusiasm on the part of all. Soon athletes from the four occupying powers and from other European countries were seen practicing in Berlin. The stadium Hitler had built for the

Olympic championships was gaily decorated. On the day preceding the meet the Soviet commandant advised his colleagues that there would be no Soviet participation. Since its team had been practicing daily this was difficult to understand. No explanation was ever given for the last-minute withdrawal.

In the spring of 1946 it still looked to the casual observer as if the Control Council was functioning successfully. We had reached agreement on additional negative measures of occupation,[11] including a law to supplant Nazi legislation which prohibited marriage on racial and other grounds, a law prohibiting military construction, the repeal of a law conferring certain arbitrary powers on the Reich Minister of Justice, a directive prohibiting obnoxious supervision and control of political activities by the police, a law for the control of scientific research, and a directive requiring declaration of Allied property in Germany.

We even agreed on a few relatively simple constructive measures which were to be implemented by each zone commander. They included the re-establishment of international postal service, the reopening of museums, the better utilization of housing, the establishment of labor courts, the restoration of co-operatives, the exchange of banking statistics between zones, the establishment of works councils, and the opening of interzonal telephone and telegraph services. This was an encouraging trend although it was becoming apparent that directives from the Control Council were implemented by each zone commander as he saw fit and all of the zone commanders did not feel obligated to execute faithfully and fully the decisions of the Council.

We also reached agreement on the evaluation formula,[12] which in large part was based on the depreciation formula used by our Treasury Department for income-tax purposes. Depreciation was to be calculated on the 1938 value in Reichsmarks for capital equipment, and 1938 commodity values increased by 5 per cent were to be used to determine the reciprocal deliveries from the Soviet Government. Quadripartite teams were designated to apply the formula to specific plants so that we could proceed with allocations.

We continued our work to complete the level of industry plan. While the deadlock had been broken with the agreement on steel capacity, each industry in turn required considerable effort before conflicting views could be reconciled. We had some trouble getting a report from the Economic Directorate which would permit us to start discussion. Sokolovsky urged that, whatever its shortcomings, an immediate report was necessary. Robertson demurred and the battle of proverbs was on. Sokolovsky felt that a perfect report would be time-consuming and that a quick look on our part might result in an agreement. As he said, "Butter cannot spoil porridge"—that is, an exact measure is unnecessary. To this Robertson replied: "If you rush your horse to the fence too quickly, you are likely to fall on your nose." This in Russian, said Sokolovsky, would be: "If you go slower you will come farther from the place you are going to." Perhaps these pleasantries did hasten the work of the directorate, for its report[13] was shortly before us. In other industries our position, which had been more restrictive with respect to steel capacity than both the French and British positions, was now less restrictive. We could not but wonder whether military and economic security were not being confused.

For example, at the March 7 meeting of the Co-ordinating Committee, there was the following discussion:

General Robertson: "We do feel very strongly on this subject of synthetic textiles. . . . The manufacture . . . does have a considerable amount of war potential in it."

General Koeltz: "As regards dyestuffs, the commercial concentrations should not be higher than it was before the war. Exports should be made through the inter-Allied agency. . . . As regards pharmaceutics, . . . we would run the risk of having people saying the Control Council left Germany with the same capacity for chemical production as it had before the war."

General Clay: "I cannot understand General Koeltz's objections. . . . If we carry out our objectives of breaking down the large industries, . . . it seems to me we largely solve the security problem. Particularly because of German science and skill these products [dyestuffs and pharmaceuticals] are needed throughout the world. . . . We have agreed there is a need for a certain money value in exports. Where can this be realized which represents a lesser war potential?"

Discussing limitation of electric power, I said:

"I think all of us should agree that we would not want to take any hydroelectric power away because it saves coal. . . . I feel strongly that we should increase hydroelectric power because it saves coal."

These difficulties were finally resolved on March 26. Then acceptance of the whole plan was threatened by disagreement as to the
fundamental assumptions on which it was based. Robertson and I
insisted that it must be stated clearly that the plan was based on
existing German boundaries and could not apply if the Saar or other
areas were severed from Germany; and that it was based on an
estimated population which might (and in fact did) prove smaller
than the actual population. Moreover, the restrictions, except those
which provided for specific prohibitions, were not to be considered
as permanent or binding on all parties except for reparations purposes. After considerable discussion these assumptions were accepted
for incorporation into the final agreement, which was submitted to
the Control Council and approved in a special meeting on March 26,
1946. The long-awaited and much-debated level of industry was now
in existence. There remained the determination of the specific plants
in each industry to be removed from Germany. Although no one of
us was entirely satisfied with the plan, we were happy to have
reached agreement. I remember that at this meeting of the Control
Council Sokolovsky paid a special compliment to my efforts in bringing about compromise, saying in effect that without these efforts
there would have been no plan. I bring this up to emphasize the
change in Soviet viewpoint which came two months later when we
failed to arrange an import-export program to apply to all zones.

During the early months of 1946, while we were discussing reparations, the American delegation made an unsuccessful effort to
establish more effective quadripartite control of information services
by replacing a powerless subcommittee with a committee reporting
directly to the Co-ordinating Committee.[14] In March I pointed out
what was already a trend:

"We all might as well face the facts, and we know now that the
information given to the Germans indicates certain discords and lack
of unanimity among the Allies. There have been certain recent
charges of the German Communist party that the western zones are
harboring Nazis and Fascists. . . . The papers in the western zones
resist such a charge. Surely that isn't what we are here for."

The effort failed but it is interesting to note how early in our
operations the Soviet propaganda mill started to grind.

Another failure in our attempts at unification occurred in March when the Co-ordinating Committee was unable to agree to let political parties function on a national basis.[15] Sokolovsky favored the proposal, saying: "It seems to me we should not raise obstacles for German democratic parties to form on a national all-German basis."

In reply, I stated: "So long as we have separate political parties [in each zone] . . . German political leaders will be able to exploit and will make every effort to exploit, differences in respect to the administration of the several zones."

Robertson concurred but Koeltz rejected the proposal, referring to the French position that such questions must await decisions on boundaries and related matters.

The differences between Soviet expression of a desire for a unified Germany and Soviet actions to exclude the Western Allies from east Germany were being evidenced with increasing frequency. For months we tried to obtain permission for our Graves Registration teams to enter the Soviet Zone to locate and remove our dead. We estimated that this task, properly done, could be completed in six months. We were never able to secure free entry for this purpose and in April I gave up efforts to do so in the Co-ordinating Committee. Shortly afterward I made a direct personal appeal to Sokolovsky which did result in our teams being permitted to enter the Soviet Zone, although under such restrictions as to numbers, locations to be visited, and routes to be followed that three years later many of our dead still remained buried in the Soviet Zone.

CHAPTER 7

The Control Council
Stands Still

OUR first break with Soviet policy in Germany came over reparations. The determination of the Soviet Government to exact reparations from productive output in a deficit economy was evident by the end of 1945. In spite of apparent accomplishments by the Allied Control Council, the United States and the United Kingdom were pouring food into their zones of Germany whereas the Soviet Government was not only making its zone live on its own resources but in addition was withdrawing huge quantities of raw materials and finished products. This situation could not be permitted to continue, as it represented indirect payment for deliveries to the Soviet Union by the United States and the United Kingdom. Therefore in the spring of 1946, after repeated warnings had failed, I stopped delivery from our zone. I had no choice.

We had carried out the Potsdam Protocol requirement to fix a common level of industry for Germany as a whole, but it was meaningless if the Soviet Government refused to account for capital equipment removed from its zone and to discontinue its utilization of east Germany's productive capacity to take goods without payment. We had failed to establish the German central administrative agencies which could administer a single economy. Thus we were faced with a major decision which was certain to have lasting effect on our relationship with Russia.

During the meetings of the Co-ordinating Committee I had tried repeatedly to have the common utilization of resources considered concurrently,[1] although without success. On April 8 I advised the Committee that the Soviet representative in the Economic Directorate had expressed the view that the import-export problem would have to be considered as a zonal problem until there was a favorable trade balance for Germany as a whole and reparations had been met in full. This could mean only that the Soviet Government proposed to continue to remove Germany's productive output until it had satisfied on its own valuation its claim for $10,000,000,000. I stated: "The level of industry plan was based on a balanced import-export program. If there is no such program, then the reparations plan has no validity." I felt strongly that we were being placed in the position not only of financing reparations to the Soviet Union but also of agreeing to strip our own zone (which had insufficient industrial capacity for self-support) without getting the benefits which would come from the amalgamation of all zones. On April 26 Robertson pointed out that if each zone were to be regarded as an economic entity it would mean that each zone was to support itself and any deficit would be borne by the occupying power. I stated that the boundaries of our zone gave us a great part of the scenic beauty of Germany but had been accepted only on the understanding that the economic resources of all Germany would be available to Germany as a whole. I could not accept the principle of zonal import-export programs, nor did I see how an over-all program could be administered without a central agency. General Mikhail I. Dratvin, who had now replaced Sokolovsky on the Co-ordinating Committee, argued that there was no connection between the questions. I then made the following statement, which I quote in full, for this was the beginning of the split:

"I submit that reparations was only one of the bricks that built the house. If you pull out any of the bricks the house collapses, and it seems to me we have pulled out so many already we are on the verge of collapse. I don't believe we can ever reach a solution on any one of them without reaching a solution on all of them. Certainly the question of the ability to meet the export-import program is tied up definitely with the question of reparations.

"Since it has become the practice to quote Potsdam, I would like to quote a part of Potsdam which comes before the part quoted by my Soviet colleague. Paragraph 14 requires that during the occupation Germany shall be treated as a single economic unit. During the year of occupation up to date, I would not think anyone can claim that we have done so. In Paragraph 15 it states that Allied control shall be imposed on the German economy only to the extent necessary to insure during the term of the Control Council the equitable distribution of essential commodities between the several zones, so as to produce a balanced economy throughout Germany, and reduce the need for imports. We have been here a year, but I do not believe that my colleagues would claim that we have accomplished that. And Paragraph 16 shows that the writers of this protocol foresaw what might happen and required to carry it out the establishment of German administrative machinery to proclaim and assume the administration of these controls. Would my colleagues suggest that we have lived up to this part of Potsdam? I claim that to live up to Potsdam you live up to it in whole and not in its individual parts."

Koeltz commented only to say that it was one of many questions which his government reserved to be discussed by the four foreign ministers. Robertson endorsed my statement, which drew no comment from Dratvin.

On May 3 a final attempt was made to reach agreement. Dratvin reaffirmed the Soviet position that there would be no pooling of resources until there was a balanced economy:

"Before the program will be fulfilled, each commander of the zone must be responsible for putting into operation all the industrial facilities of the zone."

This position was aggravated by Soviet refusal to give any accounting of either the plant or productive output removed from eastern Germany. So I replied:

"I think I understand the position of the Soviet delegation putting the cart before the horse instead of behind it. I can only say that, with the exception of advance reparations plants, all further reparations have been stopped in the American Zone. We will be very glad to continue preparations, but we have no intention of implementing them until the entire question has been resolved. We do not want to be put in a position where we are without plants and without an agreement."

The threatening storm had broken, the "friendly" American general who had worked so hard for a reparations agreement was now, in *Pravda* and in *Taegliche Rundschau*,[2] the "illegal General Clay."

The Council of Foreign Ministers met in Paris in April and May

1946 and again in June and July. These were the first of its meetings in which the German problem was discussed at all, and the discussions which did take place were of a more preliminary nature than desired by our representatives.

Secretary Byrnes had planned to have exploratory talks of the German problem prior to the close of the May meeting, and a full review during the June-July session. Nine months had elapsed since the Potsdam Conference, and events and discussions within Germany permitted analysis of the results.

At the time of the Potsdam Conference our strength in Europe was at its peak. Our armies were deep in Germany, Austria, and Czechoslovakia. The extent of our air and armored power was evident everywhere. New governments in Poland, Czechoslovakia, and Hungary had Communist participation, but were not Communist-dominated. Even the Balkan States were not under Communist control and Generalissimo Stalin was not sure that it could be imposed in these countries. Hence, at Potsdam, the Soviet representatives had been willing to accept a unified Germany under quadripartite control and to depend on open Communist political action to dominate its life, since the Communist party in Germany was recognized as a democratic party. Open and underground political activities would be undertaken elsewhere to implant Communism throughout Europe. Meanwhile the Soviet economy would be restored in part with German capital equipment and the pent-up consumer demand satisfied as much as possible with German productive output. If Germany ended in economic chaos it would be even more susceptible to Communist indoctrination.

While Soviet representatives supported in principle the establishment of central administrative agencies, they did not intend to permit such agencies to break down zonal barriers or to place the resources of east Germany into a common pool unless they were assured of a large share of the productive output of all Germany without payment. They expected that we would finance the deficit and accept continued reparations from production. I do not believe that either in Potsdam or in the Paris conferences the Soviet Government had a definite, long-range plan in mind. Its policy of Communist world domination which had been checked by war was brought out of moth balls and clearly formed the basis of their day-to-day planning, which was still, however, on an expediency basis.

In the spring of 1946 the situation in Europe had changed materially. Our forces had been withdrawn from Czechoslovakia and were contained in our occupation areas in Germany and Austria. While the process of redeployment still left us with a larger force in Europe than we were to have later, it was no longer the powerful military organization with which we had ended the war. Communist control of the eastern European countries was becoming stronger each day and its penetration into western Europe was gaining momentum, but even with these gains the Soviet position was not yet sufficiently entrenched to permit the clanging of the Iron Curtain and Molotov was not prepared to have serious discussion of the issues within Germany.

French unwillingness to accept central German administrations until the questions of the Saar, the Ruhr, and the future political structure of Germany had been resolved seemed of less importance as the intransigent Soviet position made it appear unlikely that these central agencies could operate successfully.

The Council of Foreign Ministers by this time recognized that the provisions of the Potsdam Protocol providing for a common policy in matters relating to German economy could not be implemented by the Allied Control Council. The Soviet representatives at Potsdam, carried away by the first sight of modern German factories, had believed that their way to economic progress and to industrialization lay in dismantling entire plants and factories in Germany for re-erection in Soviet Russia. They began this dismantling process early, and soon railroad cars were passing through Berlin laden down with equipment. They had not discovered yet that the machinery in a plant is a small part of the total investment in buildings, transport facilities, access to materials and skilled labor, and "know-how." The Soviet Government soon found that it could not reconstruct these factories quickly, if at all. Reports verified by photographs reaching our intelligence agencies in Germany showed that almost every siding in east Germany, and many in Russia, contained railway cars filled with valuable machine tools rusting into ruin.

Meanwhile the Soviet representatives had placed some of the plants remaining in Germany in production and their output was proving an important contribution to a disrupted economy. Hence, when we insisted that the Control Council proceed to carry out the Potsdam decision to place exports in a common pool, with proceeds to go in the first place toward payment of essential imports, we met with objection after objection from the Russians. They did not deny the agreement but put up a successful delaying action. Perhaps a frank explanation would have led to understanding, as certainly our country was sympathetic to Russian suffering during the war and recognized the need for rapid rehabilitation of the Soviet economy.

The American delegation at Paris, headed by Secretary Byrnes, included Senators Connally and Vandenberg, Mr. Cohen, Mr. Matthews, and Mr. Bohlen. The conference was devoted in large measure to the treaties with the satellite countries, and Germany was discussed only toward the end. Secretary Byrnes then sent for Mr. Murphy and me. Earlier in this conference he had introduced his proposal for a treaty to last for twenty-five years, which would pledge the four powers to keep Germany demilitarized.[3] He hoped that this treaty would quiet the fears of Germany's neighbors and permit a reduction in occupation forces advantageous to German economic recovery and to the growth of democracy. He told me that he had arranged a special meeting to discuss his proposal directly with Molotov, but had made no progress in obtaining the latter's support. This was surprising as Stalin had appeared sympathetic to such a proposal when Byrnes visited Moscow in December 1945.

I attended the May 15 meeting in Luxembourg Palace and sat with the American delegation at the conference table. On that day Foreign Minister Georges Bidault made it clear that the French Government required consideration and solution of the problems of the Ruhr, the Rhineland, and the Saar in the interest of security before it would consent to the establishment of central agencies in Germany.[4] He stated that the Ruhr should be under international political and economic control, the left bank of the Rhine should be garrisoned permanently by Allied troops, German territory west of the Rhine should be made into a separate province, and the Saar territory should be integrated economically but not politically with France.

Bevin expressed willingness to consider the French proposals, although he was not favorable to the political severance of the Ruhr from Germany. Molotov was noncommittal. Byrnes then proposed the immediate appointment of special deputies to consider questions of urgency before the June 15 meeting of the Council. Molotov evaded the issue and charged the British with secrecy in their Ruhr operations. Byrnes suggested that five questions be placed before the deputies:

1. What is to be done with the Ruhr and the Rhineland?
2. Are the resources left to Germany to be made available for Germany as a whole, and for exports to pay for essential imports?
3. Can agreed procedures be reached to effect economic unity in the next ninety days?
4. Can zonal boundaries be accepted only as delineating occupation areas?
5. Can tentative agreements be reached on the western boundary?

After much fruitless discussion in two separate sessions it was evident that Molotov was not prepared to appoint special deputies to consider these questions or any questions concerning Germany. The Council adjourned on May 16 and the German problem was carried over to the June meeting.

While nothing specific had developed, the discussions on Germany had proved valuable in indicating why agreement in Berlin to carry out the Potsdam Protocol had been so difficult. My attendance at the conference had given me the opportunity to explain to Byrnes the economic consequences which were already resulting from the severance of Germany into four independently operated areas, and to discuss these consequences with Connally and Vandenberg.

When Molotov charged that the Western Powers were not proceeding with the disarmament of Germany, Byrnes wired McNarney to introduce in the Allied Control Council a proposal for a quadripartite inspection of all the zones to determine the facts. When McNarney did so it was referred to the Co-ordinating Committee,[5] which for some time had been attempting to arrange for just such an inspection. Again we insisted that the inspection, to be useful, must cover all phases of disarmament including the use of German industrial production for war purposes. The only kind of inspection to which the Soviet delegation would agree was one to determine whether any German troops were still maintained in concentrated groups under their own officers. In the meeting of May 23 I challenged a Soviet accusation that German troop bodies existed in our zone:

"The United States Zone has nothing to hide. It has, with reasonable freedom, permitted access of the representatives of all zones. . . . There has not been provided like access in all other zones. . . . The Soviet Government's unwillingness to accept an examination of production prevents a comprehensive examination of disarmament . . . a partial examination would serve no useful purpose."

Our efforts to establish a disarmament mission with access to east Germany proved vain. The Iron Curtain was being lowered inch by inch and day by day.

The next meeting of the foreign ministers began in Paris on June 15. The American delegation was again headed by Byrnes and included Connally and Vandenberg. While this meeting produced only limited debate of the German problem, it was nevertheless the most important international discussion about Germany since the Potsdam Conference.

Again Murphy and I were summoned to Paris on July 9. Molotov read a prepared statement[6] directed at Byrnes's proposed treaty for the four-power disarmament and demilitarization of Germany. It was apparent that this statement was made for propaganda purposes in France and to aid the French Communists. It attacked the proposal as inadequate and insufficient, but suggested no revision other than the necessity for Germany to be kept disarmed for forty years rather than twenty-five. Molotov said in part:

"Study of the draft shows the complete inadequacy of the measures it sets forth to safeguard security and to prevent aggression by Germany in the future."

He referred to the measures already agreed to in the Potsdam Protocol which he believed adequate for this purpose if carried out, and then charged:

"The Soviet Government already proposed that investigation be undertaken in all the zones in Germany to see how the disarmament of German forces and disbandment of all other military and paramilitary organizations and establishments have been carried out in actual fact. This has not been done to this day. As to the elimination of German war and military economic potential, the position is entirely unsatisfactory—up to now no plan for the elimination of war potential of Germany has been adopted."

He accused the Allied occupying powers of failing to carry out the Potsdam decisions. He implied that since the proposed treaty did not repeat the decisions of Potsdam its purpose was to avoid carrying them out. He reiterated the demand for reparations to the Soviet Government in the amount of $10,000,000,000 and complained that just Soviet requirements were being refused by the cessation of deliveries of reparations from the United States Zone and from western Germany as a whole, as allocations could be made from the British and French zones only with American consent.

He employed his usual device of half-truths to present a completely distorted picture. It is true that his representatives in Berlin had charged British representatives with supporting enemy military organizations in Germany[7] because the British commander had maintained a German military staff to administer the discharge of German prisoners of war, and because he had kept under their own officers the Royal Yugoslavian Forces captured with the German Army in view of the difficulty involved in their repatriation under conditions which then existed in Yugoslavia. We had known that there was no military significance in these British actions, which were administratively helpful. However, we had urged, and the British representatives had agreed, that these organizations be broken up to avoid any possible basis for Soviet protest.

On the other hand, intelligence reports had convinced us that substantial quantities of war munitions were being produced for the Russians in the Soviet Zone, and we had demanded that the Soviet-proposed investigation of disarmament in all four zones include the production of war munitions. This idea met a Soviet veto each time it was proposed. Moreover, Molotov, in charging the Western Allies with failure to deliver reparations, conveniently neglected to mention that this resulted from the Soviet refusal to place German resources in a common pool and, as a corollary, to account for all exports from the Soviet Zone.[8]

Byrnes replied, not without some feeling, that the treaty he proposed was not intended to replace previous decisions regarding Germany. On the contrary, it was intended to indicate that even after these decisions were carried out there remained a need to insure continued disarmament and demilitarization. He said the proposal proved the United States did not intend to turn its back on the problem of controlling Germany, as had been done after World War I. He added that he was quite prepared to see the life of the treaty extended to forty years.

He pointed out that reparations were only a part of the Potsdam

Protocol, which also established the principles of economic unity and the utilization of export proceeds to pay for essential imports. He reminded Molotov of our readiness to join in an investigation of all phases of disarmament in Germany which had met with Soviet veto and said he would telephone Berlin from the conference room to have this offer renewed.

The following day Molotov spoke again.[9] If his statement on the first day was designed to please French Communists, then indeed his statement of the second day was designed to give aid and comfort to the German Communists. He said:

"It would be incorrect to adopt a course of Germany's annihilation as a state—including the annihilation of its main industrial centers. . . . Such a course would result in undermining the economy of Europe. Our purpose is not to destroy Germany. . . . It is easy to understand that without the Ruhr Germany cannot exist as an independent and viable state. . . . If as a result of a plebiscite throughout Germany, the German people express their wish to transform Germany into a federal state, or if as a result of a plebiscite in various former German states, the desire will be manifested to break away from Germany, it goes without saying that there cannot be any objection on our part."

Here Molotov cleverly carried water on both shoulders, since the plebiscite would hold out promise to the Germans without alarming the Poles. The Germans in the Polish-administered territory claimed by Poland had been expelled and replaced by Poles so that the results of a plebiscite in this area were certain. Molotov expressed indignation at unilateral (British) control of the Ruhr, which he wanted placed under four-power control. Then he said:

"We should not put obstacles to the increase in the output of steel, coal, and manufactured products. . . . We stand in principle for the conclusion of a peace treaty with Germany."

Thus Molotov on that first day insisted on disarmament, demilitarization, and reparations in terms pleasing to French Communists, while charging the Western occupying powers with failure to carry out the measures decided on at Potsdam and condemning their soft policy. On the second day—and you may be sure his first day's statement was not highlighted in the Soviet Zone—he became the foremost and first public advocate of Germany's reconstruction under a government of German choice and with increased industrial output. He urged a steel production of 10,000,000 tons a year, although his representatives in Germany had insisted only a few months before on an annual steel production of 4,500,000 tons. Certainly that element in America which had been supporting the Russians and attacking the leniency of American policy must have found it difficult to reconcile its position with this all-out effort made by Molotov to win popularity in Germany.

Bevin spoke briefly in favor of economic unity and his willingness to place the Ruhr under Allied control when all German industry was so controlled and no sooner.[10]

Bidault said that the demand for additional coal for the German economy should not be met at the expense of export tonnage, and that the Saar should be excluded from the administration of the occupied zones.[11]

Byrnes suggested that the acceptance of a formula of the nature proposed by Bidault might make it possible for France to agree to central administrative agencies.[12] He urged again the appointment of a council of special deputies to meet immediately to prepare a peace settlement with Germany and to report progress to the next meeting of the Council of Foreign Ministers. While Bevin and Bidault appeared willing to accept this proposal, Molotov believed further discussion in the Council of Foreign Ministers to be necessary before the special deputies were appointed.

Byrnes was convinced that the Soviet representatives not only did not intend to reach an agreement but were deliberately delaying discussion in the belief that the resulting conditions in Germany would be favorable to their expansion program. He agreed with me that the continued government of Germany as four separate zones could lead only to complete economic collapse and political deterioration. He felt that the time had arrived to move forward in the consolidation of the zones to the fullest extent possible. Thus he made the decision which was to demonstrate clearly Soviet intent to include Germany, or at least its zone, in its sphere of influence. It was the first evidence that the Western Powers would stand firmly to prevent such an accomplishment and to stop further Communist expansion westward. In carefully phrased language Byrnes expressed the unwillingness of the United States to accept responsibility for the chaotic Germany which had resulted from the four separate zones, and invited each or all of the other occupying powers to combine their zones of occupation in economic unity with our zone.

Another vital decision had been taken. It was to affect not only our German policy but also our European policy. We said in effect that we had tried for many months to pursue a common policy while the Soviet Government had pursued deliberately a policy of its own, and that we would wait no longer in the effort to reach agreement but would strive alone or with such others as joined with us for the attainment of the objectives in Germany to which we had all agreed. I think this was clearly understood by all four delegations when this meeting of the Council of Foreign Ministers adjourned on July 12.

At Byrnes's direction, his invitation was repeated, in the Allied Control Council and accepted by the United Kingdom.[13] This made possible the fusion of the British and American zones which led logically and rapidly to a close co-operation of the two military governments in Germany and of the two governments in the formulation of policy.

The June-July meeting of the foreign ministers was also useful in making clear the fact that even though France had blocked the establishment of central administrative agencies for many months the basic differences in policy for the treatment of Germany were between the United States and the United Kingdom, on the one hand, and Russia on the other. It was obvious that both the United States and the United Kingdom desired a policy which France could accept. I have stated elsewhere that I believe it would have been preferable to establish the central agencies and try to resolve our differences within the framework envisaged at Potsdam. Others do not agree. I have heard Mr. Bohlen comment that the French saved us by their early veto actions. Some time later I heard Ambassador Bedell Smith say that at the time we were too naïve politically to cope with the Russians in such a framework. I realize that if we had formed the central administrative agencies our basic differences would have remained and the same struggle would have occurred within this framework.

Although we made no progress toward economic unification, the Allied Control Council appeared to be functioning with some effectiveness during the remainder of the year 1946.

We continued our work to determine what specific plants would be made available for reparations as in excess of the agreed level of industry and to evaluate these plants so that they could be placed before the Co-ordinating Committee for allocation between East and West. When we announced that we would make no further deliveries until all had agreed to place Germany's resources in a common pool, we stated our readiness to continue preparations. The Soviet representatives, who had not felt as yet the effect of this decision, were confident, I am sure, that it was a bluff and would not be applied when the preparations for the delivery of plants were completed.

We also were able to agree on additional measures,[14] largely of a negative nature, including increased taxes on tobacco, alcohol, beer, and matches; confiscation and destruction of Nazi literature, and liquidation of Nazi memorials; principles concerning the establishment of federations of trade unions in each zone; disciplinary measures against institutions guilty of military or Nazi propaganda; authorization of elections in Berlin; the employment of women on building and reconstruction work; the authorization of a population census; dissolution of the Wehrmacht; providing conciliation and arbitration machinery in labor conflicts; procedures for implementation of Nuremberg Tribunal sentences; limitation of characteristics of German ships; establishment of administrative courts; repeal of Nazi "successions" law; arrest and punishment of war criminals, Nazis, and militarists; policy to be followed by German politicians and press in public utterances; prohibition of manufacture, import, export, transport, and storage of war materials; regulations for gift parcel post service; and other miscellaneous and even less important measures.

General Robertson and I were to try many times to obtain agreement to central German administrations only to find that there was no change in the French position. In one of our last meetings in 1946 Robertson made an eloquent plea[15] for progress in this field, pointing out that the gap between us was widening and that it could be closed in no other way. Unless it were closed, he felt, we would inevitably drift so far apart that unification would become impossible.

On December 21 and 22, 1946, the French military governor, though unable to obtain quadripartite approval because of Soviet veto, established a customs barrier between the Saar area and the rest of Germany. He advised us of his intention only a few hours before the Control Council meeting of December 20, at which he announced that action would be taken on the following day. My instructions, reaffirmed only a few days before this meeting, were clear-cut. They required me to support the French request in quadripartite negotiations, but to oppose unilateral French action. This was the position I took in the Control Council. Shortly thereafter Acting Secretary of State Dean G. Acheson announced in a public statement that my views did not represent the views of the United States Government, which was prepared to recognize the French action. This came as a complete surprise to me and I asked to be relieved from my post, as I felt that somehow I had lost government confidence. I was advised quickly that I had followed my instructions but that the State Department had informed the French Government a few months previously in a personal letter from Secretary Byrnes to Foreign Minister Bidault that while our government would not approve such action neither would it oppose it. My instructions to the contrary had been sent to me after this statement. What had happened was that the statement had not received full circulation in the State Department and had failed to reach those who were issuing instructions relative to German affairs. I could understand how this had happened and accepted it in good faith. Nevertheless, this opposition on my part, taken in full compliance with my instructions, looked as if it had been taken on my own responsibility and did much to portray me as anti-French in that country's press.

Quantitatively, the record of accomplishment of the Control Council in 1946 was excellent, largely owing to measures enacted in the first six months. A study of these shows that the pattern of 1945 was repeated. There was no real progress toward a true government of Germany. The measures were not important and their implementation after enactment was not on a uniform basis, since this continued to be left to the discretion of the zone commanders. Only in the British and American zones was there a tightening of ties as a result of the development of common economic objectives. The remaining zones were drifting further apart. The wide divergence between Western democracy and its emphasis on the rights of the individual and on human freedoms, and Soviet collectivism, which suborns the freedom and rights of the individual to the needs of the state, was becoming more evident at each meeting.

Early in 1946 three of the municipal judges in Berlin disappeared. They were said to have refused to render judgments in accord with the expressed views of the German Communist leaders. One resided in the Soviet Sector and admittedly was arrested by Soviet representatives; the other two were residents of the western sectors and were arrested in their homes by unknown German police. Of course these police were agents of the Soviet Military Administration. When this was discussed in the Co-ordinating Committee[16] in February 1946 we could get neither admission nor denial of the arrests by the Soviet representative. Robertson, Koeltz, and I protested vigorously, but we could get no satisfaction and I stated:

"I regard the entry into the American Zone by any zonal authority for such purposes and without our concurrence as an unfriendly act. It is one that will be resisted to the full."

Finally the Soviet representative agreed to a quadripartite investigation, which was never provided with or able to obtain information or data of value. It was an early indication of Soviet effort to intimidate Germans opposed to Communism, which was to lead later to many additional arrests.

A marked increase in unfriendly attacks in Soviet and Soviet-controlled papers during 1946 also indicated the trend. In the August 20 meeting of the Control Council, Marshal Sokolovsky, following the usual Soviet tactics of initiating the attack, took offense at an article which he deemed critical of his government, published in a paper in the British Sector of Berlin.[17] His complaint was referred to the Co-ordinating Committee and gave me the opportunity I had been seeking to expose the growing attacks in the Soviet-controlled press against the United States. I agreed to an investigation of the incident provided the following would also be investigated:[18]

A speech by Mr. Grotewohl published in Neues Deutschland *which discusses the progressive development in the eastern zone (as compared with lack of progress in the western zones); the article in the same paper of 26 July referring to the illegal General Clay; an article in* Berliner Zeitung *of 14 August which criticizes denazification measures in west Germany; an article in* Neues Deutschland *of 13 August which places the American press in the hands of a clique of monopolists; an article in* Taegliche Rundschau *of 18 August which accuses the American and British press of slander and lies . . . ; an article in Berlin* Vorwaerts *of 22 June which accuses American Military Government personnel of having been friends of Hitler.*

The discussion did lead to diminished Soviet propaganda attacks and to an agreement to prohibit in each zone malicious criticism of the policies of the occupying powers. It was short-lived, and in the September 23 meeting of the Co-ordinating Committee I was forced to call attention to a vicious attack in the *Neues Deutschland* of September 18 which charged us with profiteering in German exports. I branded the article as "false and malicious" and expressed the view that: "It would be regrettable if we permitted German newspapers to criticize each of the Allied Powers. On the other hand," I assured General P. A. Kurochkin, who succeeded General Dratvin as deputy on the Co-ordinating Committee for a few months only, "the American delegation does not intend to be spattered with mud without throwing mud in return. If this continues, we must assume quadripartite rules are no longer applicable."

In the September 26 meeting Kurochkin replied: "I am willing and in favor of stopping these calumnies." I believe Kurochkin really meant his statement, and it perhaps is one of the reasons why his tenure of office was cut short. During this period in the life of the Control Council our protests would stop or at least retard propaganda attacks for some time. There had not yet developed the incessant outpouring which was to prevail later.

In November 1946 General Robertson brought before the Co-ordinating Committee the matter of the organized movement of skilled workers from Berlin to Russia.[19] The Soviet representative claimed that these workers were being given contracts but refused to give us information as to their right to turn down the contracts or as to the numbers involved. Our stand in protest did develop an intense reaction in Germany which stopped for the time being any further deportations from Berlin. Our concepts of individual freedoms were never more clearly in contrast. I am sure that General Kurochkin was sincere when he explained that these workers were being given contracts and that they would be moved by special train with their belongings to the Soviet Union just as Soviet workers were moved on government orders. The forced acceptance of the contract and the forced movement had no special significance to him. The workers were needed by the state.

Outwardly there was no change in the friendly relations between the key representatives of the four occupying powers. In November 1945 General McNarney, who succeeded General Eisenhower, was welcomed by Marshal Zhukov in generous terms. When my son, a major of armed forces, was married to the daughter of my old roommate, in Berlin in January 1946, General Sokolovsky remained after the reception to join a gathering of young officers who had attended the wedding and were rounding off the evening singing Army and Air Force songs. Later Zhukov invited the three commanders in chief, their deputies and political advisers to dinner at his residence in Babelsberg. When the dinner ended, cars were brought to the front entrance for the British and French parties, but not for us. As I was looking for an interpreter to remonstrate, I found that we were being led back into the house so the party could continue. And continue it did, with the entertainers, two young soldier dancers, an accomplished Russian Wac singer, and a pianist, joining us in the attempt to sing each other's songs. Field Marshal Montgomery gave a dinner in which soldiers (from, I believe, the Black Watch) did the Highland sword dance to the tune of bagpipes. Our own Washington's Birthday party was attended by a large number of Soviet representatives who appeared to have a good time, and equally large American contingents partook of Soviet hospitality in Cecilienhof Palace in Potsdam on Red Army Day on February 23 and Revolution Day on November 7. Always at their parties senior guests joined Sokolovsky in a private room for special refreshments and generous hospitality.

In November 1945 when Zhukov was recalled to become Minister of the Soviet Ground Forces, an apparent promotion, he was succeeded by Sokolovsky. Later it was to look as if Zhukov had been "kicked upstairs" to separate him from the Army, since the military leader described by the German generals as the ablest of the Russian generals was sent shortly to an insignificant command in Odessa. At the time this transfer made no impression upon us, as we were all genuinely fond of Sokolovsky. On February 12, 1946, Montgomery was replaced by Air Marshal Sir Sholto (later Lord) Douglas. Thus the triumvirate of the three great field commanders was dissolved; the glamour had been replaced by the daily grind.

Shortly after Mrs. Clay joined me in April 1946 we were invited by Marshal and Mrs. Sokolovsky to accompany them to the Leipzig Fair. The Semeonovs (Counselor Semeonov was political adviser to Sokolovsky), General Robertson, Sir William Strang, and Mr. Murphy completed the party. We motored to Leipzig, where we were entertained at lunch and dinner, visiting the fair in the afternoon and returning by motor in the evening. Although my friend, Marshal of the Tank Corps Pavel Rotmistrov, was at my right during lunch to challenge my capacity in vodka, Sokolovsky turned him loose on the diplomats at dinner, so that I could relax and watch Murphy meet the challenge, which he did with his usual effectiveness. We had a pleasant day with the Sokolovskys, and on our return found that they had placed in the car several presents from the fair, including some Meissen china and figurines. Occasionally the Sokolovskys dined with us, and in spite of language difficulties we enjoyed their visits. Frequently Sokolovsky and I would exchange calls to discuss matters before the Co-ordinating Committee. Often on these visits I took no one with me, using his interpreter, and he did likewise when visiting me. At Christmas 1946 he loaned us a famous naval chorus which sang Soviet melodies and danced intricate folk dances in our soldiers' and officers' clubs. Our directorate and committee representatives reported that they too were getting along well with their Soviet colleagues.

When we had taken over our sector in Berlin in July 1945, we found that substantial numbers of Soviet soldiers, probably absent without leave, had remained behind to hide in their German billets in daylight and to forage at night for food and drink. The shortage of electricity prevented street lighting and travel at night on foot was dangerous. Throughout the night rifle and carbine shots could be heard frequently. Soldiers and officers carried their arms off duty. The 2d Armored Division had been replaced by the 82d Airborne, ideally fitted for cleanup purposes. It did succeed quickly in restoring law and order. Unfortunately some of the Soviet soldiers resisted arrest and it was necessary to use force, which resulted in several deaths. Soldiers, guns, and liquor make a combination headed for trouble, particularly in night clubs and resorts of dubious character. The friendly relations between General Eisenhower and Marshal Zhukov overcame these difficulties. When more normal conditions prevailed, agreement was reached that guns would be carried only by soldiers on duty; night clubs and similar resorts were placed off limits for American troops as rapidly as their own clubs could be opened. Joint Military Police patrols were established, and all Allied soldiers were welcomed in our American clubs.

Unfortunately these relationships did not last. Despite the friendship between the senior representatives of the four countries, there was no lessening of the tensions beneath. They continued difficult to define but more surely present than in 1945.

In January 1946 Soviet representatives attempted to seize twelve locomotives which we were using in the railroad yards in our sector of Berlin. In January and February omnibuses operating in our sector were held up at gun point by Soviet soldiers. In February three Soviet soldiers broke into an American party and shot one American in the hip. In January a Soviet soldier attempted to arrest a German employed in an American home in our sector of Berlin. In February our Military Police had intercepted a raid by four MVD police in our sector and had arrested and returned them. In May the police record showed 42 violations of law and order by Soviet soldiers in our sector of Berlin. In our zone, Soviet crossings of the border in small groups to raid isolated German farmhouses became frequent. Americans who left the highway to Berlin were arrested and held for hours; two were held for several days. An American civilian was killed trying to escape from arrest; however, under our quadripartite rules he had every right to be in the Soviet Sector and there was no reason for the arrest which led to his death.

In an effort to improve the situation, early in 1946 I made a gentlemen's agreement with Sokolovsky that, if either of us arrested a citizen of the other's country, that citizen would be returned forthwith with statement of charges for trial in the zone in which he belonged. I was frequently able to reach oral agreements with the Soviet representatives. I am sure this was because they feared to make commitments in writing which could not later be denied if they drew the displeasure of Moscow. For many months this agreement proved effective and it did much to relieve the growing tension at the time it was made. Later the arrangement was thought by some to have reduced the number of Soviet deserters in that it required their arrest and return to Soviet authorities. This was not correct. The agreement required no arrests, only that arrestees be returned, and Soviet deserters who entered the United States Zone were neither arrested nor returned unless they engaged in criminal activities.

Another incident which reflected the hidden tensions occurred in April 1946 when Soviet troops attempted to remove railway track in our sector of Berlin on the grounds that it was an authorized reparations item. They rejected our protest and moved armed troops into the area to protect their workers, However, the armed troops found that our Constabulary tank patrols had arrived first and that the workers had quit. The staff report records:

Although the situation was tense for several days, it was finally resolved amicably by conference between the two Commanders. No track was removed.

In the summer of 1946 we learned that discharged prisoners of war from the west, returning to their homes in east Germany, were being screened and that officers and skilled specialists were being detained.

These are only a few of the many incidents of the year. They are cited to show that we never fully attained our effort to develop friendly relationships with Soviet personnel. They were made more striking because I knew that the British were having the same difficulties with Soviet troops, whereas British, French, and Americans were serving side by side and if any incidents developed between them they were so few and so trivial as never to reach my attention.

In October 1946 the efforts of British and American representatives to obtain an elected city government were realized. When we entered Berlin the city officials in office had been selected and appointed by the Soviet authorities. In the October 20 election the SED (Socialist Unity party, a combination of the Social Democrats and Communists in the Soviet Zone forced by Soviet pressure and denounced by the Social Democrats of the western zones), was routed. The Social Democrats had received 48.7 per cent; the Christian Democrats 22 per cent; the Liberal Democrats 9 per cent; and the Soviet-sponsored SED, although encouraged in east Berlin in every possible way by the Soviet Military Administration, had received only 19.8 per cent of the votes. This election, carried out under the city-wide supervision of quadripartite inspection teams, must have stunned the Soviet authorities and made them realize that their hope of gaining Germany by normal political methods was futile. Unquestionably it changed their tactics in Germany. The just right, exercised by the new City Council, to oust Soviet-appointed Communist officials was resisted by Soviet authorities and created a growing dissension in the Allied Government of Berlin (Kommandatura).

Thus when the Council of Foreign Ministers held its next meeting in New York in November and December 1946, such change as had occurred in the relationships of the occupying powers was for the worse. Murphy and I were in Washington to attend the Anglo-American conference on bizonal fusion when the Council convened. We proceeded to New York, where we remained for approximately two weeks to be available to Secretary Byrnes.

The setting for this meeting of the Council of Foreign Ministers was one of the upper floors of the Waldorf Towers. Looking from the windows of the conference room, the tall buildings and brilliant lights made an impressive picture of the strength and wealth of America. It seemed to me a fitting location. During this meeting of the Council, Senators Connally and Vandenberg were performing double duty, as they were also participating in the work of the United Nations General Assembly. Murphy and I called on both, and as usual received fresh courage from their friendly and sympathetic support.

My stay in New York gave me an opportunity to lunch with former President Hoover, who had done so much to help us obtain additional food for Germany and to support and encourage us in our efforts to revive German economy. I had the pleasure of having tea with Secretary and Mrs. Stimson in their apartment in New York. I had called to obtain his advice and counsel, and it was not until I left that I realized that by a combination of adroit questioning and sympathetic interest he had led me into doing almost all of the talking, pouring out my perplexing problems and difficulties. I left him, feeling certain of his sympathetic understanding and that he recognized that we had tried hard indeed to meet the wise objectives he had expressed to us in Germany in the summer of 1945.

During our visit to New York, Secretary Byrnes took Maurice Couve de Murville, head of the French delegation in Bidault's absence, Turner Catledge of the New York *Times,* Robert Murphy, and me to a football game between the New York Giants and the Philadelphia Eagles. I was pleased at the warmth with which the friendly crowd greeted Byrnes. My pleasure at the game was dimmed by the knowledge that we were to drive back to the hotel the same way we had come—through New York traffic at high speed following a New York motorcycle police escort. As we swung through traffic I began to realize how quiet the German streets seemed, and I could not help but admire the complete nonchalance with which Byrnes ignored what seemed to me almost certain crashes.

While the conference again refused to consider in detail the German problem, or perhaps I should say Molotov refused to permit the conference to consider the German problem, it did agree to convene the next session of the Council of Foreign Ministers to consider German and Austrian questions at Moscow on March 10, 1947. It also agreed[20] to an agenda which included consideration of a comprehensive report to be prepared by the Allied Control Council on its work on demilitarization, denazification, democratization, economic problems, reparations, the establishment of central administrations, and other problems connected with the political, economic, and social situation under quadripartite government; liquidation of Prussia; consideration of form and scope of provisional political organization; and preparation of a peace treaty. It further agreed to appoint special deputies to hear the views of neighboring and other Allied states which had participated with their armed forces in the common struggle, to consider questions of boundaries, of the Ruhr and the Rhineland, the United States-proposed disarmament and demilitarization treaty, and the report of the coal experts.

The Allied Control Council was called upon to submit its report not later than February 25, 1947. The deputies were to convene in London on January 14, 1947, and to submit their report by February 25.

The conference adjourned on December 31. This conference was the last appearance of Secretary Byrnes at the Council of Foreign Ministers, although neither Murphy nor I had any inkling of this when we departed from New York. He had given from his high intelligence and his broad experience of government his utmost effort to allay Soviet suspicions and to create a world of peace by agreement. When he had found this impossible he had made clear our firm intent to yield no further in our views in the hope of compromise.

CHAPTER 8

The Control Council
Falters

OUR main effort now was devoted to preparing for
Moscow. Murphy was designated by Byrnes to be
special deputy for the German problem. While we were struggling
to prepare an agreed report from the Control Council for the
foreign ministers,[1] he and his colleagues were engaged in a like effort
in London,[2] besides hearing the views of the Allied states, including
Australia, Belgium, Brazil, Byelorussia, Canada, Czechoslovakia,
Denmark, Greece, Luxembourg, the Netherlands, New Zealand,
Norway, Poland, the Ukraine, the Union of South Africa, and
Yugoslavia.[3] The views of these nations emphasized once again the
conflict which had to be resolved before there could be a German
peace treaty. Eight favored moderate and constructive policies;
the five "Slav" countries, closing their eyes to Molotov's statement
designed for German propaganda in the June-July conference, supported heavy reparations, stringent political and economic restraints,
and prolonged occupation. The "Western" states favored decentralized federal government; the "Slav" states a centralized government which would be easier to control. Only two favored the
confederation type of government. No state asked for political separation of the Ruhr; all favored some degree of control. Eleven
favored reparations from production. Exclusive of the Soviet and
Polish accessions and of the Saar, claims were made for German
territory aggregating 1200 square miles with a population of
177,000.

All nations agreed on the necessity for demilitarization and military control. Some were in favor of nationalization of German industry. Some favored, and others were opposed to, excluding Germany from high-seas navigation. Several governments opposed strict controls because if exercised over an extended period they might incite German resistance, which would injure rather than foster material and spiritual reconstruction. Some wanted special guarantees for their property rights in Germany; others wanted guarantees against discriminatory measures. The one thing that was certain was that there was no concert of opinion among the sixteen nations.

The special deputies devoted many hours to the discussion of procedural questions relating to preparation of a peace treaty. They could agree on neither the nations to participate in the preparation of the treaty, nor those which, while not participating, would be consulted in its preparation; nor on other lesser procedural questions. Their field of disagreement was so broad that they were unable to agree to a report on their disagreement, and confined their joint report to summarizing the views of the Allied Nations as presented to them.[4]

Concurrently the Allied Control Council was devoting the first two months of 1947 to the preparation of its report to the Council of Foreign Ministers. Its purpose was to bring out the basic differences which had prevented quadripartite government from functioning, and thus narrow the range of issues to be discussed at Moscow.

The many questions to be considered were allocated to the appropriate directorates in December 1946, and the Co-ordinating Committee spent hours of discussion in January and February in the effort to develop agreed recommendations. These efforts were futile. The ability of the Control Council to reach such decisions had deteriorated so much that it was almost impossible to agree in the face of our instructions to the submission of a report summarizing largely our disagreements.[5]

While this report was in preparation, little else was accomplished in the Co-ordinating Committee. An interesting debate did occur on February 1947 in connection with the resignation of the Oberbuergermeister of Berlin, Dr. Otto Ostrowski, a member of the Social Democratic party elected by its majority in the city council.

He was found by his party to be too amenable to Soviet suggestion and was required to resign. Ernst Reuter, who was elected to take his place, had been secretary general of the Communist party in 1921 and before that head of the Volga Republic. He had discovered the true aim of the Communist party and had returned to the Social Democratic party in 1922 as a bitter opponent of Communism. Thus he was regarded as a mortal enemy by Soviet representatives who refused to accept him in office. Reuter, who had lived in Turkey during the Nazi regime, was an experienced administrator and an honest and capable official. While every effort was made by the three Western Powers to secure Soviet acceptance,[6] we had finally to face the fact that Soviet veto could prevent his exercise of office. In the discussion General Robertson said:

"My views are very simple. If we agree that they [the Germans] may choose by elections their representatives to perform such duties, then we should not interfere with those elections."

General Kurochkin replied that the election of Reuter "should serve as a warning . . . of the undesirability of hasty abatement of control."

I entered the debate to remark: "This is a basic principle of democracy as it stands in America. . . . We will debate at any time the question of giving election privileges to the Germans . . . or taking away such privileges which they abuse. If we give them the right to select their candidates, we ought to accept their choice unless removal by cause is agreed unanimously."

Reuter was not to take office until the Soviet actions had resulted in a divided city. Since we could not approve Reuter, we had to accept the deputy, Frau Louise Schroeder, as acting. We were unwilling to authorize another election, as we held Reuter to be duly elected and qualified to serve. Of course we were satisfied with Frau Schroeder, a woman of courage and ability, who had opposed the Nazi regime and was to stand firm against Communist efforts to gain control of the Berlin government. It was difficult to realize the strength within this quiet, motherly-appearing woman.

Perhaps the most important act of the Control Council in this period was the liquidation of the state of Prussia.[7] This was necessary to legalize the dissolution of the former state to form new states within the several zones.

The report which the Control Council submitted in nine voluminous sections recorded few agreed conclusions. It did record the differences in viewpoint both as to what had occurred and what remained to be done. It did lay down in black on white clearly and succinctly the wide divergencies which had taken place in the attempt to administer Germany as a unit by the unanimous consent of the representatives of the four occupying powers.

As even the synopsis of principal differences which accompanied the report is a lengthy document it seems desirable to record enough of these to emphasize the opposed viewpoints. On demilitarization, the Western Powers cited the large numbers of prisoners of war held in Soviet Russia, and the unwillingness of the Soviet Military Administration to permit free inspection of plants by quadripartite teams. The Soviet representatives charged the Western Powers with failure to destroy war plants and to deliver reparations. On denazification, they made a general charge of failure to denazify, while the Western Powers charged that statistics proved the opposite, and particularly that, in the Soviet Zone, joining the SED erased the "Nazism" of the joiner. The Soviet representatives charged the Western Powers with failure to agree on a decartelization program, and the Western Powers charged them with building up a large concentration of economic power through their seizure and incorporation under Soviet ownership of plants and enterprises in their zone. Although the document may have represented a monumental accomplishment in report making, it could add little to comfort the foreign ministers or to help them in solving the pressing problems which would be presented in Moscow. I think that as the report was finally signed on February 25, even Marshal Sokolovsky felt discouraged at the result.

In its preparation we had tried hard to obtain information on the extent of the capital equipment removed from east Germany, the value of the productive output exported to Russia, and the number of German prisoners of war held in Russia. We were unable to get this pertinent data from the Soviet representatives, who promised us that it would be made available at the conference by their government. The promise was not kept.

Realizing the import of the Moscow meeting to the German problem, meticulous attention was given to advance preparation. In addition to the reports of the Allied Control Council and the special deputies, Military Government had prepared 31 separate papers on subjects which ranged from provisional government and financial reform to aviation and occupation costs, which it submitted to the War and State Departments. The State Department, utilizing such of the contents of these reports as it accepted, likewise prepared a comprehensive set of papers which were returned to us in time for our comment. Also Military Government was asked to send, in addition to Mr. Murphy, experts in economics under General Draper, and in governmental affairs under General Henry Parkman and Dr. Edward H. Litchfield. I was to take over the command of the theater from General McNarney on March 15, 1947, and asked to be excused from attending the conference unless my attendance seemed necessary. I had always found it difficult to participate in these meetings, which usually lasted several weeks, not only because attendance involved long separation from my administrative duties but also because I was responsible to the War Department and hesitated to make recommendations on major issues which had not received its approval.

The United States delegation arrived in Berlin on March 8, prepared to spend two days in discussion with us. General Marshall had replaced Secretary Byrnes. The Republican party had gained control of Congress. Marshall had been unable to persuade Senators Connally and Vandenberg to leave their pressing congressional duties. He had brought with him a new member of the American delegation, John Foster Dulles. The familiar faces of Ben Cohen, "Chip" Bohlen, and Freeman Matthews were present to insure continuity.

General McNarney joined me in welcoming General Marshall and his party at the airport, and in accompanying them to the residence on the Wannsee assigned for their stay. We proceeded immediately to discuss the pending issues with Marshall and his advisers, who questioned our experts at length on conditions and relations in Germany.

While I had known General Marshall for some years, I had had very little direct personal association with him. During the war I had served directly under General Somervell and Under Secretary Patterson. On several occasions I had attended conferences called by Marshall. When I left the United States to become deputy military governor I had called to pay my respects and had been impressed with his sympathetic understanding of the difficulties I would face. I held for him the great respect and loyal affection which he had won from the whole Army. I had worked more intimately with Secretary Byrnes and not only respected his great ability but also had come to love him and Mrs. Byrnes as if I were a part of their family. I could not have other than deep regret that he had felt it necessary to resign his post while, at the same time, I recognized that he had been replaced by another great American of stature and character.

The Moscow conference convened on March 10, 1947. I received a cable from Moscow asking me to report at once. I did not know who had dispatched this message. I replied, pointing out my immediate responsibilities in Germany, and asked once more to be excused unless the Secretary of State personally felt my attendance desirable. I received a further message that my attendance was desired by the Secretary of State, so I proceeded to Moscow by air on the same day. Bedell Smith met me at the airport in the late afternoon and took me directly to the embassy, where I reported my arrival to Secretary Marshall's aide, General Marshall Carter. I then looked for Cohen to see what task, if any, he had in mind.

Space in Moscow was at a premium and space combined with security of papers and communications was unobtainable. Therefore Ambassador Smith had installed the rather large American delegation in improvised offices in the embassy residence, Spasso House. He had done his best even though the results were a bit on the inadequate side. The senior members of the delegation were installed in the billiard room. Here I found Cohen and Dulles, with desks in a small alcove, while in the room proper I found Murphy, General Mark Clark, Matthews, and my own desk. Our secretaries were in a narrow corridor leading to the billiard room. Marshall had his office and staff conference room in an upstairs living room near which Carter and Bohlen had office space. The experts, files, secretaries, clerks, and stenographers were all installed in the ballroom. The windows in this room were kept closed with drawn shades as the security officer (with what I thought rather vivid imagination and unquestioned zeal) was apprehensive that some acute hearing devices and long-distance cameras might otherwise record or photograph conversations and papers. Needless to say, rumors about security, or rather Soviet efforts to break security, flew thick and fast, including one which I could never verify that the

British had found six concealed plastic dictaphones in the walls of their office. In any event, we were instructed to discuss no matters of substance in our hotel rooms, although frequently some American fed up with security restrictions would shout rather unprintable descriptions of our hosts in the hope that they would be permanently inscribed in the record.

We were billeted in the Moskva, newest and proudest of Soviet hotels. Murphy and I followed our usual custom of sharing a suite with a common living room and bath. While the furnishings were somewhat suggestive of our hotels in the late nineties, with less modern plumbing, it was clean and comfortable. The lobby, dining room, and public rooms were massive and on the whole impressive. Food was fair, though service was very slow with the exception of room service, which was excellent.

Normally the senior members of the delegation breakfasted and lunched at Spasso House. While in effect this made it seem as if the Bedell Smiths were running a hotel, their hospitality never diminished and Mrs. Smith made each of us feel welcome. I had made a friend of their principal Chinese cook, who kept a pot of coffee always ready for my visits to the kitchen.

All of us had difficulty in adjusting to Moscow habits of work through the night and sleep in the morning. The Council of Foreign Ministers met usually at four o'clock in the afternoon in sessions which lasted from three to four hours. It amused Murphy and me to test vaunted Soviet security in entering the conference building for these meetings. I bet him that I could enter without showing my official pass. I was in uniform and each day as the guard stretched out his hand for my pass, I would draw myself to rigid attention, salute him, and move on. Always his hand would snap to the salute as I walked on, pass still in pocket. It never failed and it convinced me that Soviet soldiers are just as human as those of other countries. It might not have seemed so humorous had they stopped me. I had formed the habit of carrying a small automatic pistol in my brief case, though I am not sure why as I seldom carried the case. However, I did use it in Moscow and never realized until long after my return to Germany that this pistol in a small compartment in my brief case had accompanied me to all the meetings I attended. I am sure that Secretary Marshall would have been most indignant to know that he had an armed bodyguard even if the bodyguard did not know he was armed. When the afternoon session was over our delegation would have a hurried dinner before it met to discuss the agenda and papers for the next session. If this discussion required changes in papers—and it did as a rule—the experts would work far into the night so that the documents would be ready for the morning conference with Secretary Marshall.

Cohen would labor with us to reconcile different views before this conference, but frequently the available time would not suffice. Thus we would place the several views before Marshall. He had little time to familiarize himself with past meetings of the Council and the many German and Austrian issues. He was calm and patient as he sought to obtain and resolve our divergent stands, in the limited time in which he was not either in session with the Council or else in separate conference with Bevin or Bidault, even though our differences in opinion sometimes led to sharp exchanges. In one such exchange Dulles insisted that I make no commitments in a four-power working party to which I had been designated without approval in advance by the delegation. I felt that in my two years of negotiation with the Russians I had learned to know when I should obtain approval and that no working party could hope to negotiate an agreed report unless its members had some discretionary authority. After this exchange we apologized to each other, as both of us realized we were making mountains out of molehills. I had learned to admire and respect Dulles for his sincerity and ability. He was a formidable adversary in argument. While I knew that I could not be responsible for the execution of the policy then advocated by him, I did not question its sincerity or his right to its advocacy. Later I think our viewpoints came closer together and I was particularly appreciative of the support he was to give to our continued stay in Berlin under the blockade.

In fact the differences in opinion between Dulles and me were no more sharply drawn or frequent than the differences which developed among the members of the delegation. In retrospect it has become clear that these differences were in detail and not in principle. Many were resolved in our discussions at Moscow, and the remainder were to disappear before the London conference later that year. As an example, a proposal which we were to present as a definition of democratic government resulted in the preparation of several papers. Certainly all of us had the same concept of democratic government. Nevertheless, we argued for some hours before we reconciled our views. It seemed to me then and now that these debates served to bring out the merits and demerits of each issue and that they could have been developed in no other way.

Perhaps the major question Secretary Marshall had to resolve at Moscow was our position on the utilization of productive output for reparations. This had not been specifically prohibited in the Potsdam Protocol, although it seemed clear to us that the requirement that proceeds from exports should be used in the first place to pay for imports did exclude any such use of productive output as long as there was an adverse trade balance. I favored developing the issue in the effort to obtain a clear-cut definition of Soviet intent. Dulles believed that we should not raise the question and that if others raised it we should discuss it only to oppose its discussion. There was much merit in his view. Marshall decided in favor of a compromise which proposed an increase in the level of industry, accepted as necessary by all four powers; the plants withdrawn from reparations to make this increase possible would be compensated for by productive output of corresponding value. Although this formula offered considerable flexibility, it was either overlooked by the Soviet delegation or else, more probably, the Soviet delegation did not desire that any real agreements be reached in this conference.

The conference room was filled with familiar faces. Bevin was accompanied by Strang' and Robertson, for German discussions; Molotov by Vishinsky and Sokolovsky; and Bidault by Couve de Murville and Hervé Alphand.

All delegations introduced papers covering the many issues raised in the Control Council report, and each paper presented by representatives of the Western Powers drew new charges from Molotov. In this conference, which had as its great purpose the establishment of a common policy for Germany, he charged the British with failure to denazify Germany, citing as examples some obscure names of persons alleged to be playing "a significant role."[8] Yet such was the defensive attitude of the Western Powers that cables were dispatched to Berlin for immediate investigation so that the charges could be answered and refuted.

In another exchange Molotov accused the United States of seizing for its exclusive use German patents and trade processes.[9] Charles Kindleberger of the State Department had brought with him, in case the occasion should arise, a letter from the Soviet commercial representative in Washington to the Secretary of Commerce thanking him for the German patent data made available to the Soviet Government and asking when additional data would be published. I am sure that Marshall enjoyed reading this letter, which caught Molotov by surprise and even produced smiles on the customary poker faces of his staff.

To save time, a co-ordinating committee was designated to report the agreements and disagreements contained in the several papers presented to the Council on the form and scope of the provisional political organization of Germany. I represented the United States on this committee, which included Vishinsky, Alphand, and Robertson. We were in session from late afternoon to early morning and recessed then for a few hours to permit the report to be typed for presentation to the afternoon session of the Council.

The report[10] proved of little help, as its recital of disagreement was by now a familiar story. Again it was clear that the French, British, and Americans favored a federal government under a democratic constitution as democracy is understood in the West, whereas the Russians favored a strong central government under a provisional constitution prepared in an assembly composed of representatives of "anti-fascist" organizations. Obviously this would guarantee representation from the Communist party and its many front organizations and would provide a governmental structure lending itself to single-party domination. Although the meetings of the co-ordinating committee were attended only by the principals and a few staff assistants, habit was too strong for Vishinsky to resist making a constant attack on the Western Powers. In one of these attacks he made a sarcastic reference to the loyalty of minority groups in the United States and stated that no such problem existed in the Soviet Union, where the loyalties of all citizens were unquestioned. I had to remind him that we had found many thousand Soviet-claimed citizens fighting with the German Army and even then were being pressed to return to Russia thousands more who denied Soviet citizenship.

The Council of Foreign Ministers was likewise unsuccessful in its effort to reconcile the differences recorded in the report of the special deputies on the procedures to be followed in the preparation of the peace treaty.

While the foreign ministers met in session after session, they were able to reach agreement on only a few matters hardly worth listing, since they were all included in the Potsdam understanding and were discussed only as a result of charges and countercharges as to the effectiveness of their accomplishment. I did not stay for the duration of this meeting, as Secretary Marshall had approved my request to return to my duties in Germany on March 31.

While I was going back to Germany because I believed that I should not stay away from my administrative responsibilities too long, I must admit that I was glad to leave Moscow. There had been occasional diversions from the grind of conference. Mr. and Mrs. Molotov had entertained the delegation at a formal dinner, followed by a reception. Each of the foreign ministers had proposed toasts which expressed their hopes for international understanding and friendship. Secretary Marshall, to indicate his desire for co-operation, wore the decoration of the Order of Suvorov, awarded to him by the Soviet Government for his war contribution, on his dinner coat. Molotov also entertained the three other foreign ministers, the ambassadors, and the commanders in chief in Germany at a ballet performance of *Romeo and Juliet,* exquisitely staged and danced by the incomparable Russian Ballet. Nevertheless, I had found Moscow presenting a dreary appearance, with the winter snow which was piled everywhere covered with thick black soot from soft-coal fires. While there were life and movement in the streets, there was no lightness evident anywhere, and happy smiling faces were rarely seen and then only among the young children. I could not estimate how much of this resulted from the long war years with their exacting sacrifice and how much of it was the reflection of the police state.

When I left Moscow the earlier sessions had convinced all of us that there would be no real progress. The agreements[11] which were reached were sent to us subsequently in Berlin. They called for the acceleration of destruction of German military matériel and installations; the liquidation of plants suitable only for production of munitions; the determination of progress in demilitarization activities by quadripartite inspections; the acceleraton of denazification and trials of war criminals; and the encouraging of German authorities to adopt uniform legislation for completion of denazification; the completion of land reform; the establishment of a free exchange of information between all zones; affirmation of the right of accredited representatives of interested nations to visit displaced persons centers and the prohibition of propaganda campaigns directed from these centers; the care and return of deceased United Nations nationals; the acceleration of repatriation of displaced persons; a restudy of the question of transfers of population into Germany; the publication of reparations lists; and the repatriation of German prisoners of war by December 31, 1948. The Control Council was instructed to study the size of the armed forces of the occupation forces in Germany. Since the zone commanders claimed to have met the requirements in most of these matters, quadripartite inspections throughout Germany were essential to permit comparison in accomplishment but Soviet acquiescence to such inspections was never obtained except under restrictions which destroyed their value.

As General Marshall said in his radio talk to the nation on April 28, 1947:

"Agreement was made impossible at Moscow because, in our view, the Soviet Government insisted upon proposals which would have established in Germany a centralized government adapted to the seizure of absolute control."

He had talked to Generalissimo Stalin and still had hope, as the latter had said: "These were only the first skirmishes and brushes of reconnaissance forces on this question." Nevertheless, Secretary Marshall told the American people: "The patient is sinking while the doctors deliberate."

The Moscow conference had significant if not immediately tangible results. The foreign ministers of all four powers had accepted the need for a higher level of industry in Germany. However, the principal result was to convince the three foreign ministers representing the Western Powers of the intransigence of the Soviet position. This led them to work more closely together in the future.

I do not believe that our delegation had any illusions as to the outcome of the conference. Our difficulties in preparing the report of the Allied Control Council had demonstrated Soviet unwillingness to seek a settlement. Also, Soviet expansion in Europe was still gaining ground and Soviet representatives were confident that

Germany would be included. While we had not yet embarked on a positive program of assistance to the free countries of Europe, I believe that it was at Moscow that Secretary Marshall recognized the necessity of stopping the Communist advance in Europe before the German problem could be settled.

After the Moscow conference the meetings of the Allied Control Council continued. They seemed to have lost substance and I, for one, felt that we were merely going through meaningless motions. Although we had received definite instructions from the Council of Foreign Ministers, we could not agree as to how we would carry them out. In our meeting of May 31 we discussed the report which we were instructed to prepare on the size of the occupation forces. The lack of progress is clear from the debate which ensued: [12]

Marshal Sokolovsky: "As to the figure of 200,000 men for the Soviet Zone, it is simply substantiated. In the center of the Soviet Zone of Occupation we have the capital of Germany, the city of Berlin, a major political as well as military strategic point. The city of Berlin represents a very essential junction of railways, waterways, and highway transport and in order to have necessary—for the purpose of security as well as for the purpose of fulfilling the task of occupation—the Soviet authorities require additional facilities in order to implement the tasks of occupation. The additional 100,000 men are required to be left with the Soviet Zone in order to safeguard against any eventualities which might occur in such an important center as Berlin. There are no other capitals of Germany in any other zone. We have one capital in Germany. It is located in the Soviet Zone. And for these reasons I see no necessity for an additional amount of troops for these zones."

General Clay: "Mr. Chairman, I thought that when we came into Berlin we took a quadripartite responsibility for Berlin. If there is any question as to the American unwillingness to share that responsibility I am prepared to increase our garrison in Germany immediately. I don't think that we have as yet quadripartitely agreed that Berlin is necessarily the future capital of Germany, but I do want to emphasize that in accepting the responsibility for its quadripartite government we also accepted the responsibility for its security. If it should be considered that

100,000 troops are necessary for security in Berlin I would certainly be prepared to give serious consideration to contributing our portion of the share, so that this burden of occupation can be on an equitable basis among all of us."

Marshal Douglas: "My conception of the solution is the same as General Clay's, that the security of Berlin is a quadripartite responsibility and we are ready to contribute."

Marshal Sokolovsky: "The assurances made by General Clay to the effect that he is in a position to send any additional amount of troops to Berlin, a view which was also supported by the French member, in my opinion are unfounded and for the following reasons: We all know that there is no place to live in Berlin and the Soviet commander is forced not to locate his troops within the city on account of the lack of accommodation. The scanty survived living space has already been recognized by various agencies of the occupation authorities and to find a certain additional amount of living space is practically impossible."

Marshal Sokolovsky was charged with having made his figures equal the French, British, and American combined total, which he denied. I then said:

"I am not very good at arithmetic, Mr. Chairman, but regardless of the principle that I use . . . the figures in this column come out the same. I don't think it is logical that all the zones must have the same strength. I am not even arguing against the necessity for the Soviet forces to aggregate 200,000. However, the principle that whatever may be determined to be necessities of the British, French, and American zones, the necessary strength in the Soviet Zone is 100,000 in addition thereto to protect Berlin, does not appear logical to me."

Needless to say, we could reach no agreement.

We were able to agree on a few more negative measures and some rather insignificant constructive measures,[13] such as repeal of Nazi law providing debt relief caused by total war; repeal of Nazi legislature on hereditary farms; termination of German insurance operations abroad; law for disposition of property belonging to Nazi organizations; exchange of parcels between Berlin and the zones of occupation; law to combat venereal disease; law for liquidation of

Krupp steelworks; repeal of certain provisions in German criminal law; and a law providing for interzonal exchange of printed matter and films. These results did not prevent me from reporting on August 1947: "No substantial progress was obtained toward the settlement of major problems before the Allied Control Council."

We also continued our work to list the plants in excess of the agreed level of industry to be made available for reparations and to evaluate these plants. Meanwhile, on August 29, 1947, we fixed a new level of industry for the bizonal area,[14] which required General Robertson and me to advise our colleagues that the plants to be made available for reparations purposes from the British and American zones would be reduced in number. We accepted the allocation of plants between East and West from a partially completed list so that the Inter-Allied Reparations Agency[15] could proceed with the suballocation made to the West. Deliveries remained suspended. Soviet representatives realized at last that there would be no further deliveries of plants from the United States Zone until economic unity and common utilization of resources were achieved, and that plants allocated to the East in the British Zone were not being dismantled.

We tried to obtain agreement in the Control Council to currency reform.[16] The Soviet representatives insisted on two sets of plates, so that printing could be done from one set in Leipzig in the Soviet Zone and from the other in the United States Sector of Berlin. Marshal Sokolovsky said:

"Printing of currency should be done in Berlin and in Leipzig. I do not see the necessity . . . that . . . printing will be done under quadripartite control."

In the hope of obtaining agreement, I offered to segregate the printing plant in the United States Sector and make it a quadripartite enclave. We had suffered badly when we made available to the Soviet Government a set of plates to print Allied military marks, and we had never been able to find out the total value of Soviet notes, large amounts of which we had redeemed in dollars. Our government did not intend to repeat this mistake, and my instructions were specific.

In August Air Marshal Douglas and I furnished the Control Council with the revised "bizonal level of industry." Marshal Sokolovsky charged us:[17]

"The very appearance of this document is witness to the fact that U. S. and British military administrations have taken the road of a complete breaking away from the decisions of the Potsdam Conference. . . . The agreement can only lead to a situation in which to the detriment of the German people's interest . . . wealth will be wrested from her and will be used for . . . foreign monopolies."

I said only: "For two and a half years the American delegation has tried desperately to get economic unity. The record speaks for itself. We do not propose to let continued and indecisive discussions draw the U. S. Zone into a state of economic chaos which would retard recovery of Europe as a whole. Our invitation to our colleagues to join still stands."

It had become obvious that the Allied Control Council had failed to function as the governing body for occupied Germany and that it was no longer an effective instrument unless the Council of Foreign Ministers could find some unexpected way out of the impasse. Even this seemed less likely in view of the deteriorating relationship in Germany, where meetings of the Control Council were used with increasing frequency by Soviet representatives to launch vicious and unfounded attacks on the Western representatives for propaganda purposes. An indication of the volume and nature of Soviet propaganda is given by a few samples of headlines taken from the Soviet and Soviet-controlled press in Germany:

Neues Deutschland, April 11—American capital is exploiting Germany.

Taegliche Rundschau, April 13—True meaning of American democracy illustrated by its treatment of negroes.

Taegliche Rundschau, April 17—China is now an American colony.

Berliner Zeitung, April 24—Munich-New York, Cardinal Faulhaber-Cardinal Spellman axis.

Vorwaerts, May—Pictures showing peaceful labor groups in Russia—Violent strike scenes in United States.

Berlin Am Mittag, May 10—Clay democracy imperialistic.

Taegliche Rundschau, June 20—Denounced Acheson's accusations against Russia.

Berliner Zeitung, July 4—Dulles and Schacht in accord.

Vorwaerts, July 8—Attacks Harriman—enveloped in dollar millions—son of smart railway king—No. 1 polo player—What is he up to now?

Taegliche Rundschau, August 8—American capitalism calling itself democracy in South America.

Day in and day out, in the press and on the radio, we heard the continuing chant: Imperialists—Monopolists—Exploiters. Protests were useless. During this entire period I had kept our information service on a constructive note, pointing out the advantages of Western democracy without attacking Communism in principle, or indeed in action, as it was even then portraying its ugly reality in neighboring countries. On October 25 I authorized Colonel Gordon E. Textor (director of Information Control Division, OMGUS) to attack Communism in every form wherever it existed and to cite each exposed example of its day-to-day work. We still would not attack governments or individuals; we would not sling mud, but we would no longer refrain from exposing Communist tactics and purposes.

In other fields, relations also deteriorated in 1947. We began to hear of the Von Paulus "National Committee for Free Germany." In August we found theodolites (for rocket recording) being manufactured for Soviet Military Administration by the Ascania Works in our sector of Berlin, in violation of the agreement prohibiting such production. A Soviet corporation was formed to mine uranium ores, and stories of forced labor in this work began to reach us. Other Soviet corporations were absorbing German industry.

In October and November we found that newspapers and magazines from the United States Zone were being confiscated in the Soviet Zone. In March, June, and August kidnapings of Germans in the United States Sector by German police from the Soviet Sector were reported. Five of these police were captured in the act and sentenced to five years by our courts.

The kidnaping situation became even more serious as Germans in the western sectors seemed unable to refuse to answer a summons or to accompany police to the Soviet Sector, so strong was their instinct to obey authority. We had to persuade the press to publish advice to the Germans in the western sectors to refuse to accompany strange callers or to answer in person summons from the Soviet Sector, and to cry for help if needed. This simple advice was followed and effectively reduced, if it did not break up, the kidnapings. In 1947 the Soviet Administration gave up its pretense that the CDU and LDP (Liberal Democratic party) were independent political parties in the Soviet Zone, and virtually forced the removal of Jakob Kaiser, Ernst Lemmer (chairman and deputy chairman, respectively, of the CDU in the Soviet Zone), and other leaders they could not control; thus following normal Communist pattern in the approach to a one-party state. The Soviet representatives organized a Soviet-owned bank in Berlin to acquire real estate and other properties.

Throughout 1947 our friendly relationships and social meetings gradually lessened. While the change was not immediately noticeable, it soon became apparent that fewer Russians were attending Allied social functions, and informal meetings between senior representatives came to a standstill. In May General Koenig invited the three military governors, their deputies, and political advisers to visit him in Baden-Baden and to accompany him on a visit to Alsace, including Strasbourg. It was a delightful trip with noted Alsatian hospitality at its best. However, neither the Soviet military governor nor his deputy, nor his political adviser accepted, and the Soviet representative was a lesser figure. This is a common Soviet way of indicating displeasure. A press attack on General Koenig limited French attendance at the Soviet party on Revolution Day in October to a single minor official. At the end of the year Soviet representatives refused to participate in the quadripartite Christmas party which had been held the previous two years.

In the early months of 1947 the Soviet press started rumors of Soviet military and air strength in Germany, and their fighter planes were flown over Berlin. So on May 30 I had a fighter group fly over Berlin in a formation making the letters "U.S." It diverted somewhat the trend in the war of nerves. On July 2, I ordered several of our B-29s over Berlin. This drew a protest from Marshal Sokolovsky, to which I replied that in view of the concern that Soviet occupation forces be large enough for the safety of Berlin, I believed it necessary to determine the effectiveness with which we could participate in its security arrangements.

During the period of worsening relationships which followed the Moscow conference the Communist pattern had become clear and the effort to dominate Europe was approaching its peak. In Paris and New York in 1946 their representatives had refused to consider the German problem. In Moscow they could refuse to discuss Germany no longer, but it was clear that they did not seek a solution of the problem. They believed time to be on their side. They had been startled when President Truman asked Congress to extend aid to Greece and Turkey in March. The anti-Communists in Poland were forced from government with only a few escaping to safety. The coups to throw anti-Communists in Czechoslovakia out of office and to drive Michael from Rumania were ready for execution. The Communists, under direct control of the Kremlin, dominated most of eastern Europe. Their political strength remained strong in western Europe. They were to cause a general strike in France in December, and they were already organizing to win the forthcoming general elections in Italy.

Then, at Harvard in June, Secretary Marshall offered financial assistance to the countries of Europe willing to co-operate in the common good. The Soviet Government recognized the threat to the further advance of Communism represented by this offer. It did not dare to permit our economic missions to enter the satellite countries with financial assistance. Therefore, in Paris in July, Mr. Molotov rejected our help and shortly under instructions from Moscow the satellite countries did likewise.

Time was required for Marshall aid to materialize. However, time was now on our side and there was no further advantage to be gained by the Soviet Government from delaying tactics. It was in Soviet interest to permit relationships to deteriorate, to wage a war of nerves re-creating the fear in Europe which alone could make possible the further advance of Communism. The program of the Cominform was made public in the fall. Clearly it was directed at the domination of Europe but there were two obstacles: the thin screen of British and American troops in Germany which could not be penetrated without war and which prevented the fear engulfing eastern Europe from spreading into western Europe, and the promise of financial aid which in bringing about a more normal economy would restore the will to be free of all of the people of western Europe. Therefore the Soviet Government decided that a break in Germany was desirable. It might be possible to force us out of Berlin, thus creating doubt as to our intent to hold our position in Europe.

There seemed little hope that the Council of Foreign Ministers would accomplish much at its November meeting in London. We became sure of this in the November 21 meeting of the Control Council only a few days before the London conference, when Marshal Sokolovsky really "threw the book" at us.

He charged that demilitarization had not been carried out in the western zones; that in the British Zone military formations of the Germany Army were being held intact, and in the American Zone the sports program for German youth was a cover for military training, and war plants were still in operation. He charged us with failure to carry out reparations, with the removal of German equipment and manufactured goods, and with deliberately exporting German products, paying low prices for these products while selling them in world markets at high prices for huge profits. He accused us of fostering war propaganda and of using denazification procedures to rehabilitate criminal elements. He charged us with an unlawful act in prohibiting the activities of the Socialist Unity party in western Germany, and with failure to carry out a land-reform program. He then attacked bizonal fusion as an undertaking deliberately designed to break up quadripartite government and to split Germany. He argued that we had so run the German economy as to transform Germany into a raw materials exporting country, which would have to import its equipment from the United States.

His charges, utterly unfounded in fact, were published immediately in the Soviet-controlled press. They were certainly not designed to create an atmosphere in which understanding might be possible. I attached great importance to his statement. Sokolovsky, normally witty and pleasant, had read it with utmost gravity and I seemed to feel at the time a complete change in his attitude. Of course I reported the serious view with which I regarded his statement, stating that I believed it foretold the Soviet position in London. The three Western representatives made no reply to these charges. General George Erskine, sitting in General Robertson's absence, did remark that he had been trying to find a reason why he had listened to so much invective and that the only reason he could find was courtesy and even that was severely taxed.

Between November 6 and 27 Mr. Murphy was in London, where the special deputies were engaged in a futile effort to prepare an agenda for the forthcoming meeting. There too the Soviet representative was inflexible.

In contrast, Secretary Marshall delivered a calm and measured speech in Chicago on November 19. He brought out the divergencies of purpose concerning the future of Europe between the United States and Soviet Russia, and his belief that the restoration of Europe as a solvent and vigorous community would decide the issue. He referred again to our desire for co-operation with every nation, pledging a generous effort to the common cause of European recovery. He expressed regret over the vituperative attacks of Soviet representatives in the United Nations. He stated that German recovery under adequate security controls was essential to European recovery. He fixed United States policy on the Ruhr by expressing his belief in the necessity of safeguards to see that the resources of the Ruhr should not be exclusively under German control. He ended by emphasizing that the United States would enter the London conference with open mind and would avoid statements for mere popular or propaganda effect. His restrained, studied words were both an invitation to co-operation and a reaffirmation of our determination that our efforts in Europe should not be delayed pending further failures to reach accord.

I think we all knew that the Control Council was dead when we left Berlin to attend the London conference. Fortunately, however, we had not permitted failure in the Control Council and worsening relationships with Soviet representatives to slow our efforts to improve the economic life of the British and American zones. The invitation to other occupying powers to join their zones with our zone extended by Secretary Byrnes in Paris in July 1946, and accepted by the United Kingdom, resulted in the development of a bizonal German administration under our joint control. The account of its progress in this period of quadripartite failure is heartening, and shows the feasibility of international co-operation where there is mutual good will.

CHAPTER 9

We Join the British
and American Zones

BYRNES'S economic fusion invitation was accepted by the United Kingdom on July 30, 1946. It became the second of three phases in the political reconstruction of Germany, the first being the establishment of zonal political life, and the third, West German Government.

The joint administration of the two zones was started not in the interest of political reconstruction but as a practical step toward better economic conditions within the area, thus reducing the burden of support borne by the occupying powers. The situation in the British and American zones had worsened with the receipt of over 7,000,000 expellees from Poland, the Polish-administered territory in Germany, Czechoslovakia, and Hungary. Neither of these zones had the agricultural resources to support a prewar population of approximately 34,000,000. Now their plight was serious.

Without questioning the justification for this mass movement of people (it may be questioned), it gave us an enormous additional burden.

As a result and because the food supply was insufficient to maintain the productive capacity of the worker, economic recovery in the British and American zones was proceeding slowly. This was even truer in the British Zone, which included the great Ruhr industrial area with its concentration of inhabitants and which had even less agricultural resources than did the American Zone. Of course it was clear from the beginning of the occupation that the recovery of

Germany and of Europe depended on the restoration of coal and steel production in the Ruhr.

Economically, the British and American zones complemented each other to a greater degree than any other two zones. The basic industries of Germany were in the Ruhr while the productive capacity in the American Zone was largely devoted to the assembly of finished products. The manufacturers in our zone could therefore get back into production only when they had received materials and components from the Ruhr. A minimum food supply for the British Zone required larger imports at greater cost than a minimum food supply for the American Zone. Without this minimum the Ruhr could not produce. So a merger of the two zones was of mutual advantage. While the outside support required by the American Zone would be less for some years than for the British Zone, in the long run Germany's ability to become self-supporting would depend on output from the Ruhr. British Military Government was allocating products of the Ruhr to our zone but it was not to be expected that this would be continued in view of the large deficit in its area being borne by its government.

It had been recognized at Potsdam that only a unified German economy could recover rapidly. Our efforts to bring about unification, started in the opening sessions of the Control Council, made no progress. Instead the administration of economic matters on a zonal basis was making the amalgamation of such services as transport and communications more difficult.

A review of the events which led to the economic fusion of the British and American zones starts on September 22, 1945, when the French representative, General Koeltz, rejected our proposal for a central transport administration. He claimed that railroads represented a war potential and that an administration in charge of their operation was as dangerous as the German General Staff. In reply I pointed out our willingness to unite the railroads in our zone with those of any other zone and added that the Control Council could govern Germany effectively only if it had German administration which it could hold responsible for carrying out its instructions. This suggestion was repeated on December 21, 1945, and at other meetings in late 1945 and early 1946.

In the report which I submitted to the War Department on May 26, 1946, I pointed out the consequences which were developing from the treatment of Germany as four small economic units and suggested the amalgamation of as large an area as possible into an economic unit by mutual agreement among two or more of the occupying powers. Mr. Murphy and I had discussed our views with Secretary Byrnes in Paris in April 1946, and had emphasized the conditions in Germany which were leading to economic chaos. We had told Byrnes that we believed a merger of our zone with the British Zone confined to economic matters would not result in the breakdown of the Allied Control Authority. We found Byrnes convinced that the Soviet Government did not intend to treat Germany as an economic unit and he agreed that the fusion of our zone with other zones was desirable. He did not wish to take such a step before he had extended an invitation to all the occupying powers in a meeting of the Council of Foreign Ministers.

The April meeting did not provide an appropriate occasion. However, when Molotov had used the July conference to attack the Western Powers, Byrnes believed that Soviet intent was clear and further delay in consolidating the western areas of Germany would increase economic distress and make political reconstruction impossible. In inviting any or all of his colleagues to merge their zones economically with our zone, he made it clear that the administration of these zones would be limited to economic matters and would not function as a government, and that the merger would last only until agreement was reached for the treatment of all Germany as an economic unit. For these reasons German organizations established in the bizonal area were never made responsible to the German people through the election process.

When Byrnes returned to the United States he reported the Paris conference in a nationwide broadcast on July 15 which referred not only to this invitation but stated also that Mr. Bevin had expressed the intent to accept it. He added that no views had been expressed by either French or Soviet representatives. On July 18 we were advised by radio dispatch to repeat the invitation in the Allied Control Council:

Since the zones of Germany are not self-supporting of themselves, and since treating two zones or more as an economic unit would better this situation in the zones concerned, the US representatives in Germany will join with the representatives of any other occupying power or powers in measures to treat their respective zones as an economic unit, pending four-power agreement to carry out the Potsdam provision regarding the treatment of all Germany as an economic unit and the reaching of a balanced economy throughout Germany. You should also declare that you are ready to cooperate with any or all of the other three occupying powers in setting up appropriate administrative machinery for this purpose. Administrative arrangements would seem to be required in such fields as finance, transportation, communications, industry and foreign trade to assure the economic unification of the zones concerned and they should be susceptible, upon the adherence of all four zones, to become the central German administrative departments headed by State Secretaries called for in the Potsdam Protocol. In offering this proposal the U.S. does not intend to divide Germany but to speed up its functioning as an economic unit. Whatever is agreed with one government will be offered on identical terms to the governments of other zones at such time as they become ready to participate. The U.S. government is convinced that Germany must not be administered longer in four airtight compartments without free economic exchange between the zones, and further that maintaining present conditions will lead certainly to economic paralysis in Germany. The U.S. government is not prepared to permit this creeping paralysis when it may be possible to develop economic cooperation between some of the zones as a prelude to the economic unification of all Germany.

In this same message we were instructed:

If this offer is refused by any of the participating representatives, you are instructed and expected to proceed any way to negotiate with the representatives of the occupying powers of any zone or zones which may accept to agree on arrangements to accomplish these principles which will make possible the treatment of such zones as an economic unit. With respect to the French zone, you are instructed, in accordance with the statements made by Secretary of State in Paris, to arrange details with the French representative in the understanding that the Saar territory will be excluded in any arrangements for economic unity that may be mutually accepted.

Please advise State and War Departments of course of such negotiations and submit for approval here your agreed recommenda-

tions and plans. For background purposes the following may be helpful: The U. S. government has approved OMGUS plan for central German agencies. You may use this for basis of the negotiations you undertake with any other zonal authorities. When the CFM met on July 11, Secretary of State stated substantially: U. S. government does not want a peace of vengeance and it is convinced that the economic recovery of Germany along peaceful lines is necessary to the economic revival of Europe. It desires the denazification of Germany which will encourage democratic forces who otherwise may feel they cannot assert themselves with a fair chance. The sure way to encourage the growth of democratic forces in Germany is to refuse in definite terms the conditions of settlement, to fix German disarmament measures, and the reparations which it must pay. The German people will then realize that the harder they work the sooner they will be allowed to share in the benefits of European recovery. Germany's future boundaries should likewise be defined so that the German people may know that as long as they adhere to the settlement, no interference will be given to their reconstruction efforts, which will help both themselves and all of Europe. While controls and security forces must remain for a long time in Germany, mass occupation and military government continued over a long period could defeat our own purposes. The German people must have the opportunity to minimize the certain difficulties and hardships of their situation by their own efforts so that they will not learn to blame their trials on Allied occupation but rather and properly to the devastating war of aggression which their leaders let loose. The Allied duty is to set up machinery for the peace settlement and the U. S. Government has urged the establishment of special deputies for this purpose.

Molotov then made a lengthy explanation of the Russian position and refused to consider any proposals other than his own. Another meeting of the CFM on the German question was subsequently arranged to be held immediately after the general assembly of the UN. At this state of discussion, Bevin stated that UK government would be forced to take steps to protect British taxpayers; it could not continue to purchase dollars in order to send food into the British zone in Germany from which British were trying to meet the requirements of the neighboring countries for coal. The UK government would, however, keep within the limits of the agreed level of industry agreement in its effort to increase German output.

Secretary of State replied that he hoped the situation suggested by Bevin could be avoided. The U. S. government still hoped that arrangements could be made for the central administrative agencies which were necessary for economic unity. It had agreed that Saar would be excluded from this area to be administered by the French until the frontiers were finally fixed. However, if such agreement proved impossible, the U. S. government proposed to join its zone with any other to provide as broad a basis as possible for economic recovery.

The invitation was extended to his colleagues by General McNarney at the Allied Control Council meeting of July 20, 1946.[1] At the next meeting on July 30, 1946, our proposal was accepted by the representative of the United Kingdom.

Immediately the British and American deputy military governors held several informal conferences to arrange for early merger. On August 9, 1946, they agreed that they would comprise a Bipartite Board to work out details which would ensure a common standard of living, a common consumer ration, and a pooling of their resources. German authorities in both zones would be charged with the execution of a common economic policy subject to direction and supervision by the two military governments.

General Robertson and I were mindful of our instructions and determined to avoid any justification for charges by our colleagues of political amalgamation. We went to great lengths not to create such an impression. We decided against the establishment of a common assembly or council, and to put the several agencies which we would create in different cities to avoid the appearance of a bizonal capital. Any organization founded on such a basis could be only partially effective as it was incapable of complete co-ordination of economic effort. Nevertheless, this first step represented the extent to which we felt we could proceed without jeopardizing our efforts to secure quadripartite control. Two further steps were necessary before the German administration was given sufficient authority to conduct economic affairs effectively. The second step, establishing an Economic Council with some legislative authority, was taken in May 1947, and the third step, conveying additional legislative authority and substantial executive power, in February 1948.

The military government organization to which we agreed consisted of the Anglo-American Bipartite Board, having under it a secretariat, six bipartite panels composed of our advisers in the several economic fields which were to formulate policy guidance, and six bipartite control groups which were to be located in the same cities as corresponding German administrative agencies.

German administrative agencies[2] headed by executive committees were established: for Economics at Minden, for Food and Agriculture at Stuttgart, for Transport at Bielefeld, and for Communications, Civil Service, and Finance at Frankfurt. Each of the executive committees by agreement between the Laenderrat of the United States Zone and the Central (German) Office for Economics of the British Zone was composed of one representative from each of the eight states of the two zones. They were empowered to elect an additional member to serve as chairman of the committee and chief executive of the agency.

Final arrangements were completed by September 17, 1946. The weaknesses of this organization were obvious from the start but the several agencies did much to unify the services for which they were responsible. While the lack of co-ordinating executive authority and of a responsible legislative body did restrict their effectiveness, the reasonably competent departments with trained personnel which did develop proved of substantial value later when the administration was strengthened.

Robertson and I were careful to tell the Allied Control Council what we were doing and at frequent intervals to invite the Soviet and French members to join us.

Although he and I had been able to organize and start the agencies to work promptly, it proved much more difficult to agree to the financial responsibility for the support of the combined zones which each of us was to assume.

In early meetings with Robertson's predecessor, General Weeks, prior to the withdrawal of our forces from the Ruhr, we had decided to divide between us the SHAEF grain reserve which came largely from American sources and likewise to place our export proceeds in a common pool. At that time it was clear that coal from the Ruhr would form our chief export asset for many months. We wanted to be sure how its proceeds were to be utilized before it was transferred to British control, and before we made the grain purchased with our funds available for its support. In September 1945 Robertson had confirmed this understanding and our informal arrangement was likewise approved by the State Department and the British Embassy in Washington.

When we agreed to economic fusion, neither side had as yet placed its export proceeds in the common pool. We had held ours intact but the British Government had spent its receipts in partial compensation for the food brought into its zone. Settlement was further complicated by a British announcement that the agreement to pool export proceeds was ineffective after March 1, 1946. We refused to accept this unilateral cancellation of a bilateral agreement. Also we could not agree as to the proportion of financial responsibility each was to assume. We wished the proportion to be based on population in view of the lower population in the American Zone, whereas the British insisted on at least an equal arrangement and even urged that the United States bear 60 per cent of the burden.

There were valid arguments on both sides. The United States Zone had a greater agricultural production and required fewer imports per capita than the British Zone. Hence, even in accepting a responsibility proportioned on a population basis, the merger would result in adding to our financial burden as the per capita requirement was increased. On the other hand, the great industrial area in the British Zone had to have food to produce the exports which would bring both zones to self-sufficiency. As the weeks dragged on without agreement, our joint enterprise was operating without capital and, naturally, with little progress. This led Mr. Bevin to raise the subject with Secretary Byrnes, and on October 14, 1946, I received the following letter from Byrnes from Paris:

Dear Lucius:

When I confer with Bevin on the subject referred to in the enclosed memorandum, I shall want you to be present. I think, therefore, we ought to make it about the 15th of November.

Before that time we will have an idea as to when the Council of Foreign Ministers will meet to discuss the German problem. Recently Molotov told Bevin he would prefer to have the discussion as to Germany taken up somewhere in Europe. Bevin stated that he would have to discuss that with me inasmuch as I had spent so much time in Europe. I will not agree to it unless I am satisfied it is to be a thorough discussion of all phases of the subject which would justify my returning to Europe in December. I am going to insist on the discussions starting there, and will wait to talk with you before they start.

Of course, Mrs. Clay will have to come with you.

With best wishes to you both, I am

Sincerely yours,
/s/ James F. Byrnes

The attached memorandum listed for discussion the estimated cost of financing the Anglo-American zones and the division of these costs between the two governments. The discussions were to include the determination of our respective procurement responsibilities. They were to take place in Washington and in view of their importance the British Embassy staff was to be reinforced by experts. Mr. Bevin and Secretary Byrnes, who had planned to be present, were in New York for the Council of Foreign Ministers meeting but were able to keep in touch with the discussions.

Mr. Murphy and I arrived in Washington with several members of our staff in time for the opening conference on November 13, 1946.

Secretary Patterson had designated me to speak for the War Department group. The meeting was opened in plenary session with a welcome from Acting Secretary of State Acheson to which Edmund Hall-Patch responded for the British. The agenda was approved and the plenary session was adjourned to permit smaller groups to meet. Our delegation was headed by Assistant Secretary Hilldring. It included Howard Petersen from the War Department, Murphy, Riddleberger, and myself as well as representatives from Treasury, Agriculture, and the Reconstruction Finance Corporation. The British had indeed reinforced their embassy staff with Mr. Hall-Patch and Patrick Henry Dean of the Foreign Office, Sir David Waley of Treasury, General Robertson and Sir William Strang from Germany, and Sir Mark Turner and Major General Ian Stanley Playfair of the British Control Office of Germany.

The British objectives were to maximize the money to be made available for German support including the provision of capital for expanded export operations; to minimize their payment of export proceeds owed to the common pool, to obtain a joint control of food procurement which would prevent invasion of markets being utilized by the British; and to accept as small a proportion of the financial liability as possible. The United States delegation was realistic with respect to the funds which it might be able to secure from appropriations or in loans from the Reconstruction Finance Corporation, and desired that past proceeds of exports from both zones be paid into a joint capital account. It believed that financial responsibilities should be proportionate to occupation responsibilities.

Our estimates showed that export proceeds from the American Zone came to about $14,500,000 to the end of 1946, and from the British Zone to about $155,000,000, mainly from the export of coal. Equalizing these receipts would require a cross payment in favor of the United States of approximately $70,000,000. The British, of course, accepted no liability to make payments for export proceeds received after March 1, 1946.

On the other hand, the greater food requirements for the British Zone meant an increased annual cost to the United States after fusion. Moreover, we had on hand in Germany food stocks desperately needed in the British Zone, and the British claimed inability to pay for food in dollars or to obtain it otherwise. The United States delegation realized the critical dollar position of the British Treasury and knew that our government was concurrently considering means to provide assistance.

After days of discussion an agreement[3] was reached and incorporated in a memorandum which General Robertson and I presented to Secretary Byrnes and Mr. Bevin in New York at the Waldorf-Astoria on December 2, 1946. At this meeting Bevin made a further plea for the United States to bear 60 per cent of the annual cost, basing his stand on the British financial position and the increased responsibility resting upon them for the Ruhr industrial area. Byrnes insisted on parity and suggested further our readiness to trade occupation areas with the British and take over the Ruhr. Bevin assumed this to be in the nature of a joke, although I was sure that Byrnes was at least partly serious. He remembered earlier American desire to occupy the British Zone, which had been given up at the second Quebec Conference only at British insistence. Moreover, he realized that control of the Ruhr was important to European recovery and believed that we were entitled to at least share in this control. With fusion, this resulted and gave us a much more influential voice in German affairs. Bevin, in signing, was a thorough sportsman and wished Robertson and me luck. British payments were to be made as needed, to be converted to dollars only when needed supplies could not be obtained with pounds sterling. I promised Bevin to take as many months as possible for the conversion, and tried in every way to do so.

The agreement provided, in general, that the United States should make proceeds from exports in the amount of $14,500,000, together with $29,300,000 to be paid to the United States in equalization from British Zone export proceeds, available for the capital account of the Joint Export-Import Agency. The British would make a corresponding amount available either in needed goods from the sterling area or in pounds sterling convertible into dollars on demand. Certain payments due from Sweden under the agreement of July 18, 1946, for the extinguishment of German assets in that country, were likewise to be placed in the capital account. Thus the Joint Export-Import Agency was provided with a capital fund of about $121,000,-000, of which about $90,000,000 would be paid in immediately. The agreement established a joint supply committee in Washington and authorized the opening of foreign exchange accounts with approved banks in foreign countries. It was to be reviewed every year.

The first phase of bizonal fusion was thus completed and Robertson and I returned to Germany to push vigorously the export program which we had submitted to the conference. It is interesting to note that we promised an export program of $350,000,000 in 1947; $675,000,000 in 1948; and $900,000,000 in 1949. We actually made exports worth $225,000,000 in 1947; $600,000,000 in 1948; and if the monthly rate for the first half of the year is sustained, worth more than $1,000,000,000 in 1949. In spite of the severe winter of 1946–47 which retarded our early efforts, we almost fulfilled our promise for the full period.

Our initial fears over the weakness of the bizonal organization were confirmed by experience and in the spring of 1947 we knew that it had to be strengthened. Even competent executive authority could not co-ordinate six agencies located in four widely separated cities and we did not have competent authority. State governments which were responsible to elected parliaments felt that they represented more nearly the will of the German people and therefore accepted the rulings of the bizonal agencies reluctantly and sometimes only after they were required to do so by Military Government.

Robertson and I worked on the problem for some time but hesitated to move ahead before the Moscow conference of Foreign Ministers in the spring of 1947. This conference convinced Secretary Marshall and Mr. Bevin that further delay would serve no purpose. Marshall cabled me to be at the airport on his arrival in Berlin from Moscow on April 25 and to arrange for a place in which we could have a private talk. He, Bohlen, Murphy, and I met for approximately an hour in the airport building at Tempelhof. I was instructed to proceed vigorously with the strengthening of the bizonal organization in conjunction with Robertson, and to expedite the upward revision of the level of bizonal industry to ensure the self-sufficiency of the area. It seemed possible that a wider economic unity in Germany might not take place for years.

So on May 29 we promulgated an improved and strengthened German administration for the bizonal area[4] as the second step in transfer of responsibility to German hands. We still wanted to avoid the impression of governmental authority and the creation of a capital for western Germany and our objective remained limited.

The new organization created an Economic Council to convene in Frankfurt, composed of fifty-two delegates elected by the Landtage of the several states on the basis of one delegate to every 750,000 persons. This Council, subject to approval of its actions by the Bipartite Board (Robertson and I continued on the Board when we became military governors), was charged with responsibility for adopting and promulgating ordinances in the fields of economics, transport, finance, communications, food and agriculture, and for the regulation of its own civil service.

Its decisions were to be carried out by an Executive Committee composed of one representative from each of the states designated by state governments. This Committee was empowered to make recommendations for legislation to the Economic Council, to issue implementing regulations, and to co-ordinate and supervise the several administrative agencies. The committees which had hitherto headed the administrative agencies were replaced by executive directors nominated by the Executive Committee and confirmed by the Economic Council.

Since Robertson and I were unable to leave Berlin for extended periods, we established a Bipartite Control Office in Frankfurt to act as our day-to-day representative with the German administration.

Members of Congress frequently made tours of inspection. Here General Clay sits with the Senate Appropriations Committee.

Russian General Tserenmanov flourishes a pistol before presenting it to Major General Raymond S. McLain in commemoration of the link-up between Russian and American armies.

Russian soldier hugs American GI as the two armies join near Grabow, Germany.

American tanks pass in review before Major General Vladimir S. Kuznetsov, commander of the Russian 40th Infantry Corps.

The Bipartite Control Office had under it bipartite control groups for each of the German administrative agencies. Thus we had a legislative body with specific if limited powers, an executive head to the extent that a committee can exert executive authority over all administrative agencies, and responsible single executive control for each of the administrative agencies.

The Executive Committee was formed of an equal number of representatives from the several states to ensure observance of their rights. Unfortunately the majority of its representatives belonged to a different political party (SPD) than the majority (CDU) in the Council, in which the more heavily populated states had greater representation. Political antagonisms made mutual co-operation between Council, Executive Committee, and the administrative agencies difficult. Nevertheless, it was a great improvement over the initial organization. The administrative agencies were growing in experience and ability, and the Council gained practice in debate and in the consideration and enactment of legislation. Furthermore, the Bizonal Agency was authorized to adopt measures which must be accepted by the states or the citizens thereof. For the first time a lawmaking power, albeit limited, was entrusted to a German agency above state level.

Air Marshal Douglas and I attended the first meeting held on June 25, 1947, in an improvised assembly room in the former Frankfurt stock exchange. We congratulated the Council on the part it could now play in exercising broad responsibility for government under democratic principles and in the interests of economic recovery. We had high hopes that we had taken a constructive step in political reconstruction, and I on my part have never been disappointed in this move.

Robertson and I recognized that our second step still had not established sufficient executive powers for effective co-ordination of the German agencies. We reported to our governments that the new organization would not be fully effective until it became something very close to a government even though it was not called one or given any powers of sovereignty. However, we felt it undesirable to proceed further or more rapidly pending the outcome of the next meeting of the Council of Foreign Ministers which was to convene in London on November 25, 1947.

The adjournment of this conference without agreement as to

when and where the foreign ministers would meet again led to another vital decision with respect to the German problem, made this time by the three Western foreign ministers. Shortly after the adjournment of the Council of Foreign Ministers, Secretary Marshall and Mr. Bevin met at Ambassador Douglas' residence, 14 Prince's Gate, at a luncheon attended also by Robertson, Frank Roberts of the British Foreign Office, Murphy, and me. After luncheon I presented orally, by agreement with Robertson, our joint views on the German problem. We pointed out that currency reform was essential to economic progress and recommended that one more effort be made immediately to obtain quadripartite approval to put it in effect throughout Germany, failing which we would proceed in western Germany if France would agree, or in the bizonal area if France held back. We further asked for authority to give political character to the bizonal administrative structure without giving it the name of government. This could be done, we believed, by the direct election in the early summer of 1948 of members of the Economic Council. We proposed to continue to participate in the Allied Control Council unless it was broken up by others. We anticipated difficulty in Berlin and recommended that we stay there regardless of any Soviet pressures. We urged that our governments make it clear to the French Government that it was welcome to join us at any time but that no effort be made to bring any pressure on France.

Marshall and Bevin accepted all of our recommendations and specifically instructed us to improve the political organization of the bizonal area without delay, leaving the details and procedures to Robertson's and my discretion.

The way was paved to take the final step in the organization of the bizonal area. It is interesting that this step, which completed the second phase in the evolution of German administrative responsibility, was approved at the same time that the third phase, West German Government, began. Secretary Marshall told me before leaving London that he had talked with Mr. Bidault, who said the French Government was now willing to discuss trizonal fusion provided that the question of the Ruhr and the general question of security were considered concurrently. He added that an intergovernmental conference on these matters would probably take place in London early in 1948.

Robertson and I returned to Germany to develop the further

measures deemed necessary to provide a sound bizonal German administration. This involved considerable discussion between our staffs and with German officials.

In the meantime the British Government was having trouble in fulfilling its obligations under the financial agreement of December 1946. It had to get its share of the food in the United States, which took dollars, and it felt it could not stand this drain on its dollar resources. Our State and Treasury Departments were concerned and decided to meet with British representatives in Washington to review the 1946 agreement.

The American delegation met to consider our position on October 8, 1947. It included Assistant Secretary Charles E. Saltzman, Mr. Murphy, Under Secretary of Army William H. Draper, Jr., Assistant Secretary of Army Gordon Gray, and me. There were expert advisers from State, Army, Treasury and Commerce Departments, and from Military Government. Ambassador Douglas reviewed for us the financial situation confronting the British Government. The British delegation, headed by Sir William Strang, included Mr. Dean of the Foreign Office, General Nevil Charles Dowell Brownjohn of British Military Government, D. L. Anderson, Sir Gordon Munro, and other experts.

While the negotiations were quite technical, the questions to be resolved were relatively simple. The British Government wished to be relieved of all dollar liability, not only for future procurement but also for the conversion of pounds sterling held by the Joint Export-Import Agency in its capital and operating accounts. The British had insisted on the sale of German exports in pounds sterling to those countries which wished to pay in this currency, and had promised to convert pounds into dollars as they were needed to pay for imports which were not available in the sterling area and had to be paid for in dollars. This had resulted in the accumulation of a large sum in pounds sterling which would not have been accepted except for the British Government's agreement to convert on demand.

The United States delegation at the beginning of the conference held out for continuation of equal financial responsibility. In view of the British dollar position, they knew this to be unrealistic. However, they knew that if the British Government did not convert the Germany economy would lose the use of almost all of its capital. Moreover, the United States delegation believed that they were entitled to a larger voice in financial and economic matters if they agreed to accept a heavier share of the financial responsibility.

Some of the Americans urged that the United States should insist on a predominant voice in political matters as well. I argued strongly against this. By and large, British and American objectives in Germany were close, and our success in accomplishing them depended on genuine co-operation with the British. To insist on lowering their status to that of a junior partner would have made collaboration difficult if not impossible. In view of their financial position we could have forced their acceptance, but damaged British prestige in Europe was not really to our interest. This view prevailed.

Although I served as spokesman for the American delegation Murphy and I had to return to Germany on October 23 to prepare for the London meeting of the Council of Foreign Ministers. The joint conference continued for some weeks and final agreement was signed on December 17, 1947, by Acting Secretary of State Robert Lovett for the United States and Sir William Strang for the United Kingdom.[5]

In this agreement the United States accepted almost the full financial responsibility for the bizonal area except for such specific supplies as could be found in the sterling area which could not be sold elsewhere to bring in dollar revenue. The British continued their pledge to convert pounds sterling held in our capital account into dollars except that the requirement to make such conversion on demand was limited by a fixed maximum on the amounts to be converted in a given period of time. The British agreed to limit the sale of German exports for sterling to the sterling area and to furnish certain shipping for transport of supplies to Germany. Voting rights in matters relating to foreign trade and foreign exchange of the bizonal area were proportionate to the financial contribution made by each of the occupying powers, exclusive of costs of occupation forces and personnel. This, in fact, gave us the right of final decision in financial and economic matters.

General Robertson and I were ready to announce the measures to strengthen German administration soon after our return from London. We were taken by surprise when the French Government made a strong protest to our plans in an aide-mémoire, presented to our government on January 24, 1948. The French contended that the bizonal administration prejudiced the structure of future German government. We had advised them in advance of the steps we were to take. Their objections to our plans were: failure to have an upper house of equal power, granting of limited taxation powers to the bizonal administration, establishment of single heads of administrative agencies responsible to the Bizonal Council instead of placing these agencies under committees representing the several states, and establishment of a Supreme or High Court for the bizonal area. These objections were all cited directly or indirectly in the aide-mémoire, which endeavored to portray the still weak and limited administration which we were establishing as the prelude to a powerful centralized government. I stressed this fact in a memorandum to Mr. Murphy which I asked him to transmit to the State Department:

I would like to point out that our proposals, acting under our instructions, have been presented to the Germans and of course to the French. Any substantial change at this late date would be most damaging. Moreover, the French concept of a loose confederation would not be resolved as it is our understanding that the economic and finance setup at Frankfurt is only the prelude to a government, at least of the British and American zones, to be made effective at an early date if quadripartite agreement for a unified Germany fails to materialize.

We are at a critical position in Germany and we must either move forward to give the Germans increased responsibility in the bizonal area to insure their proper contribution to European recovery, or we must move backward to increase our own forces to run a more colonial type of government. We have been in Germany three years now and have progressed very little beyond the state levels in developing responsibility upon German officials. I am quite sure that most thinking people at home will find that our bizonal organization does not go far enough in this direction, and its weaknesses largely come from our desire to meet what we knew would be French views, as much as possible consistent with effective administration. Unless we are willing to establish a working organization in which the Germans are given real responsibility, we would have to expand our own organization many times to take care of the additional export trade which we fully hope will materialize in the coming months. Delay now will prove most expensive in the months to come.

I did not believe that the French protest was really designed to stop the bizonal reorganization. It was a French custom, and an effective one, to state publicly their position prior to attending an international conference in order to develop popular support for the French stand at that conference. Perhaps they also thought some favorable world opinion would result. They had grasped this opportunity to expound the position they were to take initially in the London tripartite conference on the political organization of western Germany, which was scheduled for the following month. In this conference they were to refer frequently to the effect of specific proposals on French public opinion, an opinion which had certainly been influenced by their protest.

The French aide-mémoire did not develop any substantial public support in the United States or in the United Kingdom, where the major comment was that we were already late in establishing effective German administration in the bizonal area. Our government on February 2 answered the French point by point and affirmed our intent to proceed, although it assured them that we were establishing a provisional administration not designed in any way to prejudge the German constitution. The government of the United Kingdom did likewise.

Thus, on February 9, 1948, General Robertson and I were able to issue Proclamation No. 7,[6] which completed the final and third step in the establishment of German administration in the bizonal area.

This proclamation had been discussed in conference with the German minister-presidents of the eight states, the chairman and vice-president of the Economic Council, and the chairman and vice-chairman of the Executive Committee, on January 26 and again on January 28. The suggestions of the German officials were given careful consideration and many were incorporated in the final plan.

The proclamation enlarged the popular base for the Economic Council by increasing its membership to a total of 104. It established to protect state interests an upper house or Laenderrat composed of an equal number of representatives (two) from each state designated by the state governments. The Laenderrat was given the power to initiate legislation other than revenue and appropriation bills and the right to veto Economic Council legislation unless the veto was overridden by an absolute majority of the Council. The Executive Committee was reconstituted to be composed of a chairman and the heads of the administrative agencies.

This was a realistic political structure[7] of the federal type even though it had no sovereign powers, was limited in its authority to fiscal and economic measures, and its acts were subject to Military Government approval. There was a legislature, with broad authority in fiscal and economic fields, composed of a lower house whose members were elected by the state parliaments and were at least indirectly responsible to the people, and an upper house representing the states. There was a chairman of the Executive Committee (roughly, the chairman corresponded to a Prime Minister and the Committee to a Cabinet) responsible to the legislature. Provisions were made for a personnel office, a statistical office, and an office of legislative counsel. Subsequent amendments extended the administrative powers to even broader fields. We had the machinery for government, if not a government.

Concurrently, Proclamation No. 8[8] was issued, establishing a High Court which was charged with the interpretation and enforcement of legislation and was thus in a position to protect both the rights of the individual and of the states within the range of legislative authority granted to the Economic Council. This court was made independent from Executive control and was served by an Office of Solicitor General.

On March 1 Military Government Law No. 60[9] was enacted to charter the Bank deutscher Laender as the central bank in a new banking system which corresponded in many ways to our own Federal Reserve System. This gave the German administration an essential tool for effective financial and economic administration of the bizonal area.

Our British-American organization in Frankfurt (the Bipartite Control Office) was concurrently changed from a joint to an integrated staff except for the deputies to General Robertson and me, who served as co-chairmen of the office.

About this time I decided to transfer gradually my military headquarters from Frankfurt to Heidelberg, thus making room in Frankfurt for all of the German administrative agencies and for the supervising Anglo-American staffs. This movement was completed in July 1948. It resulted immediately in improved co-ordination and effectiveness of the German administrations, previously located in four cities.

In addition to the Bipartite Control Office, three joint agencies were established in fields in which the German administration had not been granted authority to function. These agencies, whose development and work will be described later, were the Joint Export-Import Agency,[10] which was in direct control of foreign trade; the Joint Foreign Exchange Agency, which was responsible for the handling of all foreign exchange transactions; and the Joint Coal Control Group[11] in Essen.

From the start of the bizonal German administration, Robertson and I left a large part of the work with German officials to our deputies: General Sir Gordon Macready and General Adcock. However, we felt it important to maintain some personal touch and therefore arranged to meet on the middle of each month with the German Executive Committee and the chairmen and vice-chairmen of the Council and Laenderrat. While these talks never developed the informal relationship which I had enjoyed with the Laenderrat in our zone, they were useful indeed for exchange of information and as a forum where decisions could be explained and discussed.

Soon the pattern for the Frankfurt meetings of the military governors became fixed. Robertson and I would each meet with his own staff early in the morning to discuss the agenda of the day. Then we would get together in a formal meeting of the Bipartite Board to reconcile British and American views on a wide range of problems. Robertson and I learned that compromise was the only way to progress in bipartite matters, except in those fiscal and economic matters in which the United States had and chose to use the majority voice because of its heavier financial contribution. We were usually able to reach decisions on a large agenda in a relatively short time. We had learned to avoid argument for argument's sake and to proceed immediately to the essential points.

In the early afternoon, accompanied by our principal staff directors, we would meet with the German officials across the table. We would hear their appeals from our decisions and their reports of progress. Robertson and I divided the subjects to be discussed. So well did we work together that with a few whispered words between us each was able to cover his subject from the joint viewpoint. So it was seldom necessary to delay or defer discussion to permit us to reconcile our views. I think this was really a major reason for progress in bizonal administration. After the official meeting we would join the Germans for tea and coffee.

The next day Robertson and I would talk with the principal staff directors of our integrated control staff to hear their reports and future plans and to answer when practicable the questions which were raised.

Later we were also to meet on the second day with the French military governor to discuss problems of trizonal interest.

On the last two days of each month we would meet again with our staffs and then with the minister-presidents of the eight states instead of the officials of the bizonal German administration. The meetings with the minister-presidents were less formal and particularly informative of actual conditions in Germany as the daily tasks of these men kept them keenly aware of local conditions and problems.

Between the Frankfurt meetings, Robertson and I would meet several times in Berlin as members of the Bipartite Board. Our close relationship made it frequently possible to reach Board decisions in telephone conversations, certainly a welcome change from the frustrations of the Allied Control Council.

The minister-presidents from the British Zone were interesting personalities. Lower Saxony was represented by Heinrich Kopf, a courageous, shrewd politician with lionlike head and carriage. North Rhine-Westphalia was represented by Karl Arnold, a liberal member of the Christian Democratic Union. Arnold was active, intelligent, and sincere. Somewhat lacking in a sense of humor, he had a strong religious approach and a deep interest in social problems. Hermann Luedemann, the minister-president from Schleswig-Holstein, with his pointed beard, could have played the part of Mephistopheles without make-up. An old civil servant, he understood the mechanics of government well indeed but was inclined to play his part behind rather than in front of the scenes. The strongest personality was undoubtedly Max Brauer from Hamburg. An old trade-unionist, he had fled to America, where he had established himself successfully as an American citizen. Distressed by the destruction in Hamburg, imbued with democratic understanding and faith, he had returned to Germany and resumed his former citizenship to devote his life and energy to the reconstruction of democracy in Germany.

It is difficult for those of us who worked so closely with the bizonal administration to judge fully its performance in relation to democratic development of government. It did develop into a fairly efficient administration which welded the bizonal area into an economic whole, and without its machinery, I doubt if currency reform, wage and price controls, allocation procedures, and other major fiscal and economic programs could have been accomplished successfully.

Even more important, it provided an arena in which political parties could express their views and thus develop valuable experience for future government. These political battles were real and continuous, although legislation usually represented a compromise of views which both major parties could support.

When the Parliamentary Council convened to draft a provisional constitution for all western Germany some of the members of the bizonal administration saw the end of their activities in sight. As the drafting progressed, these men became more and more political-minded and less willing to act promptly in those legislative measures which were necessary to a disrupted economy but which might not prove popular with the voters. This was a natural reaction but it resulted in the early part of 1949 in measures which, while popular, were inflationary in effect. They were adopted in the almost certain knowledge that they would receive the disapproval of Military Government. Appropriation bills were seldom accompanied by revenue bills. However, in spite of this tendency in the latter stages of its existence, there is no question that the bizonal administration made possible major financial and economic progress in the bizonal area and at the same time created effective machinery of government and restored the art of politics to a wide area of Germany.

CHAPTER 10

Financial and Economic
Reconstruction before
Currency Reform

MOST of us take for granted the everyday results of a modern complex industrial economy without thinking of the elaborate financial and business structure which makes it possible. We go to our place of work on public transport, receive our earnings in the form of a check which is deposited to our account in a local bank, order from neighboring stores, or perhaps by money order from the nearest post office. We expect public utilities and services to be available and if gas or electricity fail we resort to the telephone to summon aid. We give little thought to the banking structure or to the procedures through which raw materials are procured, processed into finished materials, manufactured into consumer goods, and then placed in the distribution stream to be available to our easy access as consumer goods. When such a system collapses it breaks into so many pieces that it seems almost impossible to find the right piece with which to start to put it together again.

Prewar Germany had developed a complex, industrialized economy which provided a high standard of living for the German people. Always closely controlled either through industrial cartels directed by a few financial institutions or in the war years by government, it had collapsed almost completely when the controls were broken by defeat. Transportation and communications were disrupted, factories were closed, credit institutions had ceased to function, economic life had apparently come to an end on May 7, 1945, when Germany surrendered.

In this chaotic condition it was perhaps natural that our first efforts were directed to the rehabilitation of communications and transport facilities. Their difficulties were tangible and physical and it was obvious that their restoration was essential to any kind of economic life.

The German communications system was government-owned and -operated. Quickly, local offices of the Reichspost, later to be called the Deutsche Post, were reopened. By August 1945 post offices were receiving and delivering mail locally and conducting the financial transactions necessary to the postal savings and checking accounts. Approximately 40,000 telephones had been released for local use. By the fall of 1945 state administrations had been given limited jurisdiction over the communications system in each state. With the formation of the Laenderrat, it was possible to establish a unified control of communications throughout the United States Zone early in 1946. By that time telephone service was available to 115,000 subscribers and calls exceeded 900,000 monthly.

Mail service, restored throughout the United States Zone, was handling 70,000,000 pieces of letter mail and 668,000 parcel-post packages monthly. In October 1945 agreement[1] was reached in the Allied Control Authority for interzonal exchange of mail, and in February 1946 for interzonal telephone and telegraph services. In April 1946 international mail[2] limited to business letters up to 20 grams was restored except to Japan and Spain. In June 1946 one-way international parcel post into Germany was reinstated and 95,000 relief parcels arrived from the United States in the first shipment. By the end of 1946 there were 440,000 telephones available in the United States Zone and long-distance telephone calls exceeded 6,000,000 monthly.

In March 1947 as a result of bizonal fusion the communications systems of the United States and United Kingdom zones were merged into a single system. Also, in the spring of 1947, international telephone and telegraph services were resumed and the financial services of the postal system were extended throughout the three western zones. In May 1947 in the bizonal area more than 600,000 telephones were in service, handling almost 11,000,000 calls monthly, and monthly telegrams in the area exceeded 1,500,000. A million and a half relief parcels were received from the United States and distributed through the postal system in that month. It was apparent that communications in the bizonal area were normal and capable of sustaining their part in economic life. In fact by the end of 1947 the mail load in the United States Zone exceeded the prewar load, and telephone and telegraph traffic was more than twice the prewar volume. Service in the bizonal area had reached almost 1,500,000 telephones with a monthly volume of 150,000,000 calls, quite a growth from the less than 100,000 available for German use in July 1945. This resulted in part from inflation. Huge quantities of money were in circulation; there was a shortage of goods to purchase with this money while communications services under controlled rates were available and, in terms of inflated currency, cheap. Families had been separated by war and the desire to keep in touch with each other was strong. When money in circulation was reduced through currency reform, and the cost of communication services became relatively high, their use decreased substantially.

In the international field of communications, only a few restrictions remained, and these were gradually removed.

The operations of the Deutsche Post were, except for the few early months after occupation, conducted at a profit until the currency reform of June 1948. Then the shortage of money which reduced traffic volume caused some apprehension among Deutsche Post officials. This proved only a temporary decline, for the telephone and telegraph users returned in part to mail, and the Deutsche Post was soon in good financial shape. Furthermore, by April 1949 its international communications services had earned the bizonal economy $15,000,000 in import credits.

It is a simple story, this redevelopment of the communications network in Germany. However, assistance provided by the loan of Army equipment, the tireless work of our own personnel in encouraging German leadership, and the difficult international negotiations which made it possible are less simple to describe. General Frank Mead, P. J. Schardt, vice-president of the Southern Railway System, and E. H. Merrill were among the many Americans who worked assiduously to accomplish our purpose—the earliest possible restoration of an adequate communications system under German administration. Their fulfillment of this objective was one of the principal contributions toward economic recovery.

Hand in hand with the restoration of the communications system went the restoration of transport facilities. Perhaps in no other field was the breakdown so disastrous to the German economy. The north German ports—Hamburg, Emden, and Bremen (the latter including Bremerhaven and three or four minor Weser River ports)—had been bombed repeatedly. Harbors were filled with sunken craft; the Rhine network was closed to navigation because of destroyed bridges, locks, and craft sunk in the navigable channels. Railway marshaling yards were badly damaged and 885 railway bridges had been destroyed. In the United States Zone, for example, a survey found 393 serviceable barges, 577 afloat but unserviceable, and 754 sunk. A survey of railway equipment in the United States Zone showed 2632 serviceable locomotives and 108,921 serviceable railroad cars, whereas there were 5588 locomotives and 41,398 cars so badly damaged as to be unusable without extensive repairs. Of the main-line railway trackage in our zone, 21.4 per cent was damaged. Conditions were comparable in the other zones.

Immediate steps were taken to restore local and divisional railway operating offices. In the fall of 1945 these offices were placed under the state administration and early in 1946 the Laenderrat was given general supervision in order that there might be a co-ordinated system in the United States Zone. In January 1947, with bizonal fusion, the rail lines of the United States and United Kingdom zones were merged into a common system. Special attention was given to the repair problem, which was hampered by acute shortages of materials and inadequate shop facilities, and to the improvement of operating efficiency.

By the end of 1945 practically all main-line trackage was restored to usage, although the volume of traffic which could be handled was substantially reduced by the temporary one-way bridges which had been provided to replace those destroyed. The availability of rolling stock had been increased by the transfer of some 25,000 American-owned railway cars brought into Germany by the U. S. Army.

Strenuous efforts were made to improve port and water transport facilities. By July 1945 the Rhine was open to limited navigation throughout the United States Zone; by April 1946, it was open throughout its entire length. Emergency repairs to tugs and barges had restored a usable fleet. Great strides had been made in reopening the ports as, for example, in Bremen, which by the end of the year was handling 10,000 tons of cargo per day.

Highway transport was given added impetus in the spring of 1946 through the sale of 12,500 U. S. Army trucks to the German economy on a deferred-charge basis. Destroyed highway bridges had been largely replaced by that time, and emergency repairs had been made to arterial highways rendered impassable by bombing and other war damage.

In spite of all efforts, only 35 per cent of locomotives, 43 per cent of passenger cars, and 58 per cent of freight cars were capable of even limited service at that time and neither the limited freight services necessary to a stricken industry and to relief efforts nor the more substantial passenger demands were being met. Only by use of waterborne transport, which in the fall of 1946 reached almost 600,000 tons monthly, was the distribution of essential food and coal possible. That fall the collection of harvests, which were threatened with spoilage in the fields, required thirty of our Army truck companies to assist in moving grain and potatoes from farm to warehouse.

The winter of 1946–47 heavily taxed our transport facilities. It was the most severe winter Germany had experienced in more than fifty years. Waterways (including the Rhine, the Elbe, the Weser, and the Danube) were frozen by December, adding another burden to the crippled railway system. Many of the poorly maintained locomotives froze on tracks or in open and unheated roundhouses, and frequently two locomotives were required to do the work done in normal weather by one. To avoid general calamity and unbearable suffering, freight traffic had to be restricted to the movement of food, fuel, military supplies, and international transit shipments. It was not until April that relief from subfreezing temperatures came and waterborne traffic was resumed.

With the advent of spring, conditions began to improve but adverse weather had not ended. The severe winter of 1946–47 was followed by one of the driest summers in Germany's history, resulting in low water levels which in the early fall stopped practically all water traffic and greatly curtailed the production of hydroelectric power, on which not only industry but in some regions railways depended for efficient operation.

In 1947 our export proceeds permitted us to contract for rolling-stock repairs in Czechoslovakia and in Belgium; German repair shops increased their output and new trucks in substantial numbers were beginning to be produced for use on the German highways. Early in 1948 we were sufficiently satisfied with the repair program to authorize the use of steel for new rolling stock to be manufactured in Germany and, with the promise of ECA aid, sufficiently well off financially to order additional new cars from Austria, Belgium, Czechoslovakia, Italy, and one or two other countries.

When currency reform was effected on June 20, 1948, our transportation system was for the first time meeting all essential needs. The German seaports had proved their ability to handle 2,500,000 tons of traffic per month, and arrangements had been made to utilize the Low Country ports and for exchange with other countries of Rhine shipping services to and from these ports. Waterways in the bizonal area, with a rehabilitated fleet of 721 tugs and 4145 serviceable barges with an aggregate capacity of 2,580,000 tons, were able in June 1948 to carry 4,724,300 tons of freight. Coastal vessels having a total capacity of nearly 200,000 gross registered tons were in operation. The 6000 serviceable German locomotives and the 210,000 serviceable German railway cars in the bizonal area of occupation in July 1945 had increased to 7189 locomotives and 233,730 cars in June 1948, and were further increased to 8193 locomotives and 247,854 cars by the end of 1948. Moreover, turn-around time of freight cars had been reduced from more than ten days in 1945 to 6.2 days in June and to 5.1 days in November 1946 through improved operating efficiency. Highway trucks, although old, were adequate in number and German manufacture was providing an average of over 3000 trucks each month for replacement.

It was apparent, therefore, that the German transportation system, while not fully back to normal, was prepared to meet the needs of the German economy and that another major contribution to economic recovery had been made.

An unsettled question still disturbing the German railway system concerns the exchange of cars with Germany's neighbors. There has always been an exchange of railway cars between European nations, and without it, transportation across the many European frontiers would be retarded. This was a co-operative service until the Germans overran most of Europe, when it came under their control. At

General Clay speaks to Jewish leaders and Bavarian officials at the consecration of a synagogue.

The famous Pariser Platz—after the Battle for Berlin. To the left, the Brandenburger Tor. On the right, ruins of the old French Embassy.

Files containing records of former German citizens living in Greece, Poland, and Russia.

Potsdam it was agreed that Germany's external assets should become the property of the countries which had participated in the war against Hitler. Thus France had a legal basis for claiming German railway cars in France as a German external asset. It was my view that the exchange of cars was normal and that cars outside of Germany were not to be considered as external assets under this agreement. France insisted on the right to retain these cars and to have all of the French cars in Germany returned with a rental payment for their use during the occupation. German transportation did not suffice to meet the most urgent needs. It had been bolstered by the transfer of our own railway cars, and the return of the French cars without receiving an equal number of German cars meant a further increase in the cost to the American taxpayer for the support of Germany.

A conference in Paris on March 18, 1948, resulted in an agreement to a one-for-one exchange which would return all French cars in Germany and still leave a substantial number of German cars in France, since there were more of the latter than the former. At the time this conference was held, it was anticipated that the French Government might agree to return the remaining cars if a lesser number of new cars were made available to France under the European Recovery Program. This question had to be left open as ERP had not yet become effective. The conference had resulted in better understanding of this problem with French representatives. However, when the recovery program did become effective, its funds were allocated to the participating countries on planned programs, and Germany would have had to finance the railway cars to be sent to France from its allocation. Again the United States would in effect have been paying the bill for this transfer of cars. The question remained open when I left Germany.

Prior to currency reform, the railway system had more than balanced its expenditures with receipts, largely owing to an abnormally heavy short-haul passenger traffic. With currency reform, this traffic dropped to less than 40 per cent of former volume, and the railway system began accumulating a steadily rising deficit. This was not unexpected, as currency reform always results immediately in throwing people out of work, which accounts for unwillingness of political leaders to take such an action. Drastic steps were taken to economize, including a reduction of 45,000 employees, and it is hoped

that they will lead to a balanced budget and will justify the investment of additional funds in the long-range improvements which are
essential if transport is to continue to meet traffic demands. Nevertheless, the early work of General John Adams Appleton, now vice-
president of the Pennsylvania Railway, and Colonels John B.
Hughes, James B. Edmunds, and Hans W. Holmer, together with
the efforts of Sir Robert Inglis (an able and experienced British
railway executive who headed our joint transport staff) and General
Gross, was reflected in the effective German administration which
eliminated transportation as the bottleneck to recovery which it
represented in 1945, 1946, and 1947.

While Germany was prohibited from having its own civil aviation,[3]
fifteen international airlines were delivering passengers and air
cargo to and from Germany by 1949, and in addition several companies were meeting Germany's internal needs through the operation
of feeder services to the international terminals. International rail
and highway traffic, including transit traffic, was likewise meeting
all requirements. Germany was no longer isolated except for the
internal blockade forced by Soviet intransigence.

Meanwhile, slow but steady progress was being made in restoring
order to economic life. Price controls, which in the war years covered
almost the full range of commodities, were continued and within a
few months local price control offices were functioning satisfactorily.
By the fall of 1945, economic offices were functioning within state
administrations and chambers of commerce with limited functions
were re-established at local levels.[4] Strict rationing controls were
also in effect, though the ration coupon for commodities other than
food was little more than a hunting license.

Here and there factories fortunate enough to have raw materials
and coal on hand were returning to limited production and by
special efforts some manufacture of such essentials as fertilizer,
pharmaceuticals, and soap had been placed under way. It was already apparent that there were two major bottlenecks—lack of power
and lack of raw materials.

The first of these could be solved within Germany but an increase
in power was possible only through an increase in the production of
coal. Even in 1945 special provision[5] had been made for food for
the miner but with the food shortage which developed in early
1946 production of hard coal, which had reached about 180,000

tons a day, fell to less than 160,000 tons. During the remainder of 1946, in spite of minor improvements in the ration and substantial increase in the labor force, production climbed very slowly and by the end of the year was still under 200,000 tons per day.

Moreover, we were obligated to export a substantial proportion of this tonnage and the neighboring countries, all short of coal and importing at high cost from the United States, were insisting on an increase in German exports. Of course any increase would deprive the German economy of the ability to meet many of its chief needs and would retard any lasting increase in coal production. Special incentives might work temporarily but any sustained increase depended on a general revival of the supporting economy. Transportation, mine equipment, and mine supplies were as essential to coal-mining production as the coal mines, and the workers in the supporting economy could not be expected to produce as effectively as the better-fed and better-clothed coal miners.

Nevertheless, when the bizonal fusion took place in January 1947 we had no choice but to use temporary incentive schemes. They were based on a system of points earned by the worker who was assiduous in attendance at work and by mines which attended specified production targets. They led to increased output which invariably fell off when the incentive was earned until new incentives were provided.

In the Paris conference of the Council of Foreign Ministers in the spring and early summer of 1946, French, British, and American experts met at Mr. Bevin's specific request to consider ways and means to increase Ruhr coal production and also to discuss an increase in the allocation for export. While the experts agreed that increased production was essential to European recovery and understood the acute need of France and other western European countries for additional coal, they did not agree that it was possible for this coal to be made available in the immediate future. At this time the output of coal in England was far below normal and western Europe was importing coal from the United States at a very high transportation cost.

Realizing that this was not normal and fully conscious of the importance of making Ruhr coal available to Europe, General Draper, who represented us at this conference, pointed out our conviction that immediate export of more coal from the Ruhr would mean less coal for export in the long run. It was impossible to maintain a separate coal economy, although there was some advocacy of such a program. Mining depends not only on the economic well-being of the miner but also on a steady flow of supplies and transportation facilities, neither of which could be expected to improve much more rapidly than the general economy. If additional coal was exported, reducing the supply already inadequate for minimum internal needs, there could result only further debilitation of the general economy which would drag the coal output down with it. Subsequent events proved our viewpoint to be correct. Special and costly incentive schemes brought spurts of increased production. A sustained increase did not occur until the general economy had improved materially.

It was difficult to resist the French appeal, which had strong support in France, or to convince the French of the merits of our argument. In fact our stand was interpreted deliberately as evidence of unwillingness on the part of the United States Military Government to co-operate with and help the countries that had suffered at Germany's hands, whereas our position was taken in the sincere belief that it was the only sound way to really provide an increased supply for all Europe.

A year later, in March 1947, the question was again discussed during the Moscow conference between the three countries. General Robertson, Monsieur Alphand, and I, after much debate, did agree on a sliding scale for coal exports. Production in the Ruhr had increased substantially and the steps we had taken led us to expect further increases. This sliding scale[6] started at 18 per cent and rose to 25 per cent of output as production increased. These quotas were reported to the European Coal Organization, which was responsible for allocating German coal exports among the claiming nations.

The French representatives were interested in an arrangement which would exclude production in the Saar from the German export quotas. Since some of the Saar production flowed normally into the United States Zone, there was also involved a replacement with coal from the Ruhr, which would result in loss of foreign exchange to the bizonal area. In September 1947 we reached an agreement[7] with the French and the British which provided for the gradual replacement of Saar coal in the German economy with Ruhr coal, although this did require a corresponding reduction in the quantities available for export from the Ruhr. This was an amendment to the Moscow agreement which the foreign ministers had signed. It safeguarded, too, the interests of Germany's neighbors in obtaining coke. While it did not fully meet the French desires, their representatives were appreciative of our efforts and thus the understanding marked a definite improvement in the relations among the three Western Powers.

As a result of the incentive programs production climbed throughout 1947 and reached a peak of approximately 280,000 tons per day in the late fall when an incentive package of Army K and C rations and surplus clothing were particularly appealing. But with incentive earned, it quickly dropped to less than 260,000 tons per day, again proving that the incentive measures offered only a temporary solution.

During this period much progress was made in rehabilitating equipment, improving transport facilities, and bettering underground working conditions. Harry Collins, an experienced British mining expert, and in turn Max Forester, Robert Estill, and later William German, all experienced executives from the coal industry in the United States, worked hard to develop a sound German organization, perhaps in some measure because of my own strong belief that German workmen would mine more coal under German management. Finally, in December 1947, an organization[8] was established under Director Heinrich Kost to have full operating responsibility for the coal industry.

Henceforth progress, if not sensational, was steady. When currency reform was effected, production had reached over 280,000 tons a day and at this rate was keeping up with the increase in industrial output. Food was no longer in short supply and the incentive schemes were discontinued in favor of a more substantial ration for the coal workers.

Following currency reform, coal production increased steadily to production in March 1949 of almost 330,000 tons a day, approximately 86 per cent of the 1936 daily average. In view of the very bad housing conditions in the Ruhr and the still incomplete rehabilitation program for the mines, this was really a remarkable achievement. Coal ceased to be a bottleneck and the shortage was now in electric generating capacity. A number of problems in the coal industry remain to be solved. Prices are not reconciled with costs, marginal mines are maintained by government subsidies; and capital investment is badly needed for new machinery and new underground developments. The seizure of the coal mines by British Military Government which is being followed by their reorganization[9] under Law No. 75 makes it difficult to secure investment capital. These problems, however, are recognized and under active study both by the coal industry management and by the bizonal German organization. They must be solved before the German economic structure can be considered sound.

The next major bottleneck, shortage of raw materials, was the most difficult to overcome. I recognized early in 1945 that no real export program was possible unless we could obtain raw materials unavailable in Germany. We had no foreign exchange with which to buy them so we could obtain them only in exchange for German production. When in 1945 I asked General Draper to give prime attention to building up exports, I told him that all sales would have to be in dollars and that purchases must be restricted to essential raw materials which after manufacture into finished products in Germany would bring many times their cost when exported. This policy, which continued in the United States Zone, was accepted by the British for the bizonal area when we merged and remained in effect until 1948. It was admittedly an effort to pull the German economy up by its own bootstraps. I can well remember General Draper saying in late 1945 and early 1946, "It cannot be done; we must have a billion dollars to finance essential imports other than food if we are to succeed." To this my reply was that there was no such money available and that we could and must build up our own capital until it sufficed to start a real flow of raw materials. Actually, until funds became available under the European Recovery Program in the fall of 1948, the only appropriations we received were those for the prevention of disease and unrest (food, medicine, and petroleum products).

Our export policy was not popular in Europe. The European countries did not want to sell to Germany products which could be sold elsewhere for dollars and they did not want to pay in dollars for German products. To have paid the Dutch and Belgian governments in dollars for using the Low Country ports would have taken these dollars from the jealously guarded export proceeds, and would have meant less money for raw materials. Italy wanted to sell us fruit in exchange for products which had dollar value; the Dutch Government in 1947 resorted to every possible means to force us to purchase surplus vegetables. These were examples of the pressures we had to resist from without as well as within, for German officials would have approved these purchases. Food was badly needed at the time. Fruit and vegetables would have added desirable variety if we could have afforded it, but they represented no measurable increase in the food supply, whereas the several million dollars they would have cost brought in raw materials to keep factories in production for essential needs in Germany or for export. We could buy raw materials only for dollars. Thus, Sweden would sell to Germany Swedish products under trade agreements which accepted German products, and while both were evaluated in dollars, it was very nearly barter trading. Swedish iron ore, on the other hand, was a separate matter and could be purchased only in dollars. In 1948, as our export proceeds began to mount, we became less rigid in our trade policy and accepted fruit, vegetables, and other items which from 1945 to 1948 were luxuries Germany could not afford.

Another problem which made foreign trade difficult arose from the fact that the internal price structure no longer bore any resemblance to the pattern of the international market. It would have been most upsetting to an already disorganized economy to attempt quickly to bring German prices into line with world prices, so it was necessary to adopt artificial methods of pricing export in terms of dollars and imports in terms of Reichsmarks. An artificial exchange rate of ten cents to the mark, established initially for occupation troops, was quite inadequate for export pricing purposes. Military Government could not let German products be sold below world market prices without arousing justified resentment; moreover, it also wanted to obtain maximum return for German products in foreign exchange. For example, high-grade ceramics, which sold internally for RM 1000 or $100, were actually worth $500, so a "conversion factor" of fifty cents to the mark was established for such exports. On the other hand, lumber was expensive in Germany, and the conversion factor for export was therefore only about fifteen cents. Imported raw materials were sold in Reichsmarks in Germany at controlled legal prices, which meant that a German manufacturer who was allocated such materials got very high value for his mark. In general, exports earned premiums in terms of marks and imports were subsidized.

We were also under considerable pressure to release for investment and procurement purposes the funds held in Germany by foreign interests. Since the use of these funds would have resulted in a substantial increase in foreign investment or in removing from the market products which could be sold for foreign exchange, we continued to block these accounts except as they were used to rehabilitate plants and equipment. Late in 1948, after currency reform, General Robertson and I believed it timely to free these funds, which were particularly needed for capital investment, and jointly recommended their release to our governments.[10]

Early in 1945 I determined to require that the marks received from imports procured with United States appropriated funds be paid into a special account. These funds were used to pay the internal costs of all exports so that the full foreign exchange would accrue to Military Government for use in Germany. While these funds belonged to Germany, since our own expenditures were considered as an obligation to be repaid by a future German government, the surplus which accrued from the excess of imports over exports could be used only with the approval of Military Government. Normally approval was given only for their use as capital investment. While we did not think of the term "counterpart funds," as they were to be called under the European Recovery Program, we had started in 1945 to require the establishment of similar funds to be used in promoting sound economic recovery.

Economic order had been restored by the end of 1945 and, in spite of severe shortages in every field, business life was being conducted through normal channels. The establishment of German state governments had made possible the functioning of price control and allocation offices as a part of these governments and early in 1946 the Laenderrat assumed the responsibility for the co-ordination of these state agencies for the United States Zone. Even with the return of order, the economic picture in our zone at the end of the year was certainly not bright. Export proceeds barely exceeded $3,000,000 and production was estimated at 22 per cent of the 1936 figure. It was apparent that our zone could improve economically only if it received additional coal and steel from the Ruhr. Within the

British Zone recovery lagged somewhat behind, because its problems were more complex. Moreover, its highly industrialized areas contained a concentration of population which could not be supported by the agricultural capacity of the zone and the British Government was having great difficulty in obtaining food to bring into Germany and in making dollars available for payment. Separated, neither zone appeared capable of self-sufficiency; combined, their chance was greater. These conditions prompted me, in the spring of 1946, to recommend the economic merger of the two zones which subsequently took place.

Under this merger the Export-Import agencies[11] of Military Government were combined into a Joint Export-Import Agency with branches in each state. It was located initially in Minden, where the German economic administration had been established in the fall of 1946. But the picture at the end of 1946 was still far from bright. Production in the United States Zone had increased from the 22 per cent of the 1936 output at the end of 1945 to 43 per cent. Export proceeds from the United States Zone were approximately $21,000,000 and from the British Zone $139,000,000, most of the latter coming from the sale of coal badly needed in the German economy. Our problem continued to be an inadequate flow of raw materials. In the fall of 1946 the United States Commodity Corporation sold to Military Government on credit cotton valued at $33,000,000. This was a high price, as were the interest and service rates, and the cotton proved to be of low quality. To obtain this credit, a priority claim had to be established on all exports. Even so, the arrival of this cotton, which made possible the revival of the textile industry, was a psychological help to all industry. In December 1946, when the bizonal fusion agreement was completed, we had for the first time some capital, of which approximately $90,000,000 was paid in, and this to us promised recovery. Except in the severe winter of 1946–47, which caused a drop in productive output, recovery has since been continuous.

Meanwhile our first joint step toward facilitating foreign trade was to reduce existing restrictions so that German firms could contract directly with their foreign customers subject to final approval of contracts by the Joint Export-Import Agency.[12] Later, as exchange rates were fixed for the mark in various industrial categories, contracts no longer required approval, although copies had to be filed with the Joint Export-Import Agency. Imports remained under the jurisdiction of central procurement. Our exports continued to increase and by the end of 1947 the bizonal area had concluded trade agreements with seventeen nations. As an incentive to export production, management was permitted to receive in foreign exchange 5 per cent of its export proceeds, which it could use for plant improvement purchases, and labor was likewise allowed 5 per cent for the import of consumer goods and foodstuffs.

In 1947 our export sales increased to $22,000,000 as compared with $160,000,000 in 1946; imports other than food were valued at $102,400,000 as compared with $2,772,000 for the United States Zone in 1946.

During the year further steps were taken to increase the effectiveness of German economic administration through the establishment of the German Economic Council.[13] The first German Administrator for Economics had been young and able Dr. Rudolf Mueller, who had set up the German organization. While he believed that the control powers to be exercised by government should be held to a minimum, there were many controls and almost all commodities were both rationed and price-fixed when he assumed office. When we established the Executive Committee to represent the several states in our second phase of organization, the Social Democratic party, which controlled a larger number of the states, obtained a majority in the Committee. Dr. Mueller was replaced by a member of that party, Dr. Viktor Agartz, who believed in a planned and controlled economy.

When General Robertson and I were arranging this step we differed on the extent to which the right to control the economy should be placed in German hands. In Moscow Mr. Bevin had consulted with Secretary Marshall after my return to Germany in an attempt to persuade the latter to accept the British viewpoint. I must admit that I felt this rather unfair. Marshall refused to accept the British proposal without consulting me and offered to cable me to return to Moscow. It was late in the conference so Bevin agreed to let the matter be returned to Germany for decision between military governments. It was at this time that Robertson and I decided we would take no measures prejudicial to the kind of economy the German people might wish to establish in the future and that they should have their choice between free enterprise and socialism.

Subsequently, in our final reorganization of the bizonal administration, the German directors of administrative agencies became responsible to the Economic Council, in which the Christian Democratic Union obtained a majority. Dr. Agartz was then replaced by Dr. Ludwig Erhard, although as a result the Social Democratic party refused to participate further in the executive work of the administration. Thus the political struggle for control of the economic machine between the CDU, which while not supporting full free enterprise wants only limited controls, and the SPD, which desires a fully controlled economy, broke into the open. It continues to be the main issue in German political life. The selection of Dr. Erhard to head the Economic Administration was to be of special significance after currency reform.

A major contribution to German economy was arranged late in 1947. Several hundred thousand tons of Army and Air Force surplus remained in Germany after other countries had bought all they wanted. These materials, increased by 40,000 tons of used but serviceable clothing from the United States, were transferred to a German public corporation formed for the purpose. The terms of credit and sale price were identical to those given other European countries. These goods are still being sold in Germany.

Throughout the first two years of military government, I had been fortunate in having General Draper as my economic adviser. He had been assisted by such able men as Dr. James Boyd, now director of the Bureau of Mines, Laird Bell, a distinguished lawyer of Chicago; Governor Menc Stephen Szymczak of the Federal Reserve Board; and Arthur Barrows, formerly vice-president of Sears, Roebuck. Draper was more than an economics adviser. He and I had worked together for four years and I relied on his ability and judgment in all fields. His devotion to public service at much personal sacrifice will always represent to me the contribution of a great public-spirited citizen. It was a blow to lose him, even though he became Under Secretary of the Army. Similarly, I lost Barrows, who became Under Secretary of Air just as he was really getting the export program under way. However, Draper's assistant, who succeeded him, Lawrence Wilkinson, although younger and therefore less experienced, proved to be of outstanding ability. I learned to lean heavily on his capable shoulders and those of his deputy, Phillip Hawkins. We were also able to get W. John Logan, a New York bank executive with broad experience, to head the Joint Export-Import Agency.

Nineteen forty-eight started off with promise. Productive output increased steadily if slowly, exports rose, and raw materials arrived in satisfactory quantities. Public finances were in excellent shape, state budgets were in balance, and food supplies were sufficient to meet the ration regularly for the first time since the occupation began. Nevertheless, the situation was far from satisfactory. For three years we had maintained price and wage controls which were really effective only for food, fuel, and rent. Price controls on other commodities and consumer goods were meaningless. The manufacturer frequently could not produce the price-controlled consumer goods and replace the raw materials used in production at the fixed selling price. No one had confidence in the currency and manufacturer and merchant preferred inventories to cash as a protection against inflation and possibly against currency reform. Barter deals threatened normal business transactions and perhaps as many goods were moving in the black market as in the legitimate market. On the whole, however, conditions were favorable to a rapid improvement. Additional coal and power were available; so were labor and raw materials. The wheels of industry should have been turning rapidly but it was evident that they would not until currency was given real value so that the public would have confidence in it and return to normal business procedures.

We were in the position to handle currency reform efficiently, for we had developed a sound banking system. We had recognized from the early days of occupation that such a system was an essential part of a healthy financial structure and that it had to be effective for currency reform to succeed.

It had not taken a financial or an economic expert on May 7, 1945, to realize that the German financial and economic structure had collapsed. While under our initial directive, JCS/1067, we could take no remedial measures, since such a collapse was deemed necessary to bring home to the German people what had been inflicted upon them by Nazi leadership, the provisions of the Potsdam Protocol did permit something to be done.[14]

The German banking system was not functioning nor was there any intention to restore it as it had previously existed. Head offices of the Reichsbank and of the six major German banks, located in the

Scviet Sector of Berlin, were closed and in Soviet hands. Our policy did not visualize the re-establishment of either the Reichsbank or the six major commercial banks which had played such an important part in controlling German industry and in directing it to support aggressive war.

While we had kept the banks in the United States Zone open, they were operating as local banks. Our Law No. 52 had been necessarily broad in blocking the accounts of the Reich, the Nazi party and its affiliated organizations, leading Nazis, industrial enterprises deemed to have contributed to the war, and cartels.

Financial paralysis had resulted from the disruption of the banking system and, since we did not intend to permit the highly centralized control of the Reichsbank to return, we had to establish a decentralized system. Regardless of Nazi responsibility for the existing conditions, mass starvation was prevented only by American aid, which would be needed indefinitely unless some degree of German economic life could be restored.

There were approximately 1300 banks open in the American Zone and by the early part of 1946 deposits were greater than withdrawals, indicating a public confidence perhaps not warranted by the facts. The currency in circulation exceeded RM 73,500,000,000, many times prewar circulation, and the internal public debt of the German Government on which service had been stopped had reached almost RM 500,000,000,000, much of which was held by the banks.

Throughout 1945 and 1946, we depended upon the use of courier service between banks to permit exchange of funds. Later a former Reichsbank branch in each state was permitted to handle the exchange of bank accounts through the Giro system and this same system was adopted for exchanges between the three western zones. The postal savings and check systems of the Deutsche Post had been restored promptly.

These measures helped to improve conditions but they were no substitute for a sound banking system. When Lewis Douglas returned home I persuaded Joseph Dodge, president of the Detroit National Bank, to take his place. We had been associated in war production, where he did an outstanding job in charge of contract renegotiation for the War Department. I asked him to develop a sound, decentralized banking system which I hoped to have adopted for all Germany by the Allied Control Council.[15] In this we were not successful. While French representatives approved the system, they were unwilling to establish a principal German bank. British representatives did not approve of the system as they believed a strong central bank with branches throughout Germany essential to a sound financial structure.

In December 1946 United States Military Government, unwilling to wait for progress in quadripartite negotiations, moved separately to establish the system in the United States Zone through laws promulgated in the several states to be effective on January 1.[16] Under this system a central bank, somewhat comparable to our Federal Reserve District Bank, was established in each state under nine directors, each of whom were appointed by the state government and one each selected by commercial banks, savings institutions, co-operatives, trade unions, industry, and agriculture. The stock, subscribed initially by the state, was to be sold to member banks in proportion to their required reserves. The State Central Bank was to assume the functions previously performed by the Reichsbank and its branches and the assets and liabilities of the latter within the state were transferred to the new bank. At the same time the branches of the Big Six Banks were made local banks and required to take new names. The state banks were not commercial institutions in any sense but were to regulate the circulation of currency and the supply of credit, insure the solvency of credit institutions and keep available reserves against deposits in such institutions, execute cash transactions for the state and other corporations created by public law, and grant short-term credits to such public agencies in so far as these tasks did not fall to other institutions.

At least we now had a banking system at the state level. An advisory council was created in our zone as a co-ordinating body between the several state banks to recommend uniform discount and interest rates, minimum reserve requirements, and uniform methods for transfers and check transactions. The new system became effective in a surprisingly short time. Both the Soviet and French zones adopted systems modeled on the one in our zone, but the British Zone continued the Reichsbank on a zonal basis. As a part of the bizonal fusion arrangements of the fall of 1946, in September, a joint Anglo-American Finance Committee was established in Frankfurt to co-ordinate the financial and banking arrangements of the two zones. This arrangement still did not co-ordinate the banks of the four zones and did not suffice for the international banking operations, which were growing in volume.

Our export sales were in dollars and under our trade and payment agreements it was necessary to open dollar accounts in the national banks of the countries with which we had such agreements. Our account in the United States was handled by the Federal Reserve Bank of New York, which does not usually undertake normal commercial operations. The two military governments handled their accounts separately, though funds could be used only for common purposes. After the failure of the Moscow conference to make any progress toward quadripartite agreement, one of the steps which we took to strengthen the bipartite organization was to set up a Joint Foreign Exchange Agency on March 31, 1947.[17] This agency was to hold all international accounts for the bizonal area and be the fiscal agent for the Joint Export-Import Agency. As the export business expanded, it became impossible for the small bipartite agency of British and American personnel, assisted by German technicians, to cope with the expanding international accounts, which now included the issuance of letters of credit in mounting volume. To indicate this volume, at the time of its dissolution the Joint Foreign Exchange Agency had accounts in thirty-five foreign banks aggregating $157,914,941.26 and outstanding letters of credit totaling $106,102,-285.32.

It became increasingly clear that we could not place a new currency in circulation without a bank of issue which could also control credit throughout the bizonal area. British representatives had witnessed the effectiveness of the structure in our zone and were now prepared to adopt it and to join us in the setting up of a co-ordinating bank for both zones.

After the failure of the London meeting of the Council of Foreign Ministers in late 1947, Bidault had agreed to join in tripartite conference looking to tripartite government. At the first conference held in London in the spring of 1948 the French representatives accepted the invitation to join us in currency reform and in a common banking system without waiting for resolution of other principles of trizonal fusion still under discussion. So on February 15, 1948, we enacted a law[18] establishing in Frankfurt the Bank deutscher Laender, which was limited to the transaction of business with its member State Central Banks and control banks of other states and of foreign countries. It was made the exclusive bank of issue. It was responsible for the development of common policies respecting banking and the regulation of credit and including interest and discount rates and the credit operations of its member State Central Banks. It was also to fix minimum reserves and arrange for the settlement of balances resulting from transfers between the states through the member State Central Banks. It was authorized to deal in foreign exchange, accept deposits, rediscount bills of exchange, and grant loans against obligations of members, treasury bills, and other public securities. It was made the fiscal agent of the Bizonal Economic Administration and of the Joint Import-Export Agency. Its Board of Directors was composed of the president of its Board of Managers and the presidents of the member State Central Banks, the former being selected by the latter. In general, the relationship of this Board of Directors to the banking system was that of our Federal Reserve Board to our system.

Simultaneously with the establishment of the bank a tripartite supervisory body known as the Allied Bank Commission was created.[19] Thus we had achieved in the three western zones a sound banking system which was to prove its worth with currency reform. On August 1, 1948, the operation of foreign exchange accounts was transferred to the Bank deutscher Laender and the Joint Foreign Exchange Agency was abolished, thus placing another major operating responsibility in German hands under Allied supervision.

There remained a need for special provisions for long-term credits, particularly as there was a marginal risk in many such credits beyond the capacity of commercial banks to absorb and yet vitally essential to the rehabilitation of bomb-damaged and worn-out German industry. The Economic Council established for this purpose the Reconstruction Loan Corporation in October 1948.[20] Its function was to supply credit institutions with medium- and long-term credits for reconstruction and economic development whenever these institutions could not finance capital investments in other ways. It was authorized to use counterpart funds (arising from the proceeds of foreign goods supplied to the combined economic area either through appropriated or European Recovery Program funds), to borrow from the German Government, and to issue fixed-interest bearer bonds. Its directors include the chairman or deputy chairman of the Board of Managers appointed by government, a representative from each of the governmental departments of Finance, Economics, and Food, Agriculture and Forestry, three representatives of the states experienced in credit matters, one representative of the Bank deutscher Laender, one representative of the credit institutions and savings banks, one representative of the trade unions, and three persons selected for their special experience in industry, agriculture, and finance. The first loans of the Reconstruction Loan Corporation were made to finance the rehabilitation of coal mines and power stations. Subsequently, in March 1949, agricultural banks and a co-operative agricultural credit association were authorized to meet the special credit problems of agriculture, rounding out the banking and credit systems.

Thus the trizonal area has a decentralized but sound financial structure which has proved by test to provide adequate banking and credit facilities.

CHAPTER 11

Financial and Economic
Reconstruction after
Currency Reform

OUR work in restoring physical facilities and in financing a flow of raw materials made economic recovery possible but we could make little real progress as long as we were confronted with the inflationary effect of worthless currency which no longer had public confidence.

We hesitated to introduce a new currency in the bizonal area which would widen the split of Germany caused by Soviet sealing of the boundary between east and west Germany.

We had expected trouble in reaching agreement on the highly technical details of currency reform. But it was not the failure to agree on these details that prevented action by the four powers. As soon as we presented a proposal for currency reform in the Allied Control Council the Soviet representatives demanded that two sets of plates be made, one to be used for printing new currency at Leipzig in their zone. While they promised to put this printing in charge of a small Allied staff, there still remained their unquestioned intent to have custody of one set of plates. My French and British colleagues were willing to run the risk. Theirs was not the financial burden for the support of west Germany which we had assumed. Moreover, we had had enough of Soviet promise in the printing of Allied military currency. We had paid dearly for the set of plates we made available to the Soviet Government in this case. We did not intend to be placed in such a position again and our government was firm in this view. The currency-printing establishment in Berlin was in our sector. To show our good faith we suggested that it be turned into an enclave under the direct control of a quadripartite group. The Soviet representatives did not accept this proposal.

A further delay in currency reform would have halted progress in economic recovery. The money in circulation in Germany had increased from about 5,000,000,000 to RM 70,000,000,000, bank deposits from RM 30,000,000,000 to 150,000,000,000, and the debt of the Reich from RM 12,000,000,000 to 400,000,000,000 during the Nazi regime. War damage and other claims exceeded 300,000,-000,000 Reichsmarks. It was evident that a substantial inflation had occurred in Germany before its surrender. Perhaps in time of full production this would have been less serious but postsurrender Germany had lost at least a third of its industry and productive capacity through transfer of territory. What remained could produce only a fraction of its potential output because of shortages in fuel and raw material.

While it had not required an expert to diagnose the need, it did require experts to plan a currency reform which would leave the amount of money in circulation and the debt carried by the German people proportionate to their productive output. The goods produced in Germany had sold at prices that reflected the actual costs of production, and it was essential to fix a foreign exchange rate which would bear a realistic relation to world market prices.

My financial adviser, Mr. Dodge, had started the study of currency reform early in 1946, bringing to Germany to assist him two able economists, Dr. Raymond M. Goldsmith and Dr. Gerhardt Colm. This group spent ten weeks in consultation with British, French, and Russian technicians, with leading German financial experts, and with Austrian and Czechoslovakian experts who had prepared the currency reforms which were introduced in those countries. The report,[1] which was presented to me on May 20, 1946, contained the elements of the plan put into effect two years later. It described the need as urgent.

A copy of this report was sent to Washington for the approval of our government, where it received further study by experts from War, State, and Treasury Departments. They had some doubt about equalization measures contained in the plan but it was approved as submitted in August 1946. At the time I felt that this delay would retard our progress, although the months of futile effort spent in trying to obtain quadripartite agreement made it inconsequential.

The report recommended a new currency and the reduction of monetary claims and obligations in the ratio of one to ten, a more liberal ratio than actually developed. The existing Reich debt was to be canceled and replaced by a new and smaller debt issue assumed by the states and allocated to banks and other credit institutions to enable them to meet their obligations. In a currency reform, holders of currency and fixed-interest-rate securities suffer immediately, whereas landowners and those who hold equities in fixed assets suffer little by comparison unless measures are taken to equalize the burden. Our program contemplated mortgages on real estate, plant equipment, and excess inventories which could be paid off over a long period of time, the proceeds being used to retire certificates issued to those who had suffered unduly in the reform or in war losses. Our government did not like the similarity of this measure to a levy on capital, and it was concerned that war losses would thus be equalized in Germany when they had not been equalized in the liberated countries.

It is difficult to make decisions in far-off capitals affecting the daily life of the individual in an occupied country. It may be asked why an occupying power is concerned. If we believed in individual rights and human freedoms we had to govern Germany in the light of these beliefs. There was no other way to democracy. Currency reform affects the everyday life of the individual as no other measure. The lifetime savings of the little man disappear. This is hard for him to understand and if he sees around him those who appear to have gained rather than lost from a new currency he feels indeed that justice has miscarried. In any country and certainly within Germany with its trend toward socialism, a currency reform which failed to provide some degree of equalization was certain to be politically unpopular and to lessen German faith in free enterprise. It permitted black market operators who had invested their huge gains in real estate and plants to escape unscathed. Legitimate holdings of physical properties including hoarded inventories were not touched.

Although our government did (like the British and French governments) approve the proposed measures, it later directed me to turn over the responsibility for their enactment to the German Economic Council. However, in December 1948 I was required to withhold approval of the first measure adopted by the Council. This change of front on our part was displeasing to labor and to the leaders of the political parties, who regarded it as inconsistent with our assertions that the problem was their responsibility. Finally we were permitted to approve the measure, amended to permit the use of equalization tax revenue for relief purposes only. Further equalization measures became a responsibility of the new West German Government. Politically, it would have been desirable to settle this matter so that the new government would not start out having to face this highly controversial issue.

Our failure to secure a quadripartite currency reform became a subject of discussion between the representatives of the three Western Powers in London when the Council of Foreign Ministers adjourned in the late fall of 1947. Mr. Bevin and Secretary Marshall instructed General Robertson and me to make a last effort in the Allied Control Council to obtain quadripartite agreement, and, if this failed, to proceed in the bizonal area. Bidault at this time expressed French willingness to accept trizonal fusion and to proceed concurrently with the bizonal area in a common currency reform. Our new proposal in the Allied Control Council did not meet with direct Soviet refusal but with their usual delaying tactics. We were engaged in these negotiations without any real hope of success when the Control Council was broken up by the Soviet withdrawal.

Before I visited the United States in October 1947, I had discussed with Robertson the possibility that a new money might be introduced in the Soviet Zone at any time. Rumors that this new currency was being printed in Leipzig were frequent. Therefore I asked State and Treasury Department officials to approve the printing of new notes which could be placed in circulation in western Germany promptly if this possibility materialized. The full cooperation of the Treasury Department made it possible for us to have this currency printed and dispatched before the end of the year. We called it "Operation Bird Dog." Although the story did reach the newspapers in the United States and Germany, delivery and storage were conducted with sufficient secrecy so that the fact that it had actually been printed was not known in Germany. We were apprehensive that public knowledge of the availability of new money would increase the hoarding of goods and inventories.

After the breakup of the Allied Control Council in March 1948 we had no difficulty in reaching an immediate agreement with British representatives on the terms of a currency reform to be effective in the bizonal area on June 1. At this time representatives of the three Western Powers were conferring in London to determine the conditions of trizonal fusion and at this conference the French representatives stated that they were ready to join the bizonal area in currency reform without waiting for full agreement on the principles of trizonal fusion. This acceptance by France created additional difficulties which made it necessary to postpone the date of issue from June 1 to June 20 and almost made the issue on that date a bizonal reform only. The French representatives did not believe that our plan provided sufficient money for their zone, where the occupation costs were an exceptionally high percentage of the state budgets. They were insistent on a larger initial distribution and on the release later for investment purposes of a larger percentage of accounts blocked at time of issue. They required what we considered a very large quantity of the new money to meet their own needs, because a part of the pay of their troops was met in German currency. The amount of money to be placed in circulation and the blocking of accounts had already been discussed in detail with the leading German officials of the bizonal area. It became necessary to reopen these matters although the German experts were "in the cage," as we called their secret working place, perfecting last-minute details.

Concurrently we were discussing the tripartite application of a tax reform measure which we proposed for the bizonal area. Income and excise taxes had been raised deliberately to very high figures by the Allied Control Council to draw off excess funds in an effort to prevent runaway inflation and obviously would prove impossible to collect with the reduction in the circulation of money which would follow currency reform. The French representatives were opposed to tax reductions, which they believed would provide their zone with revenues inadequate to meet occupation costs.

We compromised by amending the plan to a degree that had an immediate inflationary effect. We thought we had cleared the last obstacle to agreement. However, on June 15, the French commander in chief, General Koenig, sent us word that we must either accept the French tax proposals or he could not join us in the issue of the new currency. When we received this message many of the trucks were already loaded and en route to the distribution centers. Further delay was impossible. Robertson and I told Koenig's representatives that we deeply regretted the French action but had no choice other than to proceed in the bizonal area. I reported my decision immediately to the Department of the Army in a teleconference in which it was approved, and during which I received word that General Noiret, the French deputy, wished to see General Robertson and me. We met at my house with our financial experts at 11 P.M. There we found that Noiret wished to negotiate but was without authority to make specific proposals.

The London agreements for tripartite fusion and international control of the Ruhr were under discussion in the French Parliament and the vote in the French Assembly was expected hourly. In our fantastic midnight negotiation Noiret would call Koenig, who was at his home in Baden, while others of his party were telephoning Paris to find out the decision of the Assembly. Finally, in the small hours of the morning, when we had made our last concession on the tax measure, we learned that the French Assembly had supported its government. Koenig accepted our final offer of compromise,[2] and we were able to proceed trizonally.

The new currency program was made public in four separate measures.[3] In the first law, provision was made for the deposit of old currency, the exchange by each person on a one-to-one basis of sixty Reichsmarks for new Deutschemarks and for a four-day moratorium on credit transactions. The second law established the Bank deutscher Laender as a bank of issue and of credit control and fixed the total limit of its right of issue at DM 10,000,000,000. The third law permitted the conversion of credit balances on a ten-to-one basis, half to be placed in a free account, and half to be placed in a blocked account. The fourth law released 20 per cent of the blocked account, authorized 10 per cent for investment in approved medium- and long-term securities and extinguished the remaining 70 per cent. The effect of the third and fourth laws was to make 6.5 Deutschemarks of new currency available for every 100 tax-clear Reichsmarks of old currency on deposit. The third law prohibited the conversion, but without prejudice to United Nations claims, of debts of the Reich, the Nazi organizations, the Reichsbank, and certain other war obligations. It permitted United Nations nationals to accept or to defer conversion without prejudice until there was a general claims settlement. It arranged for state obligations to be issued to the banks and credit institutions to replace the non-convertible securities which they held to the extent required to cover their liabilities. On August 10 the currency reform was followed by a tax reform which reduced the anti-inflation income tax and certain excise taxes, including those on tobacco and coffee (imitation coffee).[2]

The need for equalization measures, recognized in the Dodge-Colm-Goldsmith report, was met by empowering the German Bizonal Administration to work out such measures in the bizonal area. Our governments felt this was a responsibility which should be left to German hands.

The success of the issue of the new currency and the effectiveness of the reform were evidence of the careful, painstaking work of the Allied and German experts. When Dodge returned home, he was succeeded by Jack Bennett, now governor of the Bank of Ethiopia, then on loan to us from the Treasury Department. His leadership and ability were primarily responsible for the outstanding results of one of the major currency measures recorded in financial history. It was only one of the many contributions which he made to Military Government. His associate, Sir Eric Coates, received the personal appreciation of the British Foreign Office and assurances that he would be needed at home when his work in Germany was finished. Bennett returned home only to find that he was no longer needed in the Treasury Department. Public service in our country is not always recognized and appreciated.

The introduction of currency reform combined with the redevelopment of a sound banking system created a financial structure indispensable to economic recovery.

The effect on the German economy was electric although it was given too much credit for the recovery which followed. At the time it took place production, which was then 50 per cent of the 1936 output, had been increasing each month for more than a year. Plants previously closed for lack of raw materials and power were running again, coal production had reached 74 per cent of 1936 output, and the flow of raw materials in the three months preceding currency reform and the three months following in the amounts of $140,000,000 and $147,000,000 was greater than in any corresponding periods during the occupation. The psychological impact of the European Recovery Program was particularly felt in Germany not only because of its promise of aid but also because Germany was being given the opportunity to participate in an international endeavor. While no materials financed with funds from ECA had reached Germany at the time of currency reform or were to reach Germany for several months, the knowledge that such funds were available and that the materials would arrive gave confidence in the new currency. The inertia which retarded economic recovery had been overcome before ECA aid arrived.

General Marshall's Harvard speech in June 1947 aroused much interest in Germany and both speculation and hope that Germany would be included. When the congressional committee studying the program visited the country in the late summer of 1947, west Germany now felt certain of inclusion, and enthusiasm for the program was immediate and sincere. This was due not only to the promise of material aid but also, and I think even more so, to the implied association with other nations in a common cause. Communist efforts to develop labor opposition failed completely and trade unions were quick to endorse the purposes of the program. When it was learned that Germany would participate initially only through the military governors, there had been disappointment but this was overcome in part since German technicians were allowed to work directly with those of the other participating countries.

The discussions among the European nations which led to the establishment of the Organization for European Economic Cooperation were held in Paris in the spring of 1948. The tripartite conference which was going on concurrently in London had accepted the inclusion of the French Zone and of the bizonal area in the program, and the responsibility for urging the other participating nations to agree to their inclusion.[4] United States Military Government did not take part in these early discussions, as it was believed most desirable for this organization to be formed by the representatives of the European nations without American participation. Therefore British delegates represented the bizonal area in the negotiations leading to the preparation of the charter; General Robertson, carrying with him my power of attorney, signed for the bizonal area in Paris on April 16, 1948.

Thus, for the first time since surrender, western Germany was a participant in an international undertaking, even if it was represented by Military Government. This was the first concrete evidence of the frequently expressed desire of the Western Powers to welcome the return of a peace-loving democratic Germany to the comity of nations. After the charter was ratified our representatives began to participate in the activities of the organization. We set up offices in Paris for the bizonal delegation of American and British experts headed by an American chairman and assisted by German experts. Robert Trier, who had been with us in our Trade and Commerce Branch for many months but had left us to take a year's rest in Tahiti, returned to head the delegation. Later he was succeeded by Malcolm White.

General Robertson and I signed the bilateral Economic Co-operation Agreement, under which the bizonal area became eligible to receive aid, and Mr. Murphy signed it for the United States on July 14, 1948. Somehow it seemed out of place for this document to be signed by me for the bizonal area and by Murphy for the United States, as each of us would necessarily interpret its provisions as our government required. Both Robertson and I were disappointed because all funds made available thereunder were loans and included no grants such as were made available to other countries. Unlike other participating nations which made counterpart funds available to match grants, the bizonal area was required to place in special account to be used only as approved by ECA administrator Paul G. Hoffman the counterpart funds in marks which accrued within Germany from the sale of all products financed with European Recovery funds.

The German bizonal administration established a European Recovery Program group under the president of the Economic Council to prepare the program for the two zones and to co-ordinate the activities of the German departments involved. A corresponding Anglo-American group was also established in Frankfurt as a part of the Bipartite Control Office, with a joint secretariat responsible for the collection of information and statistics pertinent to the program.[5] Special arrangements were made for adequate publicity.

The major activity of the OEEC following the approval of its charter was the division of the first appropriation. Hoffman had determined that OEEC itself should divide this appropriation among the participating nations. In the first proposed division the bizonal area was tentatively allocated only $364,000,000—less than the allocation for countries with much smaller populations such as the Netherlands and Belgium. Neither Robertson nor I could accept this figure. We knew that German recovery lagged far behind western Europe and was holding the latter back. The understandable feelings of the participating nations toward Germany had blinded them to the importance of German recovery to the program as a whole. Our general request for funds had been presented to our Congress on the basis of an estimated allocation of $500,000,000 from European Recovery Program funds, and failure to secure an amount approaching this figure would mean not only a further delay in balancing the German economy but also an increased burden to the United States Government in supporting the deficit. We were criticized severely because our refusal to accept the proposed allocation prevented the unanimous agreement required for approval, and it was alleged that our action was contrary to Mr. Hoffman's views. In fact our stand had been taken with the knowledge and approval of our government, and if there were differences in viewpoint among our governmental departments, we in Germany knew nothing of them. If the proposed allocation had been accepted, the European Recovery Program would have hurt rather than helped German recovery. As I pointed out in a teleconference to the Department of the Army on August 30, paraphrased:

I doubt if you realize full seriousness. We are giving up 275 million dollars in coal revenue and under the proposed allocation, would receive less dollars than we now have. A failure in prompt German recovery will have far reaching effects on European recovery. We are again caught in the old squeeze play with representatives of the United Kingdom working against the bizonal area in OEEC. I know my action will bring much international criticism on me but to accept would be at the expense of German recovery and extension of German burden to American taxpayer.

While Mr. Hoffman and Mr. Harriman offered at one time to negotiate better terms for the bizonal area, I had refused their offer.

I believed we should fight our own battle in OEEC if our representation was to have further effectiveness. In subsequent negotiations ending on September 10, 1948, the allocation for the bizonal area was increased to $414,000,000 although this necessitated a granting of drawing rights in the amount of $10,200,000 to other participating nations.

Near the end of June 1948 Harriman and his deputy, William Foster, visited Germany in the company of Under Secretary Draper to discuss the role to be played in Germany by the ECA special representative. Harriman proposed that the special representative be accredited to the Anglo-American Bipartite Board and have the same relationship to it as the special representatives in other countries had with their governments. I felt this to be most unwise. In view of our financial support, the bizonal fusion agreement gave us a predominant voice in foreign trade and exchange. Under these circumstances it did not seem necessary for a special representative of ECA to work directly with the British representatives in Germany. If he worked with the Americans alone, any differences could be reconciled by our government in Washington and placed into effect in Germany through the use of our dominant voice if necessary. Harriman, in a discussion which lasted late into the night, did not change his position. The next day he graciously agreed with me and later became the special representative of ECA to the bizonal area with a deputy residing in Germany who would work with the American staff. I am not sure that I persuaded him with logic; I think rather he accepted my view because of our mutual support over many months of a firm policy to check Communist expansion and penetration. Later the undesirability of separate representation in Germany for which I had stood was recognized by our government if not by Mr. Harriman. The responsibility was placed in the hands of my successor, Mr. McCloy. Harriman's deputy, Norman H. Collisson, for whose ability I had real respect, arrived in Germany in September 1948.

A second and important step taken in OEEC was the Intra-European Payments Agreement, which was signed by the participating nations on October 16, 1948.[6] While trade and payments agreements were to be executed bilaterally among the nations participating in the recovery program, the Bank for International Settlements in Switzerland became the clearinghouse through which payments were made, thus making it possible for credits and debits among countries to be offset against each other.

The program set up for spending Recovery Program funds envisaged reimbursement of expenditures by the participating nations on the presentation of proper vouchers. This was not much help to the bizonal area, which had neither dollars nor credit with which to finance its dollar procurement. So ECA representatives, accompanied by Assistant Secretary of the Army Tracy S. Voorhees, visited us in Frankfurt in the fáll of 1948 to develop procedures applicable to our special conditions. It was agreed that ECA would place funds to our account in the New York banks against approved programs and that ECA approval of contracts included in these programs would provide authorization for the issuance of letters of credit against these accounts. All this took time and delayed the flow of ECA-financed imports into Germany. This was not undesirable as a counter to the inflationary trend which followed currency reform. The real flow of ECA goods began in December 1948.

As stated previously, the immediate effect of currency reform was startling. As soon as it came into effect Director of Economics Erhard had, I think wisely, removed price and rationing controls except on food, fuel, steel, rent, essential clothing, and a few other very scarce items. Immediately goods and raw materials came out of hiding. Shopwindows and shelves filled up with goods and production lines increased overnight as hoarded raw materials were rushed to process. Of course an immediate buying spree resulted. A consumer-starved population rushed to spend its new marks. Except in the controlled fields, prices climbed rapidly. The value of the new mark in the Swiss free market fell off sharply, state budgets started to show large deficits, labor began to demand increased wages or preferably the re-establishment of price and rationing controls. My own staff became apprehensive of runaway inflation and some of its members recommended drastic measures to include a substantial increase in a rediscount rate already at 5 per cent. I could not believe that the inflation would become serious. There was insufficient money in circulation, raw materials were arriving regularly, production was increasing rapidly, and I was certain that with the exhaustion of the initial issue of currency the buying spree would stop.

This proved correct and before the end of 1948 lack of money had stopped it, consumer goods had caught up with demand or at least with the consumer's purchasing power, and prices began to fall substantially. State budgets were balanced and the value of the mark in the Swiss market rose sharply but the shortage of money did check the building program, and for the first time in months an unemployment problem developed. It was evident that the Reconstruction Loan Corporation and other financial agencies had to push a long-term investment program to provide capital repairs and new construction. Such a program, which is now under way, will be facilitated by new tax measures and also by the increase in savings which in 1949 were, for the first time since currency reform, exceeding withdrawals.

The picture at the end of 1948 was bright. Total imports for the year aggregated $1,400,000,000: $797,000,000 for food and other imports financed by direct United States-appropriated funds; $417,-000,000, financed from export proceeds; and $101,000,000 financed from ECA funds. The balance was met by the United Kingdom contribution of $70,000,000, and miscellaneous receipts from other sources. Exports for the year came to $599,000,000. Our first trade agreement, made with the Netherlands in January 1947, had expanded into twelve bilateral trade agreements with OEEC countries, ten trade agreements with other countries, and eight further contracts were in negotiation. Internally the situation had improved beyond belief. Food and consumer goods were meeting the demand. An Every Man Clothing Program to provide work clothes at reasonable prices was successful. There was a new bustle in German life, new hope and courage in German faces.

To facilitate recovery, we took several major steps in 1948 to cut red tape and to increase German responsibility. One of them was to transfer all foreign exchange accounts to the Bank deutscher Laender, which in turn arranged for its member banks to issue letters of credit direct to approved importers for accepted import programs. Likewise the licensing of exports was transferred to local banks and the exporter was free to execute contracts directly with customers.[7] The multi-exchange rates were replaced by one rate of thirty cents to the mark, which represented fair purchasing value in Germany. This stopped some exports but proved on the whole to be a fair exchange in the world market. In addition, importers could apply for credit against an over-all allocation of funds for specific import purposes and, having secured this credit, could place their orders directly with foreign suppliers. While export controls were necessarily maintained on the same items controlled by our own government, there was a major relaxation which helped materially to stimulate trade. Of course procurement under directly appropriated and ECA funds still remained centralized although distribution within Germany followed normal business channels.

Nearly all black market and barter transactions had ceased but they were replaced by another economic threat, the smuggling of money and goods. The free market in Switzerland sold marks at a lower cost than their purchasing value within Germany. Lack of central customs control made the movement of goods and money across the borders relatively easy and the amounts being moved were substantial. We established central control of customs in the bizonal area and obtained French assurance of full co-operation.[8] Control was extended to include non-Germans entering and leaving Germany.

In the fall of 1948, between October 25 and November 10, the three Western Powers met with the representatives of the Benelux countries in Paris to discuss the safeguarding of foreign interests in Germany. The American delegation, headed by Assistant Secretary of State Willard Thorp, for the first time had no Military Government representation. Mr. Hawkins, from our Economics Division, was invited to attend a few of the early meetings of the delegation in an advisory capacity. Questions at issue were vital to the German economy, and indirectly to the American taxpayer, who was supporting this economy. I felt it our responsibility to point out to the delegation those measures which would increase the burden to the American taxpayer even though they were desired by Germany's neighbors.

This conference resulted in recommendations[9] to the several governments for the decontrol of Allied property in Germany, the creation of a non-German appeal body to serve as a final judge in matters of internal restitution, and the removal of restrictions governing the reinvestment and disposal of foreign property in Germany. The first two of these measures were already in effect in our zone. General Robertson and I had submitted joint recommendations to our governments some time before the meeting of the conference to accomplish the third of these measures. Prior to currency reform we had resisted the reinvestment and disposal of foreign assets in Germany as these assets could be used to obtain control of an undue proportion of German industry. After currency reform new foreign capital, which could not be expected until foreign capital in Germany was released from restriction, was needed to facilitate recovery. Although our government had urged action for some time, it had still not acted on this when I left Germany.

Another recommendation of the conference was the delivery without further payment of goods ordered in Germany prior to its surrender which had been paid for in whole or in part by other countries. I believed that this created a privileged group and I could see no reason why their claims should have greater validity than those of people who had paid for undelivered goods which had been destroyed by war. Our financial support of the German economy entitled us to utilize goods manufactured in Germany which were there when Germany surrendered, to obtain the food and other essential imports to keep Germany alive. All claims against Germany, in my opinion, should be considered together at the time of the peace treaty. I could see no reason why we should spend our funds to rebuild a Germany which would pay for war damages and claims from its deficit income. Admittedly our policy was a hard one. It had to be if it was to reduce the cost to the American taxpayer. The acceptance of the conference report would have reversed a policy applied over three years.

The conference also asked for the conversion of Deutschemark earnings of foreign powers within Germany, perhaps as a part of the Intra-European Payments Agreement among the countries participating in the European Recovery Program. Robertson and I had recognized the necessity for an incentive to attract further investments and had recommended that a portion of the income earned by such investments be made available in foreign exchange as dividends in all cases where the investments resulted in an increase of German exports; but free transfer of Deutschemarks into foreign exchange, thus reducing the foreign exchange available to procure essential imports, seemed unthinkable to me as long as the United States was financing the German exchange deficit. It would mean that the investments of other countries in Germany would be supported by the United States and not by Germany.

A suggestion of the conference which varied with the policy we had followed for three years was for the exemption of properties belonging to members of the United Nations from tax equalization measures from war losses and the exemption of foreign-owned properties from providing any proportion of equipment made available from an industry to other plants in compensation for reparations losses. Foreign ownership had not exempted plants. We had consistently stood for a non-discriminatory policy under which foreign-owned investments in Germany would receive equal treatment under the law with German investments and had opposed special privileges. The conference likewise recommended deviation from our non-discriminatory policy to grant special privileges to foreign owners affected by land reform.

The conference desired a study by experts to fix internal coal prices for foreign-owned mines which would insure a profit to the owners, which certainly is far from non-discrimination. The fixing of internal coal prices in Germany could not be separated from the German economic problem and treated as a separate and special problem where foreign ownership was involved.

Our representatives at this conference dissented to its recommendations for the protection of foreign creditors against the reduction in value of Reichsmarks holdings caused by currency reform, the protection of the full rights of creditors when expressed in gold marks, and to the resumption of operations by foreign insurers without the re-establishment of their legal reserves. When I left Germany final governmental action had not been taken on the recommendations of this conference which needed to be resolved to remove doubt and uncertainty.

Robertson and I were disappointed that the meeting had failed to establish protection for German patents and trade processes. Our efforts to re-establish a patent office and to negotiate for external protection were blocked by French opposition. Right after surrender we had sought out new German patents and processes which were made available for general world use. Hence German manufacturers were unwilling to bring out new patents and processes and yet they are essential to industrial progress. This still unsolved problem remains a serious obstacle to recovery.

During 1949 productive output and foreign trade continued to increase although at a somewhat lesser rate. We had reached the capacity made possible by available coal and power. Long-term programs were under way to increase both, but the increases would come slowly over many months. The rise in productive output is best illustrated by steel, which more than doubled from 323,000 tons per month in May 1948, just prior to currency reform, to 752,000 tons a month in March 1949. Industrial output in the same period went from 47 per cent in 1936 to 89 per cent. Exports averaged $89,000,000 per month in the first three months of 1949 and promised to exceed $1,000,000,000 for the year, a long way from the $3,000,000 of exports made with unbelievable effort from the United States Zone in the last half of 1945.

The German economy is still a deficit economy requiring substantial outside assistance and now being provided by the United States. In order to stimulate dollar sales, thus reducing the deficit being borne by the taxpayers, Military Government held an industrial exhibit of German products in New York City in April 1949. It met with some opposition which, although understandable, would have harmed the American taxpayer rather than the Germans if the exhibit had been closed.

When the Occupation Statute comes into effect, West Germany is represented directly in OEEC and will negotiate its own bilateral agreement with the United States for ECA funds. This is timely. The German authorities have now had experience in running their economy. They have a sound banking and financial structure, and they should be given the responsibility. They have difficult years ahead. Nevertheless, with the continuance of the European Recovery Program, there is no reason why they cannot balance their economy to provide a reasonable standard of living, although it cannot for years reach their prewar standard.

There is no question in my mind that the European Recovery Program has saved the free nations of Europe and that our country can be proud that its statesmen had the wisdom to foresee its need and to provide the funds which made it possible. However, while this may not be the appropriate place, I must confess to misgivings about some aspects of the program. Perhaps this is a non-constructive approach, as I must admit I know of no alternatives which might overcome these misgivings. For example, early in the program, we acquired from the United States large quantities of tobacco which were surplus to our needs and therefore could be obtained at low-cost support prices. This purchase was resented by both Greece and

Turkey, who protested in OEEC that it was inconsistent with past patterns of trade and that, regardless of the much higher price, and to conserve dollars, we should have purchased Greek and Turkish tobacco, providing manufactured products in exchange. In fact, to alleviate their resentment, we did purchase more tobacco than the German economy could afford. A similar problem arose with respect to dried fruits and more are certain to develop in the future when surpluses exist in the United States. Bilateral trade agreements and the Intra-European Payments Agreement are supposed to provide the framework for free trade among the signatory powers. In practice, under each trade agreement, the signatory countries try to obtain a close import-export balance, and there is increasing tendency for the signatory powers to suggest that high selling prices for certain commodities which can be made available for export by one of the countries be offset by corresponding high values for selected exports from the other. Thus the trade agreements tend to become a mechanism for barter transactions which reduce the demand for products produced elsewhere at lower cost. This certainly does not tend to reopen the market place. As long as the participating countries are utilizing controlled currencies in foreign exchange there seems to be no way to carry on trade between two countries except under bilateral trade and payment agreements. Today West Germany trades freely only with the United States and to a lesser extent with Switzerland and this is possible because the dollar deficit in this exchange is borne by the United States. Moreover, national and international production programs are designed more and more to support trade agreements.

It is now the economist in a government office who with sharpened pencil and an over-all trade agreement determines what goods can be sold and to whom they can be sold. Frequently the price is related neither to the production cost nor to the world market price. No longer is there incentive for the manufacturer to develop new processes to reduce expenses, to watch production costs closely so that his product may sell in the free competition of the open market. Certainly some degree of economic planning is desirable. However, it can easily be carried into programing which makes free enterprise difficult if not impossible. That to me is the danger which we face in the present work of the Organization for European Economic Cooperation. While the planning is now directed toward increasing trade among the participating nations, it may well result in an attempt at regimentation certain to fail but which in its failure can destroy the advantages of free enterprise.

In Germany the conflict between a controlled economy and an economy of free enterprise cannot be avoided and it may prove to be the most difficult problem to be faced by West German Government. I hope that the issue can be deferred, for the German economic machine is just beginning to run and an attempt to change engines while it is in motion may reverse the trend to recovery and cause a serious economic reverse. Still it is a decision which the German people have the right to make.

The economic improvement which came about from the fusion of the British and American zones under a German Economic Administration proved to me that much more rapid political progress would result from political consolidation. However, prior to the setting up of West German Government, political affairs remained in the hands of the occupying powers. Since they could not exercise their control through the Allied Control Council, it had to be exercised separately in each zone by its military governor. Political administration in the American Zone continued in our hands during the period in which financial and economic administration was a joint Anglo-American responsibility.

CHAPTER 12

Administration in the
United States Zone

GENERAL EISENHOWER, and later General Mc-
Narney, delegated broad authority to me to administer military government. As we met the difficult problems
involved in restoring law and order, in re-establishing schools, in
informing the German people of world events, in demilitarization
and denazification, and in restitution, I was glad that I had no military responsibilities. A few months before his departure McNarney
put me in command of our troops in Berlin. Otherwise I was able to
devote my full time as deputy military governor to the organization
of military government so that it would represent us in the Allied
Control Council and also would administer our zone of occupation
and carry out our unilateral responsibilities. By the spring of 1947 I
was confident that both military government and the German administration within our zone were organized effectively for these
purposes.

I succeeded McNarney on March 15, 1947, at a small military
ceremony in Frankfurt, during which he presented me with the
Distinguished Service Medal and in the simple words of a comrade
transferred the command to my hands. He had faced the problems of
redeployment and had begun the reorganization of the occupation
forces. A sound administrator, he had established area commands or
posts in which a single commander was responsible for general administration and discipline. Prior to this action, a large city might
contain several tactical units, each reporting to separate commanders

elsewhere, which made it difficult if not impossible to fix responsibility. He had adopted and put into effect excellent programs for depots, training schools, and logistical support. He had laid the foundation for a field training program although it could not be placed under way in the larger tactical units. They were needed to maintain order because the trained German police were not yet prepared to assume this responsibility.

McNarney had given me his full support and confidence in Military Government affairs, including its separation from the Army command. I think the only difference of opinion he and I had was that he should establish his principal headquarters with Military Government in Berlin rather than at Army Headquarters, then in Frankfurt. I could never persuade McNarney to take this step which I believed essential to emphasize that our main task in Germany was government. However, I believed then as now that, fully recognizing this, he did not make the move because of his consideration for my position as deputy, which might have lost some significance with the military governor present. McNarney contributed much to our occupation. In its lasting effects, I believe that his development of the Army program for German Youth Assistance (GYA) will prove to have been one of our major contributions to a new Germany.

Immediately after the transfer of command I was summoned to Moscow for the meeting of the Council of Foreign Ministers and had little opportunity to organize my new office. The designation of the command had been changed to Commander in Chief, Europe, henceforth known as CINCEUR. While in Moscow I was promoted to the rank of general on March 28, 1947, although I could not advertise the promotion for several days as I had no extra stars with me to place on my uniform.

On my return from Moscow, I reorganized my office. While I gave a larger measure of responsibility to the competent deputy military governor, Major General Frank Keating, I retained direct control of Military Government, delegating a still broader authority in military command. I thus took the step which I had urged my predecessor to take to indicate the importance of our governing responsibility.

The major commanders in Europe—Lieutenant Generals Clarence R. Huebner, Geoffrey Keyes, and Curtis S. LeMay—were able, outstanding soldiers, experienced in combat and in garrison. I designated Huebner as my deputy and chief of staff and also as commander of the Ground Forces, thus utilizing his staff for both over-all and Ground Force Command. LeMay, later succeeded by the equally able Lieutenant General John Kenneth Cannon, who commanded the Air Forces, and Keyes, who commanded our troops in Austria, were given almost complete autonomy. Keyes was also High Commissioner for Austria, in which capacity he reported directly to our government and not through my headquarters. To maintain general control, I added to my own staff the director of intelligence, the inspector general, and the budget control officer. This arrangement, which saved me from the detailed work which goes with a large staff, proved fully satisfactory in practice.

In my first conference with major commanders and my military staff I expressed my confidence in them. I told them I had learned long ago that both officers and soldiers, given the opportunity, wanted to improve their professional ability; that they would be given this opportunity, and that, further, I did not want to hear again the words "poor soldier" as I was sure that we had good soldiers who would respond to expressed confidence in their abilities.

While this is not primarily a record of the Army in Germany, military government would not have been possible without the Army, which provided not only security but also logistical and administrative support. Few know of the problems involved in the care of 150,000 Americans in a disrupted economy from which they drew only housing, light, and fuel. Food, essential supplies, and sundries of all types had to be brought in and sold in commissary and Post Exchange, the latter doing a monthly business of approximately $8,000,000. Recreational facilities had to be provided, and since there were no appropriated funds for the purpose expenses for recreation and welfare were met from exchange profits. Still we were able to have service clubs with American hostesses for our soldiers, winter sports in the Bavarian Alps and European tours at low cost, dayrooms in barracks, bowling alleys, motion pictures, and all forms of competitive athletics. Our radio, Armed Forces Network (AFN), supported from our own finances, provides excellent programs free from commercials. They have wide popularity throughout Europe and have done much to further our objectives. Our daily newspaper, the *Stars and Stripes*, publishes factual world and local news. Our libraries are supplied with the latest books and periodicals. A complete educational system through high school is available for American children. These are but a few of the widespread activities under Army management which made our occupation possible. Friction between Army and Military Government did exist in the early days but long ago became the exception and not the rule.

Immediately after my return from Moscow I determined to inspect personally the military installations in the theater, devoting usually at least one full day and often two days a week to this purpose. This I continued throughout my command, as knowledge which can be obtained only through personal inspection is essential to the exercise of command. This direct association with young officers and soldiers was inspiring to me, and we were soon able to share our enthusiasms in developing and maintaining high standards.

I told General Huebner that we could now depend on German police to maintain law and order and that we must start a tactical training program. One combat team of the 1st Division and one regiment of Constabulary troops were released from all duty except tactical training and sent to the field. When General Bradley visited us in August and September 1947, I was proud of the combat team which he reviewed. I know of no greater soldier ever produced from our Army and to sense his satisfaction with our progress made all of us feel that our efforts had proved worth while. Later the highly mobile but lightly armed Constabulary was strengthened by changing four of its battalions to artillery units. During 1947 we continued the release of the troops from garrison duties, and by the summer of 1948 the entire 1st Division was placed on a full-time training schedule which included five months in the field. In the summer of 1948 the division in full combat strength and equipment passed in review before my colleagues, Generals Robertson and Koenig, and made a splendid impression. Then, except for two border patrol squadrons, the Constabulary, already well equipped with artillery, was relieved of the responsibility for local security and formed into three hard-hitting armored cavalry groups. Anti-aircraft units as well as supporting service units were organized and trained. Field exercises became the order of the day.

When I took command our Negro troops were largely in service units. Their disciplinary record was not good and the number of incidents involving difficulties with the Germans was excessive. Huebner had instituted an educational program which provided continuing academic advancement. This program developed a new sense of pride and proved its worth many times over. In addition I directed the transfer of Negro soldiers from service units to form three Negro infantry battalions, later incorporated into the Constabulary. They became excellent units and we saw the incident rate for Negro troops fall below the white rate. The incident rate, which records the total number of disciplinary violations that occur in a month divided by the number of thousands of troops, is a satisfactory index of the state of discipline. It includes many violations of a minor nature which would never be recorded on a police blotter. By 1949 our rate had become much lower than the police court rates in many American cities and the venereal rate had been cut in half. Our soldiers were sensing their purpose in Germany; they were becoming proud representatives of the United States.

There is much I could write of the Army's role in Germany. I have known and loved the Army and respected the American soldier for many years. Never did I know it to respond more to the demands of its commander than in my two years of command in Germany. Young though our soldiers may be, they are performing their duties admirably. Small though our forces may be, they are well trained, excellently equipped, and competent for any service they may be called on to perform, and even those soldiers with daily administrative and supply duties are trained in secondary tactical missions. What I have said about our soldiers applies to our airmen, who were equally responsive to our training objectives. I pay tribute to their work in the Berlin airlift elsewhere. Of course among 100,000 Americans there will always be a few who cause trouble. In Germany they became very few, and I am sure that visiting Americans who saw our soldiers in 1948 and 1949 returned home proud of what they had seen.

Another responsibility I assumed with command was the care and protection of displaced persons. The Allied armies advancing in Germany had uncovered almost 6,500,000 displaced persons,[1] the great majority of whom had been brought into Germany for forced labor. In an unbelievable operation, by rail, highway, and air, more than 4,000,000 had been repatriated[2] by July 31, 1945, and of the remaining 2,200,000 almost 2,000,000 were collected in assembly centers. There were large numbers who did not wish to be repatriated because of their political beliefs, including the Baltic people and the western Ukrainians, whose states had been absorbed by the

Soviet Union. In 1945 visitors from the United States, some of them members of the Harrison group, were critical of conditions in these camps.[3] This seemed unfair to the Army, which had exerted every effort for their care. It was shocking to Americans used to plenty to find conditions inevitable in the movement of more than 2,000,000 people into assembly centers, but these conditions improved rapidly. Never did the Army receive any substantial criticism from the displaced persons themselves, who were then, and remained, grateful for Army protection. By November 1945 continued repatriation had reduced this number in the United States Zone to less than 500,000 and they were being adequately fed and housed. Repatriation then became a dribble and "the haven of refuge" provided by our zone was attracting additional numbers from Poland and later from the Balkans. By the end of December the number in our zone had increased to more than 500,000. This influx continued until April 21, 1947, when further entry to the assembly centers was denied although our borders remained open.[4] Meanwhile continued efforts at repatriation, including a gift of rations for a number of days, resulted in further reductions, so that as of April 30, 1947, there remained in our zone 354,000 residents in the assembly centers, with perhaps an additional 156,000 living outside of them.

In all west Germany at the time the total number in assembly centers aggregated 649,000 of whom 165,000 were Balts, 105,000 Ukrainians, 189,000 Polish, and 138,000 Jews. It was apparent that repatriation would not solve the problem and that resettlement was the only solution.

Nineteen forty-seven was a difficult year for the DPs. Resettlement was negligible and there seemed little hope of their finding new homes and opportunities. Everything possible in a disrupted economy was being done to help them. In 1945 UNRRA had been formed and became responsible for administering the camps.[5] The Army furnished supplies to UNRRA centers and protected the camps. Displaced persons were subject to Military Government court jurisdiction. Camps were largely self-governing. In the face of despair, morale in the camps dropped off and there was a consequent breakdown in character which led to black market and similar activities. Reports concerning the extent of these activities were often exaggerated, and, considering the conditions under which these people lived, their behavior was most creditable.

In June 1947 UNRRA was dissolved. This worried us greatly as the Army was not prepared to reassume administrative responsibilities. While the International Refugee Organization[6] which was to replace UNRRA had not yet been formed under its charter, a Preparatory Commission (PCIRO) was created. On July 9, 1947, the Army contracted with PCIRO to furnish to the latter's warehouses without payment, food from the German economy to the extent that Germans received their rations from the economy and imported food was to be paid for at cost price. PCIRO also received for the displaced persons housing, transport, light, and fuel, and such other items as were available to the German economy on the same scale as the Germans, without payment. This later led to some arguments between PCIRO and Army officials, as my orders prohibited me from making available items made from imported raw materials, which would have increased the cost of our support. I believe that the Department of the Army had promised the Appropriations Committee not to augment the appropriation for IRO by indirect aid from the United States. Later, when PCIRO was replaced by IRO, a new contract embodying the same principles was executed. Without criticizing UNRRA, whose services had been most helpful, we found IRO to be a more businesslike organization, which did its work effectively and economically.

The Department of the Army consistently supported legislation to permit resettlement in the United States, believing that displaced persons would make good citizens. In the fall of 1947 a subcommittee of the House Committee on Foreign Affairs, with James G. Fulton as chairman, visited Germany to study the problem.[7] We also presented our views to the large number of congressional visitors that summer, and to a committee of the American Legion headed by then National Commander Griffith. We were pleased when Congress enacted legislation on June 25, 1948 which provided for the entry of 200,000 DPs over a two-year period.[8]

The stimulation thus provided to other countries and the creation of the new state of Israel brought a substantial increase in resettlement in 1948, and perceptible improvement in the morale of displaced persons. By March 1949 total resettlement figures by principal receiving countries were: United States, 7129; Australia, 2160; Canada, 2010; Israel, 8427, and in the United States Zone 231,000. The numbers going to the United States increased rapidly as our resettlement program hit its stride, and to Israel even more rapidly as conditions there became more stable. The newly established government of Israel, despite most difficult economic problems, courageously determined to receive large numbers of the unfortunates still remaining in Germany. We are hopeful that new legislation will double the authorized entries into the United States, since the present limit will only half meet the problem. Even then there will remain the aged, the infirm, and the incurables whom no country will want. This group of perhaps 35,000 persons constitutes a serious long-term problem for which some humane solution must be found. We have a new problem in receiving and caring for refugees who have fled from the Communist terror in Czechoslovakia.

Throughout the four years the Army gave priority in employment to DPs and used substantial numbers in labor and guard units. Idleness was always a problem in the assembly centers. Displaced persons were loath to work in the German economy and, furthermore, were remote from the labor market. Because of bomb damage their assembly centers could not be located in industrial areas. American and other relief organizations helped in arranging for self-support and handicraft activities. Jewish agencies were particularly successful in establishing vocational training.

The Army was fortunate in its several advisers on Jewish affairs: Judge Simon Hirsch Rifkind, Rabbi Philip Sidney Bernstein, Judge Louis Edward Levinthal, Professor William Haber, and Harry Greenstein. All were able, sincere men who saw the problems of both the displaced person and the Army. They proved invaluable in maintaining good relations, and I am sure that they would also testify to the Army's sincerity of purpose. Jewish relief agencies, especially the American Joint Distribution Committee, were also most helpful.

I visited a number of assembly centers informally and met from time to time with leaders of the several groups, including the Committee for Liberated Jews. I found them men of ability, reasonable in their requests and understanding when some of their requests could not be fulfilled.

The Army can be proud of its role in the care and protection of displaced persons and it can be sure of their gratitude. I shall always cherish a painting entitled *Liberation* given me by a Lithuanian camp, a small inlaid wooden tray from a Latvian camp, an inscribed

Jewish Bible, and a book of pictures with the inscription "Pictures of a few of the thousands of Jewish displaced persons who will never forget the devotion of General Lucius D. Clay." Just a day or two before my departure representatives of the Jewish groups visited me in Berlin to say good-by and to leave with me a few souvenirs, one of which was a scroll bearing their words of appreciation. I realize this was not a personal tribute, but a tribute to the American Army from a group of courageous unfortunates who saw ahead a new home and a new future.

There will remain in Germany, after the early departure of the Jewish displaced persons, Jewish communities which may contain about 20,000 persons. Earlier, because of their understandable feeling toward the Germans, there was a tendency on the part of other Jewish DPs to regard those who wished to remain in Germany as unfaithful to the Jewish cause. Fortunately Mr. Greenstein has laid the way to accord between these two groups. At my request our National Council of Christians and Jews has representatives in Germany working to prevent the regrowth of anti-Semitism there, and to develop a true spirit of tolerance. I think it a great mistake for Jewish leaders to advocate the evacuation of all Jews from Germany. They should maintain their right to remain and participate in the future Germany, helping to mold it to a life in which freedom thrives.

I visited our cemetery in Luxembourg on Memorial Day, 1947, where several thousands of our war dead, including General Patton, rest. The people of Luxembourg from their prince to humble farmers gathered in large numbers to bring flowers and to pay their simple but impressive tribute. On this visit the Grand Duchess of Luxembourg honored me with a decoration and the Foreign Minister gave us a pleasant luncheon. Our relations with that country, which was a popular shopping center for the Americans in Germany, were always friendly.

The summer and fall of 1947 were busy months. My schedule for June, for instance, placed me in Frankfurt on the second for an Army conference, in Stuttgart on the third to meet with the German Laenderrat, in Wuerzburg on the fourth, in Giessen on the ninth, in Bremen on the nineteenth, in Bamberg on the twenty-fifth, in Berchtesgaden on the twenty-ninth, and in Marburg on the same day to inspect military installations. Mrs. Clay and I visited Strasbourg on General Koenig's invitation on June 14 and 15. The rest of the time I was in Berlin, attending meetings of the Control Council on the tenth, eleventh, and thirtieth. A filled brief case accompanied me on all trips and I was able to answer letters and cables while traveling by plane or train. My Berlin office staff, Captain Margaret Allen, Miss Edna Shelley, and Captain Edloe Donnan, and Lieutenant Colonel George T. Stump who ran the Frankfurt office, cared nothing about hours in their efforts to ease my task.

We received more than eighty-five congressional visitors, including some of the major committees and subcommittees of both House and Senate. The Foreign Affairs, Armed Services, and Appropriations committees of both Senate and House were represented. The full Herter Committee, which was studying the proposed European Recovery Program prior to its consideration by Congress, passed several days with us. It left a subcommittee under Congressman Francis Case to spend several weeks in a study of German and Austrian economic problems. We made every effort to facilitate the work of these congressmen and planned schedules which always left some free time. Later we were charged (unfairly, I thought) with fixing schedules which would permit our congressional visitors to see and hear only what Military Government believed they should see and hear. Our arrangements were made to conserve their time and I am sure that there was no congressional visitor who did not feel that he had ample opportunity to investigate what he desired and to meet those Germans with whom he wished to confer. The Case Committee[9] was a hard-working, fact-finding group which made a comprehensive report on the German situation. Its members showed understanding and sympathetic attention to German matters which came before Congress.

All visiting congressmen were interested in our relations with Soviet representatives and in the importance of the European Recovery Program in preserving Western democracy. There was no one in Military Government who did not recognize that Germany must recover to make possible the growth of a peaceful democratic nation. We all believed that German recovery should be fitted into and was essential to western European recovery. We were convinced that the restoration of a normal economy in Europe would revive the will to be free and that it could come about only with our financial assistance. The provision of such assistance to the free countries of Europe would change our course of action from a passive defense against

Communist penetration along our eastern occupation border to an active attack with ideas and economic benefits from a revived western Europe. There seemed no alternative. Whether or not we helped in presenting the case is difficult to know but we spoke from conviction and complete sincerity.

Some visiting congressmen were attacked on the ground that they did not attempt to obtain information on Germany. This was unfair. We found them willing to spend long hours to get the facts, intelligent in their questioning, and understanding of complex problems. In view of the responsibility of Congress, it would have been helpful if every member of the Senate and House had visited Germany.

Obviously neither all congressmen nor all committees approved the policies being carried out by Military Government. Senator Styles Bridges, who went along on most points, did not believe in plant removals which reduced economic potential for European recovery; Congressman Case and his subcommittee reported that the severity of our denazification program interfered with economic recovery; and others had contrary views. Nevertheless, they left the impression that on the whole Congress was satisfied with the conduct of Military Government and with the broad aspects of basic policy. Some members of the Senate and House visited us as individuals and traveled through our zone to obtain information and to form their opinions. Senator William F. Knowland in 1947 and Senator Robert Taft later visited us this way. Congressman Everett M. Dirksen spent several weeks with us in the summer of 1947, during which he traveled and worked arduously to become familiar with our problems, which he presented with vigor and ability in Congress before serious eye trouble led to his departure from government life. I wish that space permitted the naming of all congressmen who came to Germany, each of whom contributed on his return home to a better understanding of the problem.

On July 15, 1947, we received the revised policy directive[10] which I had been called to Washington to discuss in the fall of 1945, and which embodied the principal points made by Secretary Byrnes in his 1946 Stuttgart speech. This directive provided, "Your authority as Military Governor will be broadly construed and empowers you to take action consistent with relevant international agreements, general foreign policies of this government and with this directive, appropriate or desirable to attain your government's objectives in Germany or to meet military exigencies." I accepted this statement at its face value and it was not modified during my tenure of office.

The new policy did not alter our objectives to demilitarize and denazify Germany. While it still demanded the punishment of war criminals, it required the speedy conclusion of trials. Likewise it required the early completion of plant removals. It continued to call for the breaking up of cartels and excessive concentrations of economic power. While retaining punitive measures, it emphasized the constructive work ahead, including the rapid transfer of governmental responsibility to German hands and the encouragement of a German government of the federal type. It specifically required maximum cultural exchange and the use of our information media to present factual information to the German people. In the economic and financial field, where under the previous directive we had to let events take their course, we were now empowered to undertake currency reform and other measures necessary to develop a balanced economy based on sound currency and credit. While much of the new policy was in effect when received, as a result of amendments from time to time in the old directive, it was helpful to have our instructions in a single document.

On October 4, 1947, our Ambassador to Belgium, Alan G. Kirk, invited me to join him in Antwerp to pay homage to the first of our war dead to be sent home. We were joined by high Belgian state, church, and town officials in a dignified ceremony which concluded as we stood at attention while the flower-bedecked ship slowly left port.

Soon after my visit to Antwerp, on November 9, 1947, Mr. Murphy and I, accompanied by Mrs. Murphy and Mrs. Clay, accepted an invitation of the Italian Government to attend an exhibition of old masterpieces which we had returned from Germany. While I had declined several such invitations, Ambassador James C. Dunn urged our acceptance in the interest of good will. Appreciative of his able work in Italy, I could not refuse. It proved to be a delightful visit. President Enrico de Nicola, Prime Minister Alcide de Gasperi and members of his Cabinet attended the exhibition to express their appreciation. We were guests at a reception in the ancient Villa Taverna, with fountains in unbelievable numbers playing everywhere in its beautiful garden. The Minister of Defense and the Chief of Staff, General Efisio Marras, gave us a formal dinner. A day or two with the Dunns is always an occasion to remember, and Murphy and I were both happy to know that Dunn believed our visit had contributed to good will.

That fall I returned home to participate in the discussions which led to the United States assuming major financial responsibility for the bizonal area. Ambassador Smith was in Washington at the time. He, Murphy, and I were summoned to appear before the National Security Council in the President's cabinet room. President Truman and the heads of the major government financial agencies attended the meeting. Smith and I reported our views of relations with Russia and answered questions as best we could. We both expressed the view at that meeting that we must be prepared for Soviet action to force our withdrawal from Berlin and that we must remain.

I was asked by Senator Kenneth S. Wherry to meet informally in his office with a group of Republican and Democratic senators to report on the German situation and to answer their questions. This gathering, which was repeated in subsequent visits, proved helpful and stimulating. I have always been grateful for Wherry's interest in arranging them.

In early January 1948 Secretary Marshall announced at a press conference that the State Department was ready to take over military government in Germany. While this had long been advocated by the Department of the Army, the timing of the announcement came as a complete surprise both to the Department and to me. Frankly, I was upset because the indefinite date at which this was to be accomplished left me dangling on a limb, a dangerous position for a negotiator under the conditions which existed in Germany.

A few days later I was again called to Washington, this time to testify before the Appropriations Committee and to appear also before the Foreign Affairs Committee of the House and the Appropriations Committee of the Senate. While primarily there to defend the appropriation for Germany, I did have the opportunity in replying to questions to express my view of the urgent need for assistance to all western Europe. While I was in Washington Justice Byrnes asked me to meet with him and the two senators from my home state, Walter F. George and Richard B. Russell. Byrnes, with their support, urged me to continue in Germany as long as possible. I could not promise, as I already had urged the Department of the Army to insist that the State Department fix a specific date for the transfer of responsibility which could be announced immediately. I arranged for a State Department team of experts to visit Germany to work out the details of transfer. I believed that these details could be worked out in a few weeks, so I requested that I be returned to the United States on April 1 for retirement. My request was approved by the Department of the Army.

On this visit Murphy and I spent an evening with General Eisenhower at his quarters in Fort Myer. He told us of the letter he was to make public the next day declaring his firm intent not to be a presidential candidate. The letter was much on his mind and it was evident that he was apprehensive that it might be considered a vainglorious action.

On my return to Germany, I set up a small committee of Military Government and Army representatives to work with the State Department group to prepare for the transfer of responsibility to the State Department with the Army to continue to provide logistical support. At long last it seemed that we could go home, and Mrs. Clay and I sent many of our clothes ahead.

Then in March came the first Soviet blockade move. On March 23 I was summoned to a teletype conference with Secretary of Army Kenneth C. Royall and General Bradley. Royall advised me that the President was releasing a statement that day explaining that in view of the existing situation no changes would be made in the administrative arrangements for Germany. He then referred to the international situation and said: "In view of this, I hope, and General Bradley joins me in this hope, that you will stay on the job at least through the present calendar year. You are urgently needed there." I replied: "I am an Army officer as long as the Department feels it needs me. I do want to retire as soon as I can, and the Army agrees. I owe too much to the Army not to remain with it if it feels I am needed. Thank you both for your confidence." This decision was a blow to Mrs. Clay, who was anxious to be home where she could see our grandchildren from time to time but as always she accepted it with outward cheerfulness.

In June 1948 currency reform in west Germany was followed by the attempted blockade of the civilian population, the long but futile negotiations with Soviet representatives, and the airlift. In July and October I made hurried trips to the United States, the latter one primarily to keep a promise to Cardinal Spellman to speak at the annual dinner of the Alfred E. Smith Memorial Foundation.

In March, when I agreed to remain in Germany, I made it clear that I had the calendar year 1948 in mind. In September, when it appeared for a short while that the blockade might be lifted, I thought this would give me the opportunity to retire just before the election. I did not want my retirement to appear to have any political significance. As an Army officer, I hold no political affiliation. When the negotiations with the Russians broke down I advised the Department of the Army that I would not ask to leave with winter ahead and Berlin dependent on air supply. When Royall visited the theater at Christmas I told him that I would like to leave as soon as it was clearly established that the airlift had sustained Berlin through the winter. It seemed to me that our initial mission had been accomplished: sound state political organizations existed in our zone; Germany had made splendid progress toward recovery as a member of OEEC; and a Basic Law was in preparation for a West German Government.

I had been associated with the restrictive measures of Military Government, such as the removal of industrial plants, the transfer of gold found in Germany, the liquidation of foreign assets, the denazification program, the trial and punishment (in many instances by death) of war criminals, and the placing of restrictions on industry. I believed that a military governor not associated with these events should be in office when the new German Government was formed. While Royall was very gracious in urging me to stay, he did say that I had earned the right to retire and that the Department of the Army would no longer oppose it. He agreed to fix a specific date after his return to Washington.

Shortly thereafter he wrote to President Truman, urging that it was timely for the State Department to accept responsibility for running Germany. Just at this time Secretary Marshall retired. As a result I was again asked to stay on a little longer until Secretary Acheson had time to become familiar with the problem. In March 1949 I asked that the date be fixed and suggested May 15 for my departure with retirement on June 1. This would give me two weeks in Washington so I could be available to the State and Army Departments for consultation. I had complete confidence that General George Hays, who had succeeded General Keating as my deputy, could carry on effectively until my civilian successor arrived. The proposal was accepted, so that my plans could be made accordingly.

In March I lost Mr. Murphy, who had been political adviser first to SHAEF and then to Military Government. For four years we had worked together daily, attended international conferences together, and traveled in Germany together. I think Murphy inspected more troops and barracks than most generals. During these four years we never had a major disagreement and we formed a lasting friendship. His knowledge of Europe, his understanding of European and German political conditions, and his basic faith in the American concepts made him a counselor of rare worth. I was fortunate, and so will be my successor, that James Riddleberger, a foreign service officer of exceptional ability and much German experience, was available to succeed Murphy. Murphy's recall to Washington to take full charge of the State Department Office for Germany and Austria was a wise move. There was no better qualified man for the task. It was to lighten my feeling over my own departure, to know that he was in charge in Washington of the still complex German problem.

While it had been agreed that I was to leave Germany on May 15, I was not permitted to announce the date until it was released by the White House on May 3. That day I was en route to a review of troops at our training area in Grafenwoehr, Bavaria, which had been scheduled for some weeks as routine, but General Huebner, who knew in confidence of my departure, had without my knowledge arranged for it to be a farewell review and he was becoming apprehensive that his plans would be jeopardized if my departure remained a secret. Fortunately the announcement came in time.

The review was presented by approximately 10,000 troops of the 1st Division and the Constabulary. The troops, their armor and equipment made a splendid appearance and were in every way a credit to our armed forces. As the ceremony ended the planes of the 86th Fighter Group, commanded by Colonel Clarence T. Edwinson, flew in formation, spelling out my name. This was the group which had flown the giant "U.S." formation over Berlin.

A farewell review is always an emotional strain to the soldier who has devoted most of his life to a military career. It seeemd to me that I could sense that the troops recognized my pride in their accomplishments and my appreciation for their appearance. In a short speech I told them that they had inherited the tradition of the Allied armies who had fought their way into Europe and remained to ensure that the peace and freedom for which they had fought would endure. I also reminded them that the transfer of military government from military to civilian hands was in accord with our traditions. I expressed my appreciation for their acceptance of the responsibility of occupation, which was bringing added luster to the reputation of our armed forces. It was difficult to say good-by and to end an association of thirty-four years with the American soldier, whom I had learned to love and respect and admire.

My last ten days in Germany were spent largely in completing with my French and British colleagues the negotiations with the German representatives of the constitutional assembly, and these led to the acceptance of its constitution. I said good-by to the minister-presidents of the American Zone with whom I had been closely associated for so many months. I also made a special trip to Frankfurt, where Dr. Koehler, president of the Economic Council, and Dr. Hermann Puender, chairman of the Executive Committee, had arranged an informal farewell party with the officials of the Bizonal Administration. This gave me the opportunity to thank them for their contribution to the reconstruction of Germany and to receive what I knew to be their sincere appreciation for the assistance rendered by the United States.

On our last Sunday in Berlin a large number of Germans braved the inclement weather to be present at the retreat ceremony which took place every Sunday in good weather. It was my last official act before boarding the plane for the United States. It was evident that these Germans, as well as Mayor Reuter, the German officials, and other Germans who were at the airport, were showing their appreciation for the airlift, which had prevented Communist domination of Berlin. As I was leaving innumerable letters from simple, unknown Germans came to me to indicate a similar appreciation. A mother of three young daughters still far from their teens sent me their photographs with their sentiments inscribed on the backs: "Our good wishes and thanks accompany you to your native country." "I am the youngest of three sisters—Father has told us how much your country has done for us children. We have nothing to offer you but our love." To this, the mother added: "We admire the magnanimous helpfulness, the moral generosity of your country. We will teach our beloved children that they should emulate its shining example and help your country to establish a better world." Another letter said that I had often been "harsh and arbitrary" but that the objectives of the United States were always clear and that "the Germans long for freedom and for the development with American help of an independent life with equal justice for all." Perhaps we had built better than we realized.

During the four years in which I was in Germany, and especially during the last two years, international relationships and negotiations among the four powers trying to reconcile their views—with the United Kingdom to establish the economic fusion of our two zones, and between the United Kingdom, France, and the United States to establish West German Government—overshadowed the solid achievements of administration which resulted from the everyday grind. In carrying out administrative responsibilities in our zone we believed that we were laying a foundation for the future. A summary of the administrative problems which we faced and did our utmost to solve within the framework of American policy is essential to the story of military government, and to an understanding of the Germany of today and what we may expect it to be in the future.

CHAPTER 13

The Restoration
of Law and Order

THE restoration of law and order and the establishment of a rule of law were difficult and major accomplishments in the administration of our zone.

The Germany which surrendered on May 7, 1945, had been under totalitarian rule for twelve years. While this rule was destroyed, its imprint remained. Hitler had recognized that a dictatorship survives only if it controls the judiciary and the police and can depend upon both to carry out its edicts. Hence he first seized the police and then put in office judges at his beck and call. Arbitrary exercise of power was common practice. A knock on the door was not to be answered quickly to greet a friend, but was a sound of terror; it might mean a visit from the Gestapo and a trip to the concentration camp.

I believed that democratic growth in Germany was possible and I determined to make military government a rule of law. This required a codification of Military Government law under which the German who violated the law would be tried in our courts. This would demonstrate the sincerity of our belief in the basic rights of the individual and would be a basic step in the establishment of democratic procedures. Further, I wanted to limit Military Government laws to offenses against the occupation and to return the trial and punishment of Germans for other offenses to German hands. In order to carry out this program Nazi legislation had to be repealed, Nazis purged from the judiciary, and a new police force developed which would be dedicated to public safety and not to the enforcement of political rule. If the Nazi purge was to last, it must be accomplished by German hands.

A large part of this task fell to the Legal Division. It had to rebuild the German judiciary system, heavily tainted with Nazi ideology in both the personnel comprising it and the laws which formed its basis. It was responsible for the codification of Military Government laws, ordinances, and regulations.[1] It searched out and abolished all undesirable Nazi laws and drafted suitable legislation in their place. It provided legal advice and opinion to all divisions of Military Government and reviewed all Military Government court cases. Later, after the quadripartite Nuremberg trials,[2] it supervised the trials in our zone.[3] We were fortunate indeed to have this work in its early stages directed by former Solicitor General of the United States Charles Fahy, and to have as his deputy and successor the able Judge Joseph Warren Madden of our own Court of Claims. Later Madden was followed by Alvin Rockwell, who had earned his spurs as counsel for the National Labor Relations Board, and by Colonel John Raymond. These lawyers believed sincerely in a rule of law even in an occupation, and in justice under the law. Their liberal and broad viewpoints permeated every phase of our activities and contributed materially to our efforts to redevelop true liberalism in German thought and spirit.

As we entered Germany the immediate problem in restoring justice and order was to provide the laws and the courts to enforce them. There were more than 300 Military Government courts in existence when Germany surrendered, primarily engaged in the trial of minor offenses against the occupation authorities, and by July 1945 they had tried more than 15,000 cases. Our summary Military Government courts were really only police courts and a large proportion of their officers were not lawyers. The intermediate court officers were lawyers, when possible with judicial experience, who like circuit judges traveled throughout their assigned areas to hear and review cases. General courts composed of three or more officers were designated to hear major cases.

Military Government courts had jurisdiction over Germans in cases involving the occupation, displaced persons who were unwilling to accept German court jurisdiction, and American dependents and visiting American and Allied civilians. While lesser German violations of Military Government laws were soon passed to German courts, there remained a substantial volume to be tried in our courts. At peak, there were 343 summary, intermediate, and general Military Government courts. They had tried approximately 385,000 cases before a new Military Government court system was established in August 1948.[4]

I was never entirely satisfied with the initial judicial system which was adopted as an emergency measure. While all criminal cases were reviewed at State Offices of Military Government and major cases reviewed as well by the Legal Division, OMGUS, the dispensation of justice was too dependent upon the capacity and ability of the individual. By and large, humane justice was rendered but uniformity was lacking and there were instances of undue punishment. To partially remedy these defects I appointed an Administration of Justice Review Board in August 1947.[5] This Board, headed by the director of the Legal Division, conducted periodic examinations of the operation of criminal justice in Military Government courts as well as in courts-martial. Finally, in January 1948, I secured the services of a former federal judge of the Third Circuit Court of Appeals, William Clark, to review our system and discover its deficiencies. As a result of his recommendations the present system was set up under which our zone is divided into eleven judicial districts. Each judicial district is provided with magistrates and district judges whose jurisdiction is determined by the magnitude of the offense. There is a Court of Appeals consisting of six associate judges presided over by Chief Judge Clark. All judges and magistrates are lawyers and as many as possible of those selected had previous judicial experience. These courts have been given criminal jurisdiction over all non-German civilian persons including those serving with or accompanying our occupation forces and may try such persons for offenses committed against applicable Control Council, Military Government, and German law. Civil jurisdiction is largely returned to the German courts; our courts maintain jurisdiction in damage cases arising out of the operation of motor vehicles not owned by the United States Government and for penalties and forfeitures. The 4th and 5th Judicial District Courts have civil and criminal judisdiction as Rhine Navigation Courts. While some objection has been directed against the new system for its use of German law in criminal cases and because there is no trial by jury, these courts maintain law and order and are organized by and staffed with competent judges.

It was not timely to return displaced persons to German jurisdiction, or to give German Courts jurisdiction over occupation personnel and bona fide foreign visitors to Germany. It was difficult to find an applicable federal code, particularly in view of the many nationals of various countries under the jurisdiction of the courts, and it therefore appeared logical to apply the German code, purged of its Nazi additions. Trial by jury was impossible as there were not enough civilians in many areas to supply an adequate jury list. I have confidence that the new system will prove to be a demonstration of American justice and intent to govern by law. In this connection greater availability of American defense counsel may be expected as a result of recent authorization for qualified attorneys to open offices in our zone and to handle cases before our courts. Meanwhile we proceeded to rebuild the German system.

By August 1945 many denazified local courts were restored and a few of the next higher, or district, courts. It was interesting to note that in December 1945 a German court tried and sentenced a Nazi political murderer who had been protected by the Nazi regime, and numerous German war crimes trials have been held since that time. In order to expedite cases of this nature, the German states in our zone enacted uniform laws to lift the bar of the Statute of Limitations, to invalidate Nazi pardons and amnesties, and to permit the reopening of certain cases. Voluntary associations of attorneys were permitted to re-form. In October 1945 high courts of appeal were authorized in each state[6] and as a further process in decentralization the authorities formerly exercised by the Reich Ministry of Justice were transferred to the newly formed state Ministries of Justice. In December law faculties were reopened at the universities. On September 17, 1946, a revision[7] of the Administrative Code to remove the Nazi additions was completed by a panel of German jurists which had been at work for three months in Heidelberg. The several states were thus able to re-establish the administrative courts.

Military Government laws assured equality before the law, due process, speedy and public trial, right to be confronted by witnesses, and right of trial. Subsequently these rights were guaranteed in the state constitutions which became effective early in 1947, and which established independent constitutional courts to protect the rights guaranteed in the constitution. Labor courts were established March 30, 1946.[8] The court system was rounded out by the establishment of the Bizonal High Court on February 9, 1948, although its functions were restricted to economic, finan̆ial, and administrative fields.

In the early days of the occupation the search and seizure operations of the occupying army were a handicap to Military Government efforts to re-establish a humane German judicial system. It was difficult to oppose searches for arms and to challenge the right of intelligence personnel to hunt for and seize persons believed to be security risks, particularly in view of the mandatory requirement in our directive for the arrest of dangerous Nazis. In January 1947, however, I was able to persuade the Army Command not to undertake searches without previous notice to Military Government. After some opposition in the General Staff, General McNarney approved my recommendation that further house search, except in hot pursuit, would require a warrant from a Military Government court. Later the detention of security risks for more than a few hours required the appearance of our Army intelligence personnel, making the arrest before a Military Government court, to show justification for the detention. On January 7, 1948, in a further effort to restore normal justice, the right of habeas corpus was extended to all persons other than security risks who came under the jurisdiction of Military Government courts,[9] and in a few months was extended to include security arrests. Thus we were trying to make our own judicial procedure an example of democratic justice and concern for the individual.

We were also interested in prison conditions. Experienced officials on our staff inspected the prisons in Germany and found their administration as medieval as their buildings. More humane treatment of prisoners became the policy. Clemency and parole, long neglected in Germany, were exercised through clemency boards, and Christmas amnesties for lesser offenders became routine. How long-lived the effects of our measures will be remains for time to determine. They reflected our interest in the individual as a human being, an element frequently lacking in German administration. When large numbers of house searches without warrant occurred in Wuerttemberg-Baden under an "imminent danger" provision in the state constitution, widespread demand developed for a legal definition of "imminent danger" which would prevent abuse of the term. Arthur Garfield Hays and Roger Baldwin of the American Civil Liberties Union visited Germany at the request of Military Government and reported that it was more zealous of German civil rights than were the Germans. If this was true it came primarily from our work in the judicial field. It was beginning to appear that certainly slowly, but perhaps surely, the German people were attaching importance to their civil rights.

The Legal Division had a major part to play in the trials of war criminals in our zone although neither Military Government nor the Army had responsibility other than to provide administrative and housekeeping services for the International Tribunal which tried the major Nazi criminals—Goering, Hess, et al, in Nuremberg. In this trial, which started on November 20, 1945, and ended on October 1, 1946, the United States was represented on the court by Judges Francis Biddle and John J. Parker, and on the prosecution by Associate Justice Robert Jackson of the Supreme Court. Military Government was responsible for full publicity in Germany including the dissemination of trial proceedings by press, radio, and motion picture. It arranged for German press representation and for German jurists and other officials to attend. When the trials were concluded it was my duty as a member of the Co-ordinating Committee to study the appeals for clemency and to pass on the sentences to the Control Council, to arrange for the execution and disposition of remains of those sentenced to death, and for the imprisonment at Spandau prison in Berlin under rotating Allied guard of those sentenced to imprisonment. The members of both the Co-ordinating Committee and the Council considered these matters in executive sessions and pledged themselves never to disclose the factors taken into consideration, the nature of last-minute appeals, the notes of the individuals, and the decision taken for the disposition of the bodies of those sentenced to death.

Much has been written about the Nuremberg trials, their legal basis, and their probable status in history. My comment will be limited to the effect of the trials in Germany. They were conducted in solemn dignity and with a high sense of justice. The mass of evidence, which exposed not only the relentless cruelty of the Nazi regime but also the grasping rapacity of its leaders, was convincing to the German people. They may have known something of the crimes committed by their own leaders, but they did not know the full extent of the mass extermination of helpless human lives, or the ruthless cruelty of the concentration camp. The trials completed the destruction of Nazism in Germany. Nationalism in some form or other may revive again but not under Nazi leadership, which was shown not only to have used murder as an everyday political tool but also to have used it as a means of personal enrichment. No one in Germany during the trial could fail to witness its effect on the German people.

Subsequent to the International Trial, much time was lost in determining whether the additional trials should be on an international or a national basis. Soviet participation in the International Tribunal had not been received happily in the nations of the world where justice prevails, and Soviet dissents in the final judgment of the International Tribunal made new international trials undesirable. It was resolved that we would proceed in the United States Zone under Military Government, and Justice Jackson's able young assistant, General Telford Taylor, was persuaded to head the prosecution staff. Great difficulty was experienced in obtaining qualified jurists for the courts and our hopes of a substantial representation from the federal judiciary were dashed by Chief Justice Fred Vinson's decision that federal judges could not be granted leave for the purpose. It took a considerable period of time to obtain qualified jurists from the state judiciary systems to form the six courts. They were to try twelve cases, carefully selected to cover the range of German political and economic life which had contributed to its aggressive policy.

These cases included the industrial combines of Flick, Krupp, and I. G. Farben; the physicians and surgeons who had used prisoners for experimental purposes; the Storm Troop leadership that had ordered mass exterminations; the military leaders who had exploited occupied territories; the Justice Ministry, which had violated all normal concepts of justice in condoning mass extermination and in its application of Nazi laws; and the Foreign Office experts who had worked to create the international situation in which aggressive war could be launched with maximum hope for success. It is still difficult to appraise the full significance of these trials or their effect on German thinking. The trials which dealt with acts of atrocity identified the defendants with mass exterminations and added to the

German knowledge of the extent of Nazi brutality. In these cases there was little sympathy for the prisoners. To prove that the industrialists had helped to provoke war was more difficult and the courts did not find the evidence submitted sufficient to convict. Punishment of the industrialists resulted for the most part from their use and abuse of slave labor. These trials which failed to convince courts likewise failed to convince the German people of the guilt of their industrial leaders in the events which led to war. The trials of the military leaders had little effect on the German people.

The involved nature of the cases required the use of many documents by both the prosecution and the defense, so that they required months for completion. It was difficult to sustain public interest over a long period of time as much of the evidence was repetitious, and this was true at home as well as in Germany. On the whole, though, those of us who were responsible for the trials feel that the full evidence will provide history with an unparalleled record of how greed and avarice attract unscrupulous hands to bring misery and destruction to the world. Perhaps an analysis of the causes thus exposed may yet reveal the cure. Certainly, in reviewing the cases which came before me, I felt no hesitancy in approving the sentences.

I tried to expedite the trials and set July 1, 1948, as the target date for completion. In 1947 substantial opposition developed in the United States to their continuance, and the Department of the Army desired them to be brought to an early close. In September 1947, I urged the Department of the Army to permit the Foreign Ministry, Military Command, and Krupp cases to be brought to trial before the program was discontinued, and to find additional judges for the requisite courts. This was approved with the understanding that no further cases would be considered. I was unable to meet my commitment of July 1948 for completion because defense counsel had to be given as much time as it desired to prepare its evidence. The last of the cases was not completed until April 1949.

Concurrently with the Nuremberg trials ran the trials of the war criminals charged with specific crimes, such as participation in the murders and cruelties of the concentration camps, in the murder of our airmen who were forced to parachute to supposed safety within Germany, and in the murder of unarmed, surrendered American soldiers. While these cases were tried at Dachau by special military tribunals and hence did not come under Military Government, I became responsible for them in March 1947 when I took over theater command. It is unfortunate that later the Malmédy case cast some discredit on these trials as a whole, although improper methods in obtaining evidence were charged only in this instance.

A number of the death sentences in the Dachau trials were handed down before I assumed command but execution was stayed pending the hearing of a petition in the Supreme Court. When the petition for review was denied decision rested in my hands. It was then that I asked for an independent review which led to the appointment of the Simpson Commission by the Department of the Army. This commission and my own Administration of Justice Review Board found that improper methods had been used to obtain evidence in the Malmédy case. Members of the prosecution staff testified to the use of stage settings, stool pigeons, and similar measures to extract evidence. Extreme brutalities claimed by the prisoners, in manifest self-interest, were denied by the prosecution staff and not borne out by other evidence. While any use of improper methods was to be deplored, the Army had been shocked beyond measure at the cold-blooded murder of our soldiers at Malmédy. When after months of search among German prisoners the members of the Storm Troop units responsible were picked up, it was found that they had been sworn to silence and this silence was difficult to break. They were the tough, hard-bitten fanatics of Nazism, and I could understand, if not condone, the treatment they received. Although certain of their guilt, I felt that I must disapprove the death penalty unless there was evidence other than that of witnesses claiming that their confessions were extorted under force and duress.

Altogether the Dachau trials, which were brought to a close on December 30, 1947, judged 1672 individuals and acquitted 256. I set aside 69 convictions, commuted 119 sentences, and reduced 138, leaving 1090 sentences; 426 of the convictions carried the death sentence. My responsibility as reviewing officer (there was no court of appeal) and as clemency officer was great, and there was no other which weighed more heavily on me. Early in the review of these cases we found that some witnesses, who had been inmates of concentration camps and who had testified before several tribunals, remembered details and events not corroborated by other testimony and covered such a wide range of time and location as to be of doubtful credibility. Later a Senate Committee criticized us for questioning the credibility of witnesses whose words were accepted by the tribunals. Since our review encompassed a larger field, it did not seem in the interest of justice to accept fully the credibility of a witness before one court when it was made doubtful by his testimony before another. I felt that evidence leading to the death sentence must be indisputable, and therefore commuted 127 to life imprisonment. The responsibility for 299 executions rested on my final judgment and in every case I pored over the record to satisfy my conscience that the sentence was deserved.

Among the 1672 trials was that of Ilse Koch, the branded "Bitch of Buchenwald," but as I examined the record I could not find her a major participant in the crimes of Buchenwald. A sordid, disreputable character, she had delighted in flaunting her sex, emphasized by tight sweaters and short skirts, before the long-confined male prisoners, and had developed their bitter hatred. Nevertheless these were not the offenses for which she was being tried and so I reduced her sentence, expecting the reaction which came. Perhaps I erred in judgment but no one can share the responsibility of a reviewing officer. Later the Senate committee which unanimously criticized this action heard witnesses who gave testimony not contained in the record before me. I could take action only on that record. Unfortunately a failure in a lower office had resulted in several months' delay in publishing my action, which I had intended to be made public when it was taken. This was the single slip in making known to the public the actions taken in 1672 cases, and it was to be expected that it would lead to accusations of attempted concealment. To be charged with deliberate softness in war trials was more difficult to understand, as I had approved the death sentences of more than 200 war criminals.

I have been asked if the Ilse Koch and Malmédy charges discredited our war trials in Germany. It is true that they were prime subjects for Communist propaganda. On the other hand, the full discussions in our press and radio and the obvious interest of the American people in justice and fair play rather impressed the German population. At least they learned that an official representing the United States must exercise his responsibilities in the bright

Mealtime in the Nuremberg jail. Hermann Goering in his cell eats off an Army mess kit and uses a chair for a table.

A member of a German civilian denazification board takes testimony from a witness.

German workmen dismantle part of a power plant at Gondorf, Germany, for shipment to Russia as reparations.

light of public discussion. This was another and valuable lesson in democracy.

While the Legal Division was re-establishing the German judicial system, the Public Safety Branch was rebuilding a decentralized German police force. The German police before the Nazi regime had been under the jurisdiction of the states, but after Himmler became chief of the German police in 1936 the state forces were gradually centralized and infiltrated with Nazis and members of the SS and SA. In the final years of the war they were, for all practical purposes, completely centralized into one force operating as an instrument of Himmler and responsible for the continued subjugation of the people of Germany and the slave laborers who had been brought into the country by force. Before the occupation we made elaborate plans for disbanding the centralized organization to free it from control by the Nazi party and the Nazi paramilitary formations. We found on surrender that there was no need to break it up because it did not exist. It had collapsed completely, its leaders were dead, prisoners, or had fled; and the organization was paralyzed. Therefore our immediate efforts were directed toward reconstituting forces which would accept some responsibility for the preservation of law and order under the occupation forces. Police jurisdiction was limited to the state level, and local autonomy was assured. Towns and cities of over 5000 persons were required to have independent police forces. Villages with populations under 5000 were permitted to contract for state protection.[10]

The police were screened thoroughly to exclude Nazis. The number of former officers in the armed services who could be used was limited. Our denazification directive required the summary removal of any former active Nazi or members of the Nazi party formations. As we knew the officer ranks had been dominated by the Hitler machine, all persons who had held rank from lieutenant upward were also removed. Probably in no other field of German life was the purge of Nazis so complete. The result was that the reconstituted forces were commanded by former policemen who had held no rank or by inexperienced persons who had qualified under the denazification directive. There was an urgent need to train these new officials and for Military Government to advise and assist. Schools were established to teach them and to stress that they were to serve and not intimidate the public.

In July 1945, while some local protection had been restored, conditions in the United States Zone were far from satisfactory. Wandering bands of displaced persons, dressed in United States Army uniforms given them to replace their rags, engaged in robbery and pillage, and their actions brought discredit to the American soldier. Since the Constabulary had not yet been formed, increased Military Police patrols were established, and the wearing of our uniform by displaced persons was declared illegal unless dyed another color. Youth delinquency increased, and the crime rate was high. In September 1945 we found it necessary to rearm the German police with light weapons and to provide them with limited ammunition.[11] German arms had been destroyed, so American carbines were loaned to them.

Concurrently we proceeded with the organization of state police to patrol rural areas and the villages and communities under 5000 population which elected to contract with the state for this service, along lines followed at home. By October 1945 there were 22,000 German police at work in the United States Zone and the increase in crime had been checked. We established a specially trained border patrol which by February 1946 was a fairly competent force of approximately 2500. At the beginning of the occupation Military Government had issued the so-called "stand fast" order[12] which prohibited residents of the United States Zone from crossing the zonal boundaries without its approval. This was done largely to prevent the escape of wanted persons and to allow for the orderly resettlement of the roving populace. Our troops enforced the order until 1946, when they were withdrawn gradually and replaced by the newly created border patrol. None of our troops remained on static duty at the borders by the summer of 1948.

It was a difficult task to recreate an effective police force. There were few uniforms available, pay was small, food was in short supply. There was little incentive, and in a disrupted economy every temptation for corruption. Not the least of the factors to be overcome was our firm policy of depriving the police of the power to punish minor offenders directly and to issue enactments having the force of law, practices which they had traditionally carried out and which had paved the way for the complete Nazi police state.[13] Slowly obstacles were overcome and by the spring of 1947 the German forces were competent, so that the Constabulary could be released from this duty. Our Military Police continued to control the activities of occupational personnel. We also retained full jurisdiction over DP assembly areas. Our Constabulary and Military Police worked closely with the Germans, and the good-natured way our soldiers exercised their authority had much to do with the development of a better spirit of service.

Our Public Safety officers in the several states began to withdraw from active control and to serve in an advisory capacity in 1946. We relied on a relatively small staff of American experts stationed at headquarters and in the state Military Government offices, which was much smaller than the staffs of the other occupying powers. Comparative statistics indicate that their work was effective. The crime rate in Germany in 1948 could not be considered excessive, and in fact did not compare too unfavorably with prewar rates.

In 1949 we sent a small number of selected German police officials to the United States to study our state and municipal procedures.[14] They were well received and I am sure that they returned convinced that the policeman had the responsibility of serving the public and that crime prevention is a major objective. These German officials were surprised and pleased to find former soldiers who had been their combat opponents willing to advise them of the ways of a democratic police force. In Madison, Wisconsin, they were introduced to the legislature. In Germany, where the respect for authority is accompanied by almost subservient awe, this would have been impossible and it made a deep impression. In Chicago they were given every opportunity to witness the workings of city government. At one time they were entertained by German-Americans of the rare type who believed Germany could do no wrong and who spoke bitterly of the occupation. The German officials were shocked at this criticism of American policy from people reluctant to admit the full evil of the Nazi regime. They defended vigorously the exclusion of Nazis from office and our efforts to obtain a democratic Germany.

The way to full police decentralization is not yet entirely clear. In some states the control of the Finance Minister over the allocation of tax receipts still enables interference in local matters. The resistance of the cities to this interference is increasing, and the desire of the cities to control their own police will, I believe, lead to a satisfactory solution.

Along with the establishment of the new police forces, the fire-fighting services were screened to exclude the real Nazis, and within a short time were providing adequate fire protection. Under the Nazis these services had been amalgamated with the police. We separated them and relegated the small German professional and volunteer fire departments to the restricted mission of fighting fires.[15] Our Military Government fire officers found that, owing to climatic conditions, types of structures and other conditions, fire-fighting activities in Germany were not comparable to our activities at home.

Public Safety offices also were responsible for implementing the denazification program, which until late 1948 took a major portion of their time. Their work, which restored law enforcement and fire protection under the unvarying application of the principles of decentralization and development of a spirit of service, was a major contribution to the occupation. We had been fortunate in having as the head of this branch Colonel Orlando Wilson, professor of criminology at the University of California, and on his departure, Theo Hall, a young but experienced police official who represented the modern school of the well-educated police official who is also an expert in public administration.

While the transfer of denazification to German hands reduced the work load, Public Safety officers supervised the Germans in this work for many months. When the Laenderrat in the United States Zone adopted the "Law for Liberation from National Socialism and Militarism" in March 1946, it accepted the responsibility of purging major Nazis from positions of leadership. It knew and we knew that the task ahead was a major one but I doubt if either recognized its magnitude. The purpose of the law was to determine who the real Nazis were so that they could be excluded from places of public influence while new German leadership was developing. It recognized that the great mass of Nazi followers could not be kept forever from German economic and public life without creating a cancerous growth in the body politic which might well destroy democratic progress in Germany. Hence the law clearly defined five classes: major offenders, to be punished by as much as ten years' imprisonment, confiscation of property, and permanent exclusion from public office; offenders subject to imprisonment, fine, and exclusion from public office but entitled to release from restriction on probation; followers or nominal Nazis who, although subject to fine, could henceforth exercise their rights of citizenship; and those exonerated as a result of the investigation. Neither the German lawmakers nor Military Government wished to punish youth subjected to Nazi indoctrination in mass, but both desired their registration.

The magnitude of the task the Germans assumed is indicated by the organization required for the implementation of the law, which at peak aggregated 545 tribunals with a personnel in excess of 22,000. The work of these tribunals was supervised by the Public Safety Branch of Military Government, which for more than a year retained the right to set aside findings and require new trials.

Altogether, under the procedure which required all persons over eighteen years of age to register and submit a questionnaire, there were more than 13,000,000 registrants in the United States Zone, of which 3,000,000 were chargeable cases under the law. Three fourths of the German population were to render judgment on the remaining one fourth; and it is fair to estimate that the one fourth had large numbers of relatives and close friends among the three fourths. Perhaps never before in world history has such a mass undertaking to purge society been attempted.

It may be too early to judge the success of the denazification law. Certainly it developed from the beginning a controversial public opinion between those who believed the German people incapable of the task and those who believed that the program was so stringent as to retard German recovery. I can remember one visiting congressman, perhaps an unreconstructed rebel, who refused to sit in a meeting with German state officials supporting the denazification program, and denounced them as traitors to their countrymen.

The Case subcommittee of the House Select Committee on Foreign Aid, in a unanimous report submitted to Congress in February 1948, recommended that proceedings be closed on May 8, 1948, with full amnesty for lesser offenders and followers. The Department of the Army was naturally responsive to the expressed views of the committee and raised the question of closure with me on several occasions but I believed the program essential and I knew that the responsible German officials desired that it be carried to conclusion. In March 1948, I stated in a cable to the Department of the Army that "each month of trials and release leaves a constantly smaller backlog, which, however, contains increasingly the really bad actors. A general amnesty would free these bad actors and would really discredit entire program."

Also in March, in a teleconference, the Department of the Army, anticipating the Case Report, asked if both denazification and the Nuremberg trials could be closed out and suggested sending a commission over to study the question to enable it to reply to congressional queries. I replied: "I cannot stop denazification except by ordering the Germans to stop. If this is an order, please advise me." I knew the question was receiving consideration in the Appropriations Committee and that the Department of the Army was apprehensive that continuance of proceedings might affect our ability to secure funds to support Germany. I could only report that my views were well known and that I would rather forgo financial support than sacrifice our objectives. While the Department of the Army had raised the question in view of the pressures to which it was properly sensitive, it continued to approve and support my position.

In August 1946 Military Government issued an amnesty to those born after January 1, 1919, except for fanatics occupying places of leadership. These young people, only fourteen years old when Hitler came into power, had had little chance to know anything but Nazi ideology and they could not be excluded from society if they were to be rehabilitated. At Christmas in 1946 amnesties were granted to the disabled and to those whose income during the Hitler regime was so small as to indicate definitely that they had not profited from their affiliation with the Nazi party. Even with these amnesties the tribunals tried over 930,000 individuals; 1549 were found guilty as major offenders, 21,000 as offenders, 104,000 as lesser offenders, and 475,000 as followers. Nine thousand were given prison sentences; 30,000 were sentenced to special labor; 22,000 were found ineligible for public office; 122,000 were restricted in employment; 25,000 were subject to confiscation of property in whole or in part; and over 500,000 were fined.

It is easy to generalize in considering the work of the tribunals. Since a large part of the population was affected, charges against them became widespread. It was common for the German who did not like his neighbor to accuse him of Nazism; for the laborer to charge the unpopular foreman, and for the civil servant to charge the civil servant he wished to replace. It was popular to assume that any German who prospered under Nazi rule was a major Nazi. Usually, as specific cases were investigated by our Public Safety officers, they found it difficult to prove improper action by the tribunals. While the law established a prima facie case against persons who held certain rank or membership in the Nazi party or its affiliates, the tribunals were loath to convict on this evidence alone and tended to require specific evidence of acts which proved the extent of the activities of the accused during the Nazi regime to support convictions as major offender, offender, or lesser offender. We sometimes forgot that the law was intended to identify the nominal Nazi who was excluded from normal life by arbitrary decision of Military Government so that he could be restored to normal citizenship and given the opportunity for self-rehabilitation.

Certainly in no other zone of Germany was a systematic search undertaken to find the real Nazi nor were penalties exacted in comparable volume. In my view, our program did prevent Nazis of any consequence from exerting public influence during the early, formative period of state government. It definitely excluded and excludes major Nazi leaders from positions of influence in German life. In criticizing German appeal courts for releasing a Schacht who had been kept in prison under the law for three years and letting a Von Papen off with exclusion from office and a heavy fine, it should be remembered that able Allied prosecution had failed to convict these men at Nuremberg. While it was common to assume that any industrialist who had successfully engaged in business during the Hitler regime had been a part of the conspiracy to wage aggressive war, the charge was difficult to prove as we found out in the cases tried by our tribunals at Nuremberg.

Looking back, it might have been more effective to have selected a rather small number of leading Nazis for trial without attempting mass trials. The selection of these Nazis would have required registration procedures. In judging the prison sentences, which appeared to be few in number in comparison to the total tried, it must be borne in mind that most of the 74,000 internees in our custody who were transferred to the German denazification ministries had been held under rugged conditions for almost three years when they were brought to trial. On the whole German public opinion and particularly the trade unions, although critical of the actions of many tribunals, supported the completion of the program as did the German officials responsible for its execution.

It takes courage to back a hard program which directly involves over 25 per cent of a population. I am convinced that major Nazi leadership was driven from hiding by the law and excluded from leadership for years to come. Certainly there was restored to citizenship a large group who now have full rights, and yet on the record can be charged as having been Nazis. As to the degree of guilt of the individual and his contribution to the growth of the Nazi party, there will ever be differences of opinion. If the nominal Nazi had not been restored to citizenship and given the opportunity to lead a normal life, we can be sure that political unrest of a serious nature would have developed sooner or later. Moreover, the punitive and exclusion measures were administered by tribunals responsible to public bodies elected by the German people. They may not have cleaned their own houses thoroughly, but they at least removed the major dirt.

CHAPTER 14

Food and Health
for the German People

FOR three years the problem of food was to color
every administrative action, and to keep the German
people alive and able to work was our main concern. From the first
I begged and argued for food because I did not believe that the
American people wanted starvation and misery to accompany occupation, and I was certain that we could not arouse political interest for a democratic government in a hungry, apathetic population.

The need to provide food and thus prevent disease and unrest
in the population behind the battle lines was recognized throughout
the war, and SHAEF had brought to Germany for this purpose
600,000 tons of grain. This supply was not to be used lightly, because
we did not know where and how more could be obtained for the
forthcoming winter. We were convinced that the prevention of
disease and unrest was as important to winning peace as it was
to winning war. Human suffering follows quickly a falling ration,
and inadequate supply brings about a deterioration in moral qualities
difficult to overcome. Laws and regulations mean little to those who
see their loved ones suffering from hunger.

Thus the provision of an adequate supply was more than a humane
consideration. It was essential to the accomplishment of our objectives. We expected German reserves to be low and to be faced with
a difficult period. To make the best of the situation we had brought
seeds into Germany with us, even though we recognized that it was

late for extensive additional planting. In July 1945 we had determined what supplies were available and found that the ration for the normal consumer had to be set at levels varying from 950 to 1150 calories per day. This allowance was only about half the caloric content deemed essential by nutritional experts to support a working population, and about one third of that available to the American people. Actually only about 950 calories per day were distributed.

The fall planting program was difficult to inaugurate even though we had seeds. The shortage of fertilizer and farm implements was acute and little could be done to improve the situation immediately. We did reopen the large nitrogen fertilizer plant at Trostberg, Bavaria, in the United States Zone. Likewise we were able to get some of the farm equipment plants in production.

In August 1945 we fixed the official ration at 1550 calories for the normal consumer. We estimated that 4,000,000 tons of imports per year would be needed to support the 2000-calorie allowance which was our goal. However, we could not meet the lesser ration, and our weighing teams operating throughout the zone were finding increasing evidence of malnutrition. Germans from every walk of life eagerly sought employment with the occupation forces because they were furnished with a hot noon meal. Still, hunger was to be seen everywhere and even the refuse pails from our messes, from which everything of value had been removed, were gone over time and time again in a search for the last scrap of nourishment.

To improve collections from the farms we charged the German regional marketing associations with establishment of farm and market quotas. In November we got the farm co-operatives[1] going again to help in this work. We divided the SHAEF stocks, although they had been purchased almost entirely with our funds, keeping 300,000 tons and sending 250,000 tons to the British and 15,000 tons to the French Zone. I agreed to this transfer because Germans in the British and French areas were existing on a ration lower than in our zone and starving Germans wherever located would delay the accomplishment of our objectives.

We had to have food. By this time the picture was clear. West Germany had never been self-supporting. Even Germany as a whole could not raise enough to sustain its people. Now their principal producing farmlands located in north central and eastern Germany were much smaller because of the severed eastern territory. Moreover, their produce was not available to the Western zones. Yet the population of these zones had increased by about 4,000,000 and was to increase still more. In the highly productive years from 1935 to 1938 the agricultural output of west Germany would have averaged only 1100 calories a day for the normal consumer, just over half the minimum need. Thus, even with maximized agricultural production, it had to export to get money to pay for the additional food to keep its people alive.

I thought that the situation was so serious in November 1945 that I made a hurried trip home to discuss it with government officials and to ask personally for their assistance in increasing the food supply. I found that the world shortage in grain resulting from war dislocation had placed heavy demands on the United States. Everyone was sympathetic but German needs could not be given a higher priority than those of the countries allied with us in our war effort.

To maximize our efforts, we proceeded rapidly to rebuild German food and agricultural agencies. In the late fall of 1945 we set up a zonal food office under the Laenderrat. This office and the tireless General Hugh Hester, chief of our Food and Agriculture Branch, had placed these agencies on a functional basis by February 1946 and had restored normal distribution channels from ship and farm to consumer. Later the zonal food office was headed by a pre-Hitler minister, Dr. Hermann Dietrich. He was an honest, able official who held the confidence of the German people. The improved distribution and the new harvest made it possible for the official ration of 1550 calories to be met for a few months in the winter of 1945–46. But in February 1946 it resumed its downward trend and reached its low point in our zone in May–June 1946, about 1180 calories per day for the normal consumer. In March the evidence of suffering was real and led me to ask General McNarney to cable General Eisenhower and personally ask the latter's support in obtaining relief. We had assured the Germans that we would bring in enough food to maintain the approved allowance. In his cable McNarney pointed out that the lowered ration could not maintain the living standard. Sickness and malnutrition were certain to result and the population would be incapable of sustained work. We could not hope to develop democracy on a starvation diet. We could not even prevent sickness and discontent.

The effect in Germany was paralyzing. Workmen could not produce a full day's work. Economic recovery was stopped and the population was becoming more apathetic each day. Our appeal received support at home and shipments by the end of June permitted a small increase to approximately 1225 calories a day. At the time some believed that this official figure did not fairly represent the food consumed by the average German, since it ignored black market purchases. Our estimates of total production indicated otherwise. The unaccounted-for supply averaged perhaps 200 calories per person per day. Evenly distributed, this would have raised the normal consumer ration to 1425 calories, far below a sustaining diet. Of course it was not evenly distributed. Black market food benefits only the few who have the means to obtain it and not the great masses. No country has ever been able to fully prevent the selfish individual who has the means from living better than the average.

I doubt if we would have obtained increased shipments of food from the United States had it not been for the support given to our requests by former President Hoover. President Truman had asked him to visit Europe to survey the food needs of the several European countries. When I heard his visit would include Germany I asked permission to pay my respects to him on his arrival in Europe. I met him and his party at Brussels and found him sympathetic and understanding but insistent on supporting data. His party included among others Dennis A. FitzGerald, an expert from our Department of Agriculture then serving with the International Emergency Food Council of the United Nations Food and Agriculture Organization. He was an outstanding expert on world food supplies and needs. Shortly they visited us in Berlin, where our agricultural experts submitted the facts. We also brought the chief German official, Dr. Dietrich, and the state ministers of agriculture, to answer questions. Hoover's exceptionally analytical mind and his grasp of figures, combined with FitzGerald's rich store of information on the world food situation, enabled them to detect inconsistencies quickly. When our presentation was completed, they congratulated us and told us they had here been furnished more convincing evidence of need than anywhere else they had been. Their assistance on their return home was invaluable to us not only in the existing emergency but also in the months to come.

Hoover was convinced that our needs were real and that the food shortage in Germany was more acute than elsewere in Europe. He recognized the menace of Communism and the possibility of its growth in a desperate Germany. Above all, he believed that there was no place for starvation where the American flag was flying and that with the raising of that flag we accepted the responsibility to maintain human values.

His trip to Germany coincided with the visit at War Department invitation of a distinguished group of American publishers which included General Julius Ochs Adler of the New York *Times,* Henry Luce of *Time* magazine, Ralph Bellamy of the Cleveland *Plain Dealer,* Roy Howard of Scripps-Howard newspapers, Frank Gannett of Gannett newspapers of Rochester, New York, and others. These publishers witnessed conditions in Germany at first hand. We dined together one evening and participated in a joint discussion led by Hoover. It seemed the general consensus that Germany must be fed and restored to a self-sustaining economic existence. These publishers returned home to give badly needed support to our effort to obtain additional food and to improve the German economy.

The harvest in 1946 provided an average yield and, with imports, enabled the American Zone to reach the allowed ration in October. While we could have maintained this ration of 1550 calories in our zone, it had a short life owing to the fusion of the British and American zones in January 1947. This placed our reserves in a common pool and the British had no reserves. Germany experienced the most severe winter in many years, with its frozen waterways closed to navigation. Short stocks and transport difficulties made distribution most difficult. In Washington we were bidding for supplies through a joint Anglo-American Committee formed under the bizonal fusion agreement. Here we ran into one of those strange inconsistencies which ever dogged our way in Germany. Despite the fact that reserves from our zone had been used to arrest shortages in the British Zone, and despite eloquent pleas for aid from my British colleague, their representative on the joint committee in Washington opposed us until British requirements were met. We were concerned because we believed the reserve stocks in the United Kingdom could be diminished safely in view of our urgent need. We were not successful and the authorized allowance in the bizonal area dropped to 1040 calories[2] a day in April 1947. Weighing teams reported malnutrition at what proved to be the worst stage in postwar Germany. The apathy of the German people was alarming.

Again Hoover and FitzGerald came to our rescue. They returned in February 1947 to survey the food needs of the bizonal area and to study its economic status. Hoover analyzed our records in Berlin with his usual care. He visited a number of places in western Germany to get on-the-spot information and to verify the data submitted to him in Berlin. He was convinced again of the validity of our requirements, which he supported vigorously before the appropriations committees of Congress, and he insisted that we be given a higher priority in obtaining allocations. Moreover he obtained the release of Army 10-in-1 rations and other high-value foods aggregating about 40,000 tons for a child feeding program. This was placed under way in the schools in April 1947 to provide a noon meal of 350 calories for more than 3,500,000 children in the bizonal area. It saved the health of German youth. Without this aid in a critical period I do not know what would have happened. Hoover was accompanied by Tracy Voorhees, who returned to Washington to take charge of food procurement. His determined and untiring efforts contributed materially to the solution of our food supply problem and they were continued when he subsequently became first Assistant and then Under Secretary of the Army.

The child feeding program did more to convince the German people of our desire to recreate their nation than any other action on our part. The expressions of gratitude from parents and children were sincere and touching.

We undertook a land reform program in our zone which was designed to provide small farms for the resettlement of refugees and expellees. However, it was mainly symbolic of our desire to help, since our area, unlike East Prussia and much of eastern Germany, was almost entirely one of small holdings. There were only a few hundred really large landowners. Our program, which we believed fulfilled our international obligation, started with a 50 per cent reduction of holdings of 300 hectares of agricultural land, and this percentage then increased rapidly for larger holdings, following the principle of the graduated income tax. Former Wehrmacht land

and confiscated Nazi holdings were included. Much of the program was devoted to making small garden plots available to many thousands. Exceptions were made for large seed and stock farms which could not be operated economically in small units. Fair compensation was required for land taken under the law. While much has been done toward carrying these measures to completion, the deficit in state finances which followed currency reform, and the well-organized resistance of the landowners, have slowed down progress. We were to be charged with failure by Soviet authorities who had confiscated holdings in excess of 100 hectares for distribution in small plots or for creation of collective farms. However, I am convinced that a statistical analysis of production will show how badly the Soviet system failed to increase production. I believe our system sound and consistent with our own views as to property rights, and as to the individual's right to enjoy the returns from his own labor.

In June 1947 we started the ration upward again. In July Secretary of Agriculture Clinton P. Anderson visited us. He was familiar with Hoover's report. He too studied our requests and, convinced that they were real, promised us the monthly imports we needed to sustain the 1550-calorie ration, a promise which he made every effort to fulfill. He was accompanied by Secretary of Commerce Harriman, who while Ambassador to Russia had always stopped on his way through Berlin to exchange information with us. He was one of the first to realize Soviet intent in Germany and consistently supported our efforts for economic recovery, which he considered essential to checking Communist expansion.

In mid-October 1947 General Hester, who had been in charge of our Food and Agriculture Branch, left us. His right hand in the difficult early days had been Colonel Stanley Andrews, who had left us to return to civil life but had responded on his arrival in Washington to urgent pleas from Secretary Anderson to help the Department of Agriculture with its food supply problem. When the emergency was over he returned to his home in Arkansas to publish an agricultural paper. At my pressing request and at great personal sacrifice he came back to Germany to take General Hester's place. Our Food and Agriculture Branch, which at its peak never exceeded 100 persons, under the inspiring leadership of Hester and Andrews, together with its British associates, reorganized German agriculture and food distribution and saved hundreds of thousands of lives. No words are adequate tribute for their tireless labor and for their understanding that our success in Germany depended upon the provision of an adequate food supply.

Obtaining funds to provide food was facilitated by the support of the many congressmen who visited us in 1947. They were touched by the conditions they saw and their post exchange rations usually found their way into the hands of German children. Congressman John Taber was criticized severely for saying in Berlin immediately after his arrival that he had seen no one suffering from hunger. His bark was worse than his bite. Gruff, insistent on data and not on talk, Taber is a difficult man to convince when the appropriation of federal funds is involved. However, he listened attentively to our presentation, visited the Ruhr, and was convinced that our needs were authentic. He and his companions, Clarence Cannon and Richard B. Wigglesworth, returned home to support our program to the last penny.

Just as we thought we were over the worst period, we experienced the severest drought in recent German history, following the hard 1946–47 winter. The total yield was reduced by 20 per cent. However, imports began to pour in to reach 542,000 tons in August 1947. As soon as stocks permitted, the ration was increased until the official allowance of 1550 calories was met in April 1948.

Our food problem was over. The harvest of 1948 was unbelievably good. It was a bumper year not only in Germany but elsewhere and the critical world shortage was ended. By July 1948 the ration was raised to the 1990 calories recommended as a minimum by nutrition experts in 1945. We had succeeded in rebuilding the German fishing fleet and the daily haul was of great value. Imports had continued to increase and in August 1948 reached a peak of 916,000 tons. Also Europe had some surplus food for the first time since the end of the war and the promise of the European Recovery Program had encouraged us to procure some of it. We now started to rebuild the livestock population. This had been reduced purposely to divert fodder acreage to human food production although it was not economically sound in the long run. It was much better for Germany to raise high-cost meat products and import cheaper grain products. A part of our rebuilding program consisted in contracting with hog producers to use imported corn to fatten 1,000,000 hogs in the bizonal area. Food was still rationed and the diet was monotonous.

A black market meal in the Femina night club in Berlin.

A German child, suffering from starvation and not expected to live, is cared for in a Berlin hospital.

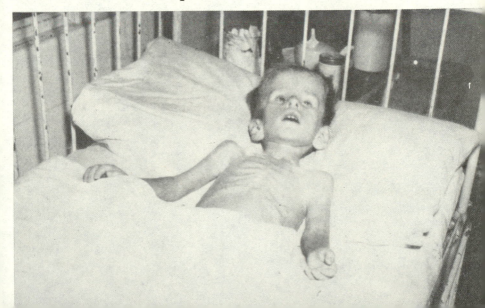

Presents are distributed to German children at a Berlin kindergarten. They were donated by Americans.

American shoes are given to these children in a Berlin orphanage.

The supply, however, sufficed to maintain a working population. The results were restored physical energy and increased output.

Collecting food in Germany during these years was difficult. Prior to currency reform money was of no real value and the farmer could obtain far more for his produce through barter. Almost every farmer had relations and friends in the city to whom he diverted a portion of his production. Trains from the city were filled with passengers carrying precious possessions to the country to exchange for food. Police controls could not prevent this. The Bizonal Administration had little positive control over state agricultural administrations. The latter, particularly in the agricultural states, were loath to invoke controls which might lose the farmer vote. At one stage we had to use the Constabulary to find hoarded supplies. After currency reform the situation improved but even then price controls were continued on farm products, and the new money, while sound, did not buy consumer goods, which were high in cost, in the same amounts the farmer had obtained through barter.

We were forced to use sanctions[3] and withhold imports from the states which failed to meet quotas. We used press and radio so that the non-agricultural population would insist that state officials exercise adequate controls. We provided special purchasing rights for fertilizer and farm implements for farmers meeting assigned quotas, and we fixed grain and potato prices at planting time[4] to encourage the farmers to plant more grain and potatoes. Many at home became convinced from these actions that we were furnishing American aid to Germans unwilling to do the utmost for themselves. This came about because we could not praise the farmer for his work; we had to continue to censure and insist on better performance. The truth is that the German farmer saved Germany in the period when world food supplies made it impossible to obtain adequate imports. Working day in and day out with his entire family, utilizing every scrap of manure, ceaselessly tilling the soil, he obtained excellent production when consideration was given to the many obstacles with which he was confronted. Against quotas which left him little for home and stock, he delivered 86 per cent in 1946–47; 83 per cent in 1947–48; and by March 15, 1949, he had delivered 25 per cent more than in the corresponding period of the preceding year.

We have also undertaken long-range measures to increase agricultural production. These include an agricultural credit bank[5] to provide long-term and a co-operative credit bank to provide short-term credits, authorized by the Bizonal Economic Council in 1949. We have encouraged additional agricultural school services. Dr. Hans Schlange-Schoeningen, director of the Bizonal Food Office, and other German agricultural officials were sent to the United States to study the advisory services which we have developed, and they were impressed with these services.

We were able, after the currency reform in June 1949, to take initial steps toward bringing German farm prices into line with world market prices.[6] There remains a need for an agency like our Commodity Credit Corporation which would purchase farm products at harvest time for resale later to the consumer, thus protecting the ration supply and at the same time stabilizing prices. For the most part, though, the food problem has been returned to German hands.

Food shortages made it more difficult and more important to take adequate measures to maintain public health for humanitarian reasons and to protect the health of the occupying forces. Bombed and partially destroyed cities, damaged water supplies, crowded dwellings, and hundreds of thousands of displaced persons, refugees, and expellees leaving and arriving daily, created the conditions in which epidemics develop. Our Military Government teams were staffed with public health specialists under the able leadership of Major General Morrison C. Stayer, and their work was little short of miraculous.

Immediate surveys showed shortages of hospital facilities, linen and bandages and medicines. We had to reopen pharmaceutical plants, repair hospitals, and allocate materials for hospital linens. German public health organizations and the medical profession had to be denazified and reorganized. In October 1945 a survey showed that the number of hospital beds, though increasing, was only about half of what was needed.

The contagious diseases like diphtheria, tuberculosis, and typhoid fever did increase, but not alarmingly, and they were held in check. In areas where diseases which could be prevented by inoculations became threatening, mass inoculations were undertaken. Water systems were repaired, chlorination was provided, or else warnings were posted to require boiling of all drinking water.

The food shortage was followed by greater evidence of malnutrition. It was necessary for some agency to continuously appraise the nutritional state of the population. Military Government had to know when signs of malnutrition appeared, how serious they were, how rapidly they progressed, and how they could be most economically corrected. It was not enough to recognize disaster when it was at hand. It was necessary to be aware of its approach in order that it might be averted. This task was accomplished through the institution of two programs.[7] One was the street weighing program which was first conducted by American and later by German personnel. This required that some 100,000 persons over twenty years of age selected at random be weighed each month. From changes in the observed weights it was possible to evaluate the broad trends. It became apparent by January 1, 1949, that this program was no longer necessary and it was discontinued. The second program was known as the nutrition team program. This was initially conducted by military personnel who formed temporary teams. They functioned in those areas where it seemed they were most needed, periodically surveying the nutritional status in cities of population over 25,000 and in the western sectors of Berlin. Anticipating the change-over from an operational to an observational, advisory, and reporting phase, Military Government in March 1946 requested the minister-presidents of the three states to establish nutritional survey teams composed of German personnel. The American teams were then withdrawn and these teams left to carry on the work.

Another problem which directly affected the health of the occupation forces was the rapid increase in venereal disease which resulted from thousands of homeless wanderers, lack of sanitary conditions and supplies, and lack of curative medicines.

We coped with these problems with every available resource. In January 1946 the reorganized German public health agencies were competent to assume local responsibility, and we withdrew our own personnel below the state level.[8] Arrangements were made to examine all refugees entering the United States Zone, to isolate contagious cases, and to apply DDT liberally as a precaution against the spread of typhus fever. In the spring of 1947 we were able to obtain enough penicillin from the United States and Great Britain to start a vigorous curative campaign for venereal disease, while at the same time working out a control program with the German authorities.

Control in our zone was helped by the enactment of Control Council Directive 52,[9] which extended the work throughout Germany. By August 1946 the sharp increase had been checked, and thereafter it decreased until it ceased to be alarming. This downward trend was brought about by the widespread use of penicillin and the setting up of 96 treatment hospitals.

Even when the lack of adequate food had brought the German population to their lowest physical energy, with indications of excessive morbidity, the birth rate remained fairly high. At the minimum it was 16.3 per 1000 population per annum in the fourth quarter of 1947, as compared to the United States average of 24.6 per 1000. The mortality rate at its peak was 15.4 deaths per 1000 population as compared to the United States average of 11.1 per 1000.

In 1946 General Stayer returned home to retire. I secured as his replacement an outstanding public health specialist, Colonel Milford T. Kubin, who continued the humane work of his predecessor.

Toward the end of 1946 our supply of insulin proved inadequate to meet the needs of diabetics, and only prompt assistance by CRALOG in bringing supplies from the United States prevented the loss of many lives. In the fall of 1947 poliomyelitis developed in Berlin. Four American specialists, six respirators, and equipment for hot-pack therapy were rushed to Berlin by air by the National Foundation for Infantile Paralysis (March of Dimes), and this humanitarian act was greatly appreciated by the German people.

Throughout 1947 the German public health organizations continued to improve and at the local level were doing excellent work. Progress at the state level was less rapid. Still, it seemed as if we were just staving off disaster.

It was not until 1948 that the state public health departments were functioning satisfactorily, medicines in adequate supply, hospitals repaired, and bed capacities beginning to meet the demand. The increase in quantity and variety of food overcame the problem of malnutrition, and with it, many accompanying problems. The tuberculosis mortality rate had declined until it was about the same as in Great Britain and below the prewar rate in France and other parts of Europe. Birth and death rates were approaching normal. School-fed children were healthy. There no longer appeared a public health threat other than that constantly facing a nation, except in

Berlin. Even there special arrangements were made to meet medical requirements by airlift, and there was no outward evidence of health deterioration. We cut our staff to a small advisory group, making public health responsibility a German matter.

Several unfinished problems still require attention. There is a constant threat to the health and economic status of the Germans in the United States Zone because 60 per cent of the cattle have tuberculosis, and the custom of pooling milk from these infected cows is a serious threat to the children through the spread of tuberculosis. Veterinary experts are working to find a solution, as the destruction of the infected cattle would be a serious blow to agricultural production. The standard of medical education is low. Medical schools were isolated from world progress and the professional standard lowered throughout the Hitler regime. The demands of war for young men prevented adequate training. German medical skill had lost its high standing.

The democratization of the Aerztekammer (Chamber of Physicians) and paramedical associations must be continued. Modern schools for training doctors and nurses in public health are important. International exchange of persons and ideas is essential to the accomplishment of these objectives. Recognizing this need, Military Government has collaborated extensively with international health agencies such as the World Health Organization, the Danish Red Cross Tuberculosis Mission which arranged for 586,000 German children to be tested for tuberculosis and for 208,000 to be vaccinated to date, and the United Nations International Emergency Fund which provides assistance for the care of mothers and children. German officials are being brought abreast of modern developments in public health through the visits of their representatives to the United States for periods of study and observation, and by the visits to Germany of our doctors, nurses, and other experts in numerous health fields. For instance, Dr. Martha Eliot, chief of the Children's Bureau, Department of Agriculture, visited Germany to advise on the development of a modern maternal and child health program, and Dr. W. W. Bauer of the American Medical Association came to plead the value of public health education. The Institute of Public Affairs through its Medical Section is helping to spread democratic techniques in health administration as well as up-to-date knowledge in medical science.

The disrupted economy that resulted from the closing days of destructive warfare and the collapse of government turned Germany into a land of wanderers and refugees. Families were separated, thousands were homeless, and hundreds of thousands of expellees[10] arrived in the four zones. It was imperative to re-establish public welfare assistance on the decentralized basis which had existed under the Weimar Republic. In the summer of 1945, 20 per cent of the German population was receiving some public assistance; child welfare bureaus and church welfare agencies were encouraged to resume their functions; and a denazified German Red Cross was active and useful in local relief work. By the fall of 1945 youth welfare bureaus were functioning on a county basis; the religious organizations were maintaining homes and schools for children without homes or parents, and the American Army was providing educational and recreational programs to combat juvenile restlessness and delinquency. Still the load increased and in December 1945 it was estimated that more than 1,000,000 persons were dependent in some measure on aid from welfare agencies.

While German welfare agencies deserved high praise for their work in the winter of 1945–46 with meager resources, there was a growing consciousness of their need for help from the United States. I was convinced that German organizations were competent to distribute supplies and that United States aid sent directly to these agencies would prove most effective.

To simplify distribution, 15 American welfare agencies at home combined to form the Council of Relief Agencies Licensed to Operate in Germany, better known as CRALOG.[11] The first shipment of supplies from CRALOG, 962 tons of food and clothing, arrived in Bremen in April 1946. Soon CRALOG was joined in similar work by the International Red Cross[12] and Swiss welfare agencies. In June 1946 Military Government concluded a contract with the Co-operative of American Remittances to Europe, known as CARE,[13] for the movement of individual food packages into Germany. Although this non-profit organization desired to set up its own distributing agency in Germany, we persuaded its representatives that a few persons operating through German relief agencies would do a more efficient job than an attempt to establish a new agency. CARE had procured a large number of 10-in-1 packages from Army surplus, and this highly concentrated and balanced food was ideal for the purpose. As these supplies became exhausted, the program was expanded to include not only a standard package of well-balanced food, but packages of baby food, kosher food, lard, woolens, blankets, knitting wool, household linens, baby layettes, and the like. Later, other agencies helped, but none provided in volume the assistance which came from these two organizations. By the end of 1948 assistance for the United States Zone alone came to almost $15,000,000 from CARE, and $14,000,000 from CRALOG. Both organizations also operated in the other zones of Germany. Two Swiss agencies provided approximately $7,000,000 worth of supplies during the same period.

The physical and psychological effects of this aid were immense. Much larger quantities of bulk food, largely grain, brought in with appropriated funds, lost their identity through processing before they reached the consumer. He knew something of the huge extent of this aid but it remained impersonal. On the other hand, when a CARE package arrived the consumer knew it was aid from America and that even the bitterness of war had not destroyed our compassion for suffering.

Relief activities reached the individual German in other ways. In the summer of 1946, and subsequent summers, children from industrial areas were given vacations in Switzerland and in recreation areas in Germany. In August 1946 statistics showed that officially approved guardians had assumed responsibility for more than 250,000 of the children made homeless by war. Late in 1946 the American Friends Service Committee organized settlement centers in Darmstadt and Frankfurt, and during 1947 in Berlin, Freiburg, Brunswick, and Cologne. These centers were places in which the Germans could help themselves. Sewing machines, club, play, and warming rooms, workshops, child care, and supervised playgrounds and nursery groups were available. Furthermore, they offered hospitality and encouraged group participation in projects of common interest. The settlement workers lived in the German economy and shared to considerable degree the hardships of the German. They assisted, too, in training German settlement workers. While the supplies which were brought in to these centers were helpful, they did not compare with the spirit of service which pervaded their work and which has made the very name of the organization to me synonymous with humility and humanity.

During the winter of 1946–47 warming centers were provided in the major cities where those who lived in homes without heat could stop to warm themselves for a few minutes and to drink a cup of hot soup or coffee substitute.

Early in 1947 Red Cross societies were granted charters on a state basis and the state societies co-ordinated their activities through a zonal committee. The Workers' Welfare Organization, which had functioned in the Weimar Republic, regained its old position as a leading relief agency, and the Catholic and Protestant welfare organizations functioned effectively. Special attention continued to be given to youth problems and a "Boys Town" was established in Bavaria. Schools for social workers reopened and their leaders met for the first time since 1933 in Stuttgart to re-form the Association of Schools of Social Work, abolished by the Nazi regime.

By the end of 1947 the relief load had decreased materially, owing to improvements in the German economy, which provided greater work opportunities, and to increased social insurance benefits. In February 1948 the American Friends Service Committee arranged for a German delegate to attend the International Conference of Social Work in Atlantic City, the first German participation in such a conference since the beginning of the war. In March a friendship train bearing relief supplies from America toured the three Western zones and was received everywhere with enthusiasm and appreciation. In the fall of 1948 thousands of children and the infirm were flown out of Berlin to the greater comforts of western Germany. Arrangements were made to pay relief transportation costs in Germany from ECA counterpart funds, thus reducing the cost to the donor. Almost $200,000 was obtained from the exhibition of German art in the United States to help in the youth program. The United Nations International Children's Emergency Fund included German children in its program.[14]

American kindness was never more generously expressed than in its aid program for Germany. Innumerable small organizations and individuals contributed. Cities like Worthington, Minnesota, adopted German cities like Crailsheim, and sent badly needed supplies of all kinds. Schools adopted schools. American enterprises sent food to their German subsidiaries, American trade unions sent food and parcels to German trade union leaders. Within Germany, American soldiers, in addition to their annual Christmas parties for hundreds of thousands of German children, provided candy and food for German youth centers. American women, organized in clubs, collected money to help hospitals and other needy projects. In my own house it was almost embarrassing, for few if any of our overseas guests escaped without leaving contributions for the Berlin Community Drive. For Christmas 1948 packages from Operation Santa Claus started by airlift pilots arrived by thousands to be sorted and delivered by our women in Berlin. Others helped, too, particularly the Swedish Red Cross with children, and the Danish Red Cross with tuberculosis vaccinations. However, America, bulging with riches, was kind indeed, and in being generous to a defeated country wrote another bright page in its history.

While it is true that without American food, bought with American money, loss of life in Germany would have been appalling, the major relief burden was carried by the German state governments and private welfare organizations. In their own misery they found means to help the needy and to organize relief work effectively. I think that the realization of Nazi brutality elsewhere had rekindled in many German hearts a feeling for the suffering of others, which all but died out under Hitler.

This was accompanied on the part of leading social workers by the desire to improve the services of their agencies and to put them on a footing with those operating in Western countries. Realizing that the modern approach to this problem placed great emphasis on the importance of the individual, they turned to us for help in this fundamental task of democratization. To meet this need and to bridge the gap between the exercise of responsibility by Military Government and its resumption by the German Government, and to provide a continuing link between the social services in the United States, other European countries, and Germany, we co-operated with German leaders in the field to place a Social Affairs Center within the Institute of Public Affairs to arrange for the international exchange of personnel and literature. As a beginning, United States and continental welfare specialists came to study and consult with German officials on measures to improve child welfare practices, reduce juvenile delinquency, and raise the level of social work training. Also able and promising German social workers were sent to the United States for study and observation under the guidance of the Federal Security Agency. Outstanding non-German literature on modern social work was made available in substantial quantities. German working committees áre preparing pamphlet material on timely subjects and emphasizing the need for a closer alignment with social science faculties in the universities.

They recognize that security without sacrifice of individual independence must be provided for those who need it and under conditions that will foster democratic thinking and action. Hitler made the most of the desire of a people for economic security to destroy their freedom. That democracy can also promise economic security without destroying the initiative of the individual is the lesson which Germany must learn. Its efforts are directed this way.

CHAPTER 15

The Way to Democracy:
The Appeal
to the German Mind

IN large measure, we knew, the accomplishment of
our objectives in Germany would depend upon our
ability to provide the German people with factual objective information and to acquaint them with the developments in the outside
world from which they had been cut off by Hitler. We did not
minimize the difficulties of this task. The 17,000,000 Germans in our
zone were dazed from the total war which preceded their defeat.
Hundreds of thousands of families were separated and homeless,
food and fuel sufficed only to maintain life. These conditions were
not conducive to the creation of interest in the ways of democracy.
Moreover, they were a hardened people as far as propaganda was
concerned, having been subjected to Goebbels' work over the years
of Nazi domination, and they had seen his promises fail, one by one,
until they were surrounded by their own ruins. We decided early
against the use of direct propaganda. On the other hand, we had
to penetrate the German consciousness to deliver our message. We
had much advice from those who professed to know the so-called
German mind. If it did exist, we never found it; German minds
seemed to us to be remarkably like those elsewhere. This meant we
had to reach them with hard, convincing facts. Only the truth constantly repeated could overcome the cynicism of a Goebbels audience. This we determined to do by every available means:

informational and educational, the magazines, the press, the radio, books, moving pictures, the theater, music, lectures, and town meetings; in the meeting halls of trade unions, in the schools, and in the churches. The groundwork for this task had been laid by Psychological Warfare Division of SHAEF, and our Information Control Division was headed initially by General Robert McClure, who had directed this work.

When we entered Germany newspapers and radio stations were ordered closed pending the screening of personnel and the rehabilitation and reconstruction of facilities.[1] Shortly after Germany surrendered we had re-established in one way or another radio outlets in Munich, Stuttgart, and Frankfurt. They were at first relay stations for Radio Luxembourg, then under U. S. Army control, and their broadcasts were devoted largely to informing the German people of developments in the outside world and to transmitting instructions and information on restrictions imposed by the occupying powers. Within a short time music and other entertainment were added to lighten the grim fare, and more constructive programs were placed under way.

The Psychological Warfare Division had established newspapers in the occupied areas during the later stages of the war;[2] we took most of them over, and by July 14, 1945, there were eight overt papers still being published. Two more were started the following month, one in Berlin and one in Stuttgart. However, we discontinued them as rapidly as we could find newspaper licensees. The overt newspapers were organs of the occupation and announced as such to the German people. It was not to be expected that they could take the place of a German press for any length of time. On July 31, 1945, we licensed the first German newspaper in the United States Zone, the Frankfurter *Rundschau,* with a circulation of 741,500, published three times a week. Licensees were carefully screened Germans, some refugees from and the majority victims of the Hitler regime. We pushed ahead so that one year later there were 38 licensed German newspapers in our zone. By the end of July 1945, 15 motion picture houses were authorized and by September 1945 approximately 100 were in operation, for which 33 American feature films, together with documentary films and commercial shorts, had been made available. A number of symphony orchestras were screened to exclude Nazis and permitted to resume operation. We were particularly careful to remove Nazis from information and entertainment media which would exert an increasing influence on the German people, in many instances in ways difficult for an occupying power to fathom.

By November 1945 more than 200 motion picture theaters had been opened. A new radio station was operating in Bremen. A United States-sponsored news service, known as DANA,[3] was established in the United States Zone. Approximately 50 books had been published, although shortage of paper limited editions to 5000 copies. There were 20 German magazines. Our overt newspapers had been cut to 3 as German-licensed papers increased, 130 theater and music licenses had been granted, and translation rights of American authors were made available. A joint weekly newsreel sponsored by American and British Military Governments was produced in Munich for distribution in both zones. Moreover, Radio Frankfurt had been built up to replace Radio Luxembourg, now released by the Army, as the key station in our German network. Meanwhile the Department of the Army had organized a news service in New York, in close co-operation with the State Department, to supply material on United States international policies and information for both periodicals and radio. The Voice of America, and particularly its excellent news reviews for radio, added to this program. Our group of political analysts, most of whom were experienced press correspondents, provided a daily local touch. Their articles were also used extensively on a voluntary basis by the German publications in the United States Zone.

In October 1945 a public opinion survey unit was created. We had much faith in these polls, although it was shattered somewhat by the election at home in November 1948. Having failed to obtain quadripartite control of Radio Berlin, which was in Soviet hands, we made a rather timid venture in the radio field in that city by installing a wire service, the Drahtfunk, which could be heard by persons who connected their radios to telephone lines. A major feature during 1945 was the opening of American libraries of information, as they were then called, in Frankfurt, Berlin, and Munich. Later these libraries were named "Amerika Haus" and were increased in number. They were supplied with American books and periodicals and became our cultural centers in Germany. Comfortable and unpretentious, as was fitting in destroyed Germany, under excellent American supervisors and with German staffs who believed in their work, they were used for lectures by local talent and visiting American experts, for documentary moving pictures of American life, American art and other activities, exhibits and musical concerts. In fact they made outstanding Americans in many fields available to volunteer German audiences and their popularity was evidenced by an attendance of 2,693,208 for the month of November 1948.

In October 1946 the news service created by Military Government, DANA (later renamed DENA), was licensed as a co-operative news service of the German press in the United States Zone and modeled along lines of our Associated Press. In April 1946 a second newspaper[4] was licensed in Frankfurt, re-establishing a competitive press for the first time in any city of our zone.

Much attention was given over the radio and in both our overt and the German press to adequate coverage of the Nuremberg trials. It was felt essential to make it difficult for German ears and eyes not to hear and see the convincing evidence presented to them. In August 1946 Justice Jackson's summation was repeated in full. Arrangements were made in Nuremberg for housing German correspondents so that they could report to their own people.

In December 1946 Marjorie Lawrence, courageous in her wheel chair, visited Berlin to give a Wagnerian selection accompanied by the Berlin Philharmonic Orchestra. It was the first presentation of Wagner since Germany's surrender, and she drew an ovation from the mixed audience of Allied and German personnel, in which even the orchestra joined. Later, other American artists, great and small, appeared before German audiences, including Menuhin, Melchior, Leonard Bernstein, and Patricia Travers. They brought examples of American culture to Germany.

On June 1, 1947, our radio station in Berlin, RIAS, was equipped with a 20-kilowatt set which enabled us to reach the Berlin audience on equal terms with the Soviet propaganda machine. This was a major move which proved of great value.[5] The listening audience increased from a mere 15 per cent of the radio listeners to 80 per cent, if polls are to be trusted. In late 1947, when it moved to a larger and better-equipped studio, its competent American director, William F. Heimlich, invited a few American and German officials to a quiet opening which, though not advertised, drew several thousand Germans to express their appreciation. RIAS developed an outstanding entertainment program, including the Berlin Philharmonic Orchestra, whose members voted against appearing on the Soviet Radio Berlin. Its news coverage and commentary program was broadened to present full and objective reporting of developments to counteract the malicious Soviet propaganda campaign against the West. The success of the RIAS approach may in part be attributed to the heavy-handedness of Soviet propaganda, which was too greatly distorted to be convincing to German audiences, and in part to our change of policy in October 1947, when, surfeited with continuous Soviet attack, our radio and press were authorized to attack Communism as such and to stress the differences between the Communist police state and true democracy.

From September 4 to 7, 1947, the German publishers in our zone met at Coburg to discuss freedom of the press and publishing problems, and were addressed by Eugene Meyer of the Washington *Post,* and Geoffrey Parsons, Jr., editor of the European edition of the New York *Herald Tribune.* We were forging ahead in our efforts to establish responsible, free, and independent information media in the United States Zone.

In June 1948 we brought a committee of five publishers from the United States, and their recommendations were helpful to the book-publishing trade which was growing rapidly in our zone and was swelled by publishers moving from Leipzig in the Soviet Zone, the traditional publishing city in Germany. In July we were able to remove restrictions on paper because of currency reform and to increase imports, and as a result many German newspapers began to publish five times a week. By the end of 1948 there were 56 German newspapers in our zone, with an average circulation per issue of 4,500,000 copies. There were more than 500 German magazines and full moving picture theater service which showed a diversified selection of French, British, American, and German pictures. Our own documentaries, prepared in Berlin, were popular. The one of the Nuremberg trials, released in late 1948 with some doubts as to its reception, was well received by large German audiences. In 1948 Military Government sent six broadcasters to the United States to observe American methods. Fifteen editors attended a six weeks' course in journalism at Columbia University.

By the end of 1948 German publishers had put out approximately

10,000 titles with a generous sprinkling of American translations. American plays were receiving excellent reception and serious American music was being played with increased frequency by German orchestras. Our Amerika Haeuser were increased to 24 in number with 126 branch libraries, and the monthly attendance in a year jumped from 266,000 to almost 2,700,000. Withdrawals from the libraries passed the half-million mark monthly, and attendance at special group programs reached 25,000 monthly. A special picturama, *America Today,* prepared by Time-Life Incorporated, drew large and receptive audiences. While the paper for our overt publications was purchased outside Germany with appropriated funds, as it was not deemed fair to cut the limited supply of the German press for this purpose, the profits of our publications were carrying the internal costs of our overt program and rightly they were not being charged as occupation costs. More and more, the Amerika Haeuser were carrying the message of America. I can think of no more constructive influence exercised by our occupation than these centers and, perhaps on a smaller scale, we should plan now for their long-term continuance in the interest of better understanding.

By the end of 1948 we had a long-range overt press and periodical program. This was based largely on our newspaper, the *Neue Zeitung,* which was printed in Munich with a circulation of 550,000, and in Berlin as a daily with a circulation of 140,000. The paper had at one time a circulation in the zone of 1,600,000. Following currency reform and removal of paper allocation, the German press was able to issue dailies. With their access to all news services and their ability to give full local coverage, it was difficult for an overt paper to compete. So we have made our paper a daily, with separate editions published in Frankfurt, Munich, and Berlin. We hope that this will develop and maintain a circulation of about 700,000, which will be adequate by comparison with the German press. It will be kept as a high-standard model effort in journalism, presenting factual news and editorials reflecting the American viewpóint. In early 1949 a crisis developed over a press campaign of mysterious origin which charged with little or no justification that the *Neue Zeitung* was becoming a mouthpiece of "German nationalism." This raised the question of whether the American editors or the German staff were responsible for editorial control. This issue was straightened out and it was made clear that the *Neue Zeitung* was an organ of Military

Government. Our magazines—*Der Monat*, of the *Atlantic Monthly* type with a circulation of 60,000; *Neue Auslese* or *New Selections*, with a circulation of 25,000; and *Heute* of the *Life* type, with a circulation of 676,000—are self-supporting and should be continued as long as possible. The *Reader's Digest* is circulated in a German edition, and ECA aid is making other American publications in English available to the German people.

It was the desire of Military Government to restore press and radio to German hands as rapidly as constitutions and laws guaranteed their freedom. As early as 1946 the start was made to obtain adequate legislation. Perhaps in no other field except school reform was the German inability truly to understand democratic freedom better illustrated. It seemed impossible to secure legislation which would not leave the press at the mercy of the government in power. Only in Bremen and in Wuerttemberg-Baden have we succeeded in obtaining laws which provide even an approximation of freedom of the press as it is understood in America, and neither of them is entirely satisfactory.[6] Although the state governments have been informed that we are prepared to give up the Military Government licensing system when they pass legislation which adequately guarantees *freedom* of the press, their approach has always been to seek methods of legalizing control. In the radio field it was almost as difficult. During late 1948 and early 1949 legislation[7] in Bremen, Bavaria, and Hesse established quasi-public corporations with board memberships representative of enough public organizations to insure a free and independent radio. In January 1949, except for time reserved for Military Government use, the radio stations in Frankfurt and Munich were turned over to the newly formed boards. In April this was done in Bremen. Wuerttemberg-Baden adopted an unsatisfactory measure but on March 31, when it was apparent that we would not transfer the Stuttgart station until satisfactory legislation was produced, a revised law was enacted. Its minister-president, Dr. Reinhold Maier, was one of the sincere democrats in Germany and yet he was blind to the importance of a free press and radio. Earlier he had been attacked (he thought unfairly) by Radio Stuttgart and not given the time he deemed adequate to reply; he was appalled that there was no government remedy at hand.

Another issue throughout the occupation was that between independent and party press. From the beginning paper allocations had been made for trade union periodicals, religious periodicals, and political pamphlets as well as for political party information bulletins, but the paper supply before currency reform was never enough to meet demands. The political parties desired full-fledged party newspapers not only for the power such a press would exert but also for revenue. While not opposed to party organs, I had a deep conviction that it was essential to first establish a free and independent press which could hold its own competitively. Hence I advised the parties that I could not approve their request. In the general election in August 1949 the independent press attacked political leaders who appealed to nationalistic passions in the electorate for their failure to present constructive programs. A political party press would have had to support the narrow attitude of party leaders. However, we were prepared to stop licensing by Military Government if adequate press laws were enacted and then the responsibility for approving a party press would be in German hands. When I left there were neither adequate laws nor party papers in our zone. The independent German publishers are protected in the use of their publishing equipment by five-year leases with three-year renewal option clauses, and that they can stand on their own feet was shown recently when the Wuerttemberg-Baden publishers asked and received public support against a state tax on newspapers. The press had appealed to us and we had told its representatives that if they could not arouse indignation over this tax among their readers they did not deserve to survive. I do not believe that this approach had occurred to them. After a few days' effort on their part, including the collecting of 500,000 signatures to a protest petition, the minister-president of Wuerttemberg-Baden suspended application of the law pending decision of its constitutionality by the Wuerttemberg-Baden Supreme Court. This was a healthy demonstration of the power of the press.

There is much to be done to develop a true consciousness in Germany of the importance of a free press and radio to the preservation of democratic freedoms and institutions. Government officials still desire to invoke official authority to silence editorial and radio criticism. On the other hand, the independent press and radio have found their voices, and it will become increasingly difficult for them to be stilled. Meanwhile, our overt papers, magazines, and radio programs should continue as long as possible not only to be the voice of America but also to serve as examples of the part to be played by press and radio in maintaining the integrity of public institutions.

In our efforts to reorient the thinking of the German people we felt it essential to develop strong and healthy trade unions. While the trade union movement is closely allied to economic development, it means so much to future German democracy that it can be discussed more appropriately along with our work to encourage democratic growth. We have made no greater or more important effort in the development of a new Germany than re-establishing a strong organized labor movement. Whereas the Soviet Military Administration created the type of organization it desired by first establishing Communist leadership, it was our policy to permit the unions to develop from the ground up through democratic processes. We wanted them, in forming a federation, to keep some degree of autonomy and to retain some control of their own finances, thus making it more difficult for unscrupulous leadership to use the movement for ideological and political purposes.

We were fortunate to have as the head of our Manpower Division General Frank Johnson McSherry, who had gained the confidence of labor leadership at home in his several years with the War Manpower Commission, and who had to assist him competent men like David Morse, later Assistant Secretary of Labor, and Leo Werts, present director of our Manpower Division. Also I had been able to persuade Joe Keenan of the American Federation of Labor, with whom I had worked closely on the War Production Board, to be my personal adviser on labor matters. Keenan was invaluable in helping the development of trade unions in the United States Zone. Later, arrangements were made for liaison representatives from the AFL and still later from the CIO to work directly with German labor leaders.

Although our endeavor was to rebuild trade unions from the ground up, we did not prohibit state- or zone-wide labor organizations. We insisted only that the membership of local trade unions be permitted to decide the type of organization they wished to have without having it imposed on them from above. Interest in employee representation was evident early in the occupation. In October 1945 elections for shop stewards were held in 3000 plants. Already able labor leaders in the United States Zone, such as Marcus Schleicher, Willi Richter, Lorenz Hagen, and Gustav Schiefer (later assisted by

Fritz Tarnow) were exercising democratic leadership and combating Communism in labor ranks.

By March 1946 trade unions were ready to federate on a state basis. At that time it looked as if a tendency was developing to form highly centralized federations in which the constituent unions would be hardly more than departments. Keenan worked with German labor leaders to persuade them of the value of autonomy. As a result, centralized local federations disappeared as autonomous state trade unions were formed. These unions, varying from 13 to 16 in number, later joined together to form federations. By the end of 1946, union membership in the United States Zone had passed the 1,000,000 mark, about 25 per cent of the estimated organizable labor force. In the spring of 1946 shop stewards were replaced by works councils elected by secret ballot of employees, both organized and unorganized. These councils were authorized by the Control Council[8] to represent the employees in matters concerning production, unemployment, and grievances in their respective plants.

Plans for trade unions on a bizonal level covering the United States and British zones were initiated by the German labor leaders in August 1947. Soon thereafter an informal Bizonal Trade Union Council was formed consisting of the senior federation officials in the two zones. Simultaneously a Bizonal Trade Union Secretariat was established. We told the American Zone labor leaders in a conference on September 8, 1947, that consolidation of trade unions with similar associations in other zones would be permitted provided certain conditions were met. These prerequisites were economic unity, freedom of movement, and the free exchange of ideas among the zones in which interzonal unions were to be formed. On December 7–8, 1947, the state labor ministers met with bizonal labor leaders and agreed to the establishment of a Manpower Department as part of the Bizonal Economic Administration.[9] This was approved by British and American Military Government and became effective on August 16, 1948.

Meanwhile labor proceeded to re-establish its schools and to devote increased attention to youth. The first Germany-wide trade union conference held since the Weimar Republic, in Bavaria on January 15–17, 1946, represented 1,200,000 union members under twenty-five years of age. Another event of significance was the participation of German labor leaders in the international conference of trade unions of Marshall Plan countries in London on March 9–10, 1948.[10] German trade unions had decisively defeated Communist opposition to the plan within their ranks and had earned this recognition. The Bizonal Trade Union Council hailed the program as a basis for European rehabilitation, lasting peace, and democracy.

The growth of the trade unions was steady if not spectacular, and by July 31, 1948, they had a total membership of about 5,000,000 in the three western zones, of whom 1,685,000, or about 35 per cent, were in the United States Zone.

On November 12, 1948, the trade unions in the British and American zones called a twenty-four-hour work stoppage as a protest against the economic policies of the Bizonal Economic Council, which halted all work in both zones except essential public utilities. It was an impressive demonstration of labor solidarity and strength, although it was received with mixed emotions by the German population, many of whom saw in it a deterrent to recovery. It was evidence that the unions had recovered their place in German life and were prepared to protect it.

Labor proceeded to form interzonal trade unions to the extent permitted by other occupying forces. The Bizonal Railway Union was formed on March 23–26, 1948, and was later admitted into the International Transport Federation. On January 27–30, 1949, representatives of public service employees' unions met at Stuttgart and formed a trizonal Public Service Union Federation. Unfortunately French Military Government refused permission to representatives from the French Zone to join, and expressed opposition to such a federation. Later it was to appear that this opposition might be withdrawn and that the Federation of Trade Unions of the three Western zones would become possible. While American and British Military Governments favored trizonal union organizations, they were prepared to accept bizonal federations if the French Zone unions could not participate.

The influence of the trade unions was helpful to the development of democratic processes in Germany. They gave sincere support to the denazification program. Prior to currency reform they held to modest requests for wage increases, fought hard against the black market, and contributed much to the prevention of runaway inflation. Currency reform substantially reduced the financial resources of the trade unions. While they did request special treatment, which was denied as it was to all others including religious groups, they were much in favor of the reform. They were opposed to the relaxation of price controls, which placed consumer goods other than a few essentials beyond the reach of the normal consumer in the early inflationary period following currency reform, and this led to the November work stoppage. Fortunately natural economic laws caused a reverse trend in late 1948 and there were reductions in prices in almost the full range of consumer goods. Nevertheless, prices remained relatively high and a demand for increased wages, if met, would have led to an increase in the cost of export items, which would have destroyed the export trade. Labor leaders wisely resisted such demands. This required courage and intelligent leadership. It was difficult for labor to see consumer goods in shopwindows, badly needed but beyond their ability to purchase, and to understand that this was in large part due to the fact that the German economy was not yet able to support a normal standard of living. It was to the credit of its leaders that they followed a restrained and conservative policy which helped to create and maintain stability, and at the same time, in each consecutive election, reduced the number of Communist officials who, in the early organizational work, had secured an undue proportion of labor offices. The climax came in 1948 when August Schmidt, the able and astute leader of the Miners' Union, succeeded in preventing the re-election not only of the Communist vice-chairman, Willy Agatz, but also of any Communist representation on the Executive Council of the union.

The relations of Military Government with labor leaders of the United States Zone were always pleasant even though we did not always agree. I met with them from time to time and our meetings were friendly and usually led to better understanding among us. One of the problems labor was anxious to solve was the return of trade union property seized by the Nazi DAF (Deutsche Arbeitsfront— German Labor Front). This property was confiscated by DAF in 1933 when independent labor organizations were suppressed by the Nazi regime. Physical property still owned by DAF at the time of its dissolution by Military Government was promptly returned. Other assets, including property purchased and resold many times, offered a difficult legal problem which we believed should be resolved by German courts. The labor leaders recognized that progress was more rapid in the United States Zone than elsewhere, and our effort to arbitrate a final solution between the state governments for the distribution of unidentifiable property was, I believe, while not wholly satisfactory, understood and accepted by the unions.

It was difficult for U. S. Military Government to be as popular with the rank and file of union members as British Military Government, which represented a Labor government. While the German trade unions, like our own, were not affiliated with any party, perhaps three fourths of its members favored the Social Democratic party and were in favor of some form of socialization of heavy industry. Our own policy was to maintain neutrality between the German political parties advocating different patterns of economic life, although it was our duty under our directive to point out the merits of free enterprise. United States Military Government never deviated from its policy of political neutrality. When our zone was merged with the British Zone, both Military Governments were in full accord that the future economic pattern of Germany should not be formed by the occupying authorities but by the German people when they had a government of their own.

Under this policy United States Military Government had to disapprove state-adopted measures giving works councils a voice in management, and British Military Government had to disapprove state socialization in North Rhine-Westphalia. In approving state constitutions which authorized public ownership of industry, I made it clear that measures in a single state which prejudged future German government could not be implemented. The German economy in the bizonal area could not recover if each state in the area developed and pursued a different economic pattern. While this reason alone impelled my disapproval of the works council legislation, there was a tendency on the part of German trade unions to have the rights of labor enacted into law. This seemed to me unwise and contrary to their own interests. Their constitutional rights were clearly established. To insist that they be further specified in legislative acts implied that they could be denied by such acts. Collective bargaining gave the trade unions the opportunity to establish the rights of works councils and other rights, and Military Government had authorized and urged its use by both employee and employer.

With the establishment of the Bizonal Department of Labor, the relationship between Military Government and the unions became more and more a joint Anglo-American problem. I learned to know and appreciate the fine qualities of men like Hans Boekler, August Schmidt, and other leaders in the British Zone. On February 15, 1949, General Robertson and I met with employers to urge a better labor-management relationship and to approve the establishment of an Employers' Association with limited functions which could represent management in conference with labor. We outlined to this group, and a few days later to the labor leaders of both zones, our common policy, and both expressed their full satisfaction. This statement of policy follows:

1. It has been the policy of Military Government since the beginning of the occupation to encourage consultation between the German Government, trade unions, employers and farmers. Military Government has followed the practice of consulting these groups in developing policies and programs.

2. The laws on the organization of the coal and steel industries provided for Military Government consultation with appropriate German bodies before designating trustees. We shall continue to ensure that the trade unions as well as employing interests are consulted in this matter, and we hope that at least some of the persons appointed will carry trade union support.

3. During the month of February, Military Government has discussed the question of consultation with the Executive Committee of the Economic Council and urged that economic groups such as the workers, employers, and farmers, be consulted through their representatives on all decisions which might affect them.

4. It is our desire to see that cooperation firmly established between German governmental authorities, employers, trade unions, and farmers.

5. It is right and proper that governments should keep themselves in the closest possible touch with organizations which speak with authoritative voices on behalf of such vitally important sections of the community as employers, workers, and farmers. It is no more than common prudence that governments should attach the greatest possible weight to the opinion of those bodies before any legislative or administrative action is taken which affects the large sections they represent in the community.

6. The occasions on which British and American Military

*Governments find it necessary to legislate in German affairs will,
no doubt, steadily decrease. But we give you the assurance that
when such occasions do arise, we will in all proper cases ascertain your views before taking any decision.*

7. *Moreover, it almost goes without saying that in matters
which concern employers and workers jointly, and there are few
occasions when their interests are separated, the work of government will be facilitated if the joint voice of employers and
workers can be heard. We need hardly stress, therefore, the
supreme importance which we attach to a body or bodies which
will enable employers and trade unions to get together, to iron
out their differences, and concert plans of action not only in
matters which may be the concern of governments but in those
for which the authority and responsibility remain with the part-
ners in industry.*

8. *Beyond these general observations, we do not propose to
lay down any rules on the relationship between governments,
employers, and trade unions. You must work them out for your-
selves, and that applied to Mitbestimmungsrecht [right of co-
determination of works councils in management]. On that
subject we have said it is not appropriate that fundamental
legislation of this type should be passed now by Laender governments in anticipation of the constitutional decision concerning
the division of powers between a federal government and the
governments of the Laender.*

9. *We feel, however, that employers, whose conduct toward
the work people they employ is governed by the consideration
that those work people have a vital interest in the prosperity of
the industry and plant in which they are employed, will not wait
upon legislation to discuss this important question frankly with
them. We have already said that we have no objection to arrangements which are arrived at by agreement between the two
sides.*

10. *Socialization. We have said, and we repeat now, that this
is a question for a duly elected German government which may
claim beyond question to have the mandate of the German peoples. We do not propose, nor do we desire, to influence that
decision one way or the other. In the United States great importance is placed upon the enterprise and initiative of the*

*private individual. In Great Britain private enterprise operates
alongside schemes of public ownership and control of industry.
Labor itself has preferred collective bargaining to legislation in
establishing its rights. Just as in these countries the people are
called upon to determine from time to time what suits their
peculiar circumstances best, so must you decide here in Germany.*

A heartening example of the contributions of organized labor
to the development of a democratic Germany was the refusal of labor
in Berlin to accept Communist domination. When we arrived in the
city the trade unions had already been organized under Soviet
leadership into a federation, the FDGB,[11] which was under Communist control. Efforts within the organization to break this control
were unsuccessful in view of the support which it received from
Soviet authorities and the by-laws under which it had been formed.
In February 1948 a working committee of independent trade unions
formed an organized opposition consisting of all non-Communist
elements. This movement was expedited in May when the results of
union elections were rejected by the Communist-dominated FDGB
executive board, and the UGO,[12] or independent trade union federation, was established. This union, which soon had a membership of
about 200,000, resisted Communist attempts to dominate Berlin and
gave wholehearted support to the airlift.

Our work with the trade unions was helped materially by the visits
of labor leaders from the United States. It is impossible to name
them all but William C. Doherty, David Dubinsky, and George M.
Harrison, of the American Federation of Labor, and Sidney Hillman,
James B. Carey, and Michael Ross of the Congress of Industrial
Organizations were among the many who came. Irving Brown, AFL
representative in Europe, was also a frequent visitor. While our
visitors did not always agree with American policy, particularly as
several felt sincerely that socialization was essential to a democratic
Germany, I am sure that they did understand and appreciate our
genuine effort to rebuild democratic German trade unions.

To some extent a punitive measure which I felt necessary to
impose in Stuttgart on October 30, 1948, was interpreted as a blow
at labor, which it was not. After a labor rally to protest against
high prices, unruly members of the audience began to break store

windows. They soon transferred their attention to passing automobiles and stoned American cars, overturning one of them. Military
Police had to assist in restoring order. I was unwilling to accept such
treatment of our own people engaged in peaceful pursuit, as acceptance might well lead to further and more serious incidents in which
bloodshed could occur. Therefore I asked Mr. LaFollette, the director of state government, to impose a curfew on the city. He did so
reluctantly, since he did not share my view that failure to do so might
lead to other and similar incidents. The speech of the German labor
leader had been inflammatory and directed against Military Government, so I sent for him to advise him that when such speeches were
followed by disorderly conduct directed against American personnel
the speaker would have to accept responsibility. I blamed neither
unions nor labor for the act of the individual but my responsibility
for the safety of occupation personnel would not permit me to let
a demonstration turn into acts of force against our personnel without warning of the strong measures which would result if there was
repetition. The officials and people of Stuttgart complied with the
curfew, which was also accepted by many of our own people, and
it was not necessary to keep it in force for more than a few days.

While trade unions were growing, our Manpower Division had
early taken hold of administrative problems in the labor field. By
July 1946 it had restored labor courts to their normal functioning in
labor disputes, and the social insurance offices were again making
deductions from wages. In August the registration of employables
was placed under way. By fall all social insurance benefits except
unemployment insurance had been re-established. German industry
was still halted and unemployment insurance benefits presented a
burden which available funds could not meet. In 1946 there was a
sharp uptrend in employment, although it resulted in large part from
the decreased output of the individual worker, who was receiving an
inadequate ration. By spring this resulted in a shortage of labor,
though production was only a small percentage of prewar output.
Absenteeism due to sickness and to the necessity for workmen to
spend hours in search of food and essentials was excessively high but
there was to be no unemployment problem until after currency
reform in the summer of 1948.

In late 1946 the states in the American Zone accepted the responsibility for the payment of unemployment insurance, thus completing

the full restoration of social insurance benefits. In April 1948 an increase not to exceed 15 per cent was authorized in wage ceilings, with the increase in each industry to be settled by collective bargaining. Thus German trade unions had a real issue in which they could represent their members in negotiations with employers. Prior to 1948 wage ceilings were raised by 10–20 per cent in coal and other mining fields, building construction, building materials, textiles, clothing, manufacturing, railroads, and forestry, which also permitted limited opportunity for collective bargaining.

Labor shortages in the Ruhr continued to hamper coal production and a recruiting program was established in the United States Zone in 1947 which furnished 50,000 workers to the Ruhr coal mines. The employment offices functioned satisfactorily in this placement program. Steps were also taken to improve relationships between German labor and United States Army employment agencies to provide an example of the desirability of satisfactory employer-employee relationships.

In general it could be said that by the end of 1947 the labor administrative agencies in the bizonal area were adequate in number and purpose, social insurance benefits were being met, and collections being made. Labor was dissatisfied with the standard of living which it could earn within established wage ceilings and with social benefits. The immediate effect of currency reform had been to increase the demand for labor. The rise of prices when released from control resulted in an inflationary threat that labor recognized and resisted. There was insufficient money in circulation to permit inflation to continue. Moreover, the increase in labor productivity due to better food and to less absenteeism enabled Germany to increase its production output by approximately 50 per cent, with a decrease in total employment. With the exhaustion of the initial cash distribution of new currency, the short supply of money stopped the inflationary trend, prices dropped, and for the first time in two years west Germany had an unemployment problem. Long-term credits, to encourage rehabilitation of plant and the construction of housing, stimulated the building trades and provided more employment.

Currently with the work of our experts in the information field and with the trade union sessions we were devoting much time and attention to liberalizing the educational structure. The work of the Education Branch was under Colonel, now Dr., John Taylor, president of Louisville University. At the start its task seemed hopeless. Many German school buildings had been destroyed, others badly damaged, and still others were occupied either by troops or by displaced persons. Teaching staffs contained many ardent Nazis; in one city more than 60 per cent of the staff had belonged to the party. Textbooks were so impregnated with Nazi ideology that even mathematics problems were expressed in military terms and logistics. German youth learned to add and subtract guns and bullets rather than apples and oranges. The hope of a new Germany rested in its youth, which was roaming the streets. It was essential that it be returned to school quickly before it formed lasting habits of indolence or violence.

Thus our Education Branch had to direct its immediate efforts to the more mechanical processes of education: the restoration and return of school buildings, the improvisation of textbooks, the screening of old and the selection of new teachers. The first school was reopened in the British Zone at Aachen, then under our Military Government, on June 4. In our zone we prepared for an October 1 opening of elementary schools.[13] We had 5,328,616 textbooks, reprints of pre-1933 textbooks; Nazis were removed from teaching staffs; priority was given to school repair and to the even more difficult task of finding housing for troops and displaced persons so that they would release buildings. With heroic efforts, schools were opened beginning October 1, and by the end of the year approximately 1,849,206 children were back in school. The number of schools was approximately half that of 1947 and they were crowded. We had screened 20,000 teachers, not more than half the number needed. Only a few schools were heated and the pupils had to sit in heavy winter clothing. Still we had accomplished our purpose. The children were off the street and juvenile delinquency was under control. German committees had been formed in each county to stimulate new or to revive pre-Hitler youth groups, and to assist in finding homes for the thousands of homeless young boys and girls wandering aimlessly over Germany and living on their wits.

We were now ready to screen the teaching staff and to open the higher schools, a program which was started with the opening of a theological faculty and three medical faculties in Heidelberg, Erlangen, and Marburg, in November.[14] As rapidly as faculties could be screened, other higher schools and universities were opened. By the spring of 1946 most·of the higher schools in the United States Zone were functioning in badly damaged buildings and with limited staffs. Also adult education, popular in Germany in pre-Hitler days, was functioning in the larger cities with regularly scheduled lecture programs.[15]

While new textbooks were being prepared by Germans we found that of 1366 submitted to us by January 1946, 163 had required amendment and 392 had to be rejected. All of the acceptable textbooks could not be printed, as there was an acute shortage of paper, and they had to share the supply with newspapers, magazines, and other publications. In 1946 we were able to print only 901,481 textbooks; in 1947, 5,574,816; and it was not until 1948, when we had paper purchased with funds provided by our Congress and were able to print 13,507,224, that the problem was solved. By December 1948 more than 19,000,000 textbooks had been published in our zone.

When Dr. Taylor returned to the United States in 1947, his deputy, Dr. Thomas Alexander, acted as head of the Education Branch. Alexander, a student and teacher of education, was an expert in German school methods. His invaluable experience and work were badly needed in the reform program, and he preferred to remain in this field. Late in 1947 I was fortunate to secure as educational adviser the president of Indiana University, Dr. Herman Wells.

At this time it was my view that the more mechanical processes of school rehabilitation had been completed. Schools were repaired; teacher staffs recruited; vocational, grade, and high schools and universities and colleges were functioning. Henceforth it was our mission indirectly to guide and influence these institutions into more progressive and democratic educational methods. This required re-awakening the interest of parents in the education of their children and, through opportunities for trips abroad, helping German educators recover from the isolation of the Nazi years. The work of the Educational Branch was extended to a broad cultural field and it was made the Educational and Cultural Affairs Division,[16] reporting directly to the military governor.

Education Service centers were established in nine locations where German educators could discuss modern teaching measures with international experts and obtain the latest textbooks and other data required in the preparation of new German textbooks. The exchange program[17] brought into Germany by March 31, 1949, more than 115 experts, of whom 90 were from the United States. In this program education was interpreted in its broad meaning and government specialists, labor leaders, experts in women's organizations and other fields of public service were included. In the same period 185 German experts and 359 German students and youth leaders were sent to the United States. Public foundations and universities at home aided the exchange, which was financed in part by appropriated funds, through the provision of scholarships and other aids. It was the foundation upon which our reorientation program was built.

Meanwhile we encouraged such efforts as the International Holiday Courses at Heidelberg, Marburg, and Munich universities, which drew 158 American, 69 foreign, and 432 German students in July 1948; and the two International Youth Conferences at Munich in which, in 1948, 800 foreign students joined with 2000 German youths in studying current problems. Citizens' school committees, akin to our Parent-Teachers Associations, began to take an active part in current educational problems. Their voices were heard in German political circles. The restoration of adult night schools in Germany was likewise encouraged, and by 1948 there were more than 200 in operation.

We gave particular attention to the use of the radio and motion picture in German school life. We were able not only to place motion picture machines in Amerika Haeuser but also to give them to our field offices for loan to schools to show documentary films. We purchased over 1000 radio sets to augment German sets in the schools and brought experts on radio instruction methods from the United States to meet with German experts. Each radio station devotes several hours each week to these programs, which have done much to inform German youth of the outside world. Educational radio is now a part of normal German life.

In May 1948 Dr. Wells, having to return to Indiana University, was able to persuade an experienced and able educator, Dr. Alonzo Grace, then commissioner of education in Connecticut, to take his place. Dr. Grace has continued with this expanding program. The interest of American educational circles in our work increased substantially when a committee of experts from the American Council on Education visited us in July 1946. This committee, under the chairmanship of Dr. George F. Zook, maintained its interest in the problem after its return home, and its members helped to build the exchange program.

School reform is still a major objective in our program but such reform obtained by order of the occupying authorities is not likely to be lasting and our hope is that it can be brought about by the German people. The state constitutions in our zone contain adequate provisions to guarantee equal educational opportunities to all children. Standard German practice was to require four years of compulsory education in the free public schools corresponding to our grammar schools. Secondary schools had tuition charges which excluded children from the poorer families, and only a small portion of the secondary school graduates entered higher schools. Thus after four years it was necessary to determine the educational future of each child. It is true that vocational schools were available for those who did not choose the secondary schools and that they were excellent technically although they needed to place much more emphasis on additional academic instruction. It is our desire to have a twelve-year public school course available for all children. Some success has been achieved, and free textbooks and tuition are now provided in the United States Zone. Experimental twelve-year programs are being carried out in all states; Berlin and Bremen have adopted the twelve-year program, and legislation adopting it in part is before the legislatures of Hesse and Wuerttemberg-Baden with cabinet approval.

Foundations in the United States are providing exchange professorships and the University of Chicago maintains a group at the University of Frankfurt.

In Berlin earnest and sincere advocates of a free educational system broke away from the Communist-dominated University of Berlin to establish with great courage in the United States Sector a new univeristy dedicated to academic freedom; it already has 140 teachers and an enrolled student body in excess of 3000.

The Educational and Cultural Affairs Division devoted special effort to encouraging youth and women's activities. German youth groups have been helped in many ways. Particular attention was given to summer camp programs, and the Army-sponsored German youth program developed competitive sports and other recreational programs designed to keep alive in German children a sense of play. Likewise, recognizing the importance of women, now greatly outnumbering men in Germany, a special group has been available to advise and assist them in organizing and playing their part through organizations in Germany's daily life. Outstanding women, including Mrs. Roosevelt and Congresswoman Woodhouse, were willing to visit Germany to talk to these organizations. Their representatives have also been sent to the United States and to European countries to confer with the leaders in women's activities.

The results of an educational program are intangible and almost impossible to evaluate immediately but they will record the success or failure of our occupation. It is difficult to produce evidence convincing to those who appropriate funds of the importance of exchange programs and the dissemination in Germany of examples of our own cultural life. I have a deep conviction that our work in the field of education is taking hold and that it may indeed succeed in creating a people more conscious of their rights and freedoms. For example, our town meetings may not become a lasting part of German life but they have already made the citizen conscious of his right to question his public officials, and the latter realize that they too can learn from the citizen the failures and successes of their administration. It is because of my belief in the value of this program that the personnel engaged in our educational activities formed the only group not being reduced in number when I left Germany. I hope that it will continue in its friendly advisory role as long as occupation continues and that even then arrangements will be made to continue Amerika Haeuser and the exchange program.

We hoped that the liberalization of the educational structure would be facilitated by a revived and invigorated religious life in Germany, although I did not believe that Military Government should take an active part in religious life. The purpose of our Religious Affairs Branch was to encourage German church leaders by helping them solve their immediate problems. We had guaranteed with the arrival of our armies full freedom of worship.

Church leaders in Germany were quick to take advantage of their opportunities, and as early as August 1945 both Catholic and Evangelical church leaders had met and expressed willingness to cooperate with Military Government.

German church leaders were the first to be permitted to attend meetings outside Germany to renew contact with the religious leaders of other countries. Early in 1946 Bishop Theophil Wurm, the head of the Evangelical Council, and the vice-president of the Council, Pastor Martin Niemoeller, attended the Geneva conference of the World Council of Churches. Michael Cardinal von Faulhaber from Bavaria, and Cardinals-elect Konrad von Preysing, Josef Frings, and Clemens August von Galen attended the Consistory at the Vatican. Leading clergymen from other countries, including our own, were encouraged to visit Germany, and religious groups at home helped with relief packages and other aid.

In early 1946, to be sure that our Religious Affairs Branch would not interfere in religious matters, I arranged for each of three faiths, Catholic, Protestant, and Jewish, to designate representatives from home to work directly with German religious leaders and to be our liaison representatives.

Theological seminaries were reopened in 1945. Jewish community life began to re-establish itself in the principal German cities and to open new synagogues and prayer rooms.

When the old problem of confessional schools arose, we insisted that this was a German problem to be settled between German officials and German church leaders.

The first international religious conference held in Germany was the Central Methodist conference in Frankfurt in November 1946, attended by Methodist leaders from Sweden and Switzerland as well as from Germany. It was the forerunner of several such conferences.

We helped the churches to resume publication of religious papers through the allocation of newsprint, although never until 1948 in adequate supply. The American Bible Society made some Bibles available, and enough cellulose was brought into Germany to print 400,000 Bibles in 1947. In that summer we scheduled time for each of the principal religious faiths to broadcast on religious subjects from each of the German broadcasting stations in the United States Zone.

Ecclesiastical leaders are playing an active role in German life, and the return to religion is marked. In general the co-operation of church leaders with Military Government has been genuine and helpful. Bishop Wurm and later Bishop Otto Dibelius, who succeeded Bishop Wurm as president of the Council of the Evangelical Church, frequently and publicly expressed their appreciation of American aid. The conference of Catholic bishops did likewise and also expressed appreciation for the new freedom which made possible the growth of Catholic youth groups. Perhaps our only major difference with church leaders came about from the open opposition of some of the leaders in the Evangelical Church to our denazification program and to the exclusion of Nazi clergymen from further pastoral activities. We were forced to carry out our program without the co-operation which we should have received from them.

The rebirth of the Jewish communities also led Military Government to request the aid of the International Council of Christians and Jews, and representatives of this Council were assigned to Germany to help develop a new spirit of tolerance. This led to the establishment of a German Council in Munich which may lead to others and to a new tolerance.

Lasting reform in Germany must come from within. It must be spiritual and moral. While Military Government has not interfered in the internal affairs of the church in keeping with our own national policy, it has recognized that religious institutions are major elements in the German social structure which must participate in any program directed to the building of a peaceful and democratic Germany if it is to have hope of success.

There is as yet little tangible evidence of a new spiritual growth in Germany. The freedom now accorded to its religious leaders, increased attendances in churches, and growing membership in religious youth groups do indicate that there is a revived interest in religious worship and teaching which may develop into a spiritual movement of deep significance in the future.

CHAPTER 16

Restitution

REMOVING Nazis from public life and providing factual information to fill the void left by twelve years of hearing and reading what a totalitarian government wanted the German people to believe were important to our objectives. They were not enough. Justice demanded that we correct as much as possible the misdeeds of the Hitler government.

Never had a nation pursued such a systematic program of loot and plunder as Germany under its gangster Nazi leaders. In the declaration of London of January 5, 1943, the Allied Nations had served warning to the German people[1] that they reserved their rights to declare transfers of plunder invalid whether they had occurred by open looting and plunder or had been covered with apparent legality. When Germany surrendered, it became necessary to develop practical procedures to carry out the London declaration and this was no simple task. It was not until January 1946 that the Allied Control Council was able to agree on a "Definition of Restitution."[2] The French had insisted not only on the return of cultural objects but also on the replacement of those that could not be found by similar objects of like value. This seemed impracticable for more than one reason. It was almost impossible to prove that a cultural item of value which could not be located was brought into and lost in Germany. If a loss was established, it was still impossible to determine what item of similar value should be offered in replacement. To have tried to do so would have meant either increasing the burden of receiving and evaluating claims or else a wholesale transfer of German cultural objects which might prevent the creation of democratic government. We could not expect the German people to understand a course that deprived them of cultural background and was akin to the Hitler policy which we condemned. We did reach a compromise which provided for replacement of lost items in special and extraordinary cases although as yet no one knows exactly what it means.

France insisted also that all items taken into Germany from the countries which it occupied be returned even if these items had not been removed by force or duress, but the London declaration had not made this mandatory. Soviet representatives opposed the French, arguing with vehemence that the transfer of these items to Germany had contributed to German war strength and that there was no equity in their return (which reduced availabilities for reparations), since the Soviet Government, whose people had suffered most from war, had no claim of this kind, having destroyed under its scorched earth policy everything in advance of the German armies which might be of help to them. After sustained argument we agreed that property in existence at the time of occupation should be presumed to have been acquired by force or duress and should be returned unless proved otherwise. Property manufactured during occupation and removed to Germany was to be entitled to consideration for return. Of course all cultural objects were to be sent back.

This decision seemed satisfactory to me. It was difficult to establish force or duress for many items purchased by Germany during occupation. Even if these articles had been charged as occupation costs, their procurement had helped to maintain a going economy in the occupied countries and frequently Germany had supplied the materials. I was influenced in my views by the financial burden which Germany represented to us and which could well have been substantially increased unless restitution procedures were based on sound legal concept including identification. In practice, claims which we rejected were seldom appealed and to most claimant nations our procedures proved satisfactory, judging from their letters of appreciation.

The search for, identification and return of cultural objects were made possible by the Monuments and Fine Arts teams of experts assembled to accompany the Allied armies entering Germany, some of whom remained with Military Government to complete the task. These cultural objects were found in huge lots, of which the Goering collection was one of the largest, and in many places: in salt mines where they were placed for safekeeping; and in old castles through south Germany. Our zone, the area in which the majority of the holdings had been placed, contained some 1500 repositories. We established collecting centers to which cultural objects could be brought for care, identification, and return, and the art experts of the looted nations were invited to participate in the work of identification. All cultural objects are of value to all the peoples of the world and equal care and attention were given as well to the safekeeping of German masterpieces.

In September 1945 we were able to make initial shipments to Belgium, France, and the Netherlands. The importance of restitution cannot be overstated. Returned masterpieces included the famous Veït Stoss altarpiece to Poland, Rembrandts, Rubens, Tintorettos, El Grecos, rare books, statues, and folklore collections. While some cultural objects were still being found in 1949, the vast majority, estimated at more than 2,000,000 in number, had been returned to fourteen nations. Their monetary value is difficult to estimate but was conservatively in the hundreds of millions of dollars.

Restitution in other fields was undertaken systematically and steadily. Germans were required by law to submit known or suspected loot and more than 25,000 declarations were filed. The nations entitled to restitution had missions in the United States Zone to present formal claims and to prove identification.[3] April 30, 1948, was fixed as the deadline on claims[4] other than cultural objects, and by that time 20,600 claims had been received. More than 42 per cent of them have been satisfied and the items identified and returned. Their variety is indicated by some of the items: household furniture, two oil cracking plants, race horses, machine tools, silver fox furs, automobiles, resin, wax, gold, silver, currency, and securities. Exclusive of cultural objects and of gold, silver, and securities, many thousand items, valued at $87,000,000 were returned. Unidentifiable monetary gold valued at $263,678,000 was placed at the disposal of the nations entitled to participate in its distribution (Norway, Yugoslavia, Albania, Belgium, Denmark, the Netherlands, France, Greece, Luxembourg, Czechoslovakia, the United States, and the United Kingdom and British Dominions). Non-monetary gold, including that taken from the helpless victims of Nazi torture in the concentration camps, valued in excess of $900,000, was given to the IRO and its predecessors to aid in the resettlement of those persecuted by the Nazi regime. Identifiable gold and silver valued at $34,765,000 was given back to Hungary and small amounts to other nations to which it belonged. This gold and silver had been captured in Germany by our Army. I suggested through the Department of the Army to the State Department that it not be returned to Hungary, because I was apprehensive that we were contributing to the Communist treasure chest and strengthening its hand for heavier attacks against Western democracy.

Currencies of Allied countries, in most instances valueless because of the issue of new money, were given back. Likewise several million securities of foreign governments and enterprises are in the process of being returned.

At the same time German cultural objects which had been taken to safe places during the war were restored first to German custody and then, where possible, to their former locations. Almost all of the really valuable German works of art had been removed. For example the famous collection of the Kaiser Friedrich Gallery in Berlin was found in the salt mines uncovered by General Patton and the Third Army. Disturbed by the possible future of Berlin and not wishing to return these masterpieces under such conditions, I sent them to the United States for safekeeping in the face of severe attack from various art groups who charged Military Government with the looting tactics of the Nazi regime. Two years later when I asked for them America was loath to give them up and did so only after sending them on tour in an exhibition which raised $180,000 to aid German children. These pictures were shown in our zone on their return and drew large German crowds who had never been able to visit Berlin to see them. Early in the occupation, art galleries and museums were opened to permit the German people to see their national treasures and to indicate our deep interest in maintaining cultural traditions and standards. Also we catalogued the most famous of Germany's national monuments, palaces, cathedrals, ancient houses, and famous homes. Our experts encouraged immediate measures to protect those that were damaged but capable of restoration and assisted in obtaining materials for this work.

Another task was the control of property, exercised by a Property

310   Decision in Germany

Control Group which in the headquarters offices and in the field never exceeded 300 American personnel. Under our directives we were required to seize all assets of the Nazi party, its affiliated organizations, and prominent Nazis, and to block their accounts.[5] Reich properties were also taken under control except for certain ones which we permitted the states to use. We took charge of the properties of citizens of the United and Neutral Nations and of all duress property;[6] that is, property acquired in the Nazi regime from persecutees of its rule. We were aided in this work by the fact that the German office corresponding to our Office of the Alien Property Custodian had maintained excellent records of United Nations-owned property which came into our possession.

The magnitude of this operation was surprising to us as it grew from 2600 properties in July 1945 to more than 107,000 at peak, valued at more than RM 11,500,000,000. Of the total, 14,600 belonged to citizens of United and Neutral Nations, 31,500 to Nazi victims, and the remainder to the Reich or to Nazis. At one time or another over 150,000 properties came under control. Included in this number was the property of the German Labor Front, which had started with the assets of trade unions and co-operatives seized by the Nazis and which had become a Nazi-financed empire that included the People's Car Plant, a retail food chain with over 12,000 outlets, a labor bank, an insurance holding company with 10 subsidiaries, 36 industrial enterprises, and substantial realty holdings in all four zones. An idea of the size and scope of the organization may be gained by noting that it is understood to have owned outright or controlled approximately 15 per cent of the German economy.

In March 1946 we called upon the Laenderrat to submit a plan for assuming custody of much of the property, which we had controlled until that time. Implementation presented a difficult personnel problem, because it was necessary to designate German custodians, and qualified officials free from Nazi affiliation were difficult to find. In joint conferences it was arranged for the several state governments to assume responsibility for all controlled property but, in order to give protection to United Nations and neutral owners, acts of custodians dealing with these properties required Military Government approval in all cases outside of the ordinary course of business. Otherwise, German custodians operated under broad directives issued by Military Government[7] and were subject only to general supervision. The transfer to state control began in May 1946 and was completed for all practical purposes in September 1946. A spot audit in August 1946 indicated that only a few of the properties were operating at a loss.

In April 1947 the Control Council enacted legislation which made possible the return of identifiable property taken by the Nazis from trade unions and co-operatives.[8] Physical assets taken directly and held in the Nazi Labor Front were identified easily and returned promptly.

In June 1947 foreign owners were authorized to designate their own agents. Their interests included such major enterprises as the Opel Motor Plant (General Motors), Standard Oil of New Jersey, National Cash Register, Kodak, Lever Brothers, and others. As there was little response, in October 1947 foreign owners were informed that they would be given until March 1948 to name their agents, after which Military Government would turn the remaining properties over to the German State Property Control Agencies and retain only general jurisdiction. This plan was carried out.

In November 1947, after months of fruitless effort to obtain a quadripartite law and also a bipartite law, United States Military Government enacted for the United States Zone a law which provided for the restitution of identifiable property taken in Germany by duress, with right of appeal in contested cases through German courts and with final right of appeal to a board of review composed of American lawyers.[9] Claims which had to be filed by December 31, 1948, exceeded 215,000, over 90 per cent of which were filed in the last month. To ensure that the property of the Jewish people who were killed in Germany and left no heirs would not benefit German holders, a Jewish successor agency, formed by recognized world Jewish organizations, was authorized to claim and receive their property, including valuable cultural property. Thus the legal course to internal restitution was established and is now in process. Approximately 1000 cases were disposed of before I left Germany, which is an indication of excellent progress.

In January 1948 the states were authorized to take title to and dispose of property confiscated in denazification proceedings, and to return property to owners cleared in these proceedings.[10]

In June 1948 captured German equipment which had been demilitarized or was not suited to military usage was transferred to a

German State Corporation for sale in the German economy.[11] This equipment, valued at RM 340,000,000, was badly needed to facilitate recovery.

In March 1949 a Military Government law was prepared to transfer title of Reich properties to the German states in which they were located, subject, however, to the retransfer of some of the properties to a future central German government under provisions which might be enacted by the West German Government.[12] Promulgation of the law was withheld until April 20, 1949, pending negotiations with the British and French military governors in the hope that they would issue parallel legislation simultaneously.

By March 1949 our staff had reduced the number of properties under control from 150,000 to 54,539, of which 30,761 were duress properties; 7131 were properties of persons still subject to denazification proceedings; 4591 were Reich-owned; and 8815 belonged to citizens of United and Neutral Nations. Most of the last group are valued at less than DM 10,000. The owners have been advised of their imminent release from control. Plans now call for the complete release of all properties, except duress properties, which must remain under control until settlement of restitution cases, and those belonging to suspected Nazi offenders, which must remain under control until their cases have been heard by the denazification authorities. The dissolution of the Property Division, except for the maintenance of the central records and a small policy staff, was scheduled to be completed by July 1, 1949. Supervision and custody of remaining duress and individual Nazi properties will thereafter be the sole responsibility of a German committee functioning under Military Government observation.

The work of the Property Division in protecting foreign properties and in helping to formulate a just internal restitution program under a rule of law has received much quiet commendation. Its prompt and vigilant action prevented concealed transfers of title with consequent loss of much Nazi property. The statistics speak for the volume of its work.

All of our administrative problems were made more difficult because of the increase in population which took place so rapidly. When economic and political life were almost at a standstill and the redeployment of troops and repatriation of displaced persons were taxing transport facilities to the utmost, we were faced with the necessity of receiving and caring for the German refugees and expellees of German origin from the liberated countries. Little has been written of this problem, which is a continuing major threat to stability in Germany and in central Europe. While it may not be considered restitution, it resulted from German exploitation of these people to create unrest.

The advance of Allied forces in Germany and the bombing of cities had changed the normal pattern of life before surrender. The United States Zone contained an estimated 1,500,000 refugees, mostly in the smaller cities of Bavaria, large numbers of whom had fled before the advancing Red Army. Far fewer refugees from the cities in our zone were living in other zones. We tried to persuade other zone commanders to exchange these refugees but when we succeeded in September 1945 it was on a one-for-one basis between zones, which was of little help to us.

When the Allied Control Council proceeded to implement the Yalta and Potsdam agreements to receive the citizens of German origin from Poland, Czechoslovakia, Hungary, and Austria, it was estimated that these expellees would exceed 3,000,000.[13] It was not contemplated that this number would be greatly increased by the expulsion of the Germans in the Polish-administered territories. However, it soon became clear that Poland did intend to expel them and regardless of agreement they soon began to arrive by the thousands and hundreds of thousands.

Under the Control Council understanding, our zone was to receive all expellees from Hungary and approximately 70 per cent of those from the Sudetenland. The balance of the Sudeten Germans were to go to the Soviet Zone and Polish expellees were to be divided between the British and Soviet zones. The French Zone was to take the expellees from Austria. Transfers were to be humane and orderly under agreements to be worked out with the responsible governments.

In my first meeting with the Laenderrat in the United States Zone, I charged it with and it accepted the responsibility for the receipt and distribution of these people. They were estimated to number 1,750,000 from Czechoslovakia and 500,000 from Hungary. The movement started in January 1946. The first trainload from Hungary was a pitiful sight. The expellees had been assembled without a full allowance of food and personal baggage, and arrived hungry and destitute. As a result of representations repeated many times, arrangements were made to permit a small baggage allowance and to provide each expellee with RM 500.[14] Difficulties were likewise experienced with the Czechs, not only in the withholding of personal possessions but also in withholding young, able workers while sending to us the aged, the women, and small children. Only after halting the movement temporarily could we remedy these conditions by negotiations. Arrivals during the early months of 1946 exceeded 125,000 monthly and their care and reception were major problems to the inexperienced state governments. Somehow housing was found and German relief agencies provided food and clothing which were inadequate in every respect but sufficient to maintain life. As the winter of 1946 approached I stopped further movements. It was impossible to transport and receive these refugees in the winter months "in an orderly and humane manner." By this time more than 1,500,000 were in the United States Zone.

In January 1947 the Laenderrat enacted for the United States Zone a "law concerning the reception and integration of German expellees"[15] which guaranteed their political rights and equal opportunities for welfare assistance and employment. They became citizens with full rights in German economic and political life. State legislative bodies set up advisory boards for refugees with half their members expellees.

I did not again open the door to expellees, except to permit the reunion of families, because it was impossible to receive large additional numbers under humane conditions. Later, after Danish pressure on our government, we accepted some of the Germans who had fled to Denmark toward the end of the war, although these refugees were principally from east Germany and did not belong in our zone. Altogether the United States Zone received 1,330,000 expellees from the Sudetenland and 168,000 from Hungary, a total of 1,498,000 which, added to an estimated 2,091,000 refugees, had increased our population by 3,589,000 persons or 20.3 per cent. The effect of this increase is obvious. If it had not taken place the United States Zone would have approached self-sufficiency. Our problem was little greater than that of the British Zone, which had received 4,288,000 expellees and refugees or an increase of 18.2 per cent. Thus the bizonal area assumed the social and economic responsibility for 7,877,000 added persons, an increase of 23.6 per cent over the normal population of 33,383,500.

The same problem did not develop in the Soviet and French zones. In the Soviet Zone large numbers of expellees were offset by the refugees who fled and continued to flee to the West from Communist terrorism. In the French Zone, owing partly to their interpretation of the four-power agreement and partly to Austrian forbearance, the additional burden proved to be small and its population in 1948 was actually 0.2 per cent less than before the war. Both General Robertson and I made repeated efforts to persuade the French to accept a fair share, particularly after its zone was included in the European Recovery Program and in our joint import-export program, but in March 1949 negotiations were still under way.

I do not wish to comment on the merits of the expulsion agreement. It is clear that it was an effort to prevent the continuance of old, or the formation of new, unassimiliated minority groups which had contributed to the undermining of their governments when Hitler moved against his eastern neighbors. It was a tragic movement of peoples from their homes, in many instances of a hundred years, to a new and unpromising environment without any resources with which to start anew. It was a cruel and heart-rending sight to witness their arrival with a handful of belongings in a country where they were not welcomed, where the available housing had been drastically reduced by bomb and artillery damage, where the food supply was inadequate prior to their arrival and where opportunities for employment in a disrupted economy were few and far between. In the early days German authorities did much to alleviate suffering. As the expellees arrived in overcrowded cities and villages and in overburdened homes their presence became an aggravation. Separated from Germany through many generations, the expellee even spoke in a different tongue. He no longer shared common customs and traditions nor did he think of Germany as home. He could not persuade himself that he was forever exiled; his eyes and thoughts and hopes turned homeward.

While some have been absorbed, many have not. Four hundred thousand are still in refugee camps in the bizonal area, living on minimum charity, without work and without hope. Already they have formed political groups, largely reactionary and certainly planning to go back home. In an overcrowded land where there is limited economic opportunity they may indeed prove to be a cause for increasing dissension. Certainly German authorities have failed to cope adequately with this problem and to develop a long-range program for its solution. They face many difficulties with limited resources. In my opinion there can be no hope for a solution unless, after the displaced persons are resettled, these expellees are granted the opportunity to migrate to other parts of the world where there is some economic opportunity. We must neither forget the problem nor pass it off lightly as a German problem. Its solution is necessary to a stable and peaceful Europe.

CHAPTER 17

Security

$\mathbf{S}$ECURITY is both abstract and relative. The desire for it is shared by all peace-loving nations and by the vast majority of all peoples. In its absence, political and economic unrest are to be expected. When the armies of Hitler and the Nazi regime surrendered on May 7, 1945, the victorious nations were determined that a Germany which twice within a quarter of a century had embarked on wars of conquest should never again be capable of similar action. With the Allies and the neutrals already pledged to the organization of the United Nations,[1] it then seemed that lasting peace could be attained if the known aggressive power of modern times could be reduced in strength so that it would no longer present a potential threat to the world.

This led logically and naturally to the adoption of security measures against Germany which are fully adequate as long as the responsible nations intend to enforce them. No measures are of greater value than this intent, which is essential to their accomplishment.

These measures within Germany came about first from the total defeat of Germany's armed forces and the unconditional surrender of the German Government. Its armies were disbanded completely, its military and paramilitary organizations dissolved, and their records destroyed. As a process of surrender, all warships, aircraft, armored equipment—in fact, all matériel of a military nature—came into the possession of the victorious Allies and were removed from

Germany or smashed. With a few exceptions to meet occupying and civil needs, airports were brought back under the plow to produce badly needed agricultural products. War plants were destroyed or removed. Fortifications and military installations not needed by the occupying forces were blown up. This included the destruction of mine fields, seacoast and inland fortifications, notably the works of the vaunted Siegfried Line, air raid shelters, bunkers, and ammunition storage depots. Hundreds of thousands of tons of war equipment, thousands of tanks and armored cars and airplanes, thousands of tons of ammunition were systematically destroyed or rendered worthless for military usage by conversion to peaceful purposes. Germany was rendered as defenseless as a nation can be, except for its manpower, trained and skilled in combat but useless for war unless equipped by others.

Manpower alone is of little value in modern warfare. There must be a supporting economy to provide the tremendous quantities of matériel needed to array it in formidable fighting units. To reduce the economic ability of Germany to support a modern fighting machine, it was deprived of much agricultural land in the east and also of the substantial industrial and coal-bearing areas in Silesia and the Saar. Its territory was decreased by 43,500 square miles, its industrial potential by a substantial amount. Within the reduced area which remains to Germany there was an officially estimated population as of January 1, 1949, of 67,900,000 persons to be supported, almost as many as lived in the original area. It may be argued that this concentration of population, which means a reduced standard of living, will result in permanent unrest, in itself a threat to security. Perhaps that would be true if such unrest were fomented by outside forces prepared to provide economic support to make it a hazard to peace. Otherwise, there can be no surplus of production which could be set aside for war except at the expense of export, which will be difficult indeed to provide in sufficient volume to meet the essential import needs of food and raw materials, and a diversion of any substantial proportions of this production to other purposes would result in immediate and severe suffering to the German people.

In addition to these general measures, specific measures have been devised to reduce Germany's war potential and agencies have been established to see that they are carried out. These steps include the removal of war and industrial plant and of gold as reparations, the placing of prohibitions and restrictions on industries readily adaptable to war production, the breaking up of cartels and excessive concentrations of power, and the liquidation of Germany's external assets. The Occupation Statute enables the High Commission and the two principal security agencies—the Ruhr Authority[2] and the Military Security Board[3]—to enforce the agreed measures.

The reparations program went through many changes before it took final form. It started at Yalta, where Russia first expressed its claim for $10,000,000,000. It continued at Potsdam, where it was decided that the German level of industry would be reduced so that its excess plant could be made available for reparations.

Even before the Potsdam decisions were made, an Allied committee on reparations[4] was appointed to develop a detailed program. Our representative was Ambassador Edwin Pauley, who was accompanied to Moscow, where the committee met, by economic and industrial experts. When the Potsdam Protocol was signed we could make little progress in developing a program in the Allied Control Council while we waited to hear from this committee. After several weeks of useless effort Pauley and his staff returned to Berlin, where they hoped to meet again in an atmosphere more conducive to agreement. Their hopes did not materialize and by the end of 1945 the Allied Reparations Committee had faded out of existence and the responsibility for the program rested with the Control Council.

Meanwhile the countries which were to receive reparations from western Germany, excluding Russia, which was to receive 25 per cent for itself and Poland, held a conference in Paris in the fall of 1945. Our delegation was headed by James Waterhouse Angell. The conference reached a formal agreement, which was signed on January 14, 1946, on our behalf by Ambassador Caffery. The eighteen participating countries had divided reparations payments into industrial equipment and all other payments and had fixed the percentage each would receive.[5] They set up a permanent Inter-Allied Reparations Agency at Brussels and arranged for the liquidation and distribution of Germany's assets in the participating countries. The conference also left the disposal of German assets in neutral Western countries to be negotiated by the governments of the United States, United Kingdom, and France. It provided for non-monetary gold found in Germany to be allocated to the support of non-repatriable displaced persons.

Monetary gold was pooled for proportionate return to the countries presenting gold claims. Earlier I had tried to borrow some of this gold to finance the import of raw materials. The loan could have been repaid long before the gold was delivered and its use would have reduced the need for American assistance. However, feelings at the time were too emotional for logic to prevail and even my motive to lower American costs was questioned, as I was charged with the desire to rebuild Germany at the expense of its neighbors.

The participating countries accepted their shares of reparations as covering all their claims and those of their nationals arising out of war, which we hoped would bring the reparations program to an early conclusion. Unfortunately this was agreed to only with the understanding that such acceptance would not prejudice the determination of the total account, including political and territorial demands, claims arising from prewar or pre-German occupation, social insurance claims, and bank notes of the Reich in Rentenbank. Thus a wide and vaguely defined field of still unsettled claims remains.

The Paris conference did not directly affect our work in Berlin. Although we reached agreement on the level of industry in the Allied Control Council, it became meaningless as a result of Soviet exploitation of eastern Germany. We were forced to suspend deliveries to Russia. This led to bitter altercation in the Control Council and in the meetings of the foreign ministers and was a major contributing factor to the breakup of quadripartite government.

When the foreign ministers failed to progress in Moscow in 1947, General Robertson and I were instructed to raise the level of industry in the bizonal area to insure its self-sufficiency. When we announced the new level of industry in August 1947[6] we were confronted with an immediate and vehement protest from the French Government, which delayed its being made effective until we had met in tripartite conference.

This we did in London from August 22 to 27, 1947. Ambassadors Douglas and Murphy and I represented the United States; Ambassador Massigli, Monsieur Couve de Murville and Monsieur Alphand the French; and Sir Thomas Gilmour Jenkins, Air Marshal Douglas, and Sir Cecil Weir the British. Our instructions called for us to give the French representatives full opportunity to express their views on the new level of industry, but to make it clear that until the French Zone had joined the bizonal area the United States and Great Britain would take final decision in matters affecting it.

While this conference was in progress Washington requested my comment on reparations and on control of the Ruhr. In my reply, cabled from London on August 25, I urged immediate publication of the new level of industry for the bizonal area so that excess plants could be removed promptly to help the claimant countries and so that German management would know what plants were to remain and could place them in order. I recommended no further deliveries to Russia until Germany was treated as a whole. I said that I saw "no objection in principle to the establishment of an international body for the allocation of coal from the Ruhr but that the functions of the allocating body should be clearly defined to interfere to the minimum with such sovereign powers as are restored to Germany, as otherwise the political effects would be damaging and cumulative." I suggested that the Board be entitled to full reports on the production and use of coal in Germany and to intervene to require additional export if justified. I favored the establishment of public trusteeships for Ruhr properties and not an early vote on public ownership which would develop a bitter political controversy that would be exploited in every possible way by the Communist party.

The London talks developed French apprehension that the increased level of industry would keep more coal in Germany and reduce the quantity available for export. Their representatives accepted the new level of industry subject to a satisfactory export guarantee being worked out by our coal experts in Berlin. This really was a tacit acceptance of the new level of industry upon the assurance of British and American representatives that the limitation on steel production would remain in effect during the period of occupation. On the whole the talks improved relationships among the representatives of the three countries. On our return to Germany, Air Marshal Douglas and I published the revised level of industry.

It provided for a productive output roughly equivalent to that of 1936, which represented a 25 per cent increase in the industrial capacity contemplated in the four-power plan. This capacity had to meet the needs of a population larger by about 8,000,000 people than in 1936 and thus was on a per capita basis only 75 per cent of the 1936 basis. We believed 12,000,000 tons of steel were required each year to make the bizonal area self-sustaining but accepted in compromise with the British view an annual production of 10,700,000 ingot tons from a retained capacity of 13,000,000 tons.

Meanwhile public opinion at home had changed materially. The European Recovery Program was designed to increase production, and a rehabilitated Germany could contribute to European recovery. Strong opposition developed in Congress to any further dismantlings and our government instructed Ambassador Douglas to ask Bevin to join us in suspending them until the program could be resurveyed, taking into consideration the plan for European recovery as a whole. A mission headed by Norman H. Collisson,[7] later ECA representative in Germany, arrived in the spring of 1948 to report to our Cabinet the plants which it felt should be left in Germany. Its recommendation for the retention of 332 plants listed to go had not been acted on when Congress charged the ECA administrator, Paul Hoffman, with a similar survey and report. Another mission of top American industrialists, headed by George M. Humphrey[8] of Cleveland, Ohio, came for this survey. Humphrey, accompanied by Averell Harriman, visited me in Berlin in October to arrange for the entry of the mission. I told Humphrey that the annual steel production of 10,700,000 tons had been fixed for the period of the occupation and was the basis for a series of other tripartite agreements which might collapse if it were changed. It was a limitation which our Allies regarded as an important security measure. I did not believe that the limitations in other industries had such serious implications but I expressed the hope that the committee would consider French and British views before submitting its report. This was done before the report was completed. It recommended that 167 plants slated to go should stay. It was transmitted to Ambassador Douglas, who reached an understanding with French and British representatives in time for it to be incorporated in the agreement of the three foreign ministers of April 8, 1949. In the United States Zone the number of plants was small in comparison with the great industrial area in the British Zone. We had completed dismantling in large part prior to the start of the European Recovery Program. More than 75 per cent of these plants were back at work in unrestricted industrial fields.

Thus I am convinced that the prohibitions and restrictions placed on German industry are more important for security. Plants become obsolete, production processes change; German production methods may even improve as a result of the removal of plants depreciated in value by several years of heavy war production. Prohibitions and restrictions on annual industrial output will not only be the measure of security but will also, in the long run, determine whether the industrial capacity left to Germany permits it to become self-supporting.

The tripartite conferences which ended in London on June 1, 1948, required the French, British, and American military governors to set up a working party to determine the prohibitions and restrictions to be placed on industry. After months of negotiation it was apparent that this determination could not be made by the military governors. We had reconciled many differences but we could not agree on the kind and amount of shipbuilding, the plants to be removed to insure that synthetic oil and rubber could not be produced, the extent that machine tool production should be licensed, the types of radio tubes which could be produced, and a number of lesser items. In general we favored fewer prohibitions and restrictions than either British or French representatives, though the latter were now less restrictive than the British. Somehow it seemed illogical to be insisting on the one hand that more than 150 industrial plants remain in Germany to facilitate European recovery, and on the other hand accepting prohibitions and restrictions which would reduce productive output. To me, even from a security viewpoint, one lot seemed to have as much war potential as the other. Germany would have to import rubber and oil to replace synthetic production, but so did Germany have to import iron ore for its steel production and almost every raw material it needed to sustain its industrial life.

Real security against Germany's industrial power being utilized for war lies in a very few major prohibitions, rigidly enforced. There will be a constant temptation to evade prohibitions and restrictions which are too numerous or too petty. When our occupation forces are removed public opinion may not support repressive measures for infractions of petty requirements. Prohibitions and restrictions must be simple to enforce and their violation must constitute so flagrant a breach of security as to warrant use of force if required. Stopping the production of war material of all kinds, of aircraft, and of atomic materials seemed to me to represent the needed range. Certainly limitations imposed on industrial output in the guise of military security which prove to be wanted for economic security will not hold the support of public opinion essential to their enforcement.

During the final days of the conference I visited Ambassador Douglas in London on March 22, 1949, at his request, to discuss its progress and to give him my views. He was trying to obtain consent at the same time to retaining in Germany the Humphrey list of plants, and while he was determined not to accept prohibitions and restrictions on industry to gain consent to further plants remaining in Germany, he had a difficult negotiation to conclude. He was able to obtain some major concessions from both the British and French representatives.

In the agreement as concluded, 159 of the 167 plants recommended for retention by the Humphrey Committee were accepted. The prohibitions[9] to be imposed on German industry in the interest of security included: no production of primary magnesium and beryllium, no synthetic rubber or butadiene, and no synthetic oil by either the Fischer-Tropsch or Bergius processes. The restrictions placed production of radioactive materials under special legislation and limited the maximum size of electronic tubes and of certain machine tools. They limited the production of aluminum to 85,000 tons per year and steel to 11,100,000 ingot tons per year; ships built in German yards were not to exceed deadweight tonnage of 10,800 tons and maximum speed of 12 knots. Capacity limitations were imposed on steel, electric steel, aluminum, shipyards, ball and roller bearings, synthetic ammonia, chlorine and styrene. All weapons, including atomic weapons, and machines designed to produce weapons, were prohibited, and electronic tubes and large machine tools were placed under licenses to be granted by the Military Security Board. All forms of aircraft were prohibited. The military governors were charged with the issuance of the requisite legislation, and enforcement was placed under the Military Security Board.

The plants to be removed from the western zones of Germany under the quadripartite agreed level of industry totaled 1546 in number, of which 336 were war plants, with an aggregate value of RM 1,980,000,000 ($600,000,000—30-cent mark). With the revision of this plan for the bizonal area in 1947, 636 plants were removed from the list. A revision of the level of industry in the French Zone led to a further removal of 51 plants. The London Agreement of April 1949 provided for a further reduction of 140 plants and portions of 19 other plants. Thus the total number of plants to be removed as excess to the required level of industry is 719. These plants have an estimated reparations value of RM 912,000,000 ($270,000,000—30-cent mark). Four hundred and forty-six of these plants have already been delivered or dismantled for storage and possible future delivery to the Soviet Government, leaving 273 plants still to be removed, of which only 16 are in the United States Zone. The prohibitions and restrictions on industry also included in the London Agreement will add an estimated 25 plants to the number to be removed from Germany.

The reparations program, when completed, will have resulted in the removal of 744 plants from Germany. Since these plants were largely in the heavy industrial or basic chemical categories, they have reduced appreciably the German industrial potential for the immediate future, and to a considerable degree for as long as the limitations are maintained. In addition one must consider not only the industrial capacity lost through transfer of territory but also the large, if unknown, removals from eastern Germany. Certainly there is not in Germany today industrial capacity beyond that necessary to its daily sustenance, and a diversion of this capacity to war production would bring great want to the German people. It is a far different picture from that presented at the close of World War I.

A third specific measure which the occupying powers considered necessary for security against Germany was the breaking up of cartels and excessive concentrations of economic power,[10] popularly known as decartelization and deconcentration of industry. It is perhaps unfortunate that these really separate measures were associated. Frequently Military Government was charged with failure to break up cartels, when it developed that the complaint was really against the failure to break up a particular enterprise. Certainly the law issued by Military Government making cartels illegal was comprehensive and, I believe the record will show, effective.

Acting under our directives, we early prepared a law to break up cartels and excessive concentrations of power, and submitted it to the Allied Control Council. In this draft we had established as the definition of an excessive concentration of power an enterprise which employed more than 3000 persons, represented more than 25 per cent of the total production in its field, or had an annual turnover of more than RM 25,000,000. Any enterprise coming within this definition was required to show cause why it should not be broken up. These were rigorous terms. British representatives were unwilling to accept them or in fact to impose any mandatory requirements. On the other hand, Soviet representatives, although at the same time forming large Soviet-owned industrial combinations in their zone, were unwilling to accept any compromise, and in fact welcomed the British position, which enabled Soviet propagandists again and again to attack the alleged British support of German monopolists and industrialists. The highly industrialized British Zone contained the majority of the large enterprises.

When after our failure to obtain a unified German economy we created the bizonal area, we had a common responsibility with the British for these matters. After considerable negotiation we reached agreement on substantially identical laws to be issued by each zone commander, the law in our zone being issued on February 12, 1947, as Law No. 56.[11]

This law had as its announced purpose the reorganization of the German economy to eliminate cartels, syndicates, trusts, combines, and other types of restrictive and monopolistic arrangements which could be used by Germany as instruments of political and economic aggression. It required that all economic enterprises with their headquarters in the United States Zone and employing more than 10,000 persons in the bizone be examined as a prima facie case of excessive concentration. It provided that any firm having its headquarters and 10,000 employees located in the United States Zone should be deconcentrated unless specifically approved by Military Government. It prohibited German participation in international cartels and the formation within Germany of cartels or other combinations in restraint of trade, which engaged in fixing of prices, allocation of market, allocation of products, the supervision of technology, the limitation of production, and other measures of the same purport.

The law enacted concurrently in the British Zone differed from the American law in two principal respects. It did not have the mandatory clause concerning firms with more than 10,000 employees in a single zone, and it exempted iron, steel, and coal firms from the reporting procedure provided in Regulation No. 1 issued under the law. The British did not wish to subject these enterprises to German administrative machinery while they were still being operated by British Military Government. They are being deconcentrated separately under the administrative procedure established under Military Government Law No. 75.[12] As will be readily appreciated, no exact definition is possible of what constitutes an "excessive concentration of economic power." Even with the larger firms, a careful study of the facts must be made and a decision reached after weighing all factors. The State Department realized this before the laws were passed, for it advised us in a teleconference of October 28, 1946, that it did not believe mandatory requirements should take the place of application of a rule of reason.

It is important to examine the situation which existed at the time the law was enacted, as even then two major measures had been taken to destroy excessive combinations of power. The first of these had been the seizure of the RM 8,000,000,000 I. G. Farbenindustrie. The assets of the huge concern in the United States Zone had been seized in July 1945. At the end of November 1945 the Allied Control Council took over throughout Germany and directed dispersion of ownership and assets.[13] The size of this enterprise is reflected in the 43 manufacturing plants and over 100 additional establishments taken under control in the United States Zone, although this property was estimated at only 15 per cent of the total Farben industry in Germany. These properties have been reorganized into 52 independent operating units each under a trustee, and steps are now under way for their sale as independent enterprises. Their sale prior to currency reform was deemed inadvisable in view of the lack of value of money in the inflated condition which prevailed. Similar measures are being taken in the French and British zones to complete the liquidation of this, Germany's largest (and one of the world's largest) industrial combination.

Another measure of perhaps even more important consequence was the dissolution of the so-called Big Six Banks and the restriction of individual banking enterprises to a single state. The Big Six Banks included the Deutsche, Dresdner, and Commerz banks, the Reichskreditgesellschaft, the Berlin Handelsgesellschaft, and the Bank der deutsche Arbeit. Their functions and powers far exceeded those of our own banks and included commercial and investment banking closely integrated with industry and the stock exchange. The assets of these six banks represented 55 per cent of the total assets of Germany's 653 commercial banks. Their trade in securities over the counter was larger than that carried on by the German stock exchanges. Through interlocking directorates, voting control of stocks, and management of new financing, they wielded unbelievable power throughout the industrial field. To a considerable degree they had profited under the Nazi regime, and they had not hesitated before the war began to acquire Jewish banking and financial enterprises at sacrifice value nor afterward to extend their holdings into the countries occupied by Germany. Their dissolution was essential to decentralization of financial and economic power in Germany and perhaps the major step to this end.

Other measures had also done much to break up excessive concentrations of power within German industry. The seizing of external assets had removed the foreign-owned subsidiaries of German corporations. Bomb damage had reduced holdings in Germany. Reparations were to reduce them still further. Prohibitions and restrictions in German industry were not only to cut down assets but for many enterprises to fix maximum productive output. The splitting of Germany into east and west further restricted the size of the enterprises with plants in both east and west Germany. Hence it is obvious that the powerful German industrial combinations no longer exist to present the same formidable picture as at the height of German power; the real task lies in preventing their re-establishment.

Although U. S. Military Government Law No. 56 formally terminates every cartel in the United States Zone by making cartel agreements illegal and unenforceable, it was considered desirable to provide by regulation that all those subject to the law should notify the other parties that they were terminated. Military Government has received copies of more than 1100 such notices. Many other contracts have been renegotiated to remove any provisions which under the law are in restraint of trade. Legal proceedings are also under way against certain enterprises which continue to follow restrictive practices, claiming that the law is not applicable to their particular arrangements. Trade associations, co-operatives, even chambers of commerce are watched closely to see that they are not used to conceal undesirable trade practices. A Military Government order outlaws the old German system by which local vested interests prevent competition by denying applicants a license to open a new business on the grounds that they do not have the necessary "qualifications."[14] Of course, under any anti-trust or anti-cartel law, violations will always be found and no one can say that cartels no longer exist in Germany. The large number broken up and the inability of any which may remain to operate in the open make it appear certain that few exist today and that cartels no longer control the German market.

In addition to the Big Six Banks and I. G. Farben, which were dissolved prior to the enactment of the law, other German firms, including Bosch, have been ordered to divest themselves of certain of their holdings. Action is being prepared which will require Degussa and Metallgesellschaft to sever their interconnecting ownership. Deconcentration actions are also being instituted against Siemens & Halske, the largest remaining German electrical concern.

The main task ahead lies in the reorganization of the great coal and steel enterprises, largely concentrated in the Ruhr, so that they will not again be dangerous concentrations of economic power but at the same time will have a chance to survive in fair competition when there are no longer shortages of steel and coal.

In view of the major importance of these industries, their reorganization is provided for in the separate law, No. 75. According to this law, all coal and steel enterprises are placed under the general supervision of tripartite coal and steel groups. Each of these groups supervises a German organization which will recommend the regroupings of assets into new companies. The assets not absorbed into these new coal or steel companies will be released into the custody of a German liquidator placed in charge of the residual assets of the combines which are considered to be excessive concentrations. Each newly formed company will be placed under a board of trustees which henceforth will be responsible for its management until it is disposed of by sale or otherwise. Proceeds will be used for the liquidation of the original parent enterprise and for eventual disposition among the recognized creditors and stockholders. The reorganized companies will be permitted such vertical integration as deemed necessary to economic survival. They will be kept within reasonable size so that free competition is assured. The enterprises to be formed under the reorganization must be held in trusteeship until a freely elected (west) German government has determined the economic pattern of ownership for these industries.

The extent of this reorganization is indicated by the number of companies which are deemed excessive concentrations of power. The law lists 26 companies as requiring liquidation.[15] About half of them have extensive holdings in both coal and steel and also many subsidiaries in related and unrelated fields. The remainder are coal-distributing syndicates whose liquidation had already been ordered by previous British Military Government action. The new steel companies formed out of this reorganization will be permitted only such coal holdings as are necessary to their steel-making activities. Neither the new coal nor the new steel companies will be permitted to hold subsidiaries in unrelated fields. Thus out of these 26 companies will be formed a much larger though not yet determined number of enterprises. It is one of the major reorganizations in world economic history. Technically the plan for development of the smaller but economically sound steel enterprises was facilitated by the studies and report[16] of a group of steel experts from the United States headed by George W. Wolf, loaned to us by the United States Steel Corporation.

Unfortunately the accomplishments in this field have been somewhat obscured by the controversial nature of the problem which resulted in disagreements and disloyalties within Military Government that have arisen in no other field of endeavor. A part of this came from my own decisions not to accept the recommendations of the decartelization group to dissolve Henschel & Sohn (manufacturers of machines) and VKF (Vereinigte Kugellager Fabriken, a ball-bearing concern). Henschel & Sohn is not a huge enterprise in comparison to some American corporations, but it does produce a large percentage of the locomotives built in Germany for which its principal customer is the state-owned railway system. I did not believe it in the interest of the emergent locomotive repair program to place this enterprise in reorganization proceedings. VKF, a Swedish-owned ball-bearing plant, was one of two large bearing plants which accounted for almost all of Germany's production. This was initially a prohibited industry and VKF was continued in interim production only, while the other enterprise, Kugelfischer, was delivered for reparations. Therefore the dissolution of VKF seemed unnecessary. Machinery had to be transferred to Kugelfischer to keep both plants in limited production. Subsequently annual bearing production in Germany was limited to 33,000,000 units per year, and the production will be divided between the two plants.

Some of the decartelization group were outraged at my decision, which was contrary to their recommendations, and one member resigned. For many months there had been constant charges from the group and letters from some of its members to Congress, alleging that their efforts were being blocked by my economic advisers. The decartelization group was composed of extremists, sincere but determined to break up German industry into small units regardless of their economic sufficiency. I did not consider their viewpoint unhealthy, since they were the prosecuting staff, but I found that some of the group wanted also to be judge and jury, and this I could not accept. I welcomed the difference in views between the very liberal Wallace supporter, James Martin, who headed the decartelization group, and the more conservative-minded Democrats and Republicans who composed the staff of my economic adviser. I expected, however, to make the major decisions when these views conflicted. Later one member of this group challenged the integrity and good faith of his superiors before an investigating committee. I attempted to discharge him and was immediately confronted with the accusation that this was in violation of his civil rights and freedom of speech. I find it hard to follow this reasoning. Any employee in an organization has the right to constructive criticism, but it seems to me that the right to accuse his superior of dishonesty can be exercised only if the employee has resigned. No organization can survive without some discipline, and if every employee has the right to openly attack any other employee, then indeed a disciplined organization is impossible.

Unfortunately, too, the reorganization of Ruhr industry suffered from the controversy. It was charged that the law was designed to return this industry to former Nazi ownership, which was so contrary to its provisions as to be preposterous to those who had read it. Later, when five German organizations recommended twelve names each as trustees, it was charged that former Nazis had been returned to responsible positions in these enterprises. Actually we had made no move to select the trustees other than to receive nominations from the Germans.

The publication of the law for the reorganization of the Ruhr industries aroused unexpectedly vehement French protest, directed in large part at the provision which left the pattern of future ownership in German hands. This was difficult to understand, as Anglo-American policy in this respect had been known for many months. The law had not been enacted when it became public at a meeting held with German representatives of the bizonal area in Frankfurt to explain its provisions.

We had discussed it with our French colleague in Germany and with representatives of the Benelux countries. The French representative knew that we did not particularly favor the inclusion of the provision relative to future ownership but that we could not logically oppose British insistence on its inclusion, since it was in accord with expressed Anglo-American policy.

Several discussions with General Koenig failed to change his opposition, so he was advised that we would have to proceed with the promulgation of the law. We allowed ample time for the French Government to protest our decision to our governments. This was done. The British Government rejected the French protest in writing. In my hurried trip to Washington on October 20, 1948, I had discussed the law with Under Secretary of State Lovett and had advised him that I had no objection to the withdrawal of the particular provision if the British consented. He authorized me to attempt to obtain General Robertson's agreement to deletion of the provision, and if I failed to proceed with promulgation. I reported to the State Department that I was unable to secure Robertson's consent and I understood that the State Department advised the French Ambassador that the French protest had been rejected.

When the law was made public French officials and press attacked us vigorously for undertaking such a measure without discussion with the French Government. They attacked the law on two contradictory terms: on the one hand it was returning the mines and steel properties to the old Nazi owners; on the other it was nationalizing the mines and steel mills, giving a German government power which could easily be used for aggressive purposes. Particularly surprising was the direction of the French attack against the United States, although French representatives knew full well that the provision was inserted at British insistence.

When I visited Secretary Marshall in Paris at his request on

November 19, 1948, to discuss the Berlin situation, I found that he had received a visit from Monsieur Schuman, the French Foreign Minister, who expressed hurt that the Ruhr reoganization had been announced without discussion with French representatives. I learned that Marshall had not been informed of the discussions with the French in Germany and in London and Washington, and had not been able to tell Schuman that he was mistaken. Subsequently, I understand, he did notify Schuman, who investigated the matter more closely and admitted frankly to Marshall that he had not been advised of the extensive discussions which had taken place. Schuman made a public statement that his government had been kept fully informed, but by that time the damage was done.

This was another instance in which the British and American representatives acted in secrecy even in consultation with French representatives to avoid wounding French feelings. I have always felt that frank public discussion of a measure of this kind while it was in preparation would have resulted in a well-informed public and would have avoided much of the misunderstanding which resulted from the French attack.

Marshall understood Schuman's position and wished to help him in any way possible. For some time British and American coal and steel groups had jointly supervised the Ruhr industries. The French had long wanted to join these groups. We had refused, because the coal and steel resources were essential to the bizonal economy and French participation in their management preceding trizonal fusion would have created obvious administrative difficulties. However, I felt that in spite of these difficulties it was now timely to extend an invitation to the French to join these groups as a gesture of good will. Secretary Marshall adopted my suggestion, which after discussion with the British he passed on to Schuman, who accepted promptly. While I must admit that neither Robertson nor I was happy over this outcome, which gave the French a measure of control in bizonal affairs while they were still unwilling to completely merge their zone with the bizonal area, we both hoped that it would lead to better relations in the problems still confronting us in effecting trizonal fusion.[17]

In the spring of 1949 we brought over a group of American experts under the chairmanship of James W. Parker of the Detroit Edison Company to work with a group of British experts in a study of the German power industry. Our group recommended the dissolution of large holding companies and the maintenance of the operating companies as they now exist.[18] It recommended the setting up of public regulatory commissions at both federal and state levels. The recommendations of this group were embodied in a proposal which we submitted to the tripartite machinery for negotiation.

The extent to which large business enterprises should be broken up into smaller enterprises is always a question of judgment, and no decision will receive unanimous approval. In the United States procedures under the anti-trust laws are re-enforced by court decisions rendered over a period of years. Many Americans will believe that we have carried the process in Germany too far, while others will believe that we have hardly moved at all. Actually cartels are now illegal; hundreds have been broken up and any which exist will be broken up as they appear. The processes of war damage, reparations, prohibitions and restrictions on industry, and the separation of east and west Germany have reduced the magnitude and power of almost all of the large German corporations. The Big Six Banks, the I. G. Farben empire, and the twenty-six large coal and steel enterprises are in dissolution, and have been or are being reorganized into a much larger number of smaller enterprises. The power holding companies are to be dissolved and certain other companies are being divested of some of their holdings. There has never before been a like effort to reduce concentration of economic power. Personally, I think the process has been carried to about the right point, and that to carry it any further would result in inability to compete in world markets, with an inevitable increase in the burden of support by the United States. Our right in this field remains a reserved power in the Occupation Statute, so that other measures may be taken if desired by the occupation authorities.

While not properly a part of the breakup of excessive concentration of power, the liquidation of Germany's external assets contributed much to this program as a fourth step taken to assure security against Germany. Although initially this responsibility was placed in a German External Property Commission under the Allied Control Council, the necessity for diplomatic negotiations with the various governments made the work of this Commission impracticable. As a result the so-called "Safe Haven" project was undertaken through diplomatic channels in those countries in which German assets were earmarked for the benefit of the Western Powers. It is interesting that Sweden, in agreeing with the United States, Great Britain, and France to seize Germany's assets in that country, insisted that 150,000,000 kroner realized from these assets be placed in deposit in Sweden for gradual use to pay for exports from Sweden to Germany, thus facilitating German recovery.

Military Government maintained an investigating staff and in addition required reports from Germans to disclose their holdings abroad. Although it is impossible at this time to estimate accurately the total amount of such assets, work of these investigators alone led to evidence of these holdings in the value of at least $75,000,000. While many of these assets belonged to individuals, others were represented by the foreign subsidiaries of German enterprises, some of which had been I. G. Farben-controlled, although I. G. Chemie, incorporated in Switzerland, claimed to own them. Certainly the seizure of these German-owned subsidiaries has gone a long way toward total elimination of those prewar operations in foreign countries which were directed toward improving the capacity of Germany to produce for war.

A Department of the Army investigating committee subsequently voiced some disapproval of our failure to carry out deconcentration measures vigorously. One member of the three-man committee particularly recommended that my economics adviser, his deputy, and the chief of the decartelization group have no longer connection with decartelization and deconcentration measures. I do not propose to reply to ill-founded charges which may have had political value at home but which were difficult for American representatives abroad, striving in full conscience to carry out our policy in international negotiation in the full light of publicity, to accept with equanimity. In this field as in all others Military Government must stand on the record.

The role to be played by the Ruhr Authority in maintaining security will be determined in part by the way in which it operates. Its creation was first discussed tripartitely in the London conference[19] that started on February 23, 1948, shortly after the Council of Foreign Ministers broke up. It was at this time that the three powers first planned German government. This conference, which adjourned on March 5, had accepted in principle the control of the products of the Ruhr through their allocation for export by an authority composed of representatives of the three occupying powers and of the Benelux countries. It had agreed to incorporate this principle into an agreement in its next session, to be held in London on April 20. It was recognized that difficulty would develop in effecting the agreement because of the French desire for a much stronger control of the Ruhr than we believed necessary. The fact that the French representatives no longer advocated separation of the Ruhr or foreign ownership of its industry was a step forward.

When the second session adjourned on May 31 it had agreed on the establishment of the Ruhr Authority,[20] which would control the allocation of coal and steel for export purposes, provided that in the period of occupation during which the United States provided financial assistance to Germany these allocations could be disapproved by the American representative in Germany if they added to our financial burden. The Ruhr Authority was given the right to certain inspections, access to production information, and enforcement powers for security measures not made a direct responsibility of other agencies. A further meeting was planned to prepare the details of its charter.

During this session British representatives proposed a direct relationship between the Ruhr Authority and the OEEC. I believed that this would prevent our exercise of the predominant voice in financial matters which we had required as a condition to our financial support of the bizonal area. In any event it would have impaired the ability of our representative in Germany to advance economic recovery. Mr. Douglas did not share my views and our arguments on this point were frequent and at times almost bitter. His instructions required him to obtain my agreement or to refer our disagreements to our government. With the aid of government, the features to which I objected were softened so that our relationship became one of mutual co-operation. In spite of this difference of opinion, he and I agreed on all other points under consideration. It was impossible for arguments to destroy our friendship. In fact it is impossible to stay angry with Douglas, whose infinite and gracious charm would soothe feelings far more hurt than mine. We were both pleased with the outcome of the conference, which we believed paved the way for the three countries to carry out a common policy in western Germany in the same friendly way that the British and ourselves had worked in bizonal fusion. Neither of us was prepared for the violent opposition to this agreement which developed in France and which led to approval of West German Government by the French Assembly by a narrow majority only after the French Government reserved the right to reopen the Ruhr question.

A final conference to perfect details was opened in London on November 11, 1948. The French protest over Anglo-American plans for reorganizing Ruhr industry was made concurrently in order to create an atmosphere favorable to the more rigid control which the French Government desired. Douglas was faced with almost the same British and French teams who had participated in the earlier conference. I thought it unfortunate that neither Mr. Saltzman, Mr. Wisner, nor Mr. Martin, who had attended the earlier conferences, could be present and that the State Department had to send Mr. Jackson and Mr. Brown in their places. While I did not doubt their competence in any way, they were new to the issue and had not participated in the earlier discussions. I was relieved to find that Fritz Oppenheimer was to return to State Department service to advise Douglas. He had left Germany when Hitler came to power and gone to London, where he was accepted as a barrister, and then to New York, where he was admitted to the bar and had established a successful practice. When war came, though in his middle forties, he enlisted as a private, won his commission in Officers Candidate School, and finished his military career as a lieutenant colonel in Military Government. At one time, when accompanying Field Marshal Wilhelm Keitel (then in our custody) on a trip, the latter had commented that the American schools must do an outstanding job in teaching the German language, to which Mr. Oppenheimer merely smiled in reply. After leaving Military Government because he felt he must return to his law practice, he had been drafted by the State Department and had resigned only a short time before the conference. At Douglas' specific request he had returned for the Ruhr talks. Although his stay in America had been short, I know no better American than Fritz Oppenheimer, and his knowledge of German language and law proved invaluable to us time and again. My economics adviser, Lawrence Wilkinson, and one of his assistants, F. S. Hannemann, represented Military Government in the discussions.

It was clear from the outset that the French were not satisfied with control of allocations. They wanted control over management. We had thought this question settled in the basic Ruhr agreement, although the French Government had reserved its right to raise the issue again. I was opposed to control of management. I believed that the control of allocations, the limiting of productive capacity, and the inspection and enforcement powers to be vested in the Military Security Board provided ample security. Foreign control of management would be galling to German pride over the years. It would be charged that its purpose was to secure industrial information and to prevent German competition in world markets. It might become the cancerous sore which would lead to passive or even active resistance, and would prevent any real *rapprochement* between Germany and the western European countries. Proposals by Ambassador Douglas to extend such controls to other western European nations did not receive favorable consideration. The French position was adamant.

Our desires for immediate trizonal fusion, for western European co-operation, and for a common German policy were sincere. Without a Ruhr agreement, they seemed impossible to achieve. Douglas reported: "The real dilemma in this situation is how to avoid taking action which would have depressing effect on German production and prevent German cooperation, while at the same time preventing so strong a French reaction as to upset French political situation and prejudice French going along with the many other important German decisions in which Three-Power cooperation is essential." I too was worried by German reaction because the first Ruhr statute had been published and a hardening of the terms would be difficult to explain.

Douglas was in frequent touch with me during the conference. I did not feel free to make specific recommendations directly to him, which I know made him think I was "jurisdictionally minded," but I had no mandate from the Department of the Army, which was directly interested in the problem, and felt that my recommendations had to go first to it for approval.

Pressures continued to rise and Douglas was confronted with the desire both in London and Washington for an early settlement. Knowing this, I submitted a specific recommendation to the Department of the Army on December 5:

It seems to follow that if the French insist on the Ruhr paper to effect Western German Government, then they are insisting on full adherence to the London Agreement and would logically have to accept the Ruhr Authority under the terms of the London Agreement. If this is the French stand, however, it would be my suggestion that the following alternative would leave the question part way open at least, while not committing us at this time to further controls. Following is my alternative proposal:

"During the control period (continuance of military government) security is assured by Military Government acting through the Military Security Board and the Coal and Steel Control Groups. Prior to the relinquishment of Military Government responsibilities which include the Coal and Steel Control Groups, the Military Security Board will study and recommend to their Governments the control responsibilities now exercised by the Steel and Coal Control Groups which should be transferred to the Ruhr Authority."

The above would bring the Security Board into the picture, and would recognize the possibility of the Ruhr Authority being given additional controls, but at the same time avoids commitments on management and ownership. In particular the Steel and Coal Groups are charged with preventing the return of management and ownership to former Nazis and with preventing cartelization of industries. They actually have no other control over ownership and their supervision of management is policy-wise at top level. It might save the situation for all if this alternative could be adopted.

With one change—the study I had proposed was to be made by the governments concerned instead of by the Military Security Board—this formula was accepted by all parties and formed the basis for the agreement which was concluded on December 19 and submitted for approval by governments. Though I had proposed it as a compromise, I was not too happy with a formula which prolonged the settlement of the issue, thus making it difficult if not impossible to obtain the investment of new capital required to rehabilitate Ruhr industry. But time has a way of developing solutions to the most perplexing problems and there was no other immediate means by which French acquiescence to trizonal fusion could be obtained. This agreement was approved formally by the three foreign ministers in Washington on April 8, 1949.

The Authority is to be established before West German Government is formed. It will have its headquarters in the Ruhr and will be composed of representatives of the six signatory governments and of Germany. Each government participating (Benelux countries for this purpose having each one vote) is to have three votes. The Authority will divide coal, coke, and steel from the Ruhr between German consumption and export. It must give due consideration to the minimum needs of a self-sustaining Germany and to the objectives and programs of the Organization for European Economic Co-operation. It has the power to prevent artificial or discriminatory trade practices. It is charged with the protection of foreign interests in Ruhr enterprises. It may subsequently take on responsibilities for security measures which are now the responsibility of the occupying authorities. This is the still undefined area of responsibility.

At present the breaking up of the powerful Ruhr industrial combinations and the supervision of production and management are vested in the tripartite coal and steel groups which report to the occupation authorities. If and as these groups cease to function, then such of their responsibilties as the occupying governments may determine will be given to the Ruhr Authority. This possible assumption of responsibility in the fields of production and management may make it difficult to obtain badly needed capital investment in the coal and steel industries. There is another danger. The control of allocation of coal and steel in a period of shortages is of value to European recovery in all countries now dependent on German coal. The end of world shortages in these commodities is in sight and, normally, German products would find their way into world markets to the extent that their costs of production could meet competition. When this develops, the countries participating in the Ruhr Authority will be tempted to hold down German production for exports, thus preventing free competition. The Ruhr Authority must never be permitted to use its power for this purpose, which would almost surely destroy its value as a security agency.

The London tripartite conference which ended on June 1, 1948, also called upon the military governors to establish a Military Security Board with broad responsibilities for the maintenance of security measures. Agreement among the military governors was reached on December 17, 1948. The Board's responsibilities cover the whole field of demilitarization and disarmament, including the prevention or revival of military or paramilitary organizations, the enforcement of prohibitions and restrictions on industry, the supervision of scientific research to the extent necessary to limit it to peaceful purposes, and the licensing of certain specified machine tool production. Its three divisions, Military, Industrial and Scientific Research, will be aided by inspection groups with access to German plants and records as may be necessary to ascertain compliance with security directives.

The powers reserved to the occupying authorities in the Occupation Statute protect the rights of the Ruhr Authority and of the Military Security Board. It must be pointed out, however, that provisions in an occupation statute or in a later peace treaty mean no more than the intent of the signatory powers to enforce the agreed terms.

Certainly Germany's neighbors have the right to demand security against the nation which has caused them so much destruction and grief. Their concern and their unwillingness to accept German economic and political recovery until adequate security arrangements had been made were understandable. Prior to the adoption of the Atlantic Pact, security was guaranteed by the troops of the occupying powers. The participation of the United States was assured by the presence of its forces in Germany. With the formation of Western European Military Union, on March 17, 1948, in Brussels, some of the fears of a revived Germany were dissipated. But it was not until the Atlantic Pact was signed in Washington on April 8, 1949, that western Europe felt assured of United States participation in a common defense against possible future German aggression and that the atmosphere was finally created which permitted the foreign ministers of France and the United Kingdom and our Secretary of State to quickly agree on a common German policy.

There can be no question that the security measures proposed against Germany, combined with the broad guarantees of the Atlantic Pact, suffice, as long as they are enforced, to prevent Germany alone from again becoming an aggressor nation. However, as I observed earlier, security is a relative term and its provision against Germany alone no longer means security against aggression.

Other aggressive forces have risen to threaten the peace of the world. Germany is not included in the Atlantic Pact. It is defenseless against aggression from the east except as it is protected by the forces of the United States and western Europe now in occupation. These observations raise still unresolved questions to which I do not propose the answers, although answered they must be by the responsible statesmen.

Here are the broader questions of security to which I refer:

Can Germany be left defenseless, subject to conquest and exploitation by others who would use its manpower and its skills for world aggression?

Are we prepared to maintain armed forces in Germany indefinitely to prevent its easy conquest by others, or are the Atlantic Pact signatory powers prepared to guarantee the defense of Germany indefinitely?

If the security of Germany is to be assured by the signatory powers to the Atlantic Pact, will Germany be expected to contribute to the common security?

These are not questions to be decided hastily, nor are they to be avoided because of animosities and apprehensions. Unless peace and stability can be achieved through a United Nations Organization with adequate strength to maintain them, then we must recognize that peace and stability remain only so long as there is a balance of powers which makes the chance of success of aggressive war unlikely. The part that Germany is to play in such a balance of power could well tip the scales one way or the other, and the wisdom of Western statesmen must be applied to find a solution which, through the years, makes it a contribution to the maintenance of peace.

Security against Germany is important indeed, but only to the extent to which it contributes to world security.

CHAPTER 18

The Control Council
Breaks Up

W HEN we started the new year of 1948 in the Allied Control Council we no longer had hope for success. It was soon evident indeed that the "wraps were off" and that there was "heavy going" ahead.

During the period in which General Robertson and I worked to organize our two zones as an economic unit and proceeded to execute our unilateral responsibilites we never stopped our efforts to obtain effective government by the Allied Control Council, although they became increasingly futile. When Marshal Sokolovsky used the Control Council just before the meeting in London of the Council of Foreign Ministers to make his most severe attack on the three powers it was apparent that the Control Council continued in form only and that its work was ended.

I think that the outcome of the London session in December 1947 was forecast by preceding events. After the Moscow conference in the spring of that year Secretary of State Marshall proposed the European Recovery Program. Molotov refused to participate and forced the satellite countries to stay out. Churchill's "Iron Curtain" had become an iron curtain in fact as Molotov announced publicly the intent of the Soviet Government to create an eastern European economic program, which meant really a continuation of Soviet domination of the economic life of eastern Europe.

The United States, in its offer of the Marshall Plan and its determination to proceed with the free countries of Europe when it was rejected by the Soviet Government and its satellites, had made its major postwar decision in foreign policy. It had determined that positive steps were necessary to stop the eastward movement of Communism in Europe and to rekindle the flame of freedom. In doing so it recognized that the thin screen of American and British soldiers in Germany symbolized the united will of two great nations that this far the threat of the Red Army would reach and no farther. Behind this screen economic progress could be achieved free from fear of the Red Army.

The Soviet Government could not risk the establishment of a free Germany under quadripartite supervision which would permit the message of freedom and economic security to reach the borders of its satellite countries. Molotov was not interested in any settlement of the German problem unless it insured Communist control of German government and the continued supremacy of the Soviet commander in eastern Germany. The record of the London conference is convincing proof of the validity of our views as to what would take place.

I reported to Secretary Marshall in London on November 23, 1947, and met immediately with his staff experts to discuss the papers they had prepared. Few changes were required in those which had been used at the Moscow conference. The American delegation contained many of the men who were at Moscow. I missed Ben Cohen, who was no longer with the State Department. I was glad, however, to find Ambassador Douglas added to the American delegation, as he was keenly interested in the German problem and able to participate actively in our discussions.

Our offices were at 5 Grosvenor Square, overlooking the park in which the erection of the memorial to President Roosevelt was under way. The conferences were held in Lancaster House.

The routine in London followed somewhat the pattern evolved in the Moscow conference. We met each morning with Marshall in his office to examine the preceding day's discussions in the council. Marshall was in top form and measured his decisions and moves in the light of the speech which he had made in Chicago to define American policy. It was evident that he enjoyed developing any divergencies in viewpoint within the delegation so that they could be weighed in reaching his decisions. I found these meetings invigorating and helpful. It was interesting to note the technique used by Marshall, who held open staff meetings and listened to conflicting views, as compared with that of Byrnes, who had preferred to discuss special issues with the several experts separately before making up his mind.

The delegations of the other powers were also composed of the same key personnel who had been present in Moscow. Vishinsky arrived a few days late, coming from New York, where he had attended the General Assembly of the United Nations.

There were pleasant interludes during the London meeting which somewhat eased the tenseness always present in the Council meetings. Dinners were given for the American delegation by the French Ambassador at his embassy residence, and by Ambassador Douglas for the other delegations. The King and Queen held a reception for all of the delegations at Buckingham Palace, which was attended by leading British statesmen including Winston Churchill. During the reception Robertson and I were escorted jointly to King George for a short conversation in which he showed a deep interest in German questions and expressed his satisfaction in the close Anglo-American co-operation which had developed in Germany. Bevin joined us and in his good-humored way counseled the King to give Robertson and me "the devil" so that we would not bother our governments so much. I had grown very fond of Bevin and understood his friendly intention.

I learned more of the gracious ways of the King and Queen, which perhaps explain to some extent the deep affection in which they are held by the British people. Mrs. Clay had flown over that day to attend the reception, but London fog had forced her plane to land some hours away and she did not arrive in time. When I was escorted to Queen Elizabeth, I remarked quite casually that I was so sorry bad weather had kept Mrs. Clay from being present. The next morning as she was sitting in our apartment a messenger arrived from our embassy with an invitation for tea with the Queen in the afternoon. We did appreciate this thoughtfulness and Mrs. Clay enjoyed her quiet talk with Queen Elizabeth even more than she would have enjoyed the reception.

During the London conference Murphy and I had managed to obtain use of an apartment in No. 3 Grosvenor Square, an apartment house next to our embassy, acquired in payment for Lend-Lease.

There we met informally with our friends both in the American and other delegations whenever time permitted.

While we did not have much time for relaxation, we enjoyed a day with General Sir Brian Robertson and Lady Robertson, driving through the country to have a pleasant luncheon with Lord and Lady Astor at beautiful Cliveden. After lunch we visited Charterhouse School, which had been Robertson's public school and where his son was now a student. We had a visit with the headmaster and then went through the school, wondering again at the rugged existence of the British public school boy as compared with the American preparatory school boy. We remained for Sunday evening services in the stately chapel to listen to readings by the senior students and to the excellent singing of the boys. Robertson's son was a likable young man, doing well in the school, and the parental pride which shone in the eyes of his father and mother as they looked at him made Mrs. Clay and me homesick: the war and after-war years had separated us so much from our own two sons and their families.

While the London conference was not as long as the Moscow conference, there were seventeen meetings before it was concluded. It soon became apparent that the Soviet representatives had no intention of yielding in the least the positions which they had taken in Moscow. On the other hand, they were prepared to go on indefinitely and they were skillful in using the meetings for propaganda to be released in some instances in Russia and in other instances in Germany. The Western Powers had been patient in Moscow, seeking a way to agreement. They all appeared to feel that a similar performance in London would be undignified and harmful to their prestige. I am sure that Marshall was determined that the London conference should cease when it became evident that progress was impossible, although he was willing to remain patient under almost daily attack as long as there was hope of even partial agreement.

At least two of the seventeen meetings[1] were taken up in settling the agenda. This resulted in some measure from the efforts of the three Western Powers to have the Austrian peace treaty considered first, in the belief that agreement could be reached on this question more readily than on the German question. The French representatives also wished to complete the economic amalgamation of the Saar with France, which had been before the Council of Foreign Ministers for some time, before proceeding to other German matters.

Molotov used the second meeting to compare the Soviet position, which he claimed would lead to a democratic peace, with the positions of other countries desiring an imperialistic peace. Marshall refused to engage in this debate, remarking that Molotov was too intelligent really to believe the allegations he had made. When Molotov, in another meeting, referred to press and radio statements that the Western Powers would proceed to form a West German Government as purposing to divide Germany, and urged that the Council of Foreign Ministers agree that such a government would not be established, Marshall replied that "to talk about unity is not enough" for the United States any longer, and that the way to unity was in taking practical measures such as the union of other zones with the bizonal area. The peacemaking procedures which had been discussed in Moscow became the subject of further discussion, and again the foreign ministers could reach no agreement other than to have their deputies study the question further, even though two previous meetings of the deputies had failed even to agree on a report.

Marshall had replied to Molotov's charge that the Western Powers were failing to carry out the Yalta and Potsdam agreements by stating that he saw no purpose in "rehashing" these old charges and that it would be to better purpose if the Council of Foreign Ministers would profit from the "tragic delays of the past two years to eliminate misunderstandings."

Molotov charged that the financial assistance being given Austria by the United States was for the purpose of economically enslaving the Austrian people, which gave Marshall the opportunity to compare our assistance with the "munificent purposes" evidenced by the Soviet Government in creating tension in Austria and elsewhere.

The Soviet representatives continued to insist on huge reparations from German production and to refuse to place the resources of east Germany in a common pool with those of west Germany until their reparations demands were met. The economic discussions ended when Marshall proposed that "the economic decision of immediate vital significance which I must press Mr. Molotov to answer" be to discontinue the removal of production output from Germany except in return for a fair payment until the German economy should be self-sustaining.

As the conference progressed Molotov resorted more and more to invective and charged that the British and other intermediaries had made huge profits from Ruhr coal. Bevin expressed his indignation at "these insults, insinuations, and accusations." Molotov, paying no attention to Bevin, then accused us of the acquisition of valuable plants in Germany. The atmosphere of the meeting had become chilly and tense. It was in this atmosphere that Molotov plunged into reading a long prepared statement which was practically a duplicate of the one made to the Allied Control Council by Sokolovsky. It leveled almost every conceivable charge against the administrative policies of the Western Powers in Germany.

Those of us who were sitting at the conference table were busy drafting suggested replies to pass to Marshall. He hardly gave them a glance as with superb and quiet dignity he told Molotov that it was evident his charges were designed for another audience and another purpose, and that such procedures in the Council of Foreign Ministers made it rather difficult to inspire respect for the dignity of the Soviet Government. This was the only time I ever saw Molotov wince perceptibly. I believe the Russian attack convinced the three Western Powers that the conference should end. Marshall took the initiative in a paper to which he added verbally:

"I proposed the adjournment, Mr. Chairman. I therefore do not think I have to express myself again. When we meet again, I hope that it will be in an atmosphere more conducive to the settlement of our differences."

No time or place was suggested for the next meeting. The Council of Foreign Ministers had broken up. It was not to meet again until May 1949.

I am sure that all of us present in London recognized that, with the Council adjourned, we were now engaged in a competitive struggle, not with arms but with economic resources, with ideas and with ideals. It was a struggle in which we desired no territory but were determined that others should not acquire further territory through the use of oppressive power, fear to dull the hearts, and distorted information to capture the minds of peoples powerless to resist. There could be no escape from the struggle. We could hope with some assurance that it would not lead to physical force. We knew not how long it would last or what turn it would take.

To those of us who had started quadripartite government in Germany with determination to make it work, who had believed for a few months that it might work, and who had tried to make it work in the face of daily obstruction and frustration, there was a special significance in the results of the London conference. While I recognized the inevitability of the course we had to follow, it was not with exhilaration but with sadness over the failure of a "noble experiment" that I left Lancaster House when the final meeting adjourned.

Nevertheless, an immediate and beneficial outcome of the London talks was the expedition of measures for the economic rehabilitation of the bizonal area and the transfer of further political responsibility within the area to German agencies. A more significant result came from French recognition that quadripartite relations no longer permitted France to remain alone in Germany and that it was timely to consider the fusion of the French Zone with the bizonal area. Thus the London conference paved the way for another vital decision in German affairs—the decision to establish West German Government.

The London conference had also provided Murphy and me with an opportunity to discuss German problems with Marshall and his staff, and for Robertson and me to discuss them with Marshall and Bevin. At the same time, it gave Douglas background information necessary to the active role he was to play in German affairs.

When we returned to Berlin we knew that the end of Control Council government was in sight. In the next three months we did manage to agree to two laws,[2] one controlling dangerous Germans and the other repealing certain Nazi laws affecting the churches. The discussions in this period were many and clearly indicated crisis ahead.

In the meeting of January 20, in the debate on the control of dangerous Germans, Sokolovsky insisted on drastic limitation by fixed percentage in the employment of former officers in specified types of employment.[3] I replied to his suggestions:

"I believe we are defeating our own purpose when we try to fix arbitrary limitations. . . . I doubt if we are going to create any anti-militaristic spirit in Germany by treating as outcasts all officers. . . . The result will almost certainly drive them to conspiracy and sabotage."

I had agreed that specific types of employment should be subject to periodic quadripartite inspections to determine whether a dangerous situation threatened to develop through an undue use of former officers, so that corrective measures could be taken.

In this meeting Sokolovsky refused to implement a directive of the
Council of Foreign Ministers calling on us to plan for the repatriation
of all prisoners of war[4] which we had been instructed to prepare by
the Council of Foreign Ministers.

"The Soviet Government," he said, "has determined its deadline—
31 December 1948. This deadline will be met."

Then he attempted to brand the voluntary employment of prisoners of war in France and Great Britain as slave labor:

"The most important thing is that all of them will return . . . by
the end of 1948. And the Soviet Union never attempted to recruit
labor for the Soviet Union, and never will do that as some of the
Western Powers have done."

It is interesting to note that the Soviet Government did not accomplish "the most important thing" and had to acknowledge its failure
to complete repatriation by the end of 1948. Also thousands of returned German prisoners, emaciated and broken, could testify to
their labor in the Soviet Union.

Robertson and I advised Sokolovsky and Koenig at this time of the
steps we were taking to strengthen the Bizonal German Administration.[5] The Soviet commander's reply was a bitter attack:

"Under pretense of reorganizing the bizonal economic agency, the
U. S. and British authorities . . . have commenced establishing a
separatist government. . . . It is well known that Generals Clay and
Robertson invited only those who support the partition . . . adherents of Adenauer, Kaiser, Schumacher. On the other hand, the
supporters of the unity of a democratic Germany are being perse-
cuted."

Both Robertson and I answered. I confined my remarks to expressing regret that Sokolovsky had spoken before he received and studied
the basic papers, and my belief that on examining these papers he
would find that his statement was not factual. The Council then went
into an executive session at my request so that I could present a proposal for currency reform,[6] which was designed to meet previous
Soviet objections to the fullest extent we believed feasible. This was
our last effort to obtain four-power agreement to this measure, essential to German and to European recovery.

Another stormy meeting took place on February 11. Robertson
had replied to a Soviet paper[7] on demilitarization which charged the

Western governments with deliberate failure to carry out agreements:

"I may as well make it clear that the U. K. delegation is not prepared to discuss any paper which commences with a string of unjustified allegations against its government and . . . its citizens."

Sokolovsky chose to ignore this statement and proceeded again to attack the Bizonal German Administration,[8] trying hard at the same time to pose as the champion of the German people:

"In these documents, there is not one word of the rights of the German people, nor of the democratization of the political order. . . . We have now a deformed anti-democratic German constitution enforced . . . through the intermediary of a small group of Germans. There is being prepared the inclusion of western Germany in a military and political Western bloc. This is a dangerous course. . . . These actions can only be explained by a fear of democracy and by a dread of the rebirth of . . . a competitor."

The Soviet Administration in Berlin had barred Western representatives from attending a political meeting in the Soviet Sector to which they were invited by the Germans. When we protested this action Sokolovsky claimed Berlin as a part of the Soviet Zone and accused the Western Powers of using "their position to prejudice their right to remain in Berlin."[9] The attempt to build a record to justify blockade was under way.

In the March 10 meeting Sokolovsky assailed the Western Powers for their refusal to recognize the SED party in the western zones.[10] Robertson and I pointed out that the SED was not admitted because it was not a voluntary amalgamation of Social Democrats and Communists, and had been rejected as such by the Social Democrats of western Germany.[11]

"However," I remarked, "the Communist party is permitted . . . and is being treated with great patience. It has engaged in many excesses . . . which would warrant its restriction. We have patience, but our patience is not inexhaustible."

To this Sokolovsky replied angrily: "The facts of life prove the opposite . . . prove that they [Americans and British] are intolerant to genuine democracy. . . . The most forward party, the Communist party, together with the best representatives of the Social Democrats, of the genuine democrats—of course not the kind of Schumacher—those people still live and are developing their ideas. . . .

Those attempts, these crusades, we can see beforehand that they will be unsuccessful just as Hitler's regime was unsuccessful when it tried by prisons. . . . General Robertson once more spoke of the iron curtain; he spoke of the Marshall Plan that is in his opinion the Star of Bethlehem for Germany. But, that the Marshall Plan is the Star of Bethlehem for the American monopolists but not in any way for the working class of Germany. It might be useful to ask the working class itself if the Marshall Plan is acceptable or unacceptable to them. The German working class most certainly does not wish to be a slave to its own monopolists. The working class knows perfectly well that it is directed to lead them to slavery. It is directed towards the creation of an imperialist block in which the monopolists wish to include western Germany. It is directed against the common democracy in general, not only in Germany, but for a new war. General Robertson has even gone so far as to quote the party of the working class a party of slavery. But who can be fooled by that; how can a worker himself preach suppression when in a capitalistic state he is a slave himself. The working class of Germany is itself a slave belonging to the landowners in Germany whose land, with the help of General Robertson, has not yet been confiscated. They are slaves of capitalistic monopolists in Germany, not only of the monopolistic capitalists in Germany but those who stretch their hands very far and wide in the branch of German industry. Yes, it is true that we have many arrests in our zone. But we know quite well that hundreds and thousands of people were arrested also in the British Zone and I regret to say that those people were not war criminals but very frequently honest democrats who express their democratic views towards making Germany peace-loving . . . and those people are now in concentration camps in the British Zone of Germany and also in other western zones of Germany. It is perfectly evident that if General Clay has declared a Hitler Communist crusade that he will not permit a party like the SED. From the statements made by General Robertson and General Clay and also from General Noiret's statement, it is quite evident that it is absolutely useless to continue the discussion . . . since they have very clearly expressed themselves as being against the creation of democratic working parties in their zones. That is all I have to say."

General Clay: "Mr. Chairman, I too hate to prolong a discussion that is so fruitless and that we have been over so many times before, but I have one observation. My government too dislikes monopolies, but it includes the political in its dislike for monopolies, and it believes that in many parts of the world where workmen can freely express their views they will also express a dislike for the political monopoly as well as other forms of monopoly. I have no further comment."

The Soviet charges became more vitriolic in each meeting and the same day, in some form or other, they would appear in their controlled press and radio. Russian statements from which I have quoted short extracts were growing lengthier while the Western replies were becoming shorter and sharper. In such an atmosphere there was no further hope for quadripartite government, or for our proposal for currency reform.

It was not the events which took place in the Allied Control Council alone which indicated the deteriorating relationships between the Western occupying powers and Soviet Military Administration. The differences between West and East came to the surface almost daily during the early months of 1948.

In January and February repeated reports reached me of the confiscation in Berlin and in the Soviet Zone of literature originating in western Germany. This was contrary to our agreement for free interchange.[12] On February 17 and 18 the Soviet police in Berlin seized copies of *Speaking Frankly* by former Secretary of State Byrnes, which had been printed in our zone. In March the trade union papers from our zone were confiscated at the Berlin newsstands in the Soviet Sector. There was also widespread burning of our periodicals in the cities of the Soviet Zone. This was a prelude to the organization in the same month of the news distribution agencies in the Soviet Zone into limited stock companies licensed to distribute the publications approved by the Soviet authorities. It was an effective tool to prevent Western literature from entering east Germany. Protest after protest presented to the Soviet authorities received courteous acknowledgment but proved completely ineffective.

Concurrently the Soviet propaganda attack against the Western Powers and particularly against the United States increased in volume and vituperation, and included the absurd charge published in *New Times*[13] on March 3, 1948, that our State Department was subsidizing the activities of Mosley and his British Black Shirts.

Meanwhile transport difficulties between Berlin and west Germany began to develop and we were convinced that these difficulties were intended as a threat or else that the pattern was already being cut. In January Soviet inspectors boarded our military trains and insisted that they had the right to check the identity of individual passengers. We had to issue orders to our train commanders and place guards on the military trains to prevent the entry of these inspectors. Attempts to board our trains were continued in February and March and frequently trains would be held on a siding for hours because of the refusal of their commanders to permit the entry of the inspectors.

Throughout my stay in Germany I had scoffed at the possibility of war with Russia and had been one of the principal supporters of the viewpoint that war, if not impossible, was most unlikely. Perhaps the situation in the Control Council and the incidents which occurred in the early months of 1948 did influence me. Nevertheless, it was not these events which led me to make a special report to the Chief of Staff early in March. Somehow I felt instinctively that a definite change in the attitude of the Russians in Berlin had occurred and that something was about to happen. From Sokolovsky down there was a new attitude, faintly contemptuous, slightly arrogant, and certainly assured. The intelligence reports which came to my desk contained nothing to arouse suspicion, and therefore it was with considerable reluctance that I determined to express my concern. In making my report to General Bradley, I pointed out that I had no confirming intelligence of a positive nature, but that I did sense a change in the Soviet position which I was certain portended some Soviet action in Germany. I did not predict what course this action would take, though I did state that I was no longer adhering to my previous position that war was impossible and felt that we could no longer preclude such a possibility.

A report of this type must be shown to a number of senior officials, which results sometimes in distorted rumors of its content. This report did lead to a speed-up in our preparations for defense. Some time later it was to be called an alarmist report which had built up the possibility of war without justification. Having used carefully restrained language in which there was no prediction of military action, I did not consider it alarmist and I knew that Bradley felt likewise. Neither he nor I wanted Pearl Harbor in Berlin. The report anticipated the blockade by a few weeks and it seemed to me that its imposition had in itself justified the report. Immediately after it took place I was convinced that this was the action I had anticipated and that military action was not likely. I reported these views promptly to the Department of the Army, even though the instance and events which accompanied the imposition of the blockade could have created war if they had been permitted to do so.

The last meeting of the Control Council took place on March 20, 1948. Sokolovsky had introduced in the Control Council the declaration[14] of the Prague conference of the foreign ministers of Czechoslovakia, Yugoslavia, and Poland a Soviet-inspired attack on the policies of the Western Powers in Germany. At the time the representatives of the three Western Powers advised Sokolovsky that this declaration had been addressed to the governments of the occupying powers and hence was not a proper subject for discussions in the Control Council. At this meeting I advised Sokolovsky that our government had stated publicly that it could see no useful purpose in considering resolutions which were based on misstatements and distortions of fact. Sokolovsky had his instructions and stated:

"If there is no desire to discuss here the declaration of the governments of the three countries that are the neighbors of Germany and which are those countries who have suffered most of all from the Hitler aggression, this proves once more that the British, French, and United States representatives do not consider the Control Council the organ of quadripartite administration of occupied Germany. They regard the Control Council merely as a suitable screen behind which they can hide the unilateral actions taken in western Germany and which are directed both against the interests of the peaceful countries and peace-loving Germans who are interested in the peaceful unity and democratization of their country. Will the members of the Control Council have any comments or observations to make on this?"

I replied: "As I have already stated, I do not care to discuss this resolution here at all. Marshal Sokolovsky has chosen this as an occasion to make very serious charges against his colleagues and the governments which they represent. A mere casual examination of that record shows when and where the work of the Control Council has been blocked in its effort to govern Germany. I think it is particularly interesting that Marshal Sokolovsky has brought up the suggestion of a screen to hide unilateral activities. If such a screen exists,

and I think it does, it is not on the western side of the border between the American and the Soviet zones. Marshal Sokolovsky has
charged that what we are doing is not in the best interests of the
German people. I make no claim to know the German people or to be
able to speak of what their best interests are. However, in my own
mind, I have no doubts that increasing numbers of them do know
what their best interests are."

Suddenly Sokolovsky demanded to be advised of all agreements
on western Germany reached by the three[15] Western Powers in
London in February and March. He was informed that this conference had been held between governments and its report had been
submitted for the approval of these governments. We considered his
request to be reasonable but we could not provide him with the
information he desired until we had heard from our governments. I
reminded him, too, of the exchange of notes in which the United
States had rejected the Soviet protest against the conference.
Sokolovsky expected our answer and barely waited for its translation
by the interpreters before reading a long statement which repeated
all of the old charges against the Western Powers in more aggravat-
ing language. The British representative started to reply as the interpreter completed the translation of the Soviet charge. Rudely inter-
rupting and without explanation, the Soviet delegation,[16] following
what must have been a prearranged plan, rose as one as Sokolovsky
declared: "I see no sense in continuing this meeting, and I declare it
adjourned." Without further word the Soviet delegation turned on its
heels and walked out of the conference room.

No chairman had ever attempted to adjourn a meeting without
the approval of his colleagues. No chairman had ever adjourned a
meeting without arranging for the date of the next meeting. And,
significantly, no chairman had hitherto left a meeting without inviting his colleagues to join him for coffee and light refreshments. We
know of course that this was no spur-of-the-moment action. It was a
last attempt to strike doubt in Western minds as to the advisability
of proceeding with the program for western Germany.

The three Western military governors remained in their seats to
invalidate the adjournment, to select a chairman, to continue the
meeting, and then to formally adjourn. The Allied Control Council
was dead. An international undertaking which, if successful, might
have contributed to lasting peace, had failed. We knew that day as

we left the conference room that quadripartite government had broken up and that the split in Germany which in view of Soviet intransigence had seemed inevitable for some months had taken place.

Sokolovsky, under the rules of the Control Council, was the chairman for the month of March and normally would have called another meeting for March 30. He had failed to propose this date when he left the conference room, so the three Western military governors waited for him to do so during the remainder of the month. He did not issue such a call. The result was that my French colleague was in favor of the Western representatives asking for another meeting. He suggested to me several times during the next month when I was in the chair that I take the step. I refused to do this unless officially requested to do so by one of my colleagues so that the meeting could be called in his name. As each of the three Western military governors became chairman for the month, he circulated prior to the normal date a note stating that there was no agenda and that the meeting would be held only if it was desired by one of the members of the Council. No request was made and it soon became apparent that further meetings would not take place. The stage had been set for the imposition of the Soviet blockade against Berlin.

CHAPTER 19

Berlin Is Blockaded
by Land and Water

ON the day before the blockade the Department of the Army, disturbed over the transport incidents and difficulties which we were reporting daily, summoned me to a teleconference to obtain my views on stopping further dependents from going to Germany and on gradually withdrawing families from Berlin and our zone. I replied that these were logical moves from a strictly military viewpoint but that we were engaged in a struggle of a political nature and these views would be disastrous politically. I said:

Withdrawal of dependents from Berlin would create hysteria accompanied by rush of Germans to Communism for safety. This condition would spread in Europe and would increase Communist political strength everywhere, and particularly in Italy [the Italian elections being only a few days off].

On the following day, March 31, 1948, the Soviet Military Administration issued an order which prevented the movement of military passenger trains across the border en route to Berlin unless baggage and passengers were checked by their personnel.[1] This was a direct violation of our right to be in Berlin and of the oral agreement with Marshal Zhukov in which it had been specified that our personnel would be subject to neither customs nor border controls. If these controls were accepted American personnel would be subject to seizure by Soviet police, and rough handling of our people might result.

The following day, in implementation of this order, Soviet representatives decreed that no freight could leave Berlin by rail unless permission had been granted by the Russian Kommandatura. This put the Soviet authorities in Berlin in full control of its trade. We could not accept this principle. As a result our incoming traffic was limited to civil and military freight, while trains returning from Berlin were empty.

The Soviet deputy military governor, General Dratvin, wrote to my deputy, General Hays, to announce the details of their search procedure. I reported this letter and my proposed reply at once in a teleconference with the Department of the Army. I suggested that we accept a compromise measure under which the train commanders would furnish certified passenger lists and documentation to Soviet inspectors. I added:

We cannot permit our military trains to be entered [for such purposes] by representatives of other powers, and to do so would be inconsistent with the free and unrestricted right of access in Berlin which was the condition precedent to our evacuation of Saxony and Thuringia.

This reply was approved and dispatched to General Dratvin. It was rejected by Soviet representatives.

I also reported my intent to send a test train with a few armed guards on board across the border to see if the Russians would actually stop it by force or by sidetracking. The train progressed some distance into the Soviet Zone but was finally shunted off the main line by electrical switching to a siding, where it remained for a few days until it withdrew rather ignominiously. It was clear the Russians meant business.

During this teleconference I thought I detected some apprehension on the part of Secretary Royall and his advisers that a firm stand on our part might develop incidents involving force which would lead to war. Therefore I expressed my opinion that weakness on our part would cost important prestige and that if war were desired by the Soviet Government it would not be averted by weakness. I added:

I do not believe this means war. . . . Please understand we are not carrying a chip on our shoulder and will shoot only for self-protection. I do not believe we will have to do so.

Because of the six hours' difference in time between Berlin and Washington these telecons usually took place in the late evening, as four o'clock in the afternoon in Washington was ten o'clock at night in Berlin. To go to this telecon I had excused myself from dinner in my home with my French and British colleagues. We had been discussing our course of action, and I rushed home to continue this discussion. General Bradley had ended the telecon with:

Thanks muchly. This has been an arduous day and we appreciate your co-operation.

I could admit that it had been already, though the discussion with my colleagues lasted for several additional hours. We agreed not to accept the Soviet restrictions and to maintain a common front.

On April 2 the Department of the Army again requested a teleconference in which it stated that pressures were rising at home for the withdrawal of our families and that many responsible persons believed it unthinkable that they should stay in Berlin. I reported that we could support the Americans in Berlin indefinitely with a very small airlift and that we should not evacuate our dependents. Just prior to a meeting with my staff a few days before, I had been told that a number of applications had been received from our officers and officials in Berlin requesting permission for their families to be returned to the United States. I took the opportunity afforded by the staff meeting to state that it was unbecoming to an American to show any signs of nervousness. If there were those who felt uneasy I would be glad to arrange for their return home and a request to this effect would not discredit the applicant. On the other hand, I wanted no one with me in Berlin who had sent his family home, and therefore a request to go home would apply to all members of the family. While I had expected some increase in applications, the result of my statement was the opposite and almost all of the applications previously received were withdrawn. Therefore I felt that I could say accurately in my reply to the Department of the Army:

Evacuation in face of the Italian elections and European situation is to me almost unthinkable. Our women and children can take it, and they appreciate import. There are few here who have any thought of leaving unless required to do so.

The next move of the Soviet representatives to extend the blockade was to stop outgoing passenger trains, including the international train, the Nord Express. This led to another teleconference with the Department of the Army on April 10 in which Royall stated that while there was no change in the Department's position that we should remain in Berlin, the question was under constant discussion in Washington and he wanted to have my views once more. In my reply I stated that we should not leave Berlin unless driven out by force. I thought that the extension of the blockade to cut food off from the German population in Berlin might succeed in forcing us out but I doubted if the Russians would be so foolish as to make a move which would alienate the German population completely. I continued:

We have lost Czechoslovakia. Norway is threatened. We retreat from Berlin. When Berlin falls, western Germany will be next. If we mean . . . to hold Europe against Communism, we must not budge. We can take humiliation and pressure short of war in Berlin without losing face. If we withdraw, our position in Europe is threatened. If America does not understand this now, does not know that the issue is cast, then it never will and communism will run rampant. I believe the future of democracy requires us to stay. . . . This is not heroic pose because there will be nothing heroic in having to take humiliation without retaliation.

So we remained in Berlin. Many British and French dependents were evacuated to their zones. While we had planned a substantial transfer in view of increased work in Frankfurt resulting from bizonal fusion, we slowed it down to avoid misunderstanding. In point of fact the international excitement which had resulted from the imposition of the blockade against Allied personnel and supplies did not last long. Our remaining in Berlin, dependent on air supply and cut off from the rest of the world by land and water, was soon taken for granted. The small airlift we started to meet our needs did not have the dramatic appeal of the great airlift that later supplied all the civilian population of western Berlin.

In April the Russians expelled our Signal Corps teams, which were stationed in the Soviet Zone to maintain repeater stations through which communication lines passed from Berlin to our zone.

They had been there since the 1945 agreement covering our entry into Berlin.

We were soon convinced that it was only a question of time until the blockade was extended against the German civilian population. In May the Soviet representatives established new and impossible documentation requirements for the movement of military and civilian freight into Berlin. In June our civil supply trains were held up on various pretexts, and occasionally cars were cut off from civilian freight and mail trains and disappeared. On June 10 Soviet representatives tried to remove switching locomotives and railroad cars from our sector of Berlin, and we had to stop them with armed guards. On June 18 they began to stop at the border a large percentage of the cars which carried freight for Berlin on the grounds of "bad order." Finally, on June 24, all rail traffic between the western zones and Berlin was stopped by the Soviet Military Administration. Technical difficulties were the alleged reason. These "technical difficulties" soon extended to canal and highway, and by August 4 the blockade by land and water was complete.

Later the Soviet representatives claimed that the blockade had been imposed to prevent the currency reform undertaken in western Germany from having an adverse effect on the economy of the Soviet Zone. We had endeavored to obtain quadripartite agreement on currency reform up to and including the last meeting of the Allied Control Council. When the Council broke up we proceeded with our plans on a tripartite basis and the law instituting the currency reform was promulgated in the three western zones on June 18 to become effective on June 20. It is important to remember that at this time all outgoing rail traffic from Berlin had been stopped by Soviet action except for the return of empty cars. Barge traffic had been stopped. Passenger traffic by rail in and out of Berlin had been stopped, and it continued on the autobahn only for those passengers who were willing to subject themselves to Soviet check. Therefore, on the day of currency reform there remained by land and water only the one-way movement of food and supplies for the civilian population of Berlin, and this movement could not in any way affect the transfer of funds by exchange of commodities between the western zones and Berlin.

When the three military governors agreed to introduce Western currency in our zones, we had decided against its introduction in

Berlin because we appreciated fully the difficulties which would develop in the use of separate currencies in the city. Our own government had expressed some doubt to me as to the advisability of continuing the use of the Reichsmark in Berlin and I had replied that in my opinion there would be less difficulty than would result from separate currencies. The Berlin situation became more difficult on June 16 when Soviet representatives followed up their withdrawal from the Allied Control Council by walking out of the Kommandatura, which was the quadripartite body responsible for the government of the city. The continuance of a common currency was possible under quadripartite control but it was difficult to understand how it could be maintained without such control.

Regardless of the conditons created by the breakup of the Kommandatura, the three Western military governors separately advised Sokolovsky[2] on June 18 that currency reform was to be placed into effect in their zones in view of our failure to obtain quadripartite agreement, but that the measure would not apply to Berlin. We expressed the hope that existing trade arrangements could be continued with the Soviet Zone, and that it would still be possible to arrange for a uniform currency for all of Germany. Sokolovsky replied on June 20, charging that we were splitting Germany and that our action had forced him to undertake urgent and necessary measures to safeguard the Soviet Zone. He expressed satisfaction that the Western currency was not to be introduced in Berlin and agreed that continued trade between west and east Germany was desirable.

When we received his letter we suggested that a meeting of the quadripartite finance and economic experts be held[3] in the Allied Control Council building on the morning of June 22 to discuss the Berlin currency situation and the continuation of trade. When our experts arrived at this conference they were informed by the Soviet representatives that a new currency would be introduced in their zone and in Berlin. This of course made impossible a separate currency for Berlin only.

Still hoping to avoid two currencies, our experts expressed willingness to accept the new Soviet mark provided our interests and the interests of the Germans in our sectors of Berlin were protected adequately. We asked for guarantees of equitable treatment of all Germans. Allied access to the new currency paid in by Berlin residents for the food and other imports which we brought into the city, and a trade agreement which would not place the industry of Berlin under Soviet domination. The experts met in a four-hour session and then adjourned for two hours to report to the military governors. They met again until eleven-thirty that night, when the representatives of the Western Powers were convinced that the new Soviet mark would be under complete Soviet control and that if we accepted it in the western sectors we would henceforth be guests in Berlin. In view of this situation the meeting broke up. The following morning Sokolovsky sent us letters,[4] which quite evidently had been written while the experts were still in session, advising us of the Soviet currency reform and the issue of the new mark in Berlin.

I was in constant communication with the Department of the Army during the period in which currency reform was being considered both tripartitely and quadripartitely. I had been advised on April 29 that if we failed to obtain agreement for the use of a common currency in Berlin, separate from that used either in west or east Germany, our government did not view the use of the Soviet currency as acceptable politically. Our acceptance would mean a recognition of Soviet sovereignty in Berlin. However, final decision was left to my discretion and I yielded to the arguments of my French and British colleagues to accept the Soviet currency in Berlin if we could participate in its control. Since Sokolovsky offered no such participation, I knew his proposal was unacceptable to our government.

Therefore I replied immediately[5] to Sokolovsky that we could not accept his proposal and that I would join with my colleagues in placing West marks in circulation in the western sectors of Berlin. Robertson had agreed with me fully. Our French associate, Koenig's deputy in Berlin, Noiret, would not agree. Koenig was not in Berlin and Robertson and I were apprehensive that the French would refuse to join us in this move. They did join us at the last moment with reluctance and advised us in writing that there was no other choice left to them but they did not wish to be associated with us in the responsibility for taking this decision.

The Soviet currency measures[6] went into effect on June 23. We made the West mark legal currency in Berlin on June 24 and arranged for the people of Berlin to exchange their old money between June 25 and 27. In taking this step we were still hopeful of a later agreement and therefore permitted the Soviet or Ostmark (East mark) to have equal status as legal currency with the Western currency or Deutschemark. Thus either one of the currencies could be used in the western sectors to pay for food, rent, taxes, electricity, and coal.

When the order of the Soviet Military Administration to close all rail traffic from the western zones went into effect at 6:00 A.M. on the morning of June 24, 1948, the three western sectors of Berlin, with a civilian population of about 2,500,000 people, became dependent on reserve stocks and airlift replacements. It was one of the most ruthless efforts in modern times to use mass starvation for political coercion. Our food stocks on hand were sufficient to last for thirty-six days and our coal stocks for forty-five. These stocks had been built up with considerable difficulty as our transportation into Berlin was never adequate. We had foreseen the Soviet action for some months. We could sustain a minimum economy with an average daily airlift of 4000 tons for the German population and 500 tons for the Allied occupation forces. This minimum would not maintain industrial output or provide for domestic heating and normal consumer requirements, and even if coal could be brought into Berlin in unlimited quantities, the electrical generating capacity in the western sectors was limited because the Russians had removed the equipment of its most modern plant before we entered the city. Electricity from the Soviet Zone was cut off when the blockade was imposed. The capacity which remained could provide electricity for essential purposes only a few hours each day, and even these hours of use had to be staggered for the various parts of western Berlin. Despite these conditions, we had confidence that its people were prepared to face severe physical suffering rather than live again under totalitarian government, that they would endure much hardship to retain their freedom.

The resources which we had within the theater to defeat the blockade were limited. Our transport and troop carrier planes, although more than 100 in number, were C-47s, twin-engine planes of about two and a half tons cargo capacity, and many of them had seen hard war service. The British resources were even more limited. There were no French transport planes to be made available.

Nevertheless, I felt that full use of our available C-47s would prove that the job could be done. I called General LeMay on the telephone on the morning of June 24 and asked him to drop all other uses of our transport aircraft so that his entire fleet of C-47s could be placed on the Berlin run. With air commanders of the stature of General LeMay and his successor, General Cannon, you have only to state what is wanted to know that their full resources will be applied to the effort. At the same time arrangements were made for the movement of food to our airports and on the morning of June 25 the first C-47s arrived in Berlin with food for its people.

On that same day the Department of the Army called for another teleconference and suggested that the introduction of Western currency in Berlin should be slowed down if there was any possibility that it might bring armed conflict but it was too late then. I pointed out in my reply that the difficulties to be expected had been reported in full and that we had been instructed to proceed with the issue of the western zone mark unless agreement was obtained to a separate Berlin currency. I added:

We do not expect armed conflict. . . . Principal danger is from Russian-planned German Communist groups. . . . Conditions are tense. . . . Our troops and British are in hand and can be trusted. We both realize desire of our governments to avoid armed conflict. Nevertheless, we cannot be run over and a firm position always induces some risk.

I also pointed out that the amazingly courageous resistance of the Berlin population would drive the Soviet Administration to extreme measures and that Sokolovsky had issued a proclamation on the preceding day declaring the end of four-power government. His purpose was to frighten the Berlin population so that they would not exchange their old currency for Western currency. I stated:

Every German leader, except SED leaders, and thousands of Germans have courageously expressed their opposition to Communism. We must not destroy their confidence by any indication of departure from Berlin. I still do not believe that our dependents should be evacuated. Once again we have to sweat it out, come what may. If Soviets want war, it will not be because of Berlin currency issue but because they believe this the right time. I regard the probability as remote, although it cannot be disregarded entirely. Certainly we are not trying to provoke war. We are taking a lot of punches on the chin without striking back.

American agents examine evidence seized in a black market raid in Heidelberg.

These German women, refugees from the Russian Zone, look for food in the garbage dump of a barracks.

Some of the fifty barges that were tied up in Berlin waters by the Russian blockade.

Before the blockade. Seed potatoes from the western zones reach the railroad yard in Berlin.

On the next day, June 26, the airlift became an organized operation.

A separate exchange of letters between Marshal Sokolovsky and General Robertson gave the latter the opportunity to suggest a meeting of the military governors to discuss the lifting of the blockade and the acceptance of the Eastern German currency in Berlin. I did not favor this move, because it seemed to me an indication of apprehension on our part. This time General Koenig agreed with me. While our government did not particularly desire the meeting, it was urged by the British Government to instruct me to participate. The British appeared to want agreement so badly that they believed it possible of attainment. The decision was left in my hands, and with some reluctance I agreed to attend.

On July 3 the three Western military governors proceeded separately to Sokolovsky's headquarters near Potsdam, picking up Soviet escort officers as we left the Berlin city limits. We were taken directly to Sokolovsky's anteroom and then into his office, where he greeted us politely but coldly. He had with him three attendants, none of whom we had seen before. Robertson expressed concern over the deterioration of our relationship which had culminated in the blockade and told him of our desire to reach an agreement on currency which would restore the situation. Sokolovsky interrupted to state blandly that the technical difficulties would continue until we had abandoned our plans for West German Government. This was the first admission of the real reason for the blockade. He did not even discuss the currency issue which was later given as the reason for the blockade by his government. It was evident that he was confident we would be forced to leave Berlin and that he was enjoying the situation. We were not. We had nothing further to gain from the conference[7] so we left after a very brief discussion, and our farewell was as cold as our reception. My British and French colleagues returned with me to my office where we prepared a report.

We believed this would be helpful to our governments because they were finding it difficult to agree as to their next step. Washington wished to advise the Russians that unless the blockade was lifted at once the issue would be placed before the United Nations. The British and French governments wanted to make a further effort to negotiate either among the military governors or through normal diplomatic channels. My own view, which I expressed to our government, was that further negotiations in Berlin would serve no useful purpose unless basic principles were resolved among governments.

The co-ordination of American thinking and the exchange of information during these somewhat trying days were superb. Our officials in Berlin, London, and Washington were in daily communication through the use of the teleconference, and each move was discussed in detail with Secretary Royall, Under Secretary Lovett, and Ambassador Douglas. While Ambassador Smith was not in the teleconference circuit, he was kept informed so that he could transmit his opinion by cable. It was more difficult to reconcile our views with those of the British and French governments, which was largely Douglas' assignment in London. The necessity for the co-ordination of three positions prior to each move and the time required for their reconciliation proved a major handicap to the progress of the discussions. Almost a month was to pass before the three ambassadors in Moscow received their instructions to protest. Thereafter they were delayed frequently for the same reason.

During this crisis Murphy and I were summoned to Washington to report to the National Security Council where, some months before, both Ambassador Smith and I had predicted trouble in Berlin. On July 20, I reported the existing situation in a meeting attended by President Truman, Secretaries Marshall, Forrestal, Royall, Symington, Sullivan, Under Secretary Lovett, and the Joint Chiefs of Staff. I asserted my confidence that, given the planes, we could remain in Berlin indefinitely without war and that our departure would be a serious if not disastrous blow to the maintenance of freedom in Europe. I asked for 160 C-54s, a plane which would carry ten tons of cargo as compared to the two and a half tons carried by the C-47. Symington and General Hoyt Vandenberg of the Air Forces said they could deliver these planes in a relatively short time. There was no dissent to my recommendations, which were approved by the National Security Council. When the Council adjourned, President Truman honored me by asking me to remain with him for further discussion, during which I told him I was sure that the Berlin population would stand fast through the coming winter if it proved necessary. I left his office inspired by the understanding and confidence I received from him.

We returned to Berlin immediately, accompanied by Mr. Bohlen, and arrangements were made for Ambassador Smith to join us in London for a full exchange of views and information. I developed an intensely painful attack of lumbago on the return air trip so this conference held its initial meeting in Berlin on Sunday, July 25. Smith and Bohlen proceeded to London with Douglas, who on July 28 concluded an agreement with British and French representatives for a simultaneous protest to be presented to the Soviet Government in Moscow by our ambassadors. In Berlin we had agreed that this was the procedure to be followed, although none of us was optimistic as to its results.

The three representatives of the Western Powers in Moscow presented our protests against the imposition of the blockade but while insisting on our equal rights with the Soviet Union to be in Berlin and to participate in its government, they expressed a willingness to negotiate a settlement of the currency problem. The discussion which followed lasted for almost a month and included two visits by the Western spokesmen to Generalissimo Stalin. These two visits had the usual result. Stalin made proposals in general terms which seemed acceptable but they were quite different when translated into specific terms by the Soviet Foreign Office. However, a directive[8] was agreed to on August 30, which returned the discussions to the military governors in Berlin.

I had urged in a radiogram that the negotiations be completed in Moscow as I could see no reason to hope that the military governors would be able to succeed in view of their previous failure. During the Moscow discussions Soviet representatives expressed clearly their desire to have another meeting of the Council of Foreign Ministers and to stop the progress of West German Government. Stalin raised this question himself, pointing out that while he could understand the economic necessity for bizonal fusion he could not understand the political amalgamation of the western zones. Of course his expression of understanding as to the necessity for bizonal fusion was much at variance with Soviet propaganda attacks which had taken place consistently against this move.

The most significant comment he made was that, without reservation, he did not object to four-power control of the German Bank of Emission (the bank of issue in the Soviet Zone and responsible for the issue of East marks). Stalin's comment was not incorporated in the written directive despite utmost effort by the representatives of the Western Powers. Our insistence in Berlin that the final agreement reflect this comment led in large part to the breakdown of negotiations.

The directive was somewhat ambiguous in its wording and unless interpreted in the light of Stalin's remark contained little to assure participation of the Western Powers in the control of Berlin currency. In my cables during the Moscow meeting I had reported that the omission of the.comment in the Moscow directive would make agreement in Berlin unlikely. I felt certain that the Soviet Foreign Office had no intention of really permitting quadripartite control of this bank for any purpose, and that our acceptance of ambiguous wording just to obtain an agreed directive would lead nowhere. Robertson was optimistic and continued to be so throughout the period of our negotiations. Neither my French colleague nor I could understand the basis for his optimism.

The directive from our governments provided that all of the restrictions recently imposed on transport between Berlin and the western zones would be removed and that the East mark would be accepted as the sole currency for Berlin. The military governors were instructed to arrange the necessary details to insure that there should be no discrimination against holders of West marks; that equal treatment should be given to currency, banking, and credit facilities throughout Berlin, foreign countries, and the western zones; that currency should be provided to meet Allied needs in Berlin; and that the regulation of circulation of currency should rest with the Soviet German Bank of Emission in Berlin. A finance commission consisting of representatives of the four occupying powers was to be established to supervise and control the carrying out of the agreement.

On the surface it appeared to be a workable document. The four military governors met in the Allied Control Council building on August 31, our first formal meeting since Sokolovsky had walked out of the Council in March, to establish subcommittees to study the various aspects of the problem. At this meeting it became apparent that Soviet representatives were in no hurry to reach conclusions, were determined not to yield an inch on the demands which they had presented before the Moscow discussions, and were even slightly contemptuous of the proceedings. The airlift had not yet proved itself, and the Russians remained confident that it would be physically impossible for the Western Allies to maintain their position in Berlin.

The discussions to implement the directive were technical. We offered to accept the East mark as the sole Berlin currency provided the city banking system was placed under quadripartite control. We insisted that we have access to reasonable amounts of East marks, which would be derived from the sale of food we brought into the city, and also the opportunity to export from the western sectors finished products to pay for the raw materials we would bring into the industrial plants. Sokolovsky rejected these proposals and brought up a point which had not previously been discussed in suggesting restrictions on the movement of commercial aircraft into Berlin. We made it very clear that we would not discuss any restrictions on the only transport facility which remained under our control. The seventh and last session of these meetings adjourned on September 7, the date on which our report had to be submitted to governments. We had spent many hours in discussions during which agreement had been reached only on technical details involved in the proposed currency change-over. The basic principles which appeared to have been solved in the Moscow directive remained unsolved and our efforts to obtain agreement had failed.

The three Western military governors submitted a joint report which said in part:

We can sum up the over-all position by reporting that after some days of little progress, Marshal Sokolovsky has given ground on most of the subsidiary issues. . . . There remain three main points of disagreement. We see no sign of an intention on the part of Soviet representatives to yield on these three points and we see no chance of real progress here until action has been taken on a governmental level.

These three points of disagreement were: Soviet rejection of a four-power finance committee with supervisory power over the issue of East marks by the German Bank of Emission; their insistence on complete control of trade with Berlin; and their demand for restrictions in civil air traffic.

In the period between the imposition of the blockade against Allied personnel and its extension against the civil population, the conditions in Berlin were more tense than at any other time. The arrests of our personnel who entered the Soviet Sector became increasingly frequent. Altogether there were 93 detained in the first half of 1948. Few if any of these arrests had any real justification and in many instances the Americans were held for hours under humiliating conditions in cells with German criminals. Occasionally they were required to clean floors and walls. I would not order the Americans in Berlin to refrain from entering the Soviet Sector since we had the right to visit any place in Berlin without hindrance. I did remind them of the situation which existed and requested their support in voluntarily staying out of the Soviet Sector. On the other hand I was not willing for the Soviet authorities to succeed in their attempt to intimidate American personnel and to push them about before German eyes. Therefore I decided to counter these measures so that both our own people and the Germans would know that we were not afraid.

Many Russians passed through our sector daily en route from their homes in Potsdam to their sector of Berlin. They drove with high speed and abandon in the German cars which had been confiscated for their use. I ordered the enforcement of a traffic safety program, knowing it would mean the arrest of a substantial number of speeding Russian drivers. I also placed road blocks on the Potsdam highway from time to time where Soviet cars would be required to stop for identification of passengers.

An amusing incident occurred when a sergeant and a private in a Military Police patrol jeep stopped a speeding Soviet officer who locked the windows of his car and refused to open them. We had instructed our non-commissioned officers to avoid using force and, if circumstances indicated force to be required, to call for an officer. The sergeant instructed the soldier to guard the vehicle while he went for an officer. The soldier looked at the sergeant in disgust and remarked: "Going to get an officer to get this guy out of the car? We don't need any officer. Let me get him out. What kind of an Army have I joined anyhow?" This was typical of the spirit of the American soldier in Berlin. He had no fears or worries of Soviet superiority in numbers.

On the twenty-sixth day of June our speed traps caught Sokolovsky, who had refused to stop for a jeep patrol which had then arranged by radio for the speeding car to be intercepted by one of our patrolling armored cars. When his car was stopped, armed

2

bodyguards who were following him in another car made the mistake of jumping out with guns in hand. Our patrol quickly put a gun in the pit of Sokolovsky's stomach and his bodyguards calmed down. He was held for almost an hour before an American officer arrived to identify and release him.

At the time I felt bad about this incident. While there was no question that Sokolovsky's car was speeding, he and I had once been friends. Therefore I called on him the same day to express my personal regrets. I expected him to treat the matter in his usual humorous way. This did not prove to be the case and our meeting was strained. The marshal was cold and indignant and charged that the arrest had been made as a plan to humiliate him. In view of these charges I did not try to convince him otherwise and said merely that I had not come to apologize officially for an act which was justified but only to explain as an old friend why it had happened.

During this same period we found that Soviet armed guards had been placed in a building in our sector which we had permitted the German railroad administration of the Soviet Zone to use.[9] We had not authorized this use of guards and under our agreement armed soldiers of other nations were not permitted in our sector. The Soviet Military Administration refused to remove its men and we found it necessary to throw a cordon of Military Police around the building to deny further entry into the premises except to carry food and water to those inside. In a few days the guards departed.

I know that these measures have the appearance of *opéra bouffe* and that it does not seem possible that they could take place between the representatives of great nations. However, surrounded in Berlin and subjected to continued and deliberate annoyances, there was no other recourse. The countermeasures were effective, and Soviet-created incidents were always reduced when we retaliated.

The tension in Berlin which had existed prior to the extension of the blockade to the German civil population on June 24 relaxed surprisingly, and few incidents occurred between Western Allies and Russians until after the Moscow discussions. This came about in part from the firmness with which the Western Powers met Soviet and Communist attempts to create disturbances and in part because the Soviet representatives seemed dismayed at their own actions and not at all sure as to what we would do in return. Frequent Soviet warnings of aerial gunnery practice and formation flying in the air corridors did not materialize in threatening form. Still I had little hope of a settlement by negotiation, and some hope that a prompt move on our part would break the blockade. If such a move were not made quickly we would have to prepare for a long and patient political struggle of months if not of years.

The care with which the Russians avoided measures which would have been resisted with force had convinced me that the Soviet Government did not want war although it believed that the Western Allies would yield much of their position rather than risk war. On July 10, I reported this conviction to our government, suggesting that we advise the Soviet representatives in Germany that under our rights to be in Berlin we proposed on a specific date to move in an armed convoy which would be equipped with the engineering material to overcome the technical difficulties which the Soviet representatives appeared unable to solve. I made it clear that I understood fully the risk and its implications and that this was a decision which could be made only by government. No armed convoy could cross the border without the possibility of trouble. In my view the chances of such a convoy being met by force with subsequent developments of hostilities were small. I was confident that it would get through to Berlin and that the highway blockade would be ended. When our government turned down my suggestion, I understood its desire to avoid this risk of armed conflict until the issue had been placed before the United Nations. I shall always believe that the convoy would have reached Berlin.

On July 19, I repeated these views in a cable which, paraphrased in part, said:

> I feel that the world is now facing the most vital issue that has developed since Hitler placed his political aggression under way. In fact the Soviet government has a greater strength under its immediate control than Hitler had to carry out his purpose. Under the circumstances which exist today, only we can assert world leadership. Only we have the strength to halt this aggressive policy here and now. It may be too late the next time. I am sure that determined action will bring it to a halt now without war. It can be stopped only if we assume some risk.

Following the report on the failure of the Berlin negotiations, the three Western governments developed their next step through normal diplomatic channels. The diplomatic representatives agreed on an aide-mémoire, presented on September 14 to the Soviet Government, stating that the talks in Berlin had failed because Marshal Sokolovsky had refused to comply with the terms of the Moscow directive. The Soviet Government replied on September 18, placing the blame for failure on the three Western governments. This note reiterated the demand first made during the Berlin negotiations by Sokolovsky that Soviet control of transport facilities be extended over civil air transport. This was a clear indication that the Russians did not seek a real agreement.

A few days later, on September 24, the Soviet Government issued a public statement which embodied its reply to the aide-mémoire. This statement was the usual combination of half-truths, distorted facts, and malicious charges.

Secretary Marshall was in Paris for the meeting of the General Assembly of the United Nations and he summoned Ambassadors Smith, Douglas, Murphy, and me so that we could exchange views and provide him with the latest information. He was discussing our next course of action with the British and French foreign ministers. We accompanied him to a meeting of September 25 at which the three Western Powers decided to dispatch a note informing the Soviet Government that the Berlin issue would be placed before the Security Council of the United Nations. Dr. Philip C. Jessup, our representative on the Security Council, was designated to present the position of the United States and he began immediate preparation for his task.

While we were in Paris we had two long discussions with Marshall, one of which, as I remember, was attended by our Ambassador to France, Jefferson Caffery, Assistant Secretary Willard Thorp, Mr. Bohlen, Dr. Jessup, and Mr. Murphy; and the other by Smith, Douglas, Caffery, Murphy, and Bohlen. Specific questions were not raised in these talks, the purpose of which was a full and frank exchange of views among our officials who, under Marshall's leadership, had most to do with relations with the Soviet Government.

Marshall directed the discussions so that they would develop fully our viewpoints, which coincided in principle, though at variance in detail. All of us were convinced that the Western Powers must remain in Berlin to preserve the courage and faith of all of those who wanted freedom, and especially to offer hope and courage to the eastern European countries in which Communist domination had concealed but had not destroyed the desires of the populations to be free. I reported my conviction that we could stay in Berlin by airlift indefinitely and that this airlift could be built up to maintain a reasonable standard of living.

At the meeting with Bevin and Robert Schuman, Bevin had expressed a concern at the slow build-up of the airlift and some doubt as to the maximum capacity it could reach. I handed Marshall a penciled memorandum stating that we had airplanes en route which would deliver 8000 tons of cargo per day in Berlin and that this was double the tonnage being obtained at the time.

In the conference of the American officials with Marshall, I expressed the view that the initial progress of the European Recovery Program offered hope that we would have an economically healthy western Europe and western Germany which would be able to assert rather than absorb pressure, and that this power when it developed would bring the Berlin blockade to an end. During this period, which might take many months, we must be prepared to continue indefinitely and to increase the airlift. I had no fear of physical aggression by Soviet forces and I was certain that Communism had lost any opportunity it may have had to capture Germany if we held our ground.

Smith agreed with my views in large measure and he too discounted any likelihood of immediate physical aggression by Soviet forces. On the other hand, while he recognized the need to remain in Berlin as a temporary measure, he was inclined to believe that it was a liability to be disposed of at the first auspicious moment. I was sure that no such moment could arise, as Berlin had become a symbol of the firmness of the free countries of the world to retreat no further in the face of Communist expansion.

Douglas felt as strongly as I did that we had to remain in Berlin up to the point of war if we were to accomplish our objectives in Europe. However, he felt that war must be avoided at all costs as a Soviet holocaust would destroy the remaining liberal thought in Europe. To me it did not seem practical to determine the point at which only our departure from Berlin would avoid war, and I was less apprehensive of a Soviet holocaust than my associates. It seemed to me a discounting of our real strength. I pointed out once again that I did not anticipate war, that a "cold war" always involves the risk that it may become "hot," and that this risk has to be assumed.

While these discussions were directed to long-range aspects of the situation, there was unanimous agreement that the airlift would be increased and that we should continue in Berlin for the present. Marshall approved this position and communicated it to the National Security Council with a recommendation for the release of additional transport aircraft.

This was to be my last official conference with Secretary Marshall. I did not realize that his retirement was at hand although he had told us that in the near future he would have to undergo an operation.

When the negotiations were returned from Moscow to Berlin, it appeared to be a signal for the resumption of annoying tactics by the Soviet authorities. We had anticipated that their next move would be through their German Communist vassals. Since the city offices were located in their sector, which was under the control of Communist-dominated German police, there was little we could do to protect them from terroristic tactics. In early September Communist-led organized gangs besieged the city hall, keeping members of the city assembly from meeting, while the police looked idly on. For this reason the city assembly sat for the last time in the city hall on September 6 and met on September 10 in the British Sector. The Soviet-dominated SED minority group in the assembly refused to attend this session, which it declared to be illegal. In doing so it started the split of the German city government.

These terroristic tactics failed in their purpose to inspire fear. The leaders of the democratic German parties called a protest rally on September 9 in the Reichstag Square located in the British Sector just across the line from the Soviet Sector. It was attended by 300,000 people who, in the face of inclement weather and with only meager transport facilities available, had responded to the call of their leaders to show their desire for freedom. Ernst Reuter and other political leaders addressed the gathered throng. On the whole the demonstration was orderly, although as it broke up a small group of German youth rushed to the Brandenberg Gate. One of them climbed it to remove the Soviet flag flying from its top. Soviet Zone police and Soviet soldiers then opened fire on the participants. While I do not like mass demonstrations, which can easily become disorderly and dangerous, there was no longer any question as to the choice made by the people of Berlin. The Communists attempted to stage a rival demonstration on Unter den Linden three days later. Attendance was compulsory for factory workers and school children, which explained the presence of approximately 100,000 people. The demonstration was lethargic and noticeably lacking in enthusiasm. It failed in its purpose.

The city assembly was required under the quadripartite-approved city constitution to arrange for the election of a new assembly in 1948, and it fixed December 5 as the date on which the election would be held. In October Soviet representatives refused to approve it. The three Western military governors would not intervene because the constitution placed this matter in German hands. The German officials proceeded with their plans. This led to further disturbances in city government. The assembly discharged the head of the city labor department, Waldemar Schmidt, who refused to leave office and was maintained in his position in the east sector of Berlin by Soviet support. On November 30, when it was evident that the election would take place and would result in overwhelming defeat for the Communist-dominated SED party, Soviet-sponsored groups set up a rump "city *Magistrat*" under Fritz Ebert, Jr., the worthless son of a worthy father who had been the first president of the Weimar Republic. Soviet action had split the city of Berlin.

On December 5 the people of west Berlin voted for the new assembly. Residents of east Berlin were not permitted to participate in the election by Soviet command, and members of the SED party in the western sectors were ordered to refrain from voting. The democratic parties had avoided partisan issues in the election so that its results would indicate the real attitude of the people of Berlin toward arrogant Soviet threats. Of those who were eligible 86.3 per cent cast their votes for a new assembly and for freedom.

The election was a sight worth recording. Before polling places in bombed-out basements in the shadow of the ruins of the city of Berlin were long lines of German voters. The old and the crippled were brought to the polls by their families and friends. They knew the meaning of their vote. The people of Berlin had learned the power of the ballot. Communist efforts to interfere through "strong-arm" measures were negated by prompt action of the members of the democratic parties, who had determined to meet fire with fire and had their own assembled groups ready to cope with any aggressive move which might develop. Their method was effective and the elections were quiet and orderly.

Ernst Reuter, who had been elected mayor after the first Berlin elections but had been kept out of office by Soviet veto, now became the mayor. Rugged, intelligent, and courageous, he held the affection of the people of Berlin and was their logical leader in this crisis. He had succeeded the brave but ailing Frau Louise Schroeder. Their determination to maintain freedom was matched by that of other political leaders, such as Dr. Otto Suhr (SPD), Dr. Ferdinand Friedensberg (CDU), Carl Hubert Schwennicke (LDP), Franz Neumann (SPD), and Jakob Kaiser (CDU). When the year 1948 ended Berlin was two cities in one, each with a separate government.

While these events were taking place the situation was under discussion in the United Nations in Paris. At the very time when Soviet-sponsored Communists were besieging the city hall and forcing the division of the city, Vishinsky and Dimitri Manuilsky, Foreign Minister of the Ukraine, were attacking the Western Powers before the United Nations and charging them with responsibility for the Berlin crisis. On October 19 Dr. Jessup placed our case before the Security Council in a precise, logical presentation and in calm and measured tones rejected the Soviet charges. The Soviet representatives refused to recognize the jurisdiction of the Security Council. This action had been anticipated and it was expected as a result that the issue would go before the General Assembly. Neutral members of the Security Council believed it possible, however, to find a solution without settling the question of jurisdiction. This led to the designation of a committee of neutral experts to attempt to find a technical way out of the currency problem.

Although the deliberations of this committee continued for many weeks it seemed to me that they had no reality from the day it was established. The broken parts of the split city could no longer be cemented by a technical solution. Even if the currency problem were solved, there would remain the question of political jurisdiction in Berlin, and it was certain that the elected government would not be recognized by the Soviet authorities. This is why the report of the committee of experts which was submitted in March 1949 had to be rejected by the Western Powers. The currency problem could not be resolved unless quadripartite government was restored in Berlin, and it was difficult to see how this restoration could take place unless the Russians backed down or unless we sacrificed the German political leaders who had chosen to stand for freedom.

Throughout the discussions among governments and in the United Nations, Soviet propaganda continued its attacks on the Western Powers and on the political leaders of western Berlin and western Germany. More and more it reflected the Cominform manifesto adopted by the European Communist parties at Warsaw on October 5, 1948. As a popular appeal to German opinion, this manifesto had advocated the unification of Germany accompanied by the withdrawal of the occupying armies to the periphery. To me, such a withdrawal by the Western Powers would have been a catastrophe, as fear would have marched in when the Allied armies marched out. Many Germans, in spite of their dislike for occupation, wanted the Allies to remain and it was too late for this Soviet propaganda to win support from people who had seen at close range the oppression of freedom in east Germany and the ruthless exploitation of its economy by the Soviet authorities.

In March 1949 the Communists of east Germany were called to a self-styled "People's Council" in Berlin which was to climax their political activity during the year of the blockade and represent an additional effort to win German support. It met to approve a constitution for all Germany which had been drafted in October 1948 by party-designated members and which, with the approval of the People's Council, was to be submitted to the people for ratification at some future date. Thus the Soviet representatives had ready a constitution for all Germany to bring forth in opposition to the western German constitution, and they believed that the appeal for German unity would render the latter constitution unpopular. This sordid attempt to block progress in west Germany was completely ineffective.

CHAPTER 20

The Airlift
Breaks the Blockade

BERLIN under blockade was like a besieged city with only one supply line linking it to the Western world, the airlift bringing food, clothing, coal, raw materials, and medicines to the 2,500,000 men, women, and children in its western sectors. Operation Vittles, as the pilots designated the airlift, grew steadily from the few outmoded planes we had in Germany to the fleet of giant flying transports which on the record day delivered almost 13,000 tons to our three airports.

At the start our C-47s had flown the clock around; pilots, plane and ground crews worked far beyond normal hours to achieve a maximum effort. This effort showed the high number of landings which could be made, thus demonstrating that with larger planes we could sustain the Berlin population. It was a welcome sight to the pilots of the C-47s when the first C-54s began to arrive on June 30, 1948, from Alaska, Panama, and Hawaii. It was impressive to see these planes with their insignia indicating the parts of the world from which they had come to participate in the airlift.

In July when I visited Washington I had been promised more planes to give us a total of 160 C-54s, and as they came in squadron by squadron, our freight to Berlin increased consistently. We proved on Air Force Day our ability with planes on hand to bring in 6987.7 tons, and the replacement of C-47s still in operation would have given us the 8000 tons which was essential to a sustaining economy in Berlin. We believed that in good weather we had to be able to carry twice the minimum quota of 4000 tons, although this provided a substantial safety factor.

By December our daily average exceeded 4500 tons. In January and February it had climbed to 5500 tons. We were over the minimum quota of 4000 tons a day by a substantial margin. This minimum provided no fuel for either domestic heating or industrial production. It did supply coal to maintain the available electric generating facilities in the western sectors.

The airlift was no makeshift operation. From the beginning it was a carefully planned split-second operation. It started with the determination of priority requirements in Berlin. The next steps were the requisition of supplies by the Bizonal Administration in Frankfurt, then the co-ordinated movement of these supplies by ship, rail, and truck to the planes at the five airports in the western zones, the airlift delivery to the three Berlin airports, and the transfer of cargo from these airports to the German authorities.

Latest radar techniques made landings possible under almost unbelievable weather conditions and with a remarkable safety record. Two systems of radar were used, one to track the plane in the air corridor and as it left the corridor to enter the approach pattern to the airport, and the other to pick up the plane in the approach pattern and bring it safely to ground. The first system was operated from the tower, the second from the ground. The latter system, known as GCA or Ground Control Approach, had always been liked by our Air Forces but was not used very much in civil aviation as the pilots preferred another system in which they remained in control instead of having to take instructions from the ground. The success of GCA in Germany did much to change the view and GCA is becoming more widely used in commercial flight.

To provide experience, pilots en route to Germany were given four-engine flight training in Montana, where a duplicate of the air corridor and approach paths was set up with navigation aids exactly like those in Germany. Moreover, pilots in the airlift flew the same pattern in good weather and bad.

I became well acquainted with the type and kind of weather under which our pilots operated the airlift, as it was necessary for me to visit our zone frequently. On one of these trips, just before the Berlin municipal election, we had run into several days of im-

A new daily tonnage record is painted on the side of a C-54 as the airlift begins to bring in more supplies than the railway carried before the blockade.

The C-74 employed its own elevators for unloading.

Here is a huge C-74 Globemaster unloading twenty tons of flour in Berlin. This plane was not part of the scheduled run.

possible flying weather. While perhaps it was vanity on my part, I felt that I must be in Berlin on the day preceding the election, rather than risk my absence having any possible deterrent effect. I was in Frankfurt and General Cannon promised to let me know when there was any momentary break in the weather. The break came at two o'clock in the morning. Mrs. Clay and I, accompanied by Murphy, Riddleberger, Wilkinson, and Donnan, arrived at the Rhine Main airport, which was closed to operations. Guided by a jeep, we penetrated the fog to find one of the airlift planes having ice scraped from its wings by its crew. We climbed into the plane and took off to Berlin. The pilots were kind enough to permit Mrs. Clay to ride in the cabin, while the rest of us sat on bucket seats in the cargo plane. I dozed off as best I could, while listening to the repartee taking place between Murphy and Wilkinson, who were playing a violent game of gin rummy. When we arrived over Berlin, both Tempelhof and Gatow airports reported equally unfavorable conditions so our pilot determined to make a pass at Tempelhof. Thanks to the effectiveness of GCA and its well-trained operators, we landed without accident but with our brakes hot. When the tower directed us to the taxiway we found the visibility so poor that we did not dare move farther down the runway. We were unable to follow the jeep that was sent to guide us and finally reached the unloading ramp guided by an airman under each wing signaling with flashlights. This was not unlike hundreds of landings made under adverse weather conditions except that ours was a lightly loaded plane and did not require the careful handling necessary for one carrying ten tons of cargo.

Immediately after the imposition of the blockade we had constructed two new and heavier runways at Tempelhof and one at Gatow in the British Sector. In September we had determined that an additional modern, well-equipped airport was necessary and had selected a site at Tegel in the French sector. My engineers reported that the new airport would be completed in March, and I found it necessary to tell them that it would be completed in December. I had visited China in 1943 on an inspection trip and to negotiate for payment of the construction costs of the airports built there for our use in bombing Japan. I had seen the work that could be done with hand labor. I knew that workers were available in Berlin and was confident that they would respond to our call. While we used the largest of our Army transports to bring in essential construction equipment such as rock crushers, which were cut into parts for the flight and welded back together on their arrival in Berlin, even with this equipment the construction of Tegel airport was largely a hand job, accomplished by more than 20,000 Berlin men and women working three shifts a day. They completed the airport on schedule.

A hazard at Tegel airport was the radio transmitting tower for Radio Berlin located only a short distance from the runway. Although the tower was in the French Sector, the transmitting station was under Soviet control. The French Commandant, General Jean Ganeval, called upon the German officials of Radio Berlin to remove it, which they refused to do. While there had been some reluctance on the part of French representatives to the strong position we had taken in Berlin, that reluctance did not apply to Ganeval. He sent out his demolition experts and blew up the tower despite a Soviet threat. As usual, nothing materialized from this threat and Tegel airport, operated by French personnel, carried a substantial part of the airlift burden.

The airports in western Germany were also enlarged, and to shorten the air travel distance many of our aircraft were based at British airports, where the ground operations were conducted by the Royal Air Forces. Later, to obtain maximum efficiency, General Robertson agreed to place British air transport in an integrated command headed by our General William H. Tunner.

Maintenance was difficult because of the coal haulage. To prevent combustion hazard, the coal had to be wet down. This made cleaning the plane a problem. At first we used the soldiers' duffel bags to carry coal but when the several million on hand were exhausted we made hemp bags in Germany and finally strong waterproofed paper bags. Always it was the coal load which gave the planes the heavy beating and which found us seeking better methods of packaging and loading.

Murphy and I visited the United States in October 1948. In view of the Berlin situation, our stay was limited to twenty-four hours. On my arrival in Washington I reported to the Joint Chiefs of Staff and secured their approval to request the National Security Council to provide us with 64 more C-54s, which would enable us to withdraw the C-47s from the airlift. This would give us 224 C-54s for the

American lift, and with the British contribution would successfully carry us through the winter. It was in the interests of safety to replace the slower-flying C-47s with C-54s to eliminate the possibilty of the faster aircraft overtaking and crashing into slower aircraft. The National Security Council approved my recommendation and shortly after the meeting, when I reported to President Truman, he advised me directly that the additional planes would be forthcoming. This made it a' very happy visit for me.

Modern radio and radar equipment, traffic control in experienced hands, well-organized maintenance and inspection, helped to make the airlift but all of these could not have done the work had it not been for the American and British personnel who flew the planes. The men who were responsible for the airlift in all of its phases— Air Force, Army, Navy, civilian, American, British, French, and German—deserve the highest praise. They had their hearts in the job. The pilots and crews who flew in all kinds of weather still bore the greatest burden; they knew the import of their mission. Airmen like Lieutenant Carl S. Halverson, who, with his crew chief and with their own funds, organized the dropping of candy by parachute to the children of Berlin and thus started Operation Little Vittles, which received enthusiastic support from home; airmen who developed Operation Santa Claus, which brought thousands of packages from home to meet the needs of Berlin—these men proved that theirs was not a mechanical task. It was inspiring and somewhat heart-rending to witness the spontaneous visits of the women and children of Berlin to Tempelhof airport to show their appreciation of the airlift, bringing with them some precious last possession as a token of their gratitude to the members of the air crews. Twenty-eight Americans gave their lives to the airlift; two of these were ground personnel caught in a collision between plane and truck. Considering the flight conditions, this was a remarkable safety record by comparison with normal Air Force and commercial flying. Nevertheless, it was not the loss of life but the constant nerve strain resulting from the handling of heavy planes under instrument conditions that was the test met by the airlift pilots.

Perhaps it had still other values which cannot yet be measured. For example parachuted candy once dropped into the yard of a German who refused to admit the children to recover it. His neigh-

bors came around to see that it was opened. Germans were beginning to understand that this was a co-operative effort, something
new in Germany, where the failure of neighbors to work together
had always been a major contributing factor to the rise of dictatorship.

When spring came in 1949, with our British colleagues we achieved
a daily average of 8000 tons, which was as much as we had been
able to bring into Berlin by rail and water prior to the blockade.
Obviously, given the larger planes now coming off the production
lines, this tonnage could be doubled, or, if maintained at the same
figure, delivered in Berlin at from 25 to 35 per cent less cost. We
were gaining invaluable experience in the use of air transport to
support military operations and for civil use. The cost of the airlift
could well be justified in its contribution to national defense.

Volumes can be written, and perhaps will be written, to cover
in detail the work of the airlift, though I doubt if they will do it
justice. Mechanically, it proved the efficiency of the Western Powers
in the air in a way that the Soviet Government could understand.
Morally and spiritually, it was the reply of Western civilization to
the challenge of totalitarianism which was willing to destroy through
starvation thousands of men, women, and children in the effort to
control their souls and minds.

During the life of the blockade the number of American dependents in Berlin had been gradually reduced by the transfer of personnel no longer needed in quadripartite activities to Frankfurt and
elsewhere in our zone where they could perform their duties more
effectively. There remained approximately 1000 dependents among
the 7000 Americans in Berlin. I do not believe that our families were
ever as content as during the blockade when they felt themselves
a part of the effort of the Western democracies. Faced with limited
electricity which resulted in a number of hours of darkness each day,
with difficult transportation owing to a very limited gasoline ration,
and with constant shortages in the items available for their needs,
they accepted gladly what they could get. There was no nervousness
or tenseness evidenced by any of the Americans in Berlin.

During the blockade we received a number of distinguished American visitors. In October Dr. Jessup came to Berlin shortly after he
had presented our case in the United Nations and used the occasion
to speak to the Germans over the German radio network in con-

vincing words of our determination to remain in Berlin as a matter of right. John Foster Dulles also came that fall just before the presidential election, intending, I am sure, to show the solidarity of American purpose. He too voiced his confidence in the airlift and expressed our determination to stay in Berlin.

We had as Christmas guests in Berlin Vice-President-elect Alben Barkley, Secretary of the Army and Mrs. Royall, Secretary of the Air Force Symington, Generals James H. Doolittle and Cannon, the Bob Hopes, the Irving Berlins, and the Tex McCrarys. They had all come to Germany to demonstrate their faith in our effort and to entertain the airlift personnel. The Hopes, Berlins, and McCrarys, with the members of their teams, performed repeatedly for our airmen and soldiers and it seemed to me that they were doing more than was really physically possible. As we were sitting down in our home to Christmas dinner, Ambassador and Mrs. Bedell Smith came in from Moscow on their way back to the United States. Their arrival added to the interesting day which started for Mrs. Clay and me with Christmas carols played by the Army band on our lawn, followed by a choral group from our Negro honor guard, and singing by the crippled children from the hospital which Mrs. Clay and the American women in Berlin had done much to help. Royall and I visited our soldiers' messes at noon and a few of the parties at which our soldiers were entertaining needy German children in gay Christmas parties. That night we joined our soldiers in listening to a splendid show put on by Bob Hope, Irving Berlin, and Jinx Falkenberg, after which a number of our Berlin friends joined a party for our guests. We wound up the evening around a large Christmas tree in the living room with everyone singing Irving Berlin's songs to the accompaniment of a small Hungarian orchestra. All in all, Mrs. Clay and I had an unusual and merry Christmas which we hoped our guests enjoyed too.

Berlin had kept its courage. We had been able to increase the food ration a little above the level which had prevailed prior to the blockade. We had not been able to continue industry at the same level, and unemployment had risen. The city administration had started work projects to tear down the ruins of bombed buildings and clean up the rubble. A neater city was to be observed everywhere. Still, it was a rough winter for the population. They had almost no coal for domestic heating. The woodcutting program of the city administration, which provided for the cutting of alternate trees along the streets, did not suffice to replace the coal. Electricity was available for only a few hours a day for cooking, in some parts of the city for only two hours, and the limited generating capacity made it necessary to stagger these hours throughout the city. We had been able to provide coal to heat schools, hospitals, and warming centers located in various parts of western Berlin.

The determination of the people did not falter. They were proud to carry their burden as the price of their freedom, and though the price was high it had brought them something in return that had become dear. They had earned their right to freedom; they had atoned for their failure to repudiate Hitler when such repudiation on their part might have stopped his rise to power.

On March 20, 1949, the three Western military governors took a step which had been requested by the German officials for many months, in making West marks the only legal tender in west Berlin. This step did not prohibit the circulation of East marks in west Berlin but they were no longer acceptable as payment for food, rent, taxes, fuel, and the like; nor would they be accepted at parity with the West marks. In the black market four to five East marks were required to purchase one West mark. For months our West marks had been flowing into the east sector and substantial amounts undoubtedly found their way into Soviet or Communist hands to purchase goods to be smuggled from or to finance Communist party activities in west Germany.

West Berlin could not balance its budget. The drop in industrial output and the loss in employment reduced income sharply while relief expenditures mounted. To make matters worse, tax payments could be made in East marks whereas city employees had to be paid in part in West marks. Labor received only one fourth of its pay in the more highly valued West marks. These factors contributed to a deteriorating financial situation in Berlin and by November 1948 we were convinced and were trying to persuade our British and French colleagues that a change-over to West marks as the sole legal tender in west Berlin was essential to its economy.

When the Soviet blockade was imposed on our traffic in Berlin I immediately placed a counterblockade on the movement of goods from west Germany into east Germany. I was joined in this move by my British colleague and we extended it to rail and water shipments from all western Europe to the Soviet Zone. This led to protest by some of the governments of western Europe, which appeared more anxious to continue trade than to create the conditions that would break up the blockade of Berlin. I doubt, however, whether these protests were expected to bring results in the American Zone, as they were not pushed vigorously. They did result in preventing my British colleague from applying the blockade to the trucks from western Europe traveling along the roads of the British Zone.

It was certain that our counterblockade would be more harmful to east Germany than to west Germany. East Germany lacked coking coal and steel and could not obtain these materials from behind the iron curtain, where the available quantities did not suffice. West Germany, included in the Marshall Plan, had access to the much greater industrial production of the Western world. I expected that a revived western economy would eventually force the lifting of the blockade. We were certain in the spring of 1949 that this pressure was being felt. While we could not obtain accurate statistical information, we did know that the economy of eastern Germany was at a standstill during a period in which the productive output of west Germany was increasing at a more rapid rate than anywhere else in Europe. The consistent attempt to purchase goods in west Germany to be smuggled into east Germany was in itself proof of the need. We had every reason to believe that if economic life in east Germany was not deteriorating it had ceased to progress. In the spring of 1949 there were many rumors that economic conditions there would result in early lifting of the blockade.

In April the People's Council of the Soviet Zone, which had approved the so-called eastern constitution, tried to arrange a meeting with west German officials to be held in Brunswick. This meeting was rejected. However, German officials from east Germany had met with some of the leading officials of west Germany in an effort to develop a common program for German unity which would stop the progress of West German Government. In these negotiations two Germans of some stature—Dr. Rudolf Nadolny, a former ambassador to Moscow, and Dr. Andreas Hermes, a pre-Hitler minister, led in this effort. Whether or not Nadolny, who lived in east Germany, was an agent of the Soviet Military Administration as some believed, the views he presented would have been an aid and comfort to the Communist program had they received any real reception in western Germany.

These efforts on the part of eastern Germans in the political field were perhaps a cover for the efforts of their economic officials to effect a resumption of trade with west Germany.

At this time informal conversations were taking place in New York between Dr. Jessup and Jacob Malik, Soviet representative to the Security Council. I knew nothing of these conversations and on the day preceding the press report of the discussions I had stated in a press conference in Berlin that I knew of no talks looking to the lifting of the blockade. Mr. Murphy, who had returned from Washington to Berlin to help me in the negotiations for the approval of the constitution of western Germany, had not felt free to tell me what he knew. I first learned of these discussions from the newspapers and subsequently from General Robertson after Dr. Jessup had included French and British representatives in the discussions. While I understood the necessity for keeping these conversations secret and the difficulties of maintaining secrecy when information passes through many hands, I was somewhat chagrined to hear the story this way.

On May 4 it was announced that the four occupying powers had agreed to lift the Berlin blockade, with trade conditions to be restored to the pre-blockade arrangements, on May 12, and that the foreign ministers would meet in Paris on May 23. I cabled to the Department of the Army immediately that we should continue the airlift until Berlin had adequate reserves of coal and food to carry it through another winter if the blockade should be resumed. This recommendation was approved and I announced it publicly in Germany on May 6.

At midnight on May 11–12 our trains and trucks crossed the borders en route to Berlin, without incident. Large numbers of correspondents from home and from other countries crossed the border in automobiles and as passengers in the first train. In Berlin it was a day of relaxation for the population with some evidence of a holiday spirit. However, the roar of the airlift still reminded them of their long siege. The blockade was lifted but the struggle for freedom was not yet over. The people had met a major test and were happy in the pride of accomplishment and determined to meet any further test in the same way. I did not meet the first incoming train, for though it represented a great victory, it was but one step forward in the fight for freedom.

Some restrictions on transport, communications, and trade had been in effect since March 1, 1948. The airlift had become a part of our daily lives. At its peak planes were arriving and departing at intervals of thirty seconds. My home in Berlin was directly under the approach to Tempelhof and I learned to sleep well under the steady drone overhead, waking only when there were no planes in the air to wonder at the cause. During this period, almost eleven months, the population of the western sectors of Berlin, including the Allied personnel, had been kept alive by the British-American airlift which, by the day the blockade was raised, had brought 1,402,-644 metric tons of food, coal, and other essential supplies into Berlin. Following the lifting of the blockade, gas and electricity were restored at once to twenty-four-hour service, and life in Berlin became more nearly normal.

I was to leave Berlin on May 15 to return to the United States. I asked General Howley to arrange for me to call on Mayor Reuter to say good-by and to express my appreciation for his courageous leadership of the people in Berlin. Reuter had returned only a short time before from a visit to the United States at the invitation of our Council of Mayors. He had made an excellent impression and had come back convinced of the sincerity of our purpose in supporting the cause of freedom throughout the world. Howley arranged the meeting for the morning of May 14. Shortly before I left the office I found that Reuter had arranged for me to appear before the city assembly, which was meeting to receive a report of a delegation from the constitutional assembly at Bonn. My British and French colleagues were invited to attend. Reuter, in saying good-by, expressed the appreciation of the Berlin people for the aid and support which they had received from the United States during the blockade. It was at this meeting that the resolution was adopted to change the name of the public square in front of the main Tempelhof building to Luftbruecke Platz (Air Bridge Square). It was announced that a memorial plaque would be placed in this square as a tribute to the airmen who had given their lives to the airlift. In my reply, which was improvised, I expressed my admiration for the courage of the people of Berlin and stated that it had regained for them the respect of the free people of the world.

The lifting of the blockade was regarded everywhere as a victory for the forces of freedom. Certainly the use of the airlift to sustain the city had proved the firmness of intent of the Western Powers and had given fresh courage to those who believe in freedom everywhere.

CHAPTER 21

Paving the Way to
West German Government

THE establishment of a government for western Germany was one of the great political developments in postwar Europe. It came about because the United States, the United Kingdom, and France could not agree with the Soviet Union on the form and scope of a government for all Germany, and were unwilling to delay further the return of self-responsibility to the German people. It completed the cycle of political reconstruction which gave the procedures of democratic government to western Germany as an initial step in its return to the family of free nations. The cycle had started in the separate zones and then moved to the fusion of the American and British zones.

The restoration of responsible German government from the village to the state within the United States Zone was a systematic, planned, and to a large extent scheduled-in-advance program to carry out our objectives. Since the agreement which established quadripartite government left zonal administration in the hands of the zone commander, it was a program which could be executed unilaterally.

The second phase, the return to German hands of responsibility for the bizonal area, had been more difficult to accomplish. It was now bilateral, which meant that each step had to be discussed between British and American representatives to reconcile any differences in Anglo-American thinking. Moreover, the two zones had developed politically and economically along different lines. In the British Zone the states had received less responsibility (when the

Basic Law for western Germany was approved, the states in the British Zone were still without constitutions),[1] and more central machinery had been established than in the American Zone. Furthermore, the fusion was limited to the creation of a larger economic entity. The appearances of political unity and establishment of government had to be avoided in view of possible effect on four-power relations. We still hoped at that time to obtain a true quadripartite government of Germany as a whole.

Although the slow inch-by-inch progress was sometimes exasperating, it was continuous. The Soviet attitude in the Council of Foreign Ministers in London in late 1947 shattered any remaining hopes for a true quadripartite government, and in doing so permitted us to move more rapidly and certainly to a really effective German administrative machine for the bizonal area. It also convinced the French representatives that it was time to participate in the establishment of trizonal fusion and West German Government.

It was apparent that this would be a more difficult task than the establishment of bizonal fusion. It is always harder to reconcile three points of view than two. Moreover, British and American objectives and viewpoints had been brought together in the many months of bizonal fusion.

Bidault agreed in London to early three-power discussions which would lead to the formation of West German Government. On January 20, 1948, it was announced that a conference would be convened in London on February 23 to discuss German affairs of mutual interest to the French, British, and United States governments. Also, for the first time, the Benelux countries because of their direct interest in the German problem were invited to participate in those items on the agenda not directly concerned with the administration of military government. This announcement drew a sharp protest from the Soviet Government on February 14 which made the usual charge that the Western occupying powers were attempting to split Germany. Each of the governments concerned formally rejected the Soviet protest and the conference met as scheduled in India House in London.

Our delegation, which was headed by Ambassador Douglas, included Assistant Secretary of State Saltzman, Samuel Reber, Murphy, and me, with a number of experts to assist in our work. These experts included several able men associated with or from Military Government, among whom were Riddleberger, E. H. Litchfield, and Donald

H. Humphrey. The British delegation was headed by Sir William Strang, captain of the British team for many conferences on Germany, Sir Yvonne Kirkpatrick, Patrick H. Dean, General Robertson, and C. E. Steel. The French delegation was headed by Ambassador René Massigli and included Maurice Couve de Murville, Monsieur Alphand, and Ambassador Tarbe de St. Hardouin. General Koenig attended from time to time. The Benelux delegation included Ambassador Jonkheer E. S. M. J. Michiels van Verduynen for the Netherlands, Ambassador Vicomte Obert de Thieusies for Belgium, and the Luxembourg Minister, André Clasen.

The French Government was unwilling to discuss the formation of a West German Government unless economic and security measures were discussed and settled concurrently. So the agenda[2] included the relationship of western Germany to the European Recovery Program, the role of its economy in the European economy and control of the Ruhr, security against Germany, reparations, and provisional territorial arrangements, in addition to the evolution of the political and economic organization for the three zones and a closer association with Benelux countries in policy matters. Only one of these items, the evolution of political and economic organization, pertained directly to the formation of West German Government.

It was not expected that this conference would produce a definitive agreement. Rather it was a preliminary exchange to develop basic principles and differences for consideration by governments and for approval in more detailed form in a subsequent conference. I attended most but not all of the meetings as the increasing tension in Berlin made me unwilling to be absent for more than a few days at a time.

Douglas had received his instructions on February 20, 1948. Our policy now recognized that the economy of east Germany was being reoriented to fit into the eastern European economic system, which left the Western Powers no choice but to undertake to integrate the economic and political life of west Germany with western Europe. We had not abandoned hope of eventually establishing economic and political unity in Germany. Although we would seek to avoid steps which might preclude its establishment, we were ready to move forward with the economic rehabilitation of western Germany under a democratic German political administration. We believed that the concept of western European unity which had been proposed publicly by Mr. Bevin had a place for such a Germany. We believed that necessary restrictions in German control of the Ruhr, which might be incorporated into an international agreement, would be more acceptable to the Germans if it embodied a contribution on their part to a large western European union to which other western European countries would also contribute.

The conference succeeded in eliminating many petty disagreements and in developing the principal differences in viewpoint.[3] All of the participating governments supported the establishment of a federal structure of government. It was clear that the British representatives wanted the federal government to have strong central powers; we favored a federal government with sufficient powers to maintain economic and political unity provided these powers were specifically defined; the French representatives desired a federal structure which was more nearly a confederation of loosely knit states with very limited powers vested in the central government. It was agreed in principle that "a federal form of government, adequately protecting the rights of the respective states but at the same time providing for adequate central authority, is best adapted for the eventual re-establishment of German unity, at present disrupted."

The conference decided against economic fusion of the bizonal area with the French Zone prior to political fusion, but agreed that there should be a closer co-ordination of economic matters in the bizonal area and the French Zone. It likewise accepted the association of both areas in the European Recovery Program and hoped that these measures would suffice to prevent divergent trends in foreign trade, customs, and related matters. Goods and persons were to move freely between the zones. It was also accepted in principle that there should be a closer association in matters of policy with the Benelux countries.

The final session of the conference was held on March 5, as Ambassador Douglas had to return to the United States to testify before the congressional committees holding hearings on the European Recovery Program. It issued a communiqué which could not be a report of agreement but expressed optimism over the progress achieved in preliminary exchanges. The delegates were to convene in April after their governments had studied their differences in viewpoint.

The conference called upon the military governors to study its discussions and to recommend to its second session arrangements for their close association with the Benelux countries and for the co-ordination of economic affairs in west Germany, the future political organization of western Germany, and the measures necessary to safeguard foreign interests. It also requested an inventory of machine tools.

As soon as the conference recessed the three military governors appointed a tripartite working party to further consider the political structure for west Germany.[4] This committee was able to make little progress on basic principles to be required in the constitution, or on the time this government was to be established. It went into such detail that it seemed to be writing the constitution itself rather than the broad principles which would be given to the German Assembly as the condition of Allied approval. Discussions among the three military governors failed to resolve the differences within the committee, though they did show that the American and British views could be resolved quickly in compromise. On the other hand, French representatives still insisted on provisions which would have made the German government a loose confederation. All of us were concerned with our inability to progress, which could only be regarded as an ill omen to the success of tripartite fusion.

While our talks were taking place Marshal Sokolovsky and the Soviet delegation walked out of the Allied Control Council. This had a profound effect on French representatives, who, I think, were convinced for the first time of the futility of further effort to obtain quadripartite agreement. They no longer believed that France could be the agent to bring East and West together, and they recognized the necessity for the economic and political rehabilitation of west Germany as a whole as an alternative to running the French Zone alone. They knew that we were ready to proceed in the three zones but otherwise were determined to go ahead in two. We were no longer willing to have a political and economic void in central Europe which would interfere with the recovery of the European countries participating in the Marshall Plan.

I received word informally that Couve de Murville of the French Foreign Office was interested in visiting me in Berlin to discuss our differences informally, and I grasped this suggestion at once. Couve de Murville had been a member of the French delegation at all the international conferences on the German problem in which the French Government had participated. Young, personable, and able, he spoke English fluently. He had won the regard of the Americans who had worked with him. I found that he was vacationing on the Riviera, where I sent my plane to pick him up. He arrived in Berlin on April 6, 1948, for a three-day visit in which he divided his stay between General Koenig and me.

Our discussions disclosed that basically the French Government, like ours, was interested in principles which would avoid the creation of powerful central control. When some of our detailed differences were raised, Couve de Murville would toss them aside as detail and irrelevant to our real purpose.

This convinced me that we should make a new approach to the problem, avoiding discussion of many details which might not necessarily develop in the German draft. We should concentrate on establishing the broad principles to be given to the German assembly for its guidance and also the principles which would be given to the military governors to guide them in determining whether the constitution conformed to these broad conditions.

With this thought in mind, on the last day of his visit I rushed to the office and dictated a simple memorandum which I felt sure my British colleague would accept. When Couve de Murville arrived later in the morning I showed it to him. He liked it and agreed to discuss it with Koenig. Later in the day he expressed the belief that it might indeed be a basis for agreement. I then stated that I would present it to the military governors and recommend that it be embodied in our report to the conference. The memorandum follows:

The Commanders in Chief of the three western zones of Germany submit herewith a paper to serve as a basis of discussion on political evolution and tri-fusion economic coordination:

1. *The several states will be advised that a constituent assembly will be held not later than 1 September 1948 to prepare a constitution for ratification by the several states.*
2. *The delegates to this constituent assembly will be elected by the people of the several states under the electoral procedures and regulations adopted by the several states.*
3. *The number of delegates from each state will be in the pro-*

portion that its population is to the total population of the participating states. The total number of delegates will be determined by dividing the total population from the last census by 750,000.

4. *The constituent assembly will be instructed as follows:*

   It will draft a democratic constitution which will establish a federal type governmental structure for the participating states which will protect the rights of the participating states and which will contain guarantees of individual rights and freedom. It will determine the boundaries of the several states which will form the federal government, recognizing traditional patterns and avoiding to the extent feasible the creation of states which are either too large or too small in comparison with the other states composing the federal structure.

5. *The constitution as prepared by the constituent assembly will be examined by the occupying powers to determine its compliance with the broad objectives outlined herein. If the constitution as prepared by the constituent assembly does meet these broad objectives, it will be submitted for ratification by the several states under such rules and procedures as these states may adopt. When the constitution has been ratified by two-thirds of the participating states, it will become the constitution for and binding upon all of the participating states. Thereafter, any amendment to the constitution must be ratified by a like majority of the states.*

6. *The constituent assembly will designate an electoral procedure committee consisting of one representative from each of the proposed states which in cooperation with the state governments will arrange for the elections provided for in the constitution to be held concurrent with the ratification of the constitution. The government so elected will take office thirty days after ratification by the requisite number of states. This government will then be charged with the responsibility for government of the participating states as provided in the constitution except to the extent its foreign relations are necessarily handled by the occupying powers pending the establishment of a peace treaty.*

7. *Except in the field of foreign relations and there only to the extent required by existing circumstances, Allied supervision*

and control will be directed to require adherence to the constitution as ratified by the several states and to exercise such other control of the war potential as may have been determined.

8. *Prior to the establishment of trizonal German government it is impracticable to establish trizonal Allied control. However, in the interim period certain steps have or will be taken to insure full economic coordination of the trizonal area and the French Zone of Occupation. The steps which have already been taken are: Joint banking policy under a tripartite Allied Banking Commission; agreement in principle to currency reform in the trizonal area. The remaining steps which should be taken as soon as details can be agreed by the Commanders in Chief are: A common export-import policy under a tripartite Allied export-import agency, and a common customs policy. Further steps are deemed impractical until the three zones have been joined under German government.*

The military governors agreed to send this memorandum, slightly modified, to the London conference to serve as a possible basis of discussion. It was in fact the basis on which agreement was reached. The military governors were also able to agree among themselves and with Benelux representatives on procedures for closer association in policy matters.

When the London conference reconvened, Saltzman was replaced by his deputy, Frank Wisner. Otherwise the delegations were the same. The meetings were held in India House, which, with the establishment of India as a member of the Commonwealth, had been taken over by the British Government. The room where plenary sessions met was heated by a coal fire in a huge fireplace, which kept the delegations seated on that side of the room very warm while the rest of us shivered. The walls were dominated by a portrait of Lord Cornwallis. Halls and conference rooms contained other portraits of early British governors and soldiers who had gained India for the British Empire. I could not but wonder at their comments if the paintings had come to life and had witnessed British representatives arguing for a progressive relinquishment of their authority and the early establishment of popular government in Germany.

Murphy and I shared a suite in the Dorchester Hotel where we could meet frequently with members of our delegation and with some of the members of the other delegations. I found it necessary to fly back and forth from Berlin frequently and as a result had a double birthday. I received in the morning a magnificent birthday cake from Mrs. Douglas in London, and in the evening on my return to Berlin found that Mrs. Clay had a birthday cake ready and our house filled with old friends and associates. During these flights between Germany and England I helped to contribute substantially to Murphy's support, as I was unable to win a single game of gin rummy from him in the entire period of the conference.

While in London I accepted an invitation to address a meeting of the members of the British Parliament belonging to the Parliamentary Union in one of the chambers of the House of Commons. After dining with a small group in the House of Commons dining room, I spoke of our joint policy in Germany and our conviction that we could stop Communist expansion without war. I also expressed gratification that the representatives of the United States and Great Britain were able to pursue a common policy in Germany because we had learned that we did not differ in principle and that compromise on detail was the essence of democratic government. I was grateful for the kind and gracious reception I received from this group of experts in debate and speech. I was honored also with a luncheon given for me by Mr. Bevin in his home. I knew that it was an expression of satisfaction over the harmonious way in which General Robertson and I had worked in the direction of bizonal affairs.

The initial meeting of the conference on April 20 agreed quickly to an agenda.[5] The arrangements proposed by the military governors for a closer association with the Benelux countries were accepted. It was determined that the safeguarding of foreign interests and the fixing of the western German frontier required special study and that the governments concerned would be requested to refer these questions to experts. This left three items for the real work of the delegates: the evolution of political and economic organization, the role of German economy in European economy and control of the Ruhr, and security against Germany.

Agreements were reached on control of the Ruhr and security against Germany and are discussed elsewhere. The French representatives would not have accepted the establishment of any kind of western German government if these two points had not been settled concurrently.

We knew that the real stumbling block would prove to be French reluctance to give the new government sufficient powers for it to be effective. As the discussions progressed this was demonstrated in their opposition to the central government's having any powers of taxation or any real police jurisdiction. They favored a national legislature in which both houses would be composed of representatives of the states, elected preferably by state legislatures. They wished to restore the traditional state boundaries although not at the expense of transfer of jurisdiction over any area under French occupational control.

In principle there was little difference in British and American viewpoints, though in degree there was much. We were both in favor of the central government's having a power of taxation limited to the raising of revenue required to carry out its tasks. We differed as to the powers to be entrusted to the central government, the British representatives supporting a wider range of functions than we believed necessary. We both favored giving the central government limited and clearly defined police powers. We desired a legislature in which the upper house was composed of members representing the several states and chosen as the states might determine, and the lower house of members elected on a national basis. The Americans were more inclined to support the French on the restoration of traditional state boundaries, provided that all areas in occupation be placed under tripartite supervision, than the British, who wished to maintain some degree of unilateral control in their zone. They did not want to give up their hold over the powerful industrial state of North Rhine-Westphalia. Further differences were to develop as to the degree of control to be retained in the Occupation Statute and as to how the military governors should reach decisions. Here we were insistent on majority rule, having experienced the frustration of a veto power wielded by any one of the four representatives on the Allied Control Council.

Although the conference had agreed quickly to refer the fixing of western German boundaries to a committee of experts, I had opposed such a move. The claims submitted by the neighboring countries were far from minor and in some instances involved territory containing substantial coal and oil reserves. While the representatives of the United States and United Kingdom had both stated that all decisions must await the peace treaty, and moreover must be limited to minor rectifications to correct anomalies, I felt that any changes would seriously affect the accomplishment of our objectives. We had argued that the eastern boundary of Germany could not be fixed until there was a peace treaty. Perhaps this made our legal position authorizing temporary changes in the western frontier consistent, but it certainly did not strengthen our moral position that further consideration would have to be given to the final delineation of the eastern boundary. Moreover, the western boundaries of Germany had been established for many years. It is true that in some instances these boundaries made the control of rivers for navigation and power development difficult. Occasionally railroads and highways of one of the neighboring countries passed through short stretches of Germany, but custom and tradition had solved or softened these problems over the years.

My main concern was that we were subjecting a patient who was still under shock from amputation to pinpricks which were of little real value to the claimants but extremely painful to him. Germany had already lost East Prussia, undetermined but large parts of east Germany including Silesia, and the Saar. These major amputations had severed 110,000 square kilometers of rich territory which had supported a prewar population of almost 10,000,000 inhabitants.

We were giving substantial aid to Germany in the interests of European recovery and with a view to its eventual integration into a union of western European nations. Therefore it seemed to me that Germany's neighbors had a stake in *rapprochement* with Germany and that the return they would obtain from small accessions of territory would not be worth the wounded feelings they would cause.

Postwar sentiment and the pressure of Germany's neighbors overruled my arguments. However, it was interesting that in 1949, after the experts had approved changes in the western boundaries, public opinion in Belgium and Luxembourg was such that both of these countries renounced the territory they had been granted and negotiated with German officials for small alterations which could be made without risking continued dissatisfaction and hatred. France likewise made a number of concessions in the interest of better understanding with Germany.

The discussions of West German Government were long and involved. They were noteworthy in portraying clearly the different conceptions of government which can exist even among countries with long democratic traditions. Free-enterprise America, Socialist Britain, and divided France were trying to agree on the principles of a constitution. Ambassador Douglas, with much experience in government and a liberal philosophy of human rights, was well fitted to head the American delegation and his persuasive powers led to compromises which, although they left many problems to be resolved in Germany, did enable agreement on paper authorizing the military governors to go ahead with the program.

When the report of the conference was approved by the three governments, a final decision had been made to establish an economically self-sustaining western Germany under a government of its own, to be drawn into close co-operation with the free countries of western Europe. This decision formulated for the three countries the common policy which had been advocated by our government for many months. There is no question that this was the most important conference for Germany since Potsdam. The report was completed for submission to governments on June 1, 1948. Three of its annexes— F, H, and I—determined the future course of West German Government.

Annex F[6] called upon the three military governors to arrange a meeting of the minister-presidents of the several states not later than June 15, 1948. The minister-presidents were to be authorized to recommend such modification of state boundaries as they believed desirable as long as they conformed to traditional patterns and did not create states either too large or too small. Their recommendations, if approved by the military governments, would be submitted for ratification to the people of the affected areas. The minister-presidents were authorized to convene a constitutional assembly not later than September 1 to prepare a constitution for ratification by the participating states; the delegates to the assembly were to be selected in each state as it might determine, on the basis of one delegate to 750,000 persons, or some similar figure agreed on by the minister-presidents. The minister-presidents were to be advised that they would be responsible for the arrangements in any new states which might be formed, that the institutions established by the constitution would come into effect thirty days after its ratification, and that prior to the convening of the elected assembly the powers to be retained by the occupying powers would be defined and made public. Annex F also contained a statement of principle to guide the German constitutional assembly, which read:

The Constituent Assembly will draft a democratic constitution which will establish for the participating states a governmental structure of federal type which is best adapted to the eventual re-establishment of German unity at present disrupted, and which will protect the rights of the participating states, provide adequate central authority, and contain guarantees of individual rights and freedom. If the constitution as prepared by the constituent assembly does not conflict with these general principles, the Military Governors will authorize its submission for ratification by the participating states. Ratification by two-thirds of the states is binding on all.

Annex H[7] was a "Letter of Advice to the Military Governors" fixing the considerations they would examine to determine the compliance of the constitution with the broad principles which it had to meet. This "Letter of Advice" recognized that there were a number of ways to set up a federal government, so that the constitution had to be examined in its whole to determine its nature. Certain features were established as desirable in whole or in part. A bicameral legislature in which one house represented the states, executive powers definitely prescribed by the constitution and with any emergency powers subject to broad legislative and court review were considered major tests of federal structure. All powers of the federal government were to be limited to those specified in the constitution and should not include education, cultural and religious affairs, local government, or public health (except when essential to safeguard the health of the people of the several states). The power of the federal government in the field of public welfare was to be limited to the co-ordination of social security measures. In the financial field it was to be limited to taxation measures necessary to raise the revenue for authorized federal government purposes, except that it might have the power to secure uniformity in other taxes provided their collection and utilization were left to the states. The power of the federal government in the police field was to be limited to measures specifically approved by the occupying powers and subsequent international agreements.

The constitution was to provide for an independent judiciary to review legislation, to review the exercise of executive power, to resolve conflict between federal government and the states or between the states, and to protect civil rights and individual freedoms. The federal government was to be authorized under the constitution to establish agencies only under circumstances which clearly indicated that state agencies would be ineffective.

The "Letter of Advice" adjured the military governors to examine the constitution in the light of all of these conditions, bearing in mind that it was the structure as a whole and not a deviation from any one of these conditions which would determine whether it provided for a federal type of government.

Annex I[8] established the principles which would govern the formulation of powers to be reserved by the occupying authorities and incorporated into an Occupation Statute which would be published prior to the formation of West German Government and would provide a guaranteed rule of law. It required the military governments to continue to conduct foreign relations but to exercise only those controls in foreign trade and in internal economic policies which affected foreign trade necessary to insure wise use of the financial assistance being provided to the German economy. It required the military governors to exercise agreed security controls or to arrange for the exercise of such controls, as for example by the Ruhr Authority; to enforce the fulfillment of reparations, the maintenance of the established level of industry, and decartelization, disarmament, and demilitarization measures. It required a control of scientific study to prevent war research, and a retention of the right to take such measures as were necessary to protect the prestige and insure the security of the occupation forces, to meet the physical needs of these forces, to insure observance of the constitution, and to resume full powers in case of emergency.

This Annex provided that amendments to the constitution would require approval of the military governors, but laws and regulations of the German Government which were not within the reserved field would become effective, unless disapproved by majority vote of the military governors, within twenty-one days. There was to be no restriction of German competence in German political life, social relations, and education, and Military Government was limited in these matters to observation and counsel to the German officials. Minister-presidents and the constitutional assembly were to be advised of these principles to guide them in their work, so that they would know in advance of the nature of the Occupation Statute, which would be promulgated concurrently with the approval of the constitution and preceding its submission to the states for ratification. Thus the constitution would be ratified in full knowledge of the provisions of the Occupation Statute.

During the conference it had been agreed[9] that the British and American military governors would consult with the French military governor on major measures taken in the bizonal area which might later affect its fusion with the French Zone. This had an unforeseen development. The understanding did not provide that such measures were to be held up in the bizonal area pending agreement. It did give the French Government the opportunity to appeal to our government and to the British Government when it opposed such decisions and to suggest conferences "at governmental level" to resolve the differences. In the past all conferences held outside of Germany had concerned broad policy questions, and internal German problems were left for settlement by the military governors. General Robertson and I always managed to get together. Now neither of us was able to resolve these internal problems with French representatives, who had found that if we could not accept their views on Germany, or were willing to accept them only in part, they would almost certainly obtain acceptance or further compromise at governmental level. Moreover, we did not have the same right with respect to the French Zone, since its actions were taken by the separate state administrations.

Sometimes a negotiation would be transferred from the military governors to a committee designated to represent the three governments, and I must admit that it was difficult for me to understand how such a move could be considered as a transfer to governmental level. The result was that negotiations in Germany with French representatives on measures to be introduced only in the British and American zones would fail. Operating decisions had to be made if the daily tasks of government were to be executed orderly and promptly. While I did not care where negotiations occurred, I was convinced that under no circumstances should they be held on the same subject in two places. Nor should each subject at issue be considered as an isolated problem out of context with the German picture as a whole.

Thus, in the period following the agreement with the French for trizonal fusion, Robertson and I had the greatest difficulty in undertaking measures in the bizonal area to facilitate the economic recovery to which we believed ourselves obligated by our inclusion in the European Recovery Program. As we tried to reach a solution we would make offer after offer of concession to receive little in return, and then the question at issue would be transferred elsewhere for negotiation, with the Anglo-American position starting from its last offer in Germany rather than from its original position. I discussed this situation with Secretary Royall on his visit to Germany in December 1948 to find that he shared my apprehensions. The record of meetings which followed the London conference will indicate the difficulties we faced.

The conference report was approved promptly by the governments of the United States and the United Kingdom. It did not receive public support in France, in part because the French Government had made no effort to present and to emphasize the many concessions it had won. Its defense of the report was limited to describing it as the best compromise that representatives had been able to obtain. Primarily the unfavorable reaction was directed toward the Ruhr agreement, and the French Government refused to accept it as final. Some members of the French delegation which had accepted the report even opposed its approval. Some of the opposition to the formation of a western German government expressed apprehension that it would offend the Soviet Government. This provided an opportunity exploited by French Communists to the full. These fears then spread to Germany and created some doubt in German minds as to the real determination of the three Western Powers to carry the program to completion. We ran into these doubts when we placed in the hands of the minister-presidents the responsibility of carrying out the London decisions.

When General Marshall announced the acceptance of the conference report by our government on June 9 he renewed the invitation to the Soviet Government for its zone to join the three western zones. He did not receive a reply. The report was accepted by the British Government on the same day. The approval of the French National Assembly was not secured until June 18, when the government position was supported by a majority of six votes only.

In spite of the lack of full support for its results, the agreement when approved by the three governments provided the military governors with the framework of a joint policy for setting up West German Government. We were to find that, while we had a common framework, we differed widely on what we wanted for the siding and the trim and the roof.

The delay in French ratification prevented the three military governors from meeting with the minister-presidents until July 1. Meanwhile rumors of the agreement, revealed in part by French opposition, had not created a favorable atmosphere. Before the meeting in Frankfurt we had prepared four documents[10] based on the London understanding to be presented verbally to the eleven minister-presidents, and then handed to them. The presentation was divided among us. In it we authorized the convocation of the constituent assembly and the modification of state boundaries. We informed them that the powers reserved to the occupying authorities would be expressed in an Occupation Statute which would be made available as soon as it was ready. We also appointed liaison officers who would be ready to assist them at all times. Dr. Reinhold Maier of Wuerttemberg-Baden replied for them and thanked us in the name of the German people. He then requested adjournment to allow time for our proposals to be studied until July 20. We approved his request.

The minister-presidents met in Coblentz from July 8 to 10 and then wrote us a letter which summed up their observations.[11] This letter expressed their conviction that the critical difficulties faced by the German people could be overcome only if they were enabled to administer their affairs on the broadest territorial basis possible at any time, and their willingness to accept the principle of trizonal fusion in this spirit. It expressed apprehension, however, at giving the character of a state to the organization for this purpose, which might widen the rift between East and West, and opposed a referendum which would give the weight of a national constitution to what they preferred to call a basic law.

The minister-presidents accepted the responsibility of recommending changes in state boundaries and expressed satisfaction that there was to be an Occupation Statute. They did not want Ruhr control placed in this statute, which they hoped would mark the end of a state of war. Specifically, they asked for the removal of all restrictions on foreign trade. The letter concluded with appreciation to the military governors for widening the possibilities for democratic political development and a declaration of their readiness to serve the peace of the world and to create a free and democratic Germany.

Unfortunately that part of the letter expressing doubt as to the advisability of calling the new organization a government was widely interpreted as an evidence of their unwillingness to accept responsibility for a separate western government. They were uncertain of German public sentiment toward the establishment of a government which would imply recognition of a divided Germany. Further, French opposition left them in doubt as to our firm intent and they thought they might be confronted with having set up a government which would never govern because of Soviet opposition. However, their letter had not refused to accept responsibility and I was confident that they would go ahead. I knew from talks with them that the minister-presidents from our zone were eager to do so.

Some of the German officials alleged that French representatives were saying that a more limited administration than contemplated in the London Agreement would lessen Soviet opposition and avoid the appearance that Germany was split into two parts. I did not investigate these allegations, as I had no desire to be involved in determining the facts in exchanges between French representatives and German officials. I was convinced that our formal approach to the minister-presidents in the first meeting had not given them confidence in our intent and I was determined that future meetings should be of the informal type to which General Robertson and I were accustomed. Such meetings would encourage the minister-presidents to go ahead rapidly.

The military governors had difficulty in agreeing on the reply to be made to this letter at the meeting of July 20, as General Koenig wanted to accept their proposal for a more limited government structure than we had intended. However, Robertson and I held him to the London Agreement.

When we met with the minister-presidents we again shared the presentation of our reply.[12] Robertson presided and kept the meeting on as informal a basis as possible. We told them that the London decisions were governmental and that marked deviations might require further governmental consideration, which would delay the whole program, and that they would have to accept responsibility for failure to return government to German hands promptly. We stressed our desire that the Germans voluntarily accept the responsibilities of government being turned over to them. We affirmed our interest in ratification by the states and preferably by referendum in each state, and expressed doubt as to the term "Basic Law" being adequate to describe the document which would establish German government. We again emphasized the need for a decision on state boundaries. We promised consideration of their views on the content of the occupation statute.

Minister-President Stock of Hesse, German spokesman at this meeting, requested adjournment so they could consider our reply. Minister-President Kaisen, disappointed at further delay, interrupted to express his anxiety at the failure to progress. Buergermeister Brauer of Hamburg supported Kaisen and suggested that the words "Provisional Constitution" might prove a satisfactory alternative to the words "Basic Law." After a recess of an hour the minister-presidents wanted still more time and asked for another meeting on July 26.

While the discussions at the July 26 meeting were long and involved, there was no longer any question of the willingness of the minister-presidents to accept responsibility. Between the two meetings I had made a hurried trip home and returned with lumbago, which may be why the discussions seemed so long. We agreed to call the group which would prepare the constitution the "Parliamentary Council" rather than the "Constituent Assembly," and the document which it would prepare the "Basic Law" followed in parentheses by the words "Provisional Constitution." We promised to ask our governments to consider its ratification by vote of the state parliaments in view of the minister-presidents' belief that a general ballot would be untimely under the existing political and economic situation.

There were no further obstacles in the way of the minister-presidents, who arranged in August for the state parliaments in the western zones to elect representatives to the Parliamentary Council, which would hold its sessions in Bonn. In the hope that it would facilitate the work of the Council, constitutional experts from the three major political parties were assembled at Herrenchiemsee to prepare a draft document.

On September 1 the delegates to the Parliamentary Council assembled formally in the old university city. High Allied officials were invited to the opening ceremony, which was simple, consistent with a disrupted economy, and yet dignified and impressive. Its sixty-five members came from six political parties of which the Christian Democratic Union and the Social Democratic party were the two major groups. Dr. Konrad Adenauer of the CDU was elected president and committees were designated to carry out the detailed work.

Dr. Adenauer is an interesting personality whose activity and energy belie his seventy-three years. Having spent a long life in the political field, during which he achieved the leadership of the Christian Democratic Union, he is a capable politician. His extensive knowledge of government and of parliamentary procedure combine with ability and intelligence to make an effective leader. His shrewdness enables him to create conditions favorable to his party and he is not above using criticism of others to further party interests. He is conservative in thought and supports free enterprise. When he rises above party politics he has the intelligence and character to act as a statesman. He exhibited this quality of statesmanship at critical periods in the life of the Council.

The other major party, the SPD, did not have its leader, Dr. Schumacher, in the Council but it did not lack able leadership in Professor Carlo Schmid and others. In view of the almost equal strength of the two parties, it was certain that the provisional constitution would come about only from compromises reached in prolonged debate.

When the Parliamentary Council had settled to its task, the Western military governors had time to consider the fusion measures which we had to work out. Committees had been appointed to prepare the Occupation Statute,[13] to work out the details of Allied fusion, including the composition, functions, and size of the joint staffs, the supervision of state governments in the three zones, and the harmonization of Military Government legislation in the reserved fields which would be uniform in the three zones after the establishment of West German Government. In this latter field, I was fortunate to have as our representative the exceptionally able and experienced Joseph Panuch, who had come to Germany to be my special adviser for major problems.

Progress in drafting the Occupation Statute was slow because of French insistence on reserving powers which the British and American representatives believed must be granted to the German Government if it was to be other than a sham. We did not believe that the French position was consistent with the London decisions.

However, I found that our government at this time desired a more restrictive statute than I felt advisable. On August 19, I cabled the Department of the Army, "The Occupation Statute should be as brief as possible if the provisions of the German constitution are fully satisfactory." I recommended that it contain a short preamble, setting forth its purpose to make possible a lasting and just peace based on free political institutions, and a general definition of the powers which the occupying powers had agreed to reserve until there was a peace treaty. I felt a long and detailed statute would make the Germans doubt our intention of returning responsibility for internal affairs to their hands, and would be difficult to enforce in practice. I also recommended the establishment of a High Court composed of representatives of the occupying powers and German jurists to which the German Government could appeal decisions of the military governors which they believed contrary to the occupation statute.

On August 29, I received the reply from the Department of the Army[14] which, while it agreed in principle with my observations, listed the restrictions it desired incorporated in the statute. They would have made it a very lengthy and legalistic document. I did not like to present it because I was sure that any proposal which we submitted would be added to in tripartite negotiations. Fortunately I was given sufficient discretion so that I was able to submit a less restrictive proposal. I was confident, too, that our government would accept any document which satisfied the French representatives.

It is of little interest to describe in detail the long hours of negotiation, the arguments and counterarguments which followed. French representatives were unyielding and were also expressing alarm at what they believed to be a trend to dangerous centralization in the work of the Parliamentary Council. General Koenig in an impassioned speech had expressed French unwillingness to proceed further until the Parliamentary Council was reminded of the limitations in its authority.

Again I believed the French position to be inconsistent with the London Agreement. Although Monsieur Schuman had endorsed this program and promised to support it, I felt that the French administration in Germany did not share his views and was determined to delay if not to thwart the establishment of West German Government. It seemed to me that a common tripartite policy was essential but that it could be obtained only at governmental level. So, on November 22, I reported by cable:

Koenig's stand in recent meeting is that French may not accept western German government as they dislike the present climate. . . . The Ruhr question by itself is not the disturbing factor; it is rather German economic recovery as a whole.

Although the French government has officially accepted German recovery as necessary to European recovery, many of the actions taken by its representatives in Germany have been to delay recovery.

While international ownership of the Ruhr could lead to the necessity for forced operation of Ruhr industries, it is my view that it would be less disruptive than foreign control of management which would prevent the responsibility of ownership being exercised in a normal way.

There is some validity in French argument that government ownership of Ruhr industries would provide too great a centralization of power in Germany. However, we can not be sure that socialization will result, as at least for the present non-socialist parties in Germany have a slight majority. If our established policy to permit the German people to resolve their own economic pattern is to be continued, any form of national ownership should be at the federal level as it is certainly unworkable to permit a single state within the federal government to own the industries which control and dominate German economic life.

The French government's comments concerning the prevention of establishment of dangerous and excessive economic concentration in the Ruhr and return of management of Nazi owners indicate misunderstanding of the law establishing the trusteeship arrangement. The full intent of the law is to accomplish a reorganization which will stop excessive and dangerous economic concentration and eliminate the Nazi influence in ownership.

I am even more concerned with the French comment that the participation of the representatives of Berlin at Bonn is threatening the political reconstruction of western Germany. We have told the French that if quadripartite government exists in Berlin at the time that the constitution is approved, we will have to disapprove Berlin participation in western German government. On the other hand, if Berlin is then a split city, it must be supported by western Germany. Careful attention must be given under the conditions which exist when the constitution is approved to including Berlin in western German government. The French do not really want a united Germany with Berlin as the capital. Our policy calls for a united Germany. Any act on our part which would indicate that we oppose a united Germany would lessen greatly our influence in western Germany.

The French say that there are evidences of a tendency to make Germany the strongest economic power in Europe and the center of the continental economy. Unquestionably this comes about from the present upturn in the German economy which has made its recovery real and no longer academic. More than 40 million people in western Germany having to bring in almost half of their food requirements can live only with a large industry having a surplus available for export. A self-sustaining Germany is impossible otherwise. Obviously, any such industry has some war potential and security must be provided by rigidly enforced disarmament agreements rather than by suppression of industry which can only cause a deficit economy, which would be borne for many years by the United States or would in itself become a greater war hazard than a self-sustaining economy.

I have sympathy with the French position on reparations and regret our continued inability to conclude an agreement for the period of occupation on prohibited and restricted industries. I support the level of industry agreed for the bizonal area because the limitation of 10,700,000 tons of steel was a commitment made to the French at London.

I found in Paris that I was charged with the authorship of the plan to raise the steel capacity and to retain additional plants in Germany. While this is not true, I have in all my conferences with the French taken the position of our government that upward changes would have to be made as found to be necessary in the interest of European recovery. We here can make no agreements on prohibited and restricted industries until Mr. Hoffman has made his decision as to what is to remain in Germany and the negotiations for its acceptance have been undertaken with the French and British governments.

I note that the French government desires a joint re-examination by governments of the general policy in Germany. This is not a question on which my comment is pertinent. I do wish to point out that there is an increasing conflict between American and French policy which leads to almost daily disagreements in our operations in Germany. We propose to re-establish a self-sustaining Germany at the earliest possible date as we believe such a Germany essential to a sound European economy and also to stop the continued need for financial support from the United States. While our efforts to this purpose have been most encouraging since currency reform, we are still far from a self-sustaining Germany and the United States will be requested for at least two more years and perhaps longer to support the annual deficit in Germany's trade. Our efforts to make this period a minimum are in direct conflict with French desires to retard German recovery. If we accept the French view, we are adding to our own financial liability in Germany, perhaps so much that our investment to date would be lost in its effectiveness to develop a self-sustaining responsible German government. As German economy recovers, we will be subject to further attack from French politicians reflecting both the real and imaginary fears of the French people and of the French government. This conflict of policy is at a critical stage. Each compromise retards our efforts for German recovery. Without compromise, we will be faced with an intensive French opposition which may develop a real anti-American sentiment in France.

There is no ready solution of this problem. I am convinced that German recovery is necessary to European recovery and to any real stability in Europe which makes for peace. If this recovery can only come about with the loss of French support, then stability would not result either. It does seem clear to me that it is difficult indeed to justify our continued financial support of Germany if it is not directed to developing self-sufficiency and responsible government which will require no further financial support as soon as possible.

A security pact will do much to allay French fears. However, the French fears are not entirely directed at physical aggression but also come at least in part from the competition promised by a recovered German economy.

I am trying to point up the problem. I recognize that recommendations for its solution are beyond my competence. It is a problem which must be resolved soon.

I received no reply to this cable. We continued our negotiations until December 17, when we agreed that the military governors could do no more to resolve the remaining differences and would have to submit them to their governments for resolution. Since our report was not utilized in the final agreement reached by the foreign ministers, it is not worth consideration except to indicate the divergencies in the viewpoints of the three military governors.

The basic disagreements[15] came from French insistence that German authorities not be permitted to legislate in the reserved fields, including finance and economics, without the prior approval in each instance of the occupying powers, and the British and American view that the German authorities must have concurrent legislative rights with the occupying authorities in these fields if their government was to function effectively. The French also insisted that occupation costs be distributed among and borne by the several states, while the British and Americans wanted these costs to be included in the federal budget. The French did not want the High Court to have other than advisory powers, nor to have German participation. The French and the Americans were together in insisting that the protection and care of displaced persons be provided for in the Occupation Statute, whereas the British wanted such protection and care limited to executing existing agreements with the International Refugee Organization. We united in urging our governments to give earnest and prompt consideration to our report so that the occupation statute could be delivered as quickly as possible to German hands.

The military governors still had to agree on the principles to govern trizonal fusion. Here, too, little progress had been made. The Department of the Army was unwilling to have the Occupation Statute considered at governmental level unless agreement was reached at the same time on these principles.[16] It was particularly concerned that our right to a major voice in matters affecting foreign trade and exchange be recognized in view of the financial aid we were providing for all three zones, and that food and agriculture and other interests which affected the extent of our aid be under tripartite rather than zonal inspection and supervision. I did not feel that our negotiations in Germany had gone far enough to develop basic differences. Moreover, I did not believe it possible for these differences to be resolved in London or elsewhere except by the foreign ministers themselves.

The three governments agreed to a conference to open in London on January 17, 1949, to consider these differences. Further progress toward West German Government thus rested with the Parliamentary Council on the one hand, and with the three governments on the other hand.

CHAPTER 22

The Way to
West German Government

I HAD expressed my anxiety over the French position
to our government on November 22, 1948. In an effort
to allay General Koenig's apprehension that the Parliamentary
Council favored a highly centralized government, I had joined
General Robertson in agreeing to send an aide-mémoire[1] to the
Council. It was dispatched on the same day as my cable home. It
gave the Council the conditions which the military governors would
examine carefully in determining whether the constitution provided
for a federal structure of government.

After receiving this letter the Parliamentary Council asked for a
meeting of its representatives with the three military governors on
December 17, 1948,[2] to discuss its provisions. At this meeting Dr.
Adenauer raised the points discussed in our letter. However, little
agreement resulted and it was apparent there was no common
German viewpoint. In point of fact SPD members charged that
Adenauer had raised these points in anticipation of a ruling from us
in support of the CDU position, which favored a federal government
of limited power. Since decentralization was the purport of our letter,
there seemed to be little reason for this meeting. We could offer no
encouragement to the SPD in its desire for centralized government.

Meanwhile little progress had been made in London. Minister
Julius C. Holmes headed the American delegation, which did not
include Military Government representation. The British and French
delegations were composed of the same persons who had attended

previous conferences. The Department of the Army's insistence that the conference discuss the principles of trizonal fusion led to a broadening of the agenda to include consideration of the French request to retain control and use of the port of Kehl across the Rhine River from Strasbourg. The French also proposed that a government dissenting from a majority decision of the military governors should have the right to appeal to the other governments and the decision should not become effective until this appeal was heard. In my opinion this was almost as bad as the veto power in the Allied Control Council which had destroyed quadripartite government. I hoped that our government would refuse to participate in any further international agreements which authorized this power of veto. In any event acceptance of the French proposal would have resulted in interminable delays, thus defeating the orderly day-to-day conduct of government.

When Secretary Royall visited Germany in late December 1948, I urged him to ask the Secretary of State to defer further consideration of all outstanding questions until the three foreign ministers could meet to discuss them in their relationship to each other and reach a "package" solution. The continued disagreements and bitter arguments among the Western occupying powers were playing into Communist hands as well as into the hands of the less scrupulous German politicians, who tried to make the most of every Allied dispute. Secretary of State Acheson agreed with the desirability of such a conference but was unwilling to discontinue the talks in London. He did promise to discuss German affairs with Bevin and Schuman when they came to Washington to sign the Atlantic Pact. By that time the several months of negotiation in London had not led to agreement on either the Occupation Statute or the principles of trizonal fusion.

Moreover the Parliamentary Council was having difficulty in reaching final agreement on the Basic Law. The charge of the SPD that the CDU had tried to use the meeting of the representatives of the Council with the military governors on December 17 to its own political advantage did not help. We no longer hoped that the constitution would be approved for ratification by the end of the year. Since we were unable to resolve our differences to give them the terms of the Occupation Statute, we could not urge greater speed. Fortunately German political leaders in the Council recognized the danger of delay and advised us in late December that it would proceed to complete the Basic Law without waiting for the Occupation Statute. A draft[3] was completed in the Main Committee in early January 1949 for submission to a plenary session, and copies were made available to our liaison representatives.

This draft was considered by the three military governors in Frankfurt on February 16.[4] In general we were satisfied that the Basic Law embodied the fundamental principles and safeguards of democracy. It guaranteed individual rights and freedoms and limited the powers of the executive. It established a parliamentary form of government and an independent judiciary which included a constitutional High Court. The upper house in a bicameral legislature represented the several states. The Basic Law had some new and interesting provisions. The federal chancellor was subject to removal on a vote of no confidence only if it was accompanied by simultaneous selection of his successor. The federal government could transfer sovereign powers to an international authority and incorporate federal territory into a system of mutual security. The general rules of international law were made a part of the federal law. Despite the excellent provisions for the protection of democratic rights and processes, the Basic Law showed the effect of frequent compromise between conflicting political views, particularly in establishing an administrative structure which might prove less than adequate for the purpose.

Our principal concern with the Basic Law came from our belief that it not only provided for too much centralization of authority but also failed to clearly distinguish between the responsibilities to be retained by the individual states and the responsibilities to be assumed by the federal government. We therefore requested the leaders of the Parliamentary Council to defer placing it before the Plenary Session until we could comment in detail.

We asked our political advisers[5] to study the document carefully and report any deviations from the provisions of the London Agreement. Their comment, which was not unanimous, pointed out that the powers granted to the federal government were excessive, particularly in the fields of public health, public welfare, labor, and the press, which had been specifically excluded from federal control in the London Agreement. They found that the revenue-raising and tax-collection powers given the federal government were also excessive to its needs and destroyed the independence of the states. Broad concurrent legislative powers were given to both federal government and states, which would prove confusing in practice unless exercised by the federal government, and this exercise of legislative rights would weaken the authority of the individual states unnecessarily. They were disturbed with the provision for the civil service which seemed to perpetuate the traditional, and certainly undemocratic, German code which we thought we had destroyed. The inclusion of Berlin as one of the federal states was inconsistent with our legal position that Berlin was under quadripartite control by international agreement.

The meeting[6] of the military governors to consider this report proved difficult. Robertson wished to accept the Basic Law as presented, except for the civil service and Berlin provisions, whereas both Koenig and I felt we could not agree to the centralization of authority which it provided. My own views in this respect were less in conflict with the British than were the French views. While we agreed quickly with respect to the modification of the provisions relating to civil service and to Berlin, there was prolonged debate on the financial and legislative powers granted to the federal government. Finally I suggested and obtained agreement on compromise proposals which, while leaving the federal government a wide range of tax powers, also left sufficient tax powers to the individual states to assure these states of financial independence. They did not abrogate the right of the federal government to legislate in the many fields specified in the Basic Law, but limited it to those matters which clearly affected two or more states.

We met with a subcommittee of the Parliamentary Council's Main Committee on March 2 to express our views.[7] In this meeting we emphasized that we were asking not for the acceptance of our wording but for amendments which would meet the spirit of our comments. Robertson presided at this meeting and acted as spokesman. There was little discussion across the table. After the meeting I talked to Carlo Schmid, leading SPD member of the subcommittee, who told me that he had expected a more rigid position from the military governors and hoped that the Parliamentary Council would be able to take action quickly on our comments.

At this meeting we had also advised the subcommittee that provisions in the Basic Law permitting changes in state boundaries could become effective only with the unanimous consent of the military governors, and that the responsibility for preparation of the initial electoral law belonged to the minister-presidents and not to the Council.

The provision relating to changes in state boundaries would have been of little importance if the military governors had been able to approve the recommendations the minister-presidents[8] had submitted at our request. Their early deliberations had showed that the existing states had developed strong loyalties which, combined with political rivalries, made major modifications unlikely. Therefore they were advised that state boundaries formed before the ratification of the Basic Law would be regarded as fixed until the conclusion of the peace treaty. On October 1, 1948, the minister-presidents recommended to the military governors that a plebiscite be held on the merger of Wuerttemberg, Hohenzollern, and Baden into a single state, or if such a proposal were rejected by the voters that the old states of Wuerttemberg (including Hohenzollern) and Baden be re-formed. I favored the plebiscite and, if the proposal were defeated, the re-establishment of the old states provided the problem of occupation responsibility could be solved.

When the French were included in the occupation of Germany they had been given a territory carved from both the original British and American zones. South Wuerttemberg and South Baden were included in this territory. This had led to our creation of the new state of Wuerttemberg-Baden, which had become popular with a large portion of the inhabitants. I offered to place Wuerttemberg-Hohenzollern-Baden as a single state or as two separate states under tripartite commission government. Failing British acquiescence, I suggested bipartite Franco-American commission government with occupation personnel below the state level remaining unchanged.

The French were unwilling to accept this solution and demanded that North Baden be transferred to their jurisdiction so that the whole state of Baden would be under French control, while South Wuerttemberg would be transferred to us so that the whole state of Wuerttemberg would be under our control. This I could not accept. Our military headquarters and main communications center were centered at Heidelberg in North Baden at great expense when we made Frankfurt available for joint military government and German government operations. In four years of occupation we had established in North Baden suitable quarters for our military personnel which were not available elsewhere. The transfer of North Baden would also have cut our lines of communication and hence was unsound for military reasons. The French were willing for our troops to remain under their Military Government, but this, I knew, would lead to inevitable friction. For security purposes our troops were available on call from Military Government and I doubted whether American commanders had the legal right to place their men under the orders of French Military Government. Furthermore, North Baden was a substantial industrial area where we had gained considerable prestige and influence which would be lost under the transfer.

I thought I had displayed a full desire to co-operate in offering to accept either a single merged state or the re-establishment of the traditional two states under tri- or bipartite control. The French representatives rejected my proposal and their government appealed to Washington for the acceptance of their proposal. While our financial support of western Germany, including the French Zone, was never on a quid pro quo basis, it was sometimes hard to understand why we were also expected to make the major concessions in effecting compromise.

Meanwhile the Parliamentary Council continued work on the Basic Law. Our comments of March 2 led to the informal presentation to our liaison officers of a new draft.[9] Actually the amendments did little to decrease the centralization of finance and legislative powers to which we had objected. In fact in the financial field the amended Basic Law authorized the federal government to transfer revenue from the more prosperous to the less prosperous states, a power which would almost certainly have destroyed the financial independence of the individual states. Our liaison officers were instructed to advise the Parliamentary Council in early April that its amendments did not meet our suggestions in spirit, that we hoped the Main Committee would proceed promptly with their reconsideration, and that we would be glad to meet with the Main Committee to discuss any further proposals prior to their submission in Plenary Session.

The trouble still was that the SPD had refused to yield its original position. It now insisted that the new proposal be submitted to a Plenary Session of the Parliamentary Council for approval regardless of our comment. The CDU would not agree and declared that compromise was essential and that refusal of the SPD to yield would delay the establishment of West German Government. The balance of power was held by the FDP, which was inclined to support the SPD. Rumors were flying about. One was that Bevin would be able to secure the support of the three foreign ministers in Washington for the SPD position. Meanwhile Communists and nationalists were making every effort to exploit the political situation to prevent the formation of West German Government.

Thus progress toward trizonal fusion and West German Government was at a standstill when the foreign ministers met in Washington in April.[10] Some positive steps had been taken which would facilitate trizonal fusion. In June 1948 the French had joined us in currency reform and in setting up the Bank deutscher Laender so that there were common financial and banking systems in the three zones. On October 18, 1948, they had joined us in the Joint Export-Import Agency which insured a common foreign trade policy in the three zones. Moreover, starting in October 1948, the three military governors met twice each month to consider mutual problems and to secure as much uniformity as possible in administration pending final fusion. These meetings had not helped the bizonal area, as General Koenig objected to many measures which General Robertson and I deemed essential to economic recovery, and his objections frequently resulted in appeals to government. We were convinced from these informal meetings that tripartite government would prove impossible unless decisions were made in Germany by majority vote.

Just before the meeting of the foreign ministers I was invited to visit Foreign Minister Schuman, who had expressed the view informally that our thinking on Germany was not unlike. As the State Department wanted me to do so, I accepted the invitation and went to Paris quietly in civilian clothes on March 20 to lunch with Schuman. Ambassador Caffery and Riddleberger were with me. We had a pleasant, friendly conversation in his apartment at the Quai d'Orsay, which is perhaps best described in a paraphrase of my cabled report:

Our conference took about one hour before and another hour after lunch. Mr. Schuman requested that I speak fully and frankly. I told him I was sure we had the common purpose to re-establish a peaceful, self-sufficient west Germany which would be attracted to western Europe and included some day in a western European Union; that neither of us would want a western Germany which, unable to live otherwise, looked to the east. Mr. Schuman agreed, remarking that the use of force had not worked after World War I and that we must try inducements this time.

I said my country is financing western Germany to achieve this objective but is retarded in its efforts by three-power disagreements. I added that the failure of the three Western powers to reach accord in the face of Soviet pressure in Germany was proving disastrous and that, having supposedly reached a full understanding in London in June 1948, nine months later we remained wide apart in interpreting our agreement. Mr. Schuman agreed this was proving disastrous and that we must reach early agreement.

I told him that present tripartite meetings were like the quadripartite meetings in the Allied Control Council—all talk and no decisions. It was urgent to have a tripartite policy under which decisions could be made in Germany without frequent appeals to government. He agreed in principle although he felt an appeal right necessary in such matters as Ruhr control and amendments to federal and land constitutions, giving as his reason for right of appeal on latter the French interest in educational provisions. I pointed out that the powers reserved for security purposes always gave governments the right to have military governors legislate to correct any decisions unhappy to governments. The requirement that Land constitutions had to conform to principles of federal constitution was a safeguard which seemed to me to obviate necessity for other safeguards than the disapproving action of Military Government. Mr. Schuman again expressed concurrence in principle and promised French position would be re-examined with a view to minimize the fields in which appeals would be permitted.

I expressed my apprehension over too many restrictions on industry, stating that effective controls must be few and major so that we would move in force if required to enforce them and that I doubted that when we left Germany any of us would return in force because Germany was building a bevel gear an inch or more oversize. Mr. Schuman agreed heartily and said there will be no trouble with France here; there may be with the United Kingdom.

I referred to Wuerttemberg-Baden situation, the military reasons why we wished to stay in North Baden, and our readiness to have a single combined state if desired by the voters, or the two restored states, placed under tri- or bipartite control. He asked if we would be willing to tell the Germans before they voted on fusion that if it failed the two states would be restored. I said yes if we have agreed on control, otherwise it would be most unfair to Germans. He agreed to this and to tri- or bipartite control in principle. I told him we favored tripartite commission of military governors at federal level with appropriate committees, and integrated staffs only for foreign trade, coal and steel controls. We also desired tripartite commissions at the state level. These would have small staffs and would not have authority over unilateral measures such as information services, restitution, et al. Below the state level, observers in each zone would be representatives of the power occupying the zone. Mr. Schuman believed this proposal satisfactory.

In discussing occupation statute, Mr. Schuman said it was too long and involved. I agreed. He asked if it could be changed now. I expressed some doubt in view of time required for change but suggested if it were not revised now we should tell the Germans on its issue that revision would be started concurrently with their formation of government to place less restrictions on the government as rapidly as it proved its capacity. Mr. Schuman agreed to this.

We discussed port of Kehl. I suggested removal of this question from present negotiation in understanding three military governors would try to set up a port authority with reasonable German participation as one of the details of trizonal fusion. I made it clear that I did not know my government's views on this proposal but believed it would be sympathetically considered. He reminded me of Strasbourg's objection to German participation. However, he thought my idea sound and would discuss it with French cabinet.

I repeated that French lead in rapprochement of West to western Germany was most desirable; that we could not hope to attract Germans to the west if each time they turned westward we "kicked them in the face." He agreed.

Meeting was most friendly and cordial. I hope Mr. Schuman will carry out his views. His subordinates in France and Germany may be expected to try to defeat his efforts.

Caffery reported that the meeting had been worth while as a contribution to better relations.

Cognizant of the situation in Germany, the foreign ministers acted quickly in Washington to send a message to the Parliamentary Council through the military governors. They told it that they would discuss the establishment of West German Government in their meeting and that they hoped it would resolve its political differences and adopt a Basic Law in the spirit of the London agreements. Their message was delivered promptly. It resulted in another effort by the CDU, joined this time by the FDP, to compromise with the SPD. The latter was still unwilling to yield, though its leaders in the Parliamentary Council felt otherwise.

On April 8 in the atmosphere resulting from the signing of the Atlantic Pact, the foreign ministers concluded their deliberations on Germany and arrived at a common policy. Their success was a pleasing contrast to the frustrating conferences of the four powers during the preceding four years. The policy to which they agreed was almost the one advocated and followed by the United States for many months.

The military governors were instructed to transmit a letter from the foreign ministers to the Parliamentary Council. It gave German authorities liberty of action in administrative and legislative matters, except in certain reserved fields. It advised the Council that Military Government would be replaced by a High Commission with a small staff at the time West German Government was formed. Again the foreign ministers urged prompt action by the Parliamentary Council in view of the major objective of the three Allied governments to "encourage and facilitate the closest integration on a mutually beneficial basis of the German people under a democratic federal state within the framework of a European association."

Likewise an Occupation Statute reduced to two and one half pages was approved by the foreign ministers and transmitted to the Parliamentary Council. I was particularly pleased with this short document. It conveyed full legislative, executive, and judicial powers to the federal state and the participating states except in the fields of disarmament and demilitarization; international controls such as the Ruhr Authority; foreign affairs; displaced persons; protection, prestige, and security of Allied forces; respect for the Basic Law; control over foreign exchange and over internal actions which would

increase external financial assistance; and control of prisoners confined by the occupying authorities. The statute specified that amendments to the Basic Law required unanimous approval of the occupying authorities; that, subject only to requirements of security, the
basic rights of the individual would be respected by the occupying
authorities; that inconsistent legislation of the occupying powers
would be repealed and retained legislation would be codified; and
that the statute would be reviewed and made even less restrictive
within eighteen months at most.

The foreign ministers announced their intent to permit the new
government to negotiate a bilateral agreement with the United
States for ECA aid and to support its becoming a member in its own
right in the OEEC. This was the most attractive immediate offer to
the German authorities.

The foreign ministers agreed concurrently on broad principles of
trizonal fusion which provided a High Commission with a small
staff. The predominant voice of the United States in financial matters
was recognized. Actions were to be taken by majority vote in the
High Commission except when decisions were involved which would
alter intergovernmental agreements. In such cases a dissenting commissioner had the right of appeal through his government to governments. Amendments to the Basic Law would require unanimity for
approval. Each state was to be under the supervision of a state
commissioner whose nationality would be that of the occupying
power in that state but who would be responsible for the execution
of tripartite policies to the High Commission.

This latter decision made it difficult to agree to a change of state
boundaries in Wuerttemberg and Baden and the question was deferred. The Parliamentary Council and the minister-presidents were
advised that delay in the ratification of the Basic Law would result
from the creation of new states and therefore it was advisable to
defer their further consideration until the new government was
formed. At that time it would be sympathetically considered. Likewise final decision with respect to Kehl was deferred until the peace
settlement with the understanding that the city itself would be
gradually returned to German administration. While the inclusion
of Berlin in West German Government was not approved, its city
administration was promised increased freedom of action.

The message of the foreign ministers and the Occupation Statute were dispatched immediately to the Parliamentary Council. A sub-committee of its Main Committee asked to meet with us on April 14 to discuss the Basic Law and the Occupation Statute, furnishing us in advance with the subjects to be considered.

The three military governors met on the morning of April 14 to consider papers[11] on these subjects prepared by liaison representatives. As was to be expected, these papers were cold, limited statements not conducive to better understanding. I proposed that our spokesman use them for guidance in replying informally to questions which the committee would raise, and was surprised at General Robertson's insistence that they be read as written. After some argument my view was accepted.

In the afternoon we met with the German committee, which was composed of representatives of the major political factions under the chairmanship of Dr. Adenauer. In replying to questions, as spokesman for the military governors, I stressed that much detail had been expressly omitted from the Occupation Statute, including provision for a High Court, because it was to be regarded as a living document approved by our governments in the intent of the foreign ministers to draw western Germany into a closer association with the free nations of Europe. I emphasized the advantages which would result from membership in OEEC and from a bilateral agreement with the United States for ECA aid; the dangers of delay in the face of unsettled world conditions. Professor Carlo Schmid, a recognized world authority on international law, was present representing the SPD and I suggested that even in his vast knowledge he could cite no precedent for three military governors trying so hard to divest themselves of authority and with so little success. I inquired as to the progress of the Basic Law and in the ensuing discussion was able to state that, although their last proposal was not a promising basis for discussion between us, we would welcome a new proposal which would permit us to negotiate an agreement across the table.

We agreed on two helpful decisions at this meeting with the representatives of the Parliamentary Council. Although we had thought in London that the electoral law should be the responsibility of the minister-presidents, the latter had advised us that they would prefer to have the Parliamentary Council establish a uniform electoral law. This recommendation of the minister-presidents was approved by the military governors. I therefore advised the representatives of the Council that it would have the power to adopt a uniform law which would fix the number of deputies in the central government, apportion the seats between the various states, and determine the electoral system to be used. The electoral machinery would remain within the competence of the state. Candidates at large would have to be selected from a list presented in each state to its electorate. Thus candidates at large could try for only one seat, and defeated candidates in one state could be placed in the Parliament only from that state.

The military governors had also agreed on the definition of federal police powers and therefore I was able to advise the German representatives that federal police agencies could be established to control frontier crossings, to collect and disseminate police information including information on subversive activities, to instigate the investigation of federal law violations, and to carry out limited internal police responsibilities, largely through the maintenance of a central office for criminal records.

The committee, after a brief recess, returned to thank us for the tone and conduct of the meeting and to request a further meeting on April 25. Professor Schmid did not believe that an earlier meeting could be arranged because there was a congress of the SPD scheduled for April 20.

This congress had a major bearing on the future of German government. Dr. Schumacher, in firm control of the party, had publicly announced his intent to resist the changes in the Basic Law urged by the military governors and to force its adoption without amendment. He believed that financial control had to be centered in the federal government if socialization measures were to follow. Fanatical, strong-minded and of integrity, Schumacher's opposition was serious. He had lost an arm in World War I and had just lost a leg through amputation and was confined to his home most of the time, though this did not appear to interfere with his political leadership. On this occasion he attended the meeting and his appearance was dramatic. He was playing for big stakes. If he and his party could defy the occupying powers and get away with it, they could go to the polls triumphantly proclaiming their success as defenders of the German people against the Allies.

This resulted in disagreement among the military governors on the delivery of a second letter from the foreign ministers. Their first letter had called upon the Parliamentary Council to resolve its difficulties in the spirit of the London decisions. The second letter, which was sent to the military governors for delivery when they believed it timely, did not change this position. It did suggest that financial measures designed to equalize relief burdens among the states, thus permitting the federal government to supplement its own revenues from revenues levied and collected by the states to make funds available for grants for education and welfare purposes, would be approved. I was unwilling to present this letter in view of Schumacher's position that he was opposed to any changes in the Basic Law necessary to meet the views of the occupying powers. Our position of political neutrality had not changed. However, in this instance the CDU favored federal government, which was also tripartite policy. The letter was certain to be interpreted by the SPD as a moral victory. My British colleague, under instructions from his government, pressed hard for its delivery. General Koenig stood with me.

To my surprise, I received a cable from Washington instructing me to deliver the message. I reminded the Department of the Army that the timing was left to my discretion and that delivery was impossible until discussions had resumed in the Parliamentary Council. I predicted that it would lead Schumacher to conduct the SPD campaign in the first general election on an anti-Western occupying powers platform. My protest had no effect and I was advised that our Secretary of State had promised Mr. Bevin that the discretionary rights given to the military governors would apply for only a few days. Fortunately these few days included April 20. While Schumacher had received an overwhelming personal endorsement in the party congress held on that date, its representatives in the Parliamentary Council won the right to discuss and negotiate amendments to the Basic Law. Thus the two parties were again at work in the Parliamentary Council when we delivered the letter on April 23. Since the parties were negotiating again, neither could use the letter to support its position and it had lost much of its political significance.

The committee representing the Council was thus ready to meet with the military governors as planned on April 25. Prior to this meeting I tried to ascertain how determined our government was to maintain a high degree of decentralization in the new government.

It was impossible to secure definitive instructions. Murphy, who had returned to the United States to be in charge of occupation matters in the State Department, returned to Germany accompanied by Goldthwaite Dorr, representing the Department of the Army, to advise me in the April 25 negotiations. In my discussions with them I found that they were also without instructions. Murphy said full discretionary powers rested in me and he felt that our government desired the prompt formation of a western German government, and it was hoped this could be accomplished with little sacrifice of the federalized structure. I did not understand why our government was in such a hurry because I did not know of the Jessup-Malik negotiation which was shortly to agree to the lifting of the blockade and the May 23 meeting of the Council of Foreign Ministers in Paris. I wanted the Parliamentary Council to complete its work quickly as I believed further delay would help the Communist cause.

As it was, the meeting of April 25 was of major import to the future of Germany and to the position of the three Western governments in the Paris conference. The three military governors met in Frankfurt in the morning to consider the position we would take. In the afternoon we met across the table from the German representatives in the conference room of our headquarters in Frankfurt. Representatives from Berlin attended as observers and not as participating members of the German committee. The proposals in the field of legislation and finance were no different than the ones that had been disapproved by our liaison officers.

As chairman for the military governors, I welcomed the German representatives and told them that we were now guided not only by the London Agreement but also by the foreign ministers' agreement, reached in Washington. The foreign ministers knew of the constitutional proposals which had been placed before us, and their comment had been made in the light of these proposals. We still objected to the broad provisions of authority granted to the federal government to secure uniformity in legal and economic fields. We also objected to the broad authority given to the federal government to provide financial equity among the states for all purposes. The military governors then withdrew so that the German representatives could consult among themselves.

On our return we found the German representatives still unwilling to make further changes. By this time General Robertson was urging acceptance of the German viewpoint. While General Koenig did not like the German proposals, he was willing to settle for whatever was satisfactory to the American delegation. This placed me in a difficult position as the extent of federalization rested in my hands, and if my decision was one which could not be accepted by the Germans I would be responsible for delaying the formation of West German Government.

I again pointed out to the German representatives that the military governors were operating under instructions from the foreign ministers, but that we were trying hard to meet the German viewpoint, and that unless a solution was found within our instructions we would have to go back to governments. Robertson supported my statement.

Dr. Adenauer, after a few minutes of discussion among the German representatives, suggested that they return to Bonn to reconsider the issue. I replied that we had arranged this meeting in the understanding that the German delegation and the military governors would negotiate across the table to reach agreement. We were here for that purpose. Adenauer yielded, and we proceeded.

I then suggested that the federal legislature be authorized to establish taxes to raise funds for education, health, and welfare and to make grants to those states unable to take care of these responsibilities with their own funds. My exact wording was:

> . . . *and may derive the requisite revenues from the Land taxes which it may specify and in the proportion which it may specify. With the approval of the Bunderat, revenues would then be transferred in the amounts thus granted to the Laender to whom granted.*

As it seemed doubtful that the German representatives fully understood the technical translation, I went over to them to explain personally what we had in mind. In a few minutes they agreed to this proposal and then accepted a suggestion from Robertson which clarified the legislative rights of the federal government to obtain legal and economic uniformity. Thus we had resolved our major differences on the constitution.

We knew that the two major political parties remained wide apart on the provisions of the constitution in the educational field and particularly on the support of parochial schools. We were apprehensive that this issue might prevent agreement in the Parliamentary Council. I told the German delegation that I might be "rushing in where angels fear to tread." It seemed to me, though, that the military governors, representing the three occupying powers, had been able to compromise. It would be a shame, therefore, if differences remaining among the Germans delayed final understanding. Obviously this was not an issue in which the military governors would take any part except to urge that the German delegation settled the question before we left the conference room.

The Germans requested a recess which lasted for approximately and hour and a half, and when the meeting reopened Adenauer told us that they had reached agreement and that he expected the passage of the Basic Law by a large majority in the Parliamentary Council. He thanked us for our understanding and wished us to know that the manner in which we had sought to reach agreement with them, combined with the contribution from the foreign ministers, had brought their work to a happy conclusion. He expected the completion of the constitution before May 15.

I replied for my colleagues and myself that this meeting had been a happy occasion for the military governors, who believed that it would also mark a happy occasion for the German people and would lead to their closer association with the free nations of Europe. Sacrifices in viewpoint had been made by all, but the fact that agreement had been reached was a good omen.

I also advised the German representatives that, while Berlin could not be included in West German Government, steps were being taken to give it the same status with respect to Allied administration as the new German Government had under the Occupation Statute.

We adjourned at eight-fifteen in the evening, after more than six hours of conference. After the meeting several German representatives came to me personally to thank me for the efforts made to bring about agreement and to express the view that we had insured a democratic structure for western Germany by our work that day.

It had been an interesting and difficult meeting, as each proposal from the German side required consultation among the party representatives before it was made, and each reply and proposal on our side required consultation among the military governors. In spite of such an obstacle we were able to make prompt decisions and I think that most of us felt as we left the conference room that we had accomplished something of lasting value.

The Parliamentary Council completed its work and adopted the constitution on May 8. This constitution or Basic Law established a parliamentary government of the federal type. As stated in the Preamble:

conscious of its responsibility before God and mankind, filled with resolve to preserve its national and political unity and to serve world peace as an equal partner in a united Europe,

it guarantees the basic rights and freedoms, and is in every sense a foundation for democratic government.

From our viewpoint, the 146 articles which it contains makes it a lengthier and more detailed document than we would desire. We forget that our short Constitution has been interpreted throughout its life by the decisions of the Supreme Court and that these decisions have kept it a living document and have safeguarded and prevented its abuse. The Germans do not have a tradition of judicial interpretation and many years would be required for a short constitution to be interpreted by judicial decision. Therefore it was logical that they should include many detailed provisions which would prevent misinterpretation and misapplication.

Several of the German leaders in the Parliamentary Council told our liaison officer that the Council had expedited completion of the constitution so that it could be presented for the approval of the military governors while I was still in Germany. I must admit that I was grateful for this gesture and that I did desire to participate in its approval.

This we did in Frankfurt on May 12, 1949, the same day that the blockade of Berlin was lifted. In this meeting we handed Dr. Adenauer a formal letter approving the constitution and saying that in our opinion, "It happily combines German democratic traditions with the concept of representative government and a rule of law which the world has come to recognize as requisite to the life of a free people."

We then advised the German representatives of the several reservations we had had to make in approving the constitution. These reservations were: that the powers vested in the federal government by the basic law were subject to the provisions of the Occupation

Statute transmitted to them and promulgated as of May 12; that the police powers could be exercised only with the specific approval of the occupying authorities; that Berlin could not be a voting member of the federation although a small number of its representatives could attend meetings of its legislative bodies. We reminded them that the reorganization of state boundaries would require the unanimous approval of the High Commissioners and that the legislative right of the federal government in taking measures for legal and economic unity would have to be exercised in such a way as not to lead to excessive concentration of authority. We thanked the Parliamentary Council for their successful completion of a difficult task performed under trying circumstances. We also advised them that we were authorizing the minister-presidents by separate letter to submit the Basic Law for ratification by the Landtage in the eleven participating states.

The Basic Law had become official. There remained its ratification, which took place quickly, and the election of the new government. Then West German Government would become a reality and we would have lived up to our expressed policy to return self-responsibility to the Germans, and to our belief that democracy can grow only when government is in the hands of the people governed.

After the meeting adjourned we joined the German representatives in a toast to the success of the new government. The structure of West German Government was thus established prior to the May 23 conference of the four foreign ministers in Paris. It served notice that the three Western Powers would no longer be thwarted in their efforts to reconstruct a democratic Germany and that this was the end of Communist expansion.

An Occupation Statute for Berlin was promulgated by our commandants on May 14.

A basis for popular government had been created. Perhaps the Basic Law did not fully satisfy anyone. It represented compromise among the German parties and between them and the occupying powers, and compromise is a principal ingredient in making a democracy. The new government is responsible to the people. The two houses in the assembly do not have equal power, but the upper house, representing the several states, has important veto powers, which will delay hasty or ill-conceived measures enacted by the lower house, and its veto cannot be overridden in certain major measures such as transfer of revenue between the states. The federal government may have too many powers to please the advocates of a weak central government. Still, its powers are defined and limited and certainly not as broad as the powers of our own government. Proportional representation still remains, but is applicable only in part and there is a direct election for a large proportion of the members of the assembly. An independent constitutional court is established to protect the constitution and to safeguard states and individuals from encroachment on their rights by the central government. The lengthy document and the compromises in administrative structure which it represents do not promise the most efficient government which might have resulted. Nevertheless, it does provide a satisfactory basis for the kind of government which we believed essential to the growth of democracy.

This government was established under Military Government and it was timely that our remaining task in Germany be transferred to civil authority. An occupying army had taken the lead in restoring self-responsibility to the German people and in encouraging the formation of democratic government. It was something of which the Army could be proud and which might well set a valuable historical precedent.

During my last few days in Germany I was in frequent touch with the Department of the Army to comment on the papers being prepared for the Paris conference of the four foreign ministers. I was dismayed with a plan which proposed that all occupying forces withdraw to the German periphery, leaving the German people to form a government for all Germany. This would have meant abandoning our efforts to set up a western German government. The plan did not consider the relationship of western Germany to the European Recovery Program or to western Europe. I believed strongly that fear would move in as our troops moved out, and Communism thrives on fear. The German people do not like their country to be occupied. Neither do they wish to be left defenseless. The people of western Germany want to unite with the people of eastern Germany, but not under circumstances in which Russia would participate in its control. We were dealing with the lives and destinies of 45,000,000 persons in western Germany. We could not change plans and policies to meet theoretical conditions. These people wanted and had been promised a government of their own. They did not want to be returned to four-power control and they were ready to forgo unification until conditions were more favorable to the creation of a German government which would be representative of the people.

Mr. Murphy, who had just returned to Washington, cabled me quickly that this plan was not in accord with the official State Department view and that Secretary of State Acheson was convinced that West German Government must go ahead and that our troops would remain until European stability was assured.

When I returned to Washington I had two long talks with Acheson and found him not only fully informed of conditions in Germany but also determined to reach no agreement with Soviet representatives which would lose the position we had attained in Europe. I believed that the Paris conference would affirm that the blockade was ended and would develop negotiations for trade exchange between east and west Germany. I was apprehensive that Soviet representatives would accept the establishment of an all-German government on our terms so that they could work from within to destroy it, and I was glad that this did not take place. When the free countries of Europe are able to defend themselves, then a stable Europe will make possible a unified Germany. Acheson had displayed the same high ability in Paris which had brought about tripartite agreement in Washington in April.

I also talked with my successor, John McCloy, on several occasions. I had learned to like and admire him when he was Assistant Secretary of the Army and thus I was not surprised to find him well informed on German matters and understanding of their import to Europe as a whole. American responsibility in Germany was in competent hands.

The first general elections have been held and West German Government is a reality. The new government faces many problems. Politically, the continued division of Germany will develop nationalism. The desire for unification is natural and to be expected from every German who loves his country. However, political leaders will appeal to the emotions of the German people as long as they are separated by promising that unification can be regained by force or by bargaining between east and west. Even in the first election, political leaders lacking constructive programs attacked the Allied occupying powers, hoping thus to arouse the sympathy of the German people and to obtain their vote. The results of the election do not indicate that these attacks were effective, and the democratic middle-of-the-road parties obtained a large majority.

The rapid economic recovery which followed currency reform and German participation in the European Recovery Program cannot continue. Increasing competition in world markets will require better and cheaper production in Germany. Economic distress can and must be avoided if Germany is not to return to political apathy.

There remains the granting of further sovereignty to the new government and its return to the family of nations. Wisely we do not push for such a return until the free countries of Europe are ready. Churchill has already urged the inclusion of West Germany in the Council of Europe. A West Germany accepted in the Council of Europe and restored to economic self-sufficiency will bring about unification. Sixty-five million people cannot be kept separated over the years against their will.

We cannot and should not forget the destruction Hitler brought to the world, nor the potential cruelty which led to concentration camps and mass exterminations. We cannot forgive the German people for permitting such things to happen. However, we must remember that the people in a police state have little to say and their moral and spiritual qualities deteriorate rapidly. Their faith in just government cannot be restored overnight, or by force. The people of Germany are industrious and able to contribute to the well-being of Europe. They are enjoying freedoms now which they have not possessed in many years. Their understanding of democracy will grow under democratic procedures if they are helped by those who know and love freedom. West German Government cannot endure over the years unless it is taken back into the family of European nations who believe that the rights of the individual are too precious to be submerged in the state.

Chronology

1945

April 17	General Clay appointed deputy to General Eisenhower for Military Government
May 7	Germany surrenders
May 14	JCS/1067 issued
June 5	First meeting of members of Allied Control Council in Berlin
July 1–4	U. S. and British troops move into Berlin
July 7	Kommandatura established
July 13	SHAEF dissolved
July 17 to August 2	Potsdam Conference issues Potsdam Protocol
July 30	Allied Control Council opened
July 31	First German newspaper in U.S. Zone licensed
August	Formation of political parties authorized
September 11 to October 2	London meeting of the Council of Foreign Ministers

October 5	Council of States (Laenderrat) formed in U. S. Zone
November 20	Nuremberg trial begins General McNarney succeeds General Eisenhower as military governor

1946

January 20	First free German elections since 1933 held in U. S. Zone
March	Denazification proceedings turned over to Germans
March 22	Level of industry plan established
April and May, June and July	Paris meetings of the Council of Foreign Ministers
September 6	Byrnes speech at Stuttgart outlines American policy for governing Germany
November	Anglo-American Conference in Washington on bizonal fusion
November 4 to December 31	New York meeting of the Council of Foreign Ministers
December 2	U.S.-British zonal merger pact signed

1947

January	Cold wave causes industrial shutdown, fuel shortage
February 27	Hoover report on food situation
March 10	Moscow meeting of the Council of Foreign Ministers

March 15	General Clay succeeds General McNarney as military governor
May 29	Economic Council formed for bizonal area
June 5	Secretary Marshall offers Europe financial assistance in speech at Harvard
August 29	Plan to raise level of industry announced
November 25 to December 15	London meeting of the Council of Foreign Ministers
December 17	U.S.-British accord fixing control over bizonal economy in proportion to share of cost signed

1948

February 6	Bizonal Economic Administration proclaimed
February 9	Bizonal High Court established
March 1	Bank deutscher Laender established
March 17	Western European Military Union formed
March 20	Last meeting of Allied Control Council
March 31	Blockade begins
April 3	ERP bill signed
April 16	OEEC established
June 7	London Agreement for administering Ruhr signed
June 20	Western Allies adopt Deutsche mark
June 25	Airlift inaugurated
July	German food ration raised
August 4	Blockade is completed
September 1	Parliamentary Council assembles at Bonn to draft constitution for West German Govt.

October 16   Intra-European Payments Agreement signed

December 17   Military Security Board established

              1949

March   Reparations Agreement signed

April 8   Atlantic Security Pact signed

April   Washington meeting of Council of Foreign
                    Ministers

May 8   Constitution for West German Government
                    adopted

May 12   Blockage lifted
                    Occupation Statute transmitted to German
                    representatives

May 15   General Clay leaves Germany

Abbreviations

AFL	American Federation of Labor
AFN	Armed Forces Network
CARE	Co-operative for American Remittances to Europe
CDU	Christian Democratic Union
CFM	Council of Foreign Ministers
CINCEUR	Commander in Chief, Europe
CIO	Congress of Industrial Organizations
CRALOG	Council of Religious Agencies Licensed to Operate in Germany
CSU	Christian Social Union
DAF	Deutsche Arbeitsfront (German Labor Front)
DANA	Deutsche Allgemeine Nachrichten Agentur (German General News Agency)
DENA	Deutsche Allgemeine Agentur
DM	Deutschemarks
DP	Displaced Person; German Party
ECA	Economic Co-operation Administration

ERP	European Recovery Plan
FDGB	Freier Deutscher Gewerkschaftsbund (Free German Federation of Trade Unions)
FDP	Free Democratic party
GCA	Ground Control Approach
GYA	German Youth Assistance
IARA	Inter-Allied Reparations Agency
IRO	International Refugee Organization
JCS	Joint Chiefs of Staff
KPD	Communist party
LDP	Liberal Democratic party
OEEC	Organization for European Economic Co-operation
OMGUS	Office of Military Government, United States
PCIRO	Preparatory Commission, International Refugee Organization
RFC	Reconstruction Finance Corporation
RIAS	Rundfunk im Amerikanischen Sektor (Radio in American Sector)
RM	Reichsmarks
SA	Sturmabteilung (Storm Troopers)
SED	Socialist Unity Party
SHAEF	Supreme Headquarters, Allied Expeditionary Force
SPD	Social Democratic party
SS	Schutzstaffel, Hitler's Elite Guard
TVA	Tennessee Valley Authority
UGO	Unabhaengige Gewerkschaft Opposition (Independent Trade Union Opposition)

UNICEF	United Nations International Children's Emergency Fund
UNRRA	United Nations Relief and Rehabilitation Administration
WAV	Economic Reconstruction party

Footnotes

CHAPTER 1

SUBJECT	DATE	REFERENCE
1. Separate Zones in Germany	2/3 to 2/11/45	Yalta Conference statement by the Prime Minister of Great Britain, President of the United States, and Chairman of the Council of People's Commissars of the USSR on the result of the Crimea Conference, Par. 2, 2
Central Control Commission		Par. 2, 2
French Participation		Par. 2, 3
Purpose of the Occupation		Par. 2, 4
Poland		Par. 6, 4
Reparation by Germany		Par. 3
Intention toward the German People		Par. 2, 5
2. Decision on Expulsion of the Germans from Poland	8/2/45	Potsdam Agreement, Section XIII
3. Three Documents Issued by the European Advisory Commission		Tripartite (US/UK/USSR) documents serving as a basis for the "Declaration on Defeat of Germany and the Assumption of Supreme Authority, Control Machinery in Germany, and the Zones of Occupation in Germany"

SUBJECT	DATE	REFERENCE
4. Assumption of Supreme Authority	6/5/45	"Declaration regarding the Defeat of Germany and the Assumption of Supreme Authority with respect to Germany by the Governments of the UK, the USA, the USSR, and the Provisional Government of the French Republic", Preamble, Par. 5
Unconditional Surrender		Preamble, Par. 1
Absence of Competent Authority		Preamble, Par. 2
Boundaries		Preamble, Par. 6
Disposal of War Potential		Article 2
Labor and Services		Article 5, I
Information and Records		Article 5, II
Transport Facilities		Article 5 (c)
United Nations Prisoners of War and Nationals and Political Persecutees		Article 6 (a)
Nazi Leaders and War Criminals		Article 11
German Officers		Article 6 (c)
Information on Mines and Mine Fields		Article 7 (b)
Property, Records, and Archives		Article 8
Demilitarization of Germany		Article 13 (a)
Additional Requirements		Article 13 (b)
Requirements of Allied Representatives		Article 13 (b)
5. Control Machinery in Germany	6/5/45	Statement by the Governments of the UK, the USA, the USSR and the Provisional Government of the French Republic on Control Machinery in Germany, Pars. 1–8
Control Council		Par. 3
Co-ordinating Committee and Control Staff		Par. 3

SUBJECT	DATE	REFERENCE
Liaison with UN Governments		Par. 5
Administration of Greater Berlin Area		Par. 7
Period of Operation of Agreement		Par. 8
6. Zones of Occupation in Germany	6/5/45	Statement by the Governments of the UK, the USA, the USSR, and the Provisional Government of the French Republic on Zones of Occupation in Germany, Pars. 1, 2
Four Zones of Germany		Par. 1
Greater Berlin		Par. 2
7. Policy to Apply in Postwar Period	5/14/45	JCS/1067/6 as amended by JCS/1067/8, Par. 1
US Representative to Urge Adoption of Principles on Control Council		Par. 1
Assumption of Supreme Authority		Part I, Pars. 2 (a), 3 (a)
Decentralization of Germany, Political and Administrative Structure, and Severance of Ties to Austria		Part I, Pars. 3 (c) and (g)
Attitude toward Defeated Germany		Part I, Par. 4 (b)
Economic Controls		Part I, Par. 5
Dissolution of the Nazi Party, Repeal of Nazi Laws and Regulations		Part I, Par. 6 (a) and (b)
Nominal Nazis and Party Property and Records		Part I, Par. 6 (c) and (d)
Demilitarization		Part I, Par. 6 (a), (b), and (c)
Lists of Categories of Security Arrests		Part I, Par. 8 (b), 1, 2, 3, 4, 5, 6, 7, 8, 9, 10, 11
Political Activities and Prohibition of Parades		Part I, Par. 9 (a) and (c)

CHAPTER 3

SUBJECT	DATE	REFERENCE
1. Provisions Relating to Germany	8/2/45	Potsdam Agreement, Section III
Veto Powers		Part A, Par. 1
Implementation of Yalta Declaration on Germany		Preamble, Par. 3
Allied Intentions toward Germany		Preamble, Par. 4
Supreme Authority in Germany		Part A, Par. 1
Uniformity of Treatment of German Population		Part A, Par. 2
Disarmament and Demilitarization		Part A, Par. 3 (1) (a) and (b)
Destruction of NSDAP		Part A, Par. 3 (iii)
Abolition of Nazi Laws		Part A, Par. 4
War Criminals and Nazi Leaders		Part A, Par. 5
More than Nominal Nazis		Part A, Par. 6
Control of German Education		Part A, Par. 7
Reorganization of German Judicial System		Part A, Par. 8
Decentralization of Political Structure		Part A, Par. 9 (i), (ii), (iii), (iv)
Freedom of Press, Speech, Religion, and Formation of Free Trade Unions		Part A, Par. 10
Prohibition of War Equipment Production, and Limitation of War Industries		Part B, Par. 11
Decentralization of Economy		Part B, Par. 12
Development of Agriculture		Part B, Par. 13

SUBJECT	DATE	REFERENCE
Germany as a Single Economic Unit		Part B, Par. 14
Allied Controls of German Economy		Part B, Par. 15
German Administrative Machinery		Part B, Par. 16
German-owned External Assets		Part B, Par. 18
Payment of Reparations to Leave Germany Able to Subsist without External Assistance		Part B, Par. 19
Reparations from Germany		Section IV
USSR and Polish Reparations Claims		Pars. 1, 2
Additional Reparations to the USSR		Par. 4 (a) and (b)
UK, USA, and Other Reparations Claims		Par. 3
USSR-Renounced Claims on Captured Gold		Par. 10
Disposal of the German Navy and Merchant Marine		Section V
Time Limit on Removals and Payment in Commodities		Section IV, Par. 6
Advance Deliveries		Par. 7
War Criminals		Section VII
Orderly Transfer of German Populations		Section XIII
2. Legislative Action of the Control Council	9/20/45	CONL/M(45)6, Min. 56, p. 1 (CONL/P(45) 36 dated 18 Sep 45)
3. Official Languages and Publication of Legislation	9/20/45	CONL/M(45)6 (CONL/P(45)35 dated 18 Sep '45)

CHAPTER 4

SUBJECT	DATE	REFERENCE
1. Establishment of Government in the German States (Laender) of US Zone	5/28/45	a. *Bavaria:* Letter, Hq Det EIF 3 COF, 3rd ECA Reg. AG 230.3
	6/24/45	b. *Wuerttemberg-Baden:* Directive, USFET, G-5 Div.
	6/24/45	c. *Hesse-Nassau:* Directive, USFET, G-5 Div.
	6/24/45	d. *Hesse:* Directive, USFET, G-5 Div.
2. Abolition of G-5 Staffs and Creation of Office of Military Government	10/8/45	General Order 283, Hq, USFET
3. Administrative Changes in Military Government	3/9/46	General Order 61, Hq, USFET
4. German Laenderrat: Co-ordination of German Land Governments and Special Administrative Services (Sonderverwaltungen) in the US Zone	10/5/45	Letter, Hq, USFET AG 014,1, GEC-AGO
5. Regional Co-ordinating Office	11/2/45	Letter, Hq, USFET, AG 322, GEC-AGO (Another letter dated 20 December 1945)
6. Prohibition of Fraternization	5/14/45	JCS/1067/6 as amended by JCS/1067/8, Part I, Par. 4 (b)
7. Dangerous Nazis to Be Located		a. Ibid., Part I, Par. 8 (a) and (b) b. SHAEF *Handbook for Military Government in Germany,* Chapter II, "Eradication of Nazism," Par. 277
Repealing of Nazi Laws	9/20/45	Control Council Law No. 1 (CONL/P(45)40)
Providing for Termination and Liquidation of Nazi Organizations	10/10/45	Control Council Law No. 2 (CONL/P(45)44)

SUBJECT	DATE	REFERENCE
Disposition of Property Having Belonged to Organizations. Listed in Control Council Proclamation No. 2 and Control Council Law No. 2	4/29/47	Control Council Directive No. 50 (CORC/P(46)281 Final)
Removal from Office and from Positions of Responsibility of Nazis and of Persons Hostile to Allied Purposes	1/12/46	CONL/P(45)64 (Final)
8. Prohibition of Employment of Members of the Nazi Party in Positions Other than Ordinary Labor and for Other Purposes	3/5/46	Military Government Law No. 8
9. Law for Liberation from National Socialism and Militarism	3/5/46	German law
10. Directive on US Objectives and Basic Policies in Germany	7/15/47	Reissued as OMGUS Directive 18 July 1947, AG-201-Gen Clay
11. General Clay's Review of the German Situation	5/26/46	Cable CC-5797

CHAPTER 5

1. Administration of Military Government in US Zone of Germany	7/7/45	Letter, Hq, USFET AG 014.1 GEC-AGO
2. Bremen Enclave	9/12/44	Protocol between Governments of US, UK, and USSR
	11/14/44	Amended: See Minutes of EAC (44) 12th Meeting
3. Establishment of State Government in Bavaria	5/28/45	Letter, Hq, Det. EIF 3, Co. F, 3rd ECA Reg. AG File 230.2
Establishment of State Government in Wuerttemberg-Baden	6/24/45	Directive, USFET, G-5 Div.
Establishment of State Government in Hessen-Nassau		Ibid.

SUBJECT	DATE	REFERENCE
Establishment of State Government in Hesse		Ibid.
Organization of Western US Military District for Military Government Purposes	8/7/45	Ibid.
Joining of Land Hesse and Province Hessen-Nassau	9/11/45	Ibid.
Proclamation No. 2, Constituting Administrative Areas within the US Zone of Occupation	9/19/45	Signed by General Eisenhower

4. Political Parties Authorized in the US Zone:

    Hq, USFET, Directives AG 014.1 GEC-AGO

a. On Kreis Level	8/27/45	
b. On Land Level	11/23/45	
c. On Zonal Level	2/28/46	

5. Approval of Laender Constitutions:

    "Constitutions of the German Laender," publication of OMGUS, CAD Division, January 1947

a. General Clay's Letter of Approval of the Wuerttemberg-Baden Constitution	10/21/46	
b. General Clay's Letter of Approval of the Bavarian Constitution	10/24/46	Ibid.
c. General Clay's Letter of Approval of the Greater Hesse Constitution	10/29/46	Ibid.

6. Ratification of Land Constitutions:

a. Statistics of Elections in Germany, 1946		Special Report of the Military Governor, 15 March 1947
b. Popular Ratification of Land Constitutions and Landtage Elections	9/17/46	Directive, OMGUS AG 000.1 (CA)

7. Relationships between Military and Civil Government (US Zone) Subsequent to Adoption of Land Constitutions

    9/30/46   Directive, OMGUS, AG 010.1 (CA)

SUBJECT	DATE	REFERENCE
8. Formation of Political Parties, Administration of Military Government in the US Zone	8/27/45	Directive, USFET AG 014.1, GEC-AGO
Organization of Political Parties on State Level	11/23/45	Ibid.
9. Laenderrat: Co-ordination of German Laender Governments and Special Administrative Services (-onderverwaltungen) in the US Zone	10/5/45	Letter, USFET AG 014.1 GEC-AGO
10. Chronology of Agreements on Bremen:		
a. Protocol among the Governments of the US, UK, and USSR, amended November 14, 1944	9/12/44	European Advisory Commission Documents, London, 1944. See Minutes EAC, 12th Meeting
b. US/UK Agreement on Bremen Modifying EAC Agreement, Entitled "Agreement on Military Government Responsibilities in the Bremen Enclave"	12/10/45	Signed by General Whieley and General Clay
c. Clay-Robertson Agreement on Enlargement of the Bremen Enclave, Prior to Creation of Land Bremen, to Become Effective January 1, 1947	10/30/46	Signed in Berlin
d. Proclamation No. 3, Constituting Land Bremen	1/2 /47	Signed by General McNarney, Military Governor, US Zone
11. Composition of Advisory Parliamentary Council:		
a. Membership:		
24 Members divided by states as follows:		
Bavaria, Wuerttemberg-Baden, and		

SUBJECT	DATE	REFERENCE

Hesse—7   members
each
Bremen—3 members

b. Political Composition:

SPD-9
CDU-5
CSU-3
KPD-2
LDP-1
FDP-1
WAV-1
DVP-1
BDV-1

CHAPTER   6

	SUBJECT	DATE	REFERENCE
1.	Control Council Law No. 2: Termination and Liquidation of Nazi Organizations	10/10/45	CONL/P(45)48
	Control Council Law No. 3: Increase in the Rates of Taxation	10/20/45	CONL/P(45)49
	Control Council Law No. 4: Reorganization of the German Judicial System	10/30/45	CONL/P(45)50
	Control Council Law No. 9: Seizure of Property Owned by the I. G. Farbenindustrie and the Control Thereof	11/30/45	CONL/P(45)62, amended by CONL/M(45)13
	Control Council Law No. 5: Vesting and Marshaling of German External Assets	10/30/45	CONL/P(45)39 (Revise)
	Control Council Law No. 8: Elimination and Prohibition of Military Training	11/30/45	CONL/P(45)60, amended by CONL/M(45)13
	Control Council Law No. 10: Punishment of Persons Guilty of War Crimes, Crimes against Peace and against Humanity	12/20/45	CONL/P(45)53

SUBJECT	DATE	REFERENCE
Control Council Order No. 3: Registration of the Population of Employable Age, Registration of the Unemployed and Their Placement at Work	1/17/46	CORC/P(45)59 (Final)
Control Council Order No. 2: Confiscation and Surrender of Arms and Ammunition	1/7/46	CORC/P(45)178 (Final)
Control Council Directive No. 11: Rationing of Electricity and Gas	11/30/45	CONL/P(45)61
Control Council Directive No. 22: Clearance of Mine Fields and Destruction of Military Installations in Germany	12/6/45	CORC/P(45)179 (Final)
Control Council Directive No. 23: Limitation and Demilitarization of Sport in Germany	12/17/45	CORC/P(45)180 (Final)
2. Level of German Steel Industry	12/13/45	DECO/P(45)120
3. Proposal for Establishment of Central German Transport Department—Positions of French, USSR, and USA	9/22/45	Reflected in CORC/M(45)9, Min. 122, p. 9
	10/12/45	CORC/M(45)13, Min. 183, p. 6 (see verbatim record)
	10/16/45	CORC/M(45)14, Min. 193, p. 7 (see verbatim record)
	11/23/45	CORC/M(45)22, Min. 291, p. 2
4. French Position on Trade Unions in Germany	10/26/45	CORC/M(45)16, Min. 212, p. 2 (see verbatim record)
5. Higher Education in Berlin	10/3/45	CORC/M(45)11, Min. 148, p. 4
6. Establishment by Four Occupying Powers of Consular Offices throughout Germany	12/6/45	CORC/M(45)25, Min. 337, p. 1

SUBJECT	DATE	REFERENCE
Reception of Allied Military Missions Accredited to the Allied Control Council	10/3/45	CORC/M(45)11, Conclusion, Min. 149, p. 6

Australia	India
Belgium	Luxembourg
Brazil	The Netherlands
Canada	New Zealand
China	Norway
Czechoslovakia	Poland
Denmark	South Africa
Greece	Yugoslavia

7. Zonal Boundaries 11/27/45 CORC/M(45)23, Min. 309, p. 3

Interzonal Travel of German Civilians 12/17/45 CORC/M(45)27, Min. 363, pp. 1, 2

8. Memorandum of Soviet Member on the Presence of Organized Units of the Former German Army in the British Zone of Occupation 11/26/45 CONL/P(45)59

UK Reply to Soviet Memorandum 11/30/45 CONL/M(45)13, Min. 109, p. 2, and Appendix "A" thereto

Molotov's Statement on Existence in British Zone of Organized Units of the Former German Army 7/9/46 Paris Peace Conference (15 June to 12 July 1946) Minutes of CFM Meeting 9 July

9. Advanced Deliveries on Account of Reparations—US Statement 10/23/45 Reflected in CORC/M(45)15 (Part I), Min. 196, p. 1

10. Quadripartite-issued Permits 9/13/46 CORC/P(46)286 (Final) Establishment of ACA Interzonal Facilities Bureau

11. Control Council Law No. 16: Marriage Law 2/20/46 CONL/P(46)13 (Final)

Control Council Law No. 23: Prohibition of Military Construction in Germany 4/10/46 CONL/P(46)26 (Final)

Control Council Law No. 11: Repealing Certain Provisions of German Criminal Law 1/30/46 CORC/P(46)33

SUBJECT	DATE	REFERENCE
Control Council Law No. 31: Police Bureaus and Agencies of a Political Nature	7/1/46	CONL/P(46)47 (Final)
Control Council Law No. 25: Control of Scientific Research	4/29/46	CONL/P(46)29 (Final)
Allied Control Council Proclamation No. 2: Agreement on Certain Additional Requirements to Be Imposed on Germany	9/20/45	CONL/P(45)36 (initially contained in Par. 19(c) of Proclamation)
Approved Paper: Draft Regulations for International Postal Service in Germany	6/14/46	CORC/P(46)208
Approved Paper: Policy concerning the Reopening of Museums in Germany	2/16/46	CORC/P(46)61
Control Council Law No. 18: Housing Law	3/8/46	CONL/P(46)18 (Final)
Control Council Law No. 21: Law concerning German Labor Courts	3/30/46	CONL/P(46)33 (Final)
Approved Paper: German Agricultural Co-operatives	3/18/46	CORC/P(46)94
Approved Paper: Uniform Banking Statistics in Germany	3/18/46	CORC/P(46)96
Control Council Law No. 22: Works Councils	4/10/46	CONL/P(46)25 (Final)
Approved Paper: Organization of Interurban Telephone and Telegraph Services between the Various Zones of Occupation in Germany	12/12/45	CORC/P(46)161 (Revised)
12. Evaluation Formula: Principles of Evaluation of Advanced Deliveries on Account of Reparations	2/26/46	CORC/P(46)8 (Final)
13. Level of German Steel Industry	12/13/45	DECO/P(45)120

SUBJECT	DATE	REFERENCE
Level of Industry Plan Pertaining to Other Industries	3/7/46	CORC/M(46)13, Min. 142, pp. 3, 4, 5
Level of Industry Plan and Assumptions on Which It Is Based	3/20/46	CORC/M(46)16, Min. 173, pp. 1, 4
Approval of Level of Industry Plan by Control Council	3/26/46	CONL/M(46)9 (Extraordinary Meeting) Min. 45, Conclusion

14. Proposal for Creation of an Information Committee — 3/18/46 — CORC/P(46)101, and CORC/M(46)15, Min. 167, p. 6

15. Draft Directive concerning National Political Parties — 3/14/46 — CORC/P(46)111

Position of USSR, US, UK, and French	3/26/46	CORC/M(46)18, Min. 186, pp. 7, 8, 9

CHAPTER 7

	SUBJECT	DATE	REFERENCE
1.	Import-Export Program: General Clay's Statement	4/8/46	CORC/M(46)20, Min. 215, p. 12
	UK Statement	4/26/46	Appendix "A" to CORC/M(46)22
	US and USSR Statements, and French Position		CORC/M(46)22, Min. 229, pp. 5, 6, 7
	USSR and US Statements	5/3/46	CORC/M(46)23, Min. 243, p. 2
2.	*Taegliche Rundschau*		Overt Paper of Soviet Army in Germany
3.	Draft Treaty on Disarmament and Demilitarization of Germany Submitted by Secretary Byrnes to CFM, Paris	4/29/46	CFM/46/21, Preamble and Articles I–V
4.	French Statement on Rhineland	4/25/46	CFM/46/1
5.	US Proposal for Appointment of Quadripartite Disarmament Commission	5/13/46	CORC/M(46)27, Min. 287, p. 9
	US and USSR Positions	5/22/46	CORC/P(46)186
	General Clay's Statement	5/23/46	CORC/M(46)27, Min. 310, p. 11

SUBJECT	DATE	REFERENCE
6. Molotov's Statement on Byrnes's Draft Treaty for Germany	7/9/46	Paris Peace Conference, Minutes of 9 July CFM Meeting
Byrnes's Reply and His Proposal to Extend Treaty to Forty Years		Ibid.
7. Soviet Charges of Existence in British Zone of Organized Units of the German Army	11/20/45	CONL/M(45)12, Min. 104
8. Common Pool for German Resources	4/5/46	DECO/M(46)22, Min. 223 (DECO/P(46)105, dated 10 March 1946)
9. Molotov's Second Statement on Germany	7/10/46	Paris Peace Conference Minutes of 10 July CFM Meeting
10. Bevin's Statement on Economic Unity of Germany	7/11/46	Paris Peace Conference CFM/46/224 and Minutes of 11 July CFM Meeting
11. Bidault's Statement on Coal for German Economy and Exclusion of Saar from the Administration of the Occupied Zones		Minutes of 11 July CFM Meeting
12. Byrnes's Statement on the Possibility of French Support for Administrative Agencies		Ibid.
Byrnes's Proposal to Appoint Deputies for Preparation of a Peace Treaty		Ibid.
13. Measures to Insure Economic Unity of Germany Statement by US Member of ACC	7/20/46	CONL/M(46)19, Min. 82, and Appendix "A" thereto
	7/30/46	CONL/M(46)20, Min. 87
14. Control Council Law No. 26: Tax on Tobacco	5/10/46	CONL/P(46)35 (Final)
Control Council Law No. 27: Tax on Alcohol	5/10/46	CONL/P(46)36 (Final)
Control Council Law No. 28: Tax on Beer and Matches	5/10/46	CONL/P(46)37 (Final)

SUBJECT	DATE	REFERENCE
Control Council Order No. 4: Confiscation of Literature and Material of a Nazi and Militarist Nature	5/14/46	CORC/P(46)130 (Final)
a. Amendment to Order No. 4	8/10/46	CONL/P(46)55 (Final)
Control Council Directive No. 30: Liquidation of German Military and Nazi Memorials and Museums	5/13/46	CORC/P(46)161 (Final)
a. Revision of Article IV of CONL Directive No. 30	7/12/46	CORC/P(46)226 (Final)
Co-ordinating Committee Directive No. 31: Principles concerning the Establishment of Federations of Trade Unions	6/3/46	CORC/P(46)193 (Final)
Co-ordinating Committee Directive No. 32: Disciplinary Measures against Managing and Administrative Staffs of Educational Institutions, Teaching Staffs, and Students Guilty of Militaristic Nazi or Anti-Democratic Propaganda	6/26/46	CORC/P(46)216 (Final)
Approved Paper: Berlin Elections	6/3/46	CORC/P(46)197
Control Council Law No. 32: Employment of Women on Building and Reconstruction Work	7/10/46	CONL/P(46)49 (Final)
Control Council Law No. 33: Census of the German Population	7/20/46	CONL/P(46)50 (Final)
Control Council Law No. 34: Dissolution of the Wehrmacht	8/20/46	CONL/P(46)56 (Final)

SUBJECT	DATE	REFERENCE
Control Council Law No. 35: Conciliation and Arbitration Machinery in Labor Conflicts	8/20/46	CONL/P(46)57 (Final)
Control Council Directive No. 35: Sentences of the International Military Tribunal	9/7/46	CORC/P(46)284 (Final)
Control Council Directive No. 33: Limitation of Characteristics of Ships Left at the Disposal of Germany	8/16/46	CORC/P(46)246 (Final)
Control Council Directive No. 37: Limitation of Characteristics of Ships Other than Fishing and Pleasure Craft Left to the Peace Economy of Germany	9/26/46	CORC/P(46)306 (Final)
Control Council Law No. 36: Administrative Courts	10/10/46	CONL/P(46)67 (Final)
Control Council Law No. 37: Repeal of Certain Statutory Provisions Relating to Successions	10/30/46	CONL/P(46)71 (Final)
Control Council Directive No. 38: Arrest and Punishment of War Criminals, Nazis, and Militarists and the Internment, Control, and Surveillance of Potentially Dangerous Germans	10/12/46	CORC/P(46)301 (Final)
Control Council Directive No. 40: Policy to Be Followed by German Politicians and the German Press	10/12/46	CORC/P(46)315 (Final)
Control Council Law No. 43:	12/20/46	CONL/P(46)82 (Final)

SUBJECT	DATE	REFERENCE
Prohibition of the Manufacture, Import, Export, Transport, and Storage of War Materials		
Co-ordinating Committee Draft Regulation on Gift Parcel Post Service into Germany	12/19/46	CORC/P(46)398
15. General Robertson's Statement on Central German Administrations	10/21/46	CONL/M(46)29, Min. 135, p. 2
16. Arrest of Judges in the Various Sectors of Berlin, US and USSR Statements	2/26/46	CORC/M(46)11, Min. 125, pp. 8, 12
17. Anti-Soviet Propaganda in the British Sector of Berlin	8/20/46	CONL/M(46)22, Min. 96, p. 7
18. Anti-United States Propaganda in the Soviet Sector of Berlin, US Statement	8/22/46	CORC/M(46)43, Min. 96, p. 7
Otto Grotewohl		Co-Chairman of Communist Socialist Unity Party (SED)
Neues Deutschland		Official Organ of SED
Berliner Zeitung and *Vorwaerts*		Soviet-licensed newspapers
Article in *Neues Deutschland,* September 18, 1946 US Statement	9/23/46	CORC/M(46)50, Min. 537, p. 10
USSR Statement	9/26/46	CORC/M(46)51, Min. 543, p. 4
19. Declaration of UK Member concerning Alleged Removal of Skilled German Workers from the Soviet Zone of Germany to the USSR	10/31/46	CORC/M(46)57, Min. 631, p. 13, and Appendix "A" thereto
USSR Position	11/4/46	CORC/M(46)58, Min. 644, p. 9
20. Agenda for the Fourth Session of Council of Foreign Ministers, Moscow	12/12/46	Ministers' Decisions, CFM/46/NY/74
Appointment of Deputies for Germany to Hear Allied States		Ibid.

SUBJECT	DATE	REFERENCE
Deputies for Germany to Consider Questions on Boundaries, Ruhr, and Rhineland, the US Draft Treaty, and Report of the Coal Experts		Ibid., Par. IV (a)
Allied Control Council Report to Council of Foreign Ministers		Ministers' Decisions, CFM/46/NY/74
Deputies for Germany Report to Council of Foreign Ministers		Ibid., Par. IV (c)

CHAPTER 8

1.	Preparation of Allied Control Council Report to the Council of Foreign Ministers	12/21/46 to 2/27/47	CONL/M(46)35 (CONL/P(46) 83) CONL/M(47)5 (ASEC(47)154)
2.	Meetings of Deputies for Germany in London Deputies: Sir William Strang, UK Robert Murphy, US Maurice Couve de Murville, France F. T. Gusev, USSR	1/14 to 29/47	
3.	Statements of Allied States to Deputies for Germany	1/14 to 29/47	Annex I to "Report by Deputies for Germany to the Council of Foreign Ministers," (CFM(D) (47)G, Serials I–XXXVIII)
4.	Summary of Views of the Allied States on the Principal Aspects of the German Problem	2/25/47	"Report by Deputies for Germany to the Council of Foreign Ministers," Part II, A
5.	Allied Control Council Report to the Council of Foreign Ministers	2/25/47	ASEC(47)154
6.	Elected Members of the Berlin Magistrat	2/5/47	CORC/M(47)6, Min. 66, pp. 4, 7
	Election of Oberbuergermeister of Berlin	7/10/47	CONL/M(47)16, Min. 74, p. 3 and CONL/P(47)40

SUBJECT	DATE	REFERENCE
7. Control Council Law No. 46: Abolition of the State of Prussia	2/25/47	CONL/P(47)10 (Final)
8. Statement by Molotov on Denazification and Democratization of Germany	3/13/47	CFM/47/M/9
Statement by Bevin on Denazification	3/29/47	CFM/47/M/84
9. Molotov's Statement on US Possession of German Patents	3/18/47	USDEL(47)M, 8th Meeting, p. 3, Par. 3
10. Report of CFM Co-ordinating Committee on Form and Scope of Provisional Political Organization for Germany	4/11/47	CFM/47/M/121 (includes CFM/47/M/101 dated 4 April 1947)
11. Acceleration of Destruction of German Military Matériel and Installations	4/23/47	Report of Deputies for Germany to Council of Foreign Ministers, Approved CFM/47/M/148, Part I, Par. (1), I
Liquidation of Plants Suitable Only for Production of War Materials		Part I, Par. (2), I
Quadripartite Inspection Teams		Part I, Par. (4), I
Acceleration of Denazification		Part I, Par. (1), II
Trial of War Criminals		Part I, Par. (4), II
German Denazification Legislation		Part I, Par. (5), II
Land Reform		Part I, Par. (1), 3, I
Free Exchange of Information		Part I, Par. (2), 3, I
Access to DP Centers		Part I, Par. (a), (1), 4, I
Propaganda in DP Camps		Part I, Par. (b), (1), 4, I
Repatriation of Deceased UN Nationals		Part I, Par. (1), 4, I

SUBJECT	DATE	REFERENCE
Acceleration of Repatriation of DPs		Part I, Par. (c), (2), 4, I
Restudy of Transfer of Population to Germany		Part I, Par. (d), (2), 4, I
Publication of Reparations Lists		Part II, A, II
Repatriation of German POWs by December 31, 1948	4/23/47	CFM/47/M/153, Par. (1); and CFM/47/M/42d Meeting
Limitation of Occupation Forces in Germany	5/10/47	CFM/47/M/158, and CFM/47/M/43d Meeting (24 April)
12. Report to the Council of Foreign Ministers on the Strength of the Occupation Forces	5/31/47	CONL/M(47)12, Min. 55, p. 1 (CONL/P(47)32)
13. Control Council Law No. 44: Repeal of the Ordinance of October 11, 1944, concerning "Extraordinary Measures on Leases, Agricultural Management and Debtor Relief caused by Total War"	1/10/47	CONL/P(47)1 (Final)
Control Council Law No. 45: Repeal of Legislation on Hereditary Farms and Enactment of Other Provisions Regulating Agricultural Forest Lands	2/20/47	CONL/P(47)4 (Final)
Control Council Law No. 47: Termination of German Insurance Operations Abroad	3/10/47	CONL/P(47)18 (Final)
Control Council Law No. 48: Supplement to Appendix to Control Council Law No. 2 Providing for Termination and Liquidation of Nazi Organizations	8/30/47	CONL/P(47)45 (Final)

SUBJECT	DATE	REFERENCE
Co-ordinating Committee Paper: Exchange of Parcels between Berlin and the Zones of Occupation	4/29/47	CORC/P(47)84/1
Control Council Directive No. 52: Combating Venereal Disease	5/7/47	CORC/P(47)20 (Final)
Control Council Directive No. 47: Liquidation of German War Research Establishments	3/27/47	CORC/P(47)77 (Final)
Control Council Law No. 55: Repeal of Certain Provisions of Criminal Legislation	6/20/47	CONL/P(47)35
Control Council Directive No. 55: Interzonal Exchange of Printed Matter and Films	6/25/47	CORC/P(47)42 (Final)
14. Revised Plan for Level of Industry for the US/UK Zones of Germany	8/29/47	BIB/P(47)89/1
15. Inter-Allied Reparations Agency	1945	a. Establishment of IARA agreed at Reparations Conference in Paris, 9 November–21 December 1945
	1/14/46	b. IARA Agreement signed
16. Report of the Co-ordinating Committee on Currency Reform	9/4/47	CONL/M(47)19, Extraordinary Meeting, Appendix "A" SECRET
17. Statement by Marshal Sokolovsky on Memorandum from General Clay and Marshal Douglas regarding the Revised Bizonal Level of Industry	8/30/47	CONL/M(47)19, Min. 93, p. 6, and Appendix "B" thereto
General Clay's Reply to Marshal Sokolovsky	8/30/47	CONL/M(47)19, Min. 93, p. 6

CHAPTER 9

SUBJECT	DATE	REFERENCE
1. Statement by the US Member on Measures to Insure the Economic Unity of Germany	7/20/46	CONL/M(46)19, Min. 82, and Appendix "A" thereto
	7/30/46	CONL/M(46)20, Min. 87
2. Preliminary Agreement on the Establishment of a German Economic Administration	9/5/46	BIB/P(46)5 (Revise)
3. Bizonal Fusion Agreement	12/2/46	Byrnes-Bevin Agreement (State Department Document)
4. a. Agreement for Reorganization of Bizonal Economic Agencies	5/29/47	Appendix "A" to Proclamation No. 5
b. Economic Council	6/10/47	Proclamation No. 5, Military Government for Germany, US Area of Control
5. Agreement between Governments of UK and USA Amending Certain Terms of the Bizonal Fusion Agreement	12/17/47	Lovett-Strang Amendment to the Byrnes-Bevin Agreement (State Department Document)
6. Bizonal Economic Administration	2/9/48	Proclamation No. 7, Military Government for Germany, US Area of Control
7. a. Order No. 1 Pursuant to Article III (5) of Military Government Proclamation No. 7	8/6/48	Military Government Order, AG 010 (LD)
b. Order No. 2 Pursuant to Article III (5) of Military Government Proclamation No. 7	9/1/48	Military Government Order, AG 010.6 (LD)
c. Order No. 3 Pursuant to Article III (5) of Military Government Proclamation No. 7	12/12/48	Ibid.

SUBJECT	DATE	REFERENCE
d. Order No. 4 Pursuant to Article III (5) of Military Government Proclamation No. 7	11/29/48	Ibid.
8. Establishment of a German High Court for Combined Bizonal Area	2/9/48	Proclamation No. 8, Military Government for Germany, US Area of Control
9. Establishment of a Bank deutscher Laender	2/15/48	Military Government Law No 60
10. Charter of Joint Export-Import Agency	1/15/48	BIB/P(48)8
11. Directive to the US/UK Coal Control Group from the Bipartite Board Pursuant to Military Government Law No. 75	11/10/48	BIB/P(48)187

CHAPTER 10

SUBJECT	DATE	REFERENCE
1. Initiation of Interzonal Exchange of Mail	10/24/45	DIAC/ACPC/PSC/P(45)7, approved in DIAC/ACPC/M(45)6
Initiation of Interzonal Telephone and Telegraph Services		
a. Telegraph	2/8/46	CORC/P(45)161 (Revise)
b. Telephone	2/25/46	DIAC/ACPC/M(46)8
2. Opening of International Mail	4/1/46	DIAC/ACPC/PSC/P(47)74, 6th Revision
Opening of One-way International Gift Parcel Post	6/1/46	Monthly Report of the Military Governor No. 12, p. 13
3. Prohibition of German Civil Aviation	8/2/45	Potsdam Agreement, III, A, 3, (1)(b)
4. Establishment of Economic Offices	7/45	Monthly Report of the Military Governor No. 1, p. 2
Re-establishment of Local Chambers of Commerce		Ibid.
5. Beginning of Miners' Incentive Scheme	8/12/45	Cable from USFET, S-17079, authorized miners' rations and clothing to be supplemented from military str (Class X) if necessary

SUBJECT	DATE	REFERENCE
6. Moscow Sliding Scale "Coal Agreement"	4/17/47	See Tripartite Agreement (TT/Berlin/47/P/2, 10 September 1947)
7. Replacement of Saar Coal in German Economy by Ruhr Coal	9/10/47	Tripartite Talks on German Coal and Coke Distribution (TT/Berlin/47/P/2)
8. Establishment of Deutsche Kohlenbergbau-Leitung (DKBL)	11/18/47 (effective date)	BIB/M(47)14, Decision 251, 11 November 1947 (BIB/P(47)124, dated 17 November 1947, contains British MG Ordinance No. 112 and US MG Ordinance No. 19)
9. Military Government Law No. 75: "Reorganization of German Coal and Iron and Steel Industries"	11/10/48	BIB/P(48)186 and 187, and BIB/M(48)21, Min. 576(iv), dated 15 November 1948
10. Joint US/UK Recommendation, Release of Foreign Funds for Investment	10/11/48	BIB/P(48)122/3 (This paper incorporated in BIB/P(49)2 (Appendix A) dated 4 January 1949, and approved in BIB/M(49)1, Min. 619, 42d Meeting held on 14 January 1949, and forwarded to US/UK/French and Benelux governments for approval)
11. Establishment of JEIA:		
a. Provisional Agreement	12/30/46	BIB/P(46)25 dated 27 December 1946, BIB/M(46)4, Min. 46
b. Final Agreement	2/3/47	BIB/M(47)2, Min. 80 (BIB/P(46)25, 1st Revision dated 28 January 1947, amended by BIB/P(46)25, 2nd Revision dated 6 February 1947)
12. German Firms Contracting with Foreign Buyers Subject to JEIA Approval	2/3/47	Ibid.
JEIA Approval for Exports Required for Only a Few Items	4/8/47	JEIA Instruction No. 1
13. Establishment of German Economic Council	5/29/47	BIB/M(47)7, Min. 158
	6/10/47 (effective date)	Military Government Proclamation No. 5

SUBJECT	DATE	REFERENCE
14. Policy Regarding German Finance	4/26/45	JCS/1067/7 as amended by JCS/1067/8 dated 10 May 1945
Finance Measures under Potsdam Agreement	8/2/45	Potsdam Agreement, Section III, 3, Par. 10, Part B
15. Proposal for Central Bank	10/10/46	CONL/P(46)69
16. German State Legislation for Creation of State Central Banks (Superseded by MG Law No. 66)	1/1/47	a. Law No. 50 of Land Government of Bavaria, 27 November 1946
		b. Law No. 55 of Land Government of Wuerttemberg-Baden, 7 December 1946
		c. Law concerning establishment of State Central Bank in Hesse, 7 December 1946
		d. Law concerning establishment of State Central Bank in Bremen, 6 March 1947
17. Establishment of Joint Foreign Exchange Agency	2/3/47	BIB/P(47)4
18. Establishment of Bank deutscher Laender	3/1/48	Military Government Law No. 60
19. Establishment of Allied Bank Commission	2/24/48	BIB/P(48)22 BIB/M(48)4, Min. 312
20. Establishment of Reconstruction Loan Corporation	10/29/48	Economic Council Ordinance No. 54

CHAPTER 11

1. A Plan for the Liquidation of War Finance, and the Financial Rehabilitation of Germany	5/20/46	Colm-Dodge-Goldsmith Report
2. Provisional Revision of Tax Legislation	1/20/48	Military Government Law No. 64
3. First Law for Monetary Reform	1/20/48	Military Government Law No. 61
Second Law for Monetary Reform	1/20/48	Military Government Law No. 62

SUBJECT	DATE	REFERENCE
Third Law for Monetary Reform	6/27/48	Military Government Law No. 63
Fourth Law for Monetary Reform	10/4/48	Military Government Law No. 65
4. Western Zones of Germany to Participate in ERP	6/7/48	Final Communiqué from Three-power Talks on Germany, London Part II, (a)
5. Creation of ERP Group in BICO	3/12/48	Cable, COBIB 39
6. Participation in Inter-European Payments Agreement	10/29/48	BISEC/Memo(48)62
7. Decentralized Export-Import Procedures	11/2/48	BIB/P(48)183/1 BIB/M(48)21, Min. 576 C, Meeting held 30 October 1948
8. Customs Control Law for Bizonal Economic Area	3/30/49	Economic Council Ordinances No. 70 and 97
Frontier Control	4/15/49	Military Government Law No. 17, Regulation 1
9. Decontrol of Property	11/10/48	Report of the Intergovernmental Working Party on Safeguarding Allied Interests in Germany (Paris), Section I, Par. 2
Appeal Body		Section I, Par. 3
Reinvestments and Disposal of Property		Section I, Par. 5
Prepaid Contracts for Goods		Section I, Par. 4
Transfer of Deutschemarks		Section V, Par. 3
Exemption from Tax Equalization		Section VII, Par. 4
Reparations Losses		Section II, Par. 5
Land Reform		Section III, Par. 2
Coal Prices		Section IV, Pars. 2, 3
Protection of Reichsmark Holdings		Section V, Par. 4(a) and (b)
Gold Marks		Section VI, Par. 5
Foreign Insurers		Section VII, Par. 6

CHAPTER 12

	SUBJECT	DATE	REFERENCE
1.	Total DPs Uncovered by Allied Forces	7/6/45	Situation Report No. 26, G-5 Division, SHAEF
2.	Early Repatriation of DPs	8/2/45	Situation Report No. 33, Combined Displaced Persons Executive, in care of G-5 Div., USFET
3.	Visitors from the United States to Inspect Assembly Centers	1945	Report of Earl G. Harrison Mission to Europe to Inquire into the Condition and Needs of those among the DPs in the Liberated Countries of Western Europe and in the SHAEF Area of Germany, with particular reference to the Jewish refugees who may possibly be stateless or non-repatriable
4.	Closing Assembly Centers to New Admissions	4/21/47	Cable WX-96142 from Department of Army to EUCOM and USFA, dated 15 April 1947
5.	UNRRA Assistance to the Army in Caring for DPs	11/29/44	SHAEF/UNRRA Agreement
		2/19/46	USFET/UNRRA Agreement
6.	Establishment of PCIRO and IRO	12/15/46	Constitution of the International Refugee Organization and Agreement on Interim Measures adopted by resolution of the General Assembly of the United Nations
	Agreement Reached between PCIRO (IRO) and Occupation Authorities	7/9/47	IRO/CINCEUR Agreement
	Revised Agreement Reached between IRO and Occupation Authorities	7/28/48	Revised IRO/CINCEUR Agreement
7.	Subcommittee of the House Committee on Foreign Affairs Visit to Germany to Study DP Problem: James G. Fulton, Chairman	11/47	Report of Special Subcommittee of House Foreign Affairs Committee

SUBJECT	DATE	REFERENCE

Jacob K. Javits
Joseph L. Pfeifer
Frank L. Chelf

8. Enactment of Displaced   6/25/48   Public Law 774, 80th Congress
    Persons Act of 1948

9. Case Committee: 9/23 to
     Francis S. Case   25/47
     John M. Vorys
     Charles W. Vursell

10. Directive on US Objectives   7/15/47   Reissued as OMGUS Directive,
    and Basic Policies in Ger-   18 July,
    many   AG 201-General Clay

    Military Government Au-   Par. 2 a
    thority

    Demilitarization and De-   Pars. 4, 9
    nazification

    War Criminals   Par. 10

    Speedy Accomplishment of   Pars. 4, 9, 10
    Objectives

    Plant Removals   Par. 16 b

    Cartels and Concentrations   Par. 21 a
    of Economic Power

    German Self-government   Par. 6 a, b, c

    Cultural Exchange   Pars. 22, 27

    Public Information   Par. 26, a, b, c

    Finance   Par. 19, a, b, c, d

CHAPTER 13

1. Codification of Military   7/14/45   Military Government Law No. 4
   Government Laws, Ordi-   and *Military Government Gazette*,
   nances, and Regulations   14 July 1945

2. Trial of the Major War   11/20/45   "Trial of the Major War Crim-
   Criminals before the In-   to   inals before the International
   ternational Military Tri-   10/1/46   Military Tribunal," published at
   bunal (Nuremberg)   Nuremberg, 1947, pursuant to
                                             the direction of the International
                                             Military Tribunal by the Secre-
                                             tariat, Vol. I, pp. 172, 365

SUBJECT	DATE	REFERENCE
3. Trial of War Criminals by US Military Tribunals	12/9/46 to 4/13/49	a. Military Government Ordinance No. 7, "Organization and Powers of Certain Military Tribunals," dated 18 October 1946, as amended by MG Ordinance No. 11, 17 Feb 1947
		b. Regulation No. 1 to above, dated 11 April 1947
		c. Judgment Military Tribunal IV, Case 11, 13 April 1949
4. US Military Government Courts for Germany	8/18/48	Military Government Ordinance No. 31, "United States Military Government Courts for Germany"
5. Administration of Justice Review Board	8/18/47	EUCOM General Order No. 90: "Administration of Justice Review Board"
6. Control Council Law No. 4: Reorganization of the German Judicial System (High Courts of Appeal)	10/30/45	CONL/P(45)50
7. Administrative Code	9/17/46	Military Government Regulations, Title 4, Part 7 (MGR 4-7200)
8. Control Council Law No. 21: Law concerning German Labor Courts	3/30/46	CONL/P(46)23 (Final)
9. Habeas Corpus	1/7/48	Military Government Ordinance No. 23, "Relief from Unlawful Restraints of Personal Liberty"
10. Level of Police Jurisdiction	2/1/46	Military Government Regulations. Title 9, Par. 2, Section A
11. Control Council Directive No. 16: Arming of the German Police	11/6/45	CONL/P(45)46
12. Stand Fast Order	3/7/45	SHAEF Law No. 161 (Military Government Regulations 23–361)
13. Penal Powers of the Police	2/1/46	Military Government Regulations, Title 9

SUBJECT	DATE	REFERENCE
14. Cultural Exchange Program for Police Officials	12/20/48	OMGUS Publication, Civil Administration Division, "The Governmental Affairs Cultural Exchange Program"
15. German Fire Services	2/17/46	Military Government Regulations, Title 9, Part VII

CHAPTER 14

1. Measures concerning the Reorganization and Development of Agricultural Co-operatives Based on Democratic Principles	12/4/45	ACA Document, Food and Agriculture Committee, FACO/M(45)10, Min. 106
2. Food Availability for Issue Averaging 1040 Calories per Day	4/47	Monthly Report of the Military Governor No. 23, p. 16
3. Sanctions Imposed in the Form of Import Withholdings for Failure to Meet Delivery Quotas	12/14/48	BICO/Memo(48)99
4. Fixing of Grain Prices at Planting Time	10/7/48	BICO/Sec(48)588, Decisions adopted by Economic Council at its 22d Meeting
Fixing of Potato Prices at Planting Time	5/4/48	BICO/Sec(48)296, "Increase in Price of Potatoes"
5. Bipartite Board Ordinance Establishment of an Agricultural Credit Bank	3/8/49	BIB/P(49)37
6. Bringing German Farm Prices in Line with World Market Prices	1/20/49	BICO/Memo(49)4, "Deutsche Mark Payments for Imported Food, Seeds, Fertilizer and Medical Supplies"
7. Nutrition Committee Reports	8/13/45	Combined Nutrition Survey of Settled Areas in British, French, and US Zones of Germany made during period 30 July–8 August 1945, in accordance with decision of deputy military governors (US/Br/Fr) at their fifth meeting, 13 July 1945, and announced in Minutes of that meeting (CDMG/M(45)5)

SUBJECT	DATE	REFERENCE
	11/5/45	October 25–November 3, 1945
	2/20/46	February 10–19, 1946
	5/22/46	May 12–22, 1946
	8/23/46	August 12–23, 1946
	12/12/46	December 1–12, 1946
	4/26/47	April 12–24, 1947
	10/25/47	October 12–23, 1947
Report of the Special Commission Appointed by Secretary of the Army Royall to Study Nutrition in Bizonal Germany	5/27/48	
8. Reorganization of German Public Health Organizations	4/1/46	Military Government Regulations, Title 6
9. Control Council Directive No. 52: Combating Venereal Disease	5/7/47	CORC/P(47)20 (Final)
10. Number of Expellees to Be Received Estimated at 3,000,000 (Not Including Polish Territory Expellees)	11/21/45	CONL/P(45)57
11. Council of Relief Agencies to Operate in Germany (CRALOG)	2/19/46	President Truman announced the formation of CRALOG, to include the following organizations: American Friends Service Committee, Inc. Brethren Service Committee, Inc. Church World Service, Inc. Committee on Christian Science Wartime Activities of the Mother Church Congregational Christian Service Committee International Migration Service, Inc. International Rescue and Relief Committee Labor League for Human Rights, A F of L Lutheran World Relief, Inc. Mennonite Central Committee, Inc. National CIO Community Services Committee

SUBJECT	DATE	REFERENCE
		Russian Children's Welfare Society
		Tolstoy Foundation, Inc.
		Unitarian Service Committee
		War Relief Services—National Catholic Welfare Conference, Inc.
12. International Committee of the Red Cross (ICRC)	3/46	International Committee of the Red Cross designated as channel for non-American agencies and agencies outside CRALOG and CARE distributing bulk relief supplies in Germany
13. Co-operative for American Remittances to Europe (CARE):	6/5/46	Agreement establishing CARE signed 5 July 1946

American Aid to France, Inc.
American Baptist Relief
American Friends Service Committee, Inc.
American Relief to Austria, Inc.
American Relief for Poland, Inc.
American Relief for Czechoslovakia, Inc.
Brethren Service Committee
Church World Service, Inc.
Congregational Christian Service Committee
Committee on Christian Science Wartime Activities of the Mother Church
Co-operative League of the USA
General Conference of Seventh-Day Adventists
Greek War Relief Association, Inc.
International Rescue and Relief Committee, Inc.
Labor League for Human Rights, A F of L
Mennonite Central Committee

SUBJECT	DATE	REFERENCE
National CIO Community Services Committee		
Paderewski Testimonial Fund, Inc.		
Save the Children Federation, Inc.		
Tolstoy Foundation, Inc.		
Unitarian Service Committee		
United Lithuanian Relief Fund of America		
United Ukranian American Relief Committee		
United Yugoslav Relief Fund of America		
War Relief Services—National Catholic Welfare Conference		
Y.W.C.A.—World Emergency and War Victims Fund		
14. United Nations International Children's Emergency Fund (UNICEF) Includes German Children in Its Program	4/2/49	UNICEF/OMGUS Agreement

CHAPTER 15

1. Closing of Newspapers and Radio Stations	1/18/45	SHAEF Law No. 191, "Suspension of Press, Radio and Entertainment, and Prohibition of Activities of the Reichsministerium fuer Volksaufklaerung und Propaganda"
2. Establishment of Overt Newspapers	4/16/45	Annex "C" of SHAEF order entitled "Directive for Psychological Warfare and Control of German Information Services"
US Overt Newspapers Still Being Published as of July 14, 1945:	7/14/45	ICD History for 1945–46, and Monthly Report of the Military Governor No. 1, "Information Control"

SUBJECT	DATE	REFERENCE
Augsburger Anzeiger, Augsburg		
Bayerischer Tag, Bamberg		
Weser Bote, Bremen		
Frankfurter Presse, Frankfurt		
Sueddeutsche Mitteilungen, Heidelberg		
Hessische Post, Kassel		
Muenchener Zeitung, Munich		
Regensburger Post, Straubing		
Additional US Overt Newspapers: *Allgemeine Zeitung,* Berlin *Stuttgart Stimme,* Stuttgart	8/16/45	ICD History for 1945–46, and Monthly Report of the Military Governor No. 2, "Information Control"
3. Establishment of US-Sponsored News Service (DANA—*Deutsche Allgemeine Nachrichten Agentur* [German General News Agency], later changed to DENA [*Deutsche Allgemeine Agentur*])	6/29/45	Information Control Monthly Report
4. Re-establishment of Competitive Press in Frankfurt (*Frankfurter Neue Presse*)	4/15/46	Monthly Report of the Military Governor No. 10
5. Growth of RIAS Audience (*Rundfunk im Amerikanischen Sektor,* Radio in the American Sector)		Opinion Surveys Report No. 135 dated 13 September 1948
6. Laender Press Legislation:		
a. Land Bremen	12/16/48	Monthly Report of the Military Governor Nos. 42 and 44
b. Wuerttemberg-Baden	3/24/49	Monthly Report of the Military Governor No. 45
7. Laender Radio Legislation:		
a. Land Bremen	11/18/48	Monthly Summary, Bremen Information Services Division, November 1948
b. Land Bavaria	7/29/48	Monthly Report of the Military Governor No. 37

SUBJECT	DATE	REFERENCE
c. Land Hesse	9/22/48	Land Hesse Military Governor Report, September 1948
Revision of Unsatisfactory Wuerttemberg-Baden Radio Legislation	3/31/49	Military Government Report No. 111, April 1949
8. Control Council Law No. 22: Works Councils	4/10/46	CONL/P(46)25 (Final)
9. British and American Military Government Approval of Economic Council Ordinance No. 44, "Ordinance concerning the Establishment of a Manpower Department for the Combined Economic Area"	8/30/48	Monthly Report of the Military Governor No. 38, p. 38 BIB/M(48)16, Min. 502(i) dated 6 September 1948
10. Participation by German Trade Unions of Three Western Zones in International Conference of Trade Unions of Marshall Plan Countries	3/9 to 10/48	Monthly Reports of the Military Governor No. 33, p. 116
11. Establishment of FDGB (Freier Deutscher Gewerkschaftsbund—Free German Federation of Trade Unions)	7 to 8/45	Soviet-sponsored trade union
12. Establishment of UGO (Unabhaengige Gewerkschafts Opposition—Independent Trade Union Opposition)	5/26/48	Monthly Report of the Military Governor No. 35, p. 17
13. Plans for Opening of Elementary Schools in US Zone	7/7/45	Directive, Hq, USFET, "Administration of Military Government in the US Zone," Section VII, Part I, Pars. 5 (2)
14. Opening of Universities and Institutions of Higher Learning in the US Zone	11/21/45	Letter to Commanding General, USFET, from OMGUS I A & C Division
15. Reactivation of Adult Education	7/46	Weekly Information Bulletin, OMGUS, Nos. 48 and 52
16. Establishment of Education and Cultural Affairs Division	2/18/48	OMGUS General Order No. 6, "Reorganization of OMGUS Functions"

SUBJECT	DATE	REFERENCE
10. Control Council Directive No. 57: Disposition of Property Confiscated under Control Council Law No. 10, or Legislation Issued Pursuant to Control Council Directive No. 38	1/15/48	CORC/P(47)226 (Final)
11. Transfer to German State Corporation for Sale in the German Economy of Captured German Equipment	1947	Military Government Regulations 11–422
12. Disposing of Properties in the US Zone of Occupation and the US Sector of Berlin Having Belonged to the Former German Reich and to the Former German States, Laender, or Provinces (Including the State of Prussia)	4/20/49	Military Government Law No. 19
13. Number of Persons to Be Expelled	11/20/45	Directorate of Prisoners of War and Displaced Persons "Plan for the Transfer of the German Population to be moved from Austria, Czechoslovakia, Hungary, and Poland into the four Occupied Zones of Germany," CONL/P(45)57, approved in Conclusion 102 of CONL/M(45) 12
14. Personal Belongings to Accompany Expellees from Hungary	12/45	OMGUS Cables CC-19914 (5 December) and CC-20818 (22 December)
Remedy of Inhuman Conditions Prevailing in Transfer of Sudetens from Czechoslovakia	4/9 to 10/46	"Agreement on the Subject of the Movement of Sudeten-Germans from Czechoslovakia to the US Zone of Germany"
Termination of Expellee Movements from Czechoslovakia and Hungary	11/6/46	OMGUS Cable, CC-10164, suspending movements as of 1 December 1946
15. Expellee Law	1/24/47	Letter, OMGUS, AG 010 (CA), "Laenderrat Draft Law concerning the Reception and Integration of German Expellees"

CHAPTER 17

	SUBJECT	DATE	REFERENCE
1.	Pledge to Establish United Nations Organization	2/3 to 11/45	Yalta Conference Communiqué, Par. 4
2.	Ruhr Authority	12/19/48	Ruhr Conference Paper, London, RC/21, Final
3.	Draft Directive on Organization of Military Security Board	12/7/48	TMS/P(48)1/3
		12/17/48	TRIB/P(49)17
4.	Commission for the Compensation of Damage	2/11/45	Yalta Conference Communiqué, Par. 3
5.	Reparations from Western Germany	1/14/46	"Agreement on Reparations from Germany, on the Establishment of an Inter-Allied Reparations Agency, and on the Restitution of Monetary Gold," Part I, Article I
	Inter-Allied Reparations Agency		Part II
	German External Assets		Part I, Article 6
	Non-Monetary Gold Found in Germany		Part I, Article 7, Par. A
	Restitution of Monetary Gold		Part III
	Settlement of Claims against Germany		Part I, Article 2, Pars. A, B, C
6.	Revised Plan for Level of Industry in UK/US Zones of Germany	8/29/47	BIB/P(47)81/1
7.	Collisson Commission: Norman H. Collisson, Chairman (later Chief of ERP Mission to Germany) Frank J. Baumis Julius E. Graf Edward Falck Commander Julius C. C. Edelstein, USN, Ret.	4/12 to 5/11/48	

SUBJECT	DATE	REFERENCE
They were later joined by Robert Myers and Thomas E. Hibbin		
Report of Collisson Commission	7/12/48	"Final Report on Dismantlement of Industrial Plants Located in the Three Western Zones of Occupation of Germany," submitted by the Cabinet Technical Commission to the Secretary of the Interior, the Secretary of Agriculture, and the Secretary of Commerce. SECRET
8. Humphrey Commission: George M. Humphrey, Chairman / Fredrich V. Geier / John L. McCaffrey / Gwilyn A. Price / Charles E. Wilson	10/24/48	
Report of Humphrey Commission	1/8/49	"Report on Plants Scheduled for Removal as Reparations from the Three Western Zones of Germany," submitted by Industrial Advisory Committee, Economic Co-operation Administration. SECRET
9. Agreement concerning Prohibited and Limited Industries	4/19/49	TRISEC/Memo(49)8
10. Elimination of Excessive Concentration of Economic Power	8/2/45	Potsdam Agreement, Section III, Part B, Par. 12
11. Prohibition of Excessive Concentration of German Economic Power	2/12/47	Military Government Law No. 56 MGR 23-335
Discussion in Control Council of Draft Law to Prevent Excessive Concentration of German Economic Power	8/17/45 to 10/9/47	*Original Submission:* CORC/P(45)6 discussed in CORC/M(45)2, Min. 16 (17 August 1945) / *Referred to DECO:* CORC/M(47)29, Min. 308 (17 June 1947) / *Withdrawn from Agenda:* DECO/M(47)38, Min. 314 (9 October 1947)

SUBJECT	DATE	REFERENCE
Economic Enterprises Employing over 10,000 Persons to Be Examined	2/12/47	Military Government Law No. 56, Article I, Par. 3
Provisions for Deconcentration of Large Enterprises Not Specifically Approved by Military Government		Ibid.
Participation in International Cartels		Article II
Formation of Cartels within Germany		Article I, Par. 2
12. Reorganization of German Coal Iron and Steel Industry	11/10/48	Military Government Law No. 75
13. Control Council Law No. 9: Providing for the Seizure of Property Owned by the I. G. Farbenindustrie and the Control Thereof	11/30/45	CONL/P(45)62, amended by CONL/M(45)13
14. Licensing Law	11/29/48	a. "Licensing" of New Business, Letter, OMGUS, AG 010 (PD)
	3/28/49	b. "Licensing," Letter, OMGUS, AG 680.44 (EH)
15. Companies to Be Liquidated	11/10/48	Schedule "A" to Military Government Law No. 75
16. Plan for Development of Steel Enterprises	9/10/48	Report, "Recommendations for Increasing Steel Production in Bizonia"
17. Official Admittance of French Members to Coal Control Groups	12/9/48	Letter to General Koenig, BISEC/Sec(48)251
18. Dissolution of Large Holding Companies and Maintenance of the Operating Companies	4/9/49	"Report of the US Power Consultant to General Lucius D. Clay and to General Sir Brian H. Robertson on the Organization of Companies on Schedule 'B', Military Government Law 75"

SUBJECT	DATE	REFERENCE
19. First Ruhr Agreement	5/26/48	International Control of the Ruhr, Annex C to London Report, TRI/16 Final, and Annex D to London Report, TRI/23 Final
20. Detailed Examination of Ruhr Problem	5/26/48	Annex C to London Report, TRI/16, Final, Par. 12

CHAPTER 18

1. Final Agenda for 5th Session of the Council of Foreign Ministers, London	11/28/47	CFM/47/L/11
French Statement on		
a. Concentration of Population	11/27/47	USDEL(47)(L), 3rd Meeting, p. 1, Par. 2
b. Saar Question		Ibid., p. 2, Par. 1, and CFM/47/L/10
Molotov's Statement on Differences between Policies of USSR and Western Countries, and US Reply	11/26/47	USDEL(47)(L), 2d Meeting, p. 1, Par. 3; and p. 4, Par. 1
USSR Proposal for Clarification of Views on Formation of Democratic Government for Germany as a Whole	11/28/47	USDEL(47)(L), 4th Meeting, pp. 5, 8, Par. 1
US Statement on USSR and US Interpretation of Yalta and Potsdam Agreements	12/3/47	USDEL(47)(L), 8th Meeting, pp. 4, 5, Par. 2
USSR Charge of Economic Enslavement of Austria, and US Reply	12/4/47	USDEL(47)(L), 9th Meeting, pp. 4, 5, Par. 2
Reparations from German Production, US Position	12/10/47	USDEL(47)(L), 14th Meeting, p. 5, Par. 2
USSR Charge of British and US Profit from Ruhr Coal	12/12/47	USDEL(47)(L), 16th Meeting, p. 2, Par. 2
USSR Charges against British and US Policies and Administration in Germany, and US Reply	12/12/47	CFM/47/L/31, and USDEL(47)(L), 16th Meeting, p. 9, Par. 3

SUBJECT	DATE	REFERENCE
Secretary Marshall's Closing Statement	'12/15/47	USDEL(47)(L), 17th Meeting, p. 4, Par. 5, and Annex "B" thereto
2. Control Council Directive No. 58: Measures Relating to the Restriction and Control of Potentially Dangerous Personnel of the Former German Armed Forces	1/15/48	CORC/P(47)239 (Final)
Control Council Law No. 62: Repealing Certain Laws, Ordinances, and Decrees Promulgated by the Nazi Government concerning Churches	2/20/48	CORC/P(47)226 (Final)
3. Study of Measures Relating to the Restriction and Control of Potentially Dangerous Personnel of the Former German Armed Forces, USSR Proposals	12/30/47	CONL/P(47)66
US Position	1/20/48	CONL/M(48)1, Min. 2, p. 2
4. Report from the Co-ordinating Committee on the Preparation of a Plan for the Repatriation of All Prisoners of War to Germany	1/20/48	CONL/M(48)1, Min. 4, p. 8 (CONL/P(47)65 dated 30 December 1947)
5. US Statement on a Meeting between General Robertson and General Clay with Representatives of Bizonal Economic Council and Minister-presidents of the British and US Zones	1/20/48	CONL/M(48)1, Min. 6, pp. 15–18
6. Monetary Reform	2/11/48	CONL/M(48)3, Extraordinary Meeting, Appendix "A" SECRET
7. Soviet Memorandum on a Plan for Disarmament, Demilitarization, and Disbandment of the Armed Forces and Liquidation of Germany's War Industrial Potential	1/29/48	CONL/P(48)3

SUBJECT	DATE	REFERENCE
UK Position	2/11/48	CONL/M(48)3, Min. 19, p. 9
8. Statement by Marshal Sokolovsky regarding the Promulgation in the US and British Zones of Proclamations Nos. 7 and 8		Ibid., Min. 22, p. 15
9. Incident Involving British Officers at a CDU Meeting	1/31/48	CONL/M(48)2, Min. 14, p. 8
10. Statement of the Soviet Delegate on the Subject of a Letter from the Chairman of the Joint Committee, SED-KPD	1/23/48	CONL/P(48)12
UK Position	3/10/48	CONL/M(48)5, Min. 30, p. 1
11. US Statement on Political Monopolies		Ibid., Min. 30, p. 9
12. Control Council Directive No. 55: Interzonal Exchange of Printed Matter and Films	6/25/47	CORC/P(47)42 (Final)
13. *New Times*		A Soviet weekly published in Moscow, in Russian, English, German, and French
14. Soviet Memorandum on the Resolution of the Prague Conference of the Foreign Ministers of Czechoslovakia, Poland, and Yugoslavia; and US Statement	3/20/48	CONL/M(48)6, Min. 36, pp. 1, 2 (Unagreed Minutes)
15. Soviet Charge that US, UK, and French Governments use Allied Control Council as Screen for Unilateral Action		Ibid., p. 3
US Reply		P. 4
US, UK, and French Reply to Soviet Questions on London Conference		Pp. 6–11
16. Final Soviet Statement in the Control Council		Ibid., p. 12

SUBJECT	DATE	REFERENCE
9. US Protest against Armed Soviet Guards in the Reichsbahn Building in the US Sector	4/3/48	Letter from US Deputy Military Governor to Soviet Deputy Military Governor

CHAPTER 21

SUBJECT	DATE	REFERENCE
1. Powers of States in the British Zone	12/1/46	British Military Government Ordinance No. 57
Zonal Advisory Council	1/10/47	British Military Government Ordinance No. 80
2. Three-power Talks on Germany, Agenda as Adopted at First Meeting of Conference	2/23/48	London Conference Paper TRI/1
3. Agreed Report of the Working Party on Item F (Evolution of the Political and Economic Organization of Germany) of the Agenda	3/4/48	London Conference Paper TRI/4
Communiqué regarding First Session of London Talks	3/6/48	London Conference Paper TRI/9 (Final)
Request to Military Governors to Make Arrangements for Association with Benelux	3/6/48	Reply of US, UK, and French Delegations to Benelux, approved at 11th Meeting of Six Power Conference, London
Request to Military Governors to Study and Report on Co-operation and Coordination of Economic Affairs	3/4/48 3/5/48 3/5/48	a. TRI/4, Par. 2 (b) b. USDEL Min. (L)(G)/48/10, pp. 2, 3 c. TRI/8, Record of Decisions
Request to Military Governors on the Future Political Organization of Germany		Ibid., a, b, c
Request to Military Governors on Safeguarding of Rights of Foreign Powers in Germany	3/4/48	USDEL Min. (L)(G)48/9, pp. 4, 5

SUBJECT	DATE	REFERENCE
4. Formation of Working Party to Consider · the Future Political Organization of Western Germany as Set Out in TRI/4	3/20/48	Military Governors Conference, MGC/P(48)1, Berlin Par. 5, "Terms of Reference of Working Parties set up in Berlin in accordance with decisions of London Conference"
Final Report of Working Party No. 5	4/9/48	Military Governors Conference, MGC/P(48)8, Berlin
5. Agenda of Second Session of Three-power Talks on Germany	4/20/48	London Conference Paper TRI/12
Association of Benelux Countries in Policy regarding Germany	4/16/48	a. Annex B to London Report TRI/11 b. USDEL Min. (L)(G)48/14, Conclusion 7
Committee of Experts to Consider Reparations	4/16/48	USDEL/Min. (L) 48, Prelim. 4
Germany's Western Boundaries	5/26/48	Annex K to London Report TRI/20 (Final), "Provisional Territorial Arrangements"
6. Annex F to London Report on "Political Organization"	5/31/48	Talks on Germany (Resumed Session), Final Report of the Drafting Committee of the US, French, and UK Delegations as amended, TRI/13, Final (London)
Modification of State Boundaries		Par. 2 (See also Annex G, TRI/19)
Minister-presidents Authorized to Convene a Constitutional Assembly (Parliamentary Council)		Par. 3
Elections in Any New States		Par. 8
Coming into Effect of Institutions Established by the Constitution		Par. 9
Powers Retained by the Occupying Powers		Par. 19
Basic Principles of the Constitution		Par. 6

SUBJECT	DATE	REFERENCE
Ratification of the Constitution		Par. 7
7. Annex H to London Report, Letter of Advice to Military Governors regarding German Constitution	5/12/48	Talks on Germany (Resumed Session), TRI/15, Final (London)
8. Annex I to London Report, Letter of Advice to Military Governors regarding Powers of Civil and Military Government, as Amended	5/11/48	Talks on Germany (Resumed Session), TRI/17, Final (London)
9. Consultation of UK/US Military Governors with French Military Governor on Major Measures in the Bizonal Area	6/1/48	Final Report on Three-Power Talks on Germany, London, Part III
10. Document I, "Constituent Assembly"	7/1/48	Meetings of Military Governors and Minister-Presidents of the Western Zones on Future German Political Organization, MGMP/P(48)1 (Frankfurt)
Document II, "Land Boundaries"	7/1/48	MGMP/P(48)2
Document III, "Occupation Statute"	7/1/48	MGMP/P(48)3
Presentation of London Decisions to Minister-Presidents	7/1/48	Minutes of 1st Meeting, MGMP/M(48)1
11. Reply by the Minister-Presidents to Documents on German Political Organization	7/10/48	MGMP/P(48)5, published in Berlin on 12 July 1948
Administration of German Affairs		Par. 3
Western Zones as a German State		Par. 4
Relation of Western and Eastern Germany		Par. 5
German Position on a Referendum		Par. 6
Appellation of Constitution		Par. 6

SUBJECT	DATE	REFERENCE
Land Boundaries		Pars. 7, 8, 9
German Satisfaction with Promise of an Occupation Statute		Par. 10
Ruhr Control		Par. 13
Occupation Statute to Mark the End of a State of War		Par. 15
Removal of Restrictions on Foreign Trade		Par. 12
German Determination to Create a Free and Democratic Germany		Par. 17
12. Presentation of Comments by the Military Governors regarding the Observations of the Minister-Presidents to the London Decisions	7/20/48	Meetings of the military governors and minister-presidents of the western zones on future German political organization, MGMP/M(48)2 (Frankfurt)
Opening Statement of General Robertson		Ibid.
General Koenig's Statement, Comment to German Reply regarding Document I (Constituent Assembly)		Ibid.
General Robertson's Statement, Territorial Reorganization (Document II)		Ibid.
Stock's Request for Adjournment		P. 7, Subpar. 5
Kaisen's Statement on the Desire of Minister-Presidents to Speed Up Developments		P. 7, Subpar. 6
Determination of Name for Constitution, "Basic Law (Provisional Constitution)"		P. 9, Subpar. 5(1)
Ratification of Constitution by Landtage		P. 9, Subpar. 5(2)

SUBJECT	DATE	REFERENCE
13. Committee on the Occupation Statute: Dr. E. H. Litchfield, US Mr. Chaput de Saintonge, UK M. Sabatier, France	9/9/48	
a. Consideration of the First Integrated Tripartite Draft	10/18/48	Tripartite Committee on the Occupation Statute, Berlin, TOS/P(48)1
Committee on Allied Controls:	10/9/48	Tripartite Committee on Allied Controls, Berlin,
Mr. J. A. Panuch, US Major General Brownjohn, UK M. Sabatier, France		TOS/M(48)1
14. Department of Army's Reply to General Clay's Cable of August 19	8/29/48	Cable from CSCAD, Department of Army, Reference No. WX-88372
15. Basic Disagreements regarding the Occupation Statute	12/17/48	Report of the military governors to governments, TRIB/P(48)14/1 (Frankfurt) TOS/P(48)1/6, Appendix "A" thereto
German Legislative Authority		Par. 3(c)
Occupation Costs		Par. 3(f)
Appeal Court		Par. 3(g)
Protection and Care of Displaced Persons		Par. 3(b)
16. Occupation Statute and Trizonal Agreement	1/13/49	Cable from SAOAS, Department of Army, Reference No. W-82656

CHAPTER 22

1. Aide-mémoire Left with President of the Parliamentary Council in Bonn regarding Criteria for Approval of Basic Law by Military Governors	11/22/48	Documents on Military Governors-Parliamentary Council Meetings, Bonn

SUBJECT	DATE	REFERENCE
2. Meetings between Military Governors and Delegation from Parliamentary Council to Discuss Criteria for Approval by the Military Governors of the Basic Law (Provisional Constitution)	12/16 to 17/48	MGPC/M(48)1 and 2 (Published in Frankfurt, 20 December)
3. Draft Basic Law as Passed in Third Reading by the Main Committee of the Parliamentary Council at Bonn	2/10/49	Agreed Anglo-American translation prepared by Civil Administration Division, OMGUS, 14 February 1949
4. Discussion of Basic Law by Military Governors at Frankfurt	2/16/49	TRIB/C(49)2, Conclusions of the Meeting
5. Committee of Political Advisers: Dr. E. H. Litchfield, US Mr. C. E. Steele, UK M. Sabatier, France		
Report of the Political Advisers Committee on the Basic Law, Modified and Agreed by the Military Governors	3/2/49	"Memorandum on the Basic Law," handed by military governors to Parliamentary Council Delegation in Frankfurt
6. Exchange of Views on Draft Basic Law by Military Governors	2/16/49	TRIB/USDEL/M(49)2, Frankfurt
7. Meeting of Three Military Governors with Parliamentary Council Delegation to Transmit Views on the Draft Basic Law	3/2/49	TRIB/USDEL/M(49)3, Frankfurt
Military Governors' Position on State Boundary Changes	3/2/49	"Memorandum on the Basic Law," handed by military governors to Parliamentary Council Delegation in Frankfurt, p. 5, Par. 9
Military Governors' Position on the Electoral Law	3/2/49	Statements made by military governors to Parliamentary Council Delegation

SUBJECT	DATE	REFERENCE
8. Recommendation of the Minister-Presidents of the Three Western Zones on State Boundaries	10/1/48	"Resolutions on the Questions Raised by Document II adopted by the Minister Presidents at a conference held in Jagdschloss Niederwald"
9. Counterproposals to the "Memorandum on the Basic Law" of March 2	3/10/49	a. Official text of proposals made by Parliamentary Council "Committee of Seven" on the basis of the 2 March Memorandum, Bonn
	3/17/49	b. New counterproposals formulated by "Committee of Seven," Bonn
10. Meeting of the Foreign Ministers of the US, UK, and France in Washington	4/1 to 8/49	
Message of the Foreign Ministers of the US, UK, and France to the Parliamentary Council Recommending Speedy Adoption of Basic Law	4/5/49	
Message from the Foreign Ministers of the US, UK, and France to the Parliamentary Council Setting Out Main Points of Tripartite Agreement Reached in Washington	4/8/49	
Shortened Occupation Statute	4/8/49	"Occupation Statute defining the Powers to be Retained by the Occupation Authorities," Paper №4 of the Washington Agreements
Principles of Trizonal Fusion	4/8/49	"Agreement as to Tripartite Controls" (Final Text), Paper №5 of the Washington Agreements
Wuerttemberg-Baden Boundary Changes	4/8/49	"Agreed Minute on Wuerttemberg-Baden Plebiscite," Paper №7 of the Washington Agreements

Index

Access to Berlin, difficulties, 115, 353–54, 358–62; lack of provision for, 15, 25–27

Acheson, Dean G., as Acting Secretary of State, 133, 171; as Secretary of State, 241, 420, 439

Adcock, Major General C. L., 53, 182

Adenauer, Dr. Konrad, 92, 412, 419, 430, 434–36

Adler, General Julius Ochs, 267

Administration, in United States Zone, 227–62; see also German administrations

Adult education, 300

Advisory Parliamentary Council of Laenderrat, 94, 95

AFN (Armed Forces Network), radio programs of, 229

Agartz, Dr. Viktor, 200–1

Agatz, Willy, 292

Agricultural conditions at beginning of occupation, 31, 264–65

Agricultural needs of British Occupation Zone, 39

Agricultural production, maximization under Potsdam Protocol, 41; under Western Allies, 264–65, 267–72

Airlift, for relief of Allied personnel, 361; for relief of civilian population, 365–67, 381–92

Air traffic, Soviet protests concerning, 115

Alexander, Dr. Thomas, 300

Allen, Captain Margaret, 236

Allied Bank Commission, trizonal, 206

Allied Control Council, 8, 14–15, 24; accomplishments of *1946*, 131–33; breaking up, 349–57; conflict between Western and Soviet policy, 120–22, 134–35; early functioning period, 106–14, 116–20; failure to implement Potsdam Protocol, 39–40; initial meetings of, 33–36; initial period of active functioning, 45–46; after Moscow conference, 154–62, 343–44; policy control placed in, 52–53; under Potsdam Protocol, 43; quadripartite currency reform proposed in, 211; report prepared for Foreign Ministers, 141–45; U. S. proposal for organization of, 29–30

Allied Government of Berlin. See Kommandatura

Allied Nations, views on German occupation policies, 142–43

Alphand, Hervé, 150–51, 194, 320, 395

America. See United States

American Bible Society, 304

American Civil Liberties Union, report on legal procedures under OMGUS, 250

American Council of Education, visiting committee from, 301–2

American Joint Distribution Committee, 234